D0218017

The Very Nature of God:

Baroque Catholicism and Religious Reform in Bourbon Mexico City

WITHDRAWN
UTSA LIBRARIES

The Very Nature of God

Baroque Catholicism and Religious Reform
in Bourbon Mexico City

BRIAN R. LARKIN

University of New Mexico Press ✢ Albuquerque

©2010 by the University of New Mexico Press
All rights reserved. Published 2010
Printed in the United States of America
15 14 13 12 11 10   1 2 3 4 5 6

LIBRARY OF CONGRESS CATALOGING-IN-PUBLICATION DATA

Larkin, Brian R., 1969–
The very nature of God : baroque Catholicism and religious reform in Bourbon
Mexico City / Brian R. Larkin.
p. cm.
Includes bibliographical references and index.
ISBN 978-0-8263-4834-0 (pbk. : alk. paper)
1. Catholic Church—Mexico—Mexico City—History—18th century.
2. Christianity and culture—Mexico—Mexico City—History—18th century.
3. Church renewal—Catholic Church—History—18th century.
4. Wills—Mexico—Mexico City—History—18th century.
5. Mexico City (Mexico)—Religious life and customs.
6. Civilization, Baroque—Mexico—Mexico City.
I. Title.
BX1431.M49.L46 2010
282'.725309033—dc22
2009052897

Brian Larkin, "The Splendor of Worship: Baroque Catholicism, Religious Reform,
and Last Wills and Testaments in Eighteenth-Century Mexico City," originally
published in *Colonial Latin American Historical Review* 8, no. 4 (1999): 405–42.

Brian Larkin, "Liturgy, Devotion, and Religious Reform in Eighteenth-Century
Mexico City," *The Americas* 60, no. 4 (2004): 493–518.

DESIGN AND LAYOUT: MELISSA TANDYSH
Composed in 10/13.5 Minion Pro
Display type is Bernhard Modern Std

Library
University of Texas
at San Antonio

To Terese

CONTENTS

ILLUSTRATIONS

TABLES

PREFACE AND ACKNOWLEDGMENTS

I must confess that, although this book relies heavily on the last will and testament as a source, I have not written my own will. I had cause to do so. In spring 2003, while conducting more research to transform my dissertation into this book, I was diagnosed with a rare and aggressive form of cancer. I thought about writing my will, but avoided doing it. To me, writing my will would have signaled resignation to illness and acceptance of death, and I wanted to avoid it unless it was absolutely necessary. Fortunately, after successful surgery and treatment, I haven't needed to. Although I haven't written my own will, facing the very real possibility of needing to do so has changed my relationship with my research. When I began reading wills in 1996, I saw them merely as (complex) repositories of data for researching religion in colonial Mexico. Now, I have a much more visceral connection with them—so visceral that I couldn't return to them for over a year. I now have tremendous appreciation for the individuals whose wills have served as a window into colonial Mexican piety for me and the difficulties many of them must have faced when, as death was imminent, they called a notary to their bedsides to compose their wills. Writing their wills, as I argue in the appendix, was intimately related to dying and formed part of the rituals of death in Bourbon Mexico. To write a will for most people of the time acknowledged the proximity of death, and it must have been an act that very few took lightly. It is only because of the fortitude of those people as they faced death that this study is possible.

This study began as a dissertation at the University of Texas at Austin, and I am greatly indebted to my professors who guided my studies and research. Both Susan Deans-Smith and Ann Ramsey proved excellent models of scholarly rigor and human kindness. Both helped me craft this study and commented extensively on it. William Taylor kindly agreed to serve on my dissertation committee, although as an outside reader, he had no obligation to do so. I thank all three for their perceptive comments and suggestions. I also wish to thank my fellow graduate students at UT-Austin who read parts of the dissertation as it was in progress and encouraged with me their friendship. In no particular order, I thank Doug Sofer, Catherine Nolan-Ferrell, Sean Kelly, Hal Langfur, and Marc McLeod.

Many friends and scholars were instrumental in helping me revise my manuscript as a book. I especially would like to thank Steve Perkins, who carefully read and edited the entire manuscript. Martin Nesvig likewise read the entire work and provided insightful comments. My colleagues at the College of St. Benedict and St. John's University were unfailing in their support and I would particularly like to thank Annette Atkins, Ken Jones, and Greg Schroeder for reading various early versions of this work and encouraging me to finish the project. I also thank Kelly Donahue-Wallace for guiding me through the complexities of permissions and copyrights for the publication of photographs. Last, I thank the readers at the University of New Mexico Press for their helpful comments and suggestions.

I would like to thank the staff at the archives where I conducted research. I am particularly indebted to the staff at the Archivo General de Notarías in Mexico City. When it became clear that, after more than a year of working there, I would not be able to finish my dissertation research, they graciously allowed me to microfilm many wills from 1696, 1737, and 1813. This unusual permission allowed me to complete my research. I would also like to thank Rebeca Ortega, a former archivist at the Archdiocesan Archive in Mexico City, who cultivated the most hospitable atmosphere I've ever encountered as a researcher and who also introduced me to other members of the archdiocesan staff.

I also wish to thank two assistants who helped me complete additional research for this book in the notarial archive of Mexico City in 2002. Alberto Álvarez Ferrusquia transcribed many wills from 1796, and Patricia Barriaga transcribed many from 1717. I thank Jason Lowry and Patrick Timmons for helping to facilitate this arrangement.

I would not have been able to conduct research without financial aid. A Fulbright-Hayes Doctoral Dissertation Fellowship funded my initial research in 1996–97, and generous grants from the College of St. Benedict and St. John's University Faculty Development and Research Fund allowed me to spend much of the summers of 2001 and 2002 in the archives of Mexico City. St. Ben's and St. John's also awarded me a precious course release in fall 2007 as I was finishing the manuscript. Likewise, the schools provided the resources to pay for the photographs that adorn this book.

Some of the material in this book has previously been published. I thank *The Colonial Latin American Historical Review*, *The Americas*, and the University of New Mexico Press for allowing me to include portions of previous articles and essays here. Material from the following appear throughout this book: Brian Larkin, "The Splendor of Worship: Baroque Catholicism, Religious Reform, and Last Wills and Testaments in Eighteenth-Century Mexico City," originally published in *Colonial Latin American Historical Review* 8, no. 4 (1999): 405–42; Brian Larkin, "Liturgy, Devotion, and Religious Reform in Eighteenth-Century Mexico City," originally published in *The Americas* 60, no. 4 (2004): 493–518; and Brian Larkin, "Confraternities and Community: The Decline of the Communal Quest for Salvation in Eighteenth-Century Mexico City," originally published in *Local Religion in Colonial Mexico*, ed. by Martin Austin Nesvig (Albuquerque: University of New Mexico Press, 2006).

I would also like to thank my family and friends for their support over the many years that I took to complete this project. My parents always encouraged my endeavors, as did my sister and brother. My in-laws good naturedly awaited the completion of this book, and my friends patiently engaged in many conversations about baroque Catholicism.

Most important, however, I thank Terese Van Orsow, my wife. She unfailingly supported me through graduate school, various stages of research, and many moves. She assisted me every day in the notarial archive in 1996–97 after it became clear that the scope of my research and the minimal cataloguing of the archive necessitated her aid. She catalogued many of the wills I use and transcribed a good number of them. She has read several versions of this work and offered critical assessment. She has endured my sometimes obsessive focus on work and countless conversations about religion. For all these reasons, I dedicate this book to her.

Introduction

✝ FEARING DEATH, JOSÉ ANDRÉS LINAN CALLED THE NOTARY, MIGUEL Leonardo de Sevilla, to his home in Mexico City to record his will on October 11, 1696. José was ill, probably from the typhus epidemic that ravaged the capital of New Spain in that year, and confined to bed. After the notary had written the will preamble, which contained a profession of faith and an invocation of saintly aid at the time of death and judgment, José designed his funeral. He wanted his corpse to be dressed in the habit worn by the discalced Franciscan friars of the monastery of San Diego and buried in the church of the Augustinian colegio (school/priory) of San Pablo, specifically in the chapel of Our Lady of Guadalupe. He also asked that a requiem mass be sung in the chapel with his corpse present. He then directed his executors to commission four hundred low masses for his soul and those of his parents and that the masses be celebrated as quickly as possible so that "my soul may benefit [goze] from such a great [soberano] suffrage." After this, José dictated eight secular clauses in which he enumerated his debts and credits and obliquely referred to his property. Before closing his will, however, he returned to pious issues. He donated fifty pesos "to Our Lady of Guadalupe located in said colegio of San Pablo" and stipulated that his gift be used to purchase liturgical "ornaments for saying mass" in the chapel. He also commissioned an altar cloth worth up to twelve pesos for the saint. Although José

1

began to close his will by naming his executor, he had not yet completed his pious bequests. Because he was a bachelor, had no children, and his parents had already died, he named the blessed sacrament as his heir. He mandated the sale of his entire estate to pay for the "adornment" (adorno) of the altar of Our Lady of Guadalupe, on which the sacrament of the eucharist was celebrated, and her chapel. He asked that friar Juan Navarro, probably the sacristan of the chapel, purchase any item of "adornment that the sacristy may require." José then closed his will by renouncing any other verbal or written testament he may have composed and signed the document in the presence of four witnesses and the notary.[1]

Almost 120 years later, on July 5, 1813, Andrés Acosta dictated his will before the notary Juan Mariano Díaz. Andrés, like José, did not state his occupation in his will, but the fact that he did not sign the document because he did not know how to write, an infrequent condition among the testators of Mexico City, indicates that he probably fell within the lower range of the social hierarchy. Andrés failed to mention whether he was healthy or ill at the time he wrote his will, an uncommon occurrence. As was customary, after the preamble Andrés addressed his funeral arrangements. He asked to be buried in a religious habit from the order of St. Francis and that his funeral be celebrated "in the style of the poor without the din of any pomp." He then immediately dictated seven secular clauses in which he mentioned his debts and credits, gave a small sum to his sister, referred to his two marriages, and admitted that he had an illegitimate daughter. Only after completing these mundane matters did Andrés turn his attention to spiritual concerns. He instructed his executors to remit one hundred pesos to the Franciscan monastery of San Diego to pay for an equal number of masses. Andrés also bequeathed one hundred pesos for the pious work administered by the Mercedarian order of ransoming Christian captives held prisoner by the Islamic nations of North Africa and gave the same amount to support the work of the Franciscans who maintained the holy sites of Jerusalem. He then donated fifty pesos to the hospital of San Lázaro, a hospital dedicated to those afflicted by leprosy, and another fifty pesos to the hospital of San Juan de Dios, a large general hospital under the direction of the hospital order of the same name. Andrés closed his will by naming Ignacio Ruíz Vibar, "my loyal friend and generous benefactor," as his executor and requesting that the remainder of his estate be employed as alms for masses for his soul, alms which were to be distributed only to priests who suffered the "greatest necessity." Because he could not sign, the five witnesses who attended the notarization of the document did so in his place.[2]

These two testaments reveal much about the changing nature of religious experience in Mexico City during the eighteenth century. Although both José and Andrés were eminently concerned with arranging matters on earth to expedite their eternal salvation, the pious directives they commissioned had different aims and thus reveal differing conceptions of how to best ensure salvation through good works. José donated all his wealth to adorn a chapel and altar. He was primarily concerned with enhancing the splendor of Catholic liturgy, thus honoring Christ in the eucharist and the Virgin of Guadalupe whose chapel and altar he ornamented. In contrast, Andrés specifically requested a humble funeral without splendor or "pomp." He also donated much of his personal estate to charitable causes, the freeing of Christian captives and hospitals that cared for the ill and poor, rather than to ecclesiastical institutions for the enhancement of Catholic ritual.

These two testators who wrote their wills on the opposite ends of the eighteenth century exemplify the subject of this book: the changing practices and meanings of Catholicism in Bourbon Mexico. At the beginning of the eighteenth century, baroque Catholicism with its exuberant ornamentation of sacred space and lavish rituals dominated both ecclesiastical and lay religious practice in New Spain. During the second half of the eighteenth century, a group of reforming bishops attempted to remake religious culture, to move the faithful away from baroque Catholicism to a simpler and, in their minds, more interior piety. In this book, I examine baroque Catholicism, the project to reform religious culture in Mexico, and the new pious practices that reformers and the faithful negotiated as the colonial period moved toward a close. I argue that baroque and reformed Catholicism rested on different understandings of the very nature of God. I also contend that religious reform coincided with secular reforming projects, all of which participated within and influenced new forms of epistemology and subjectivity that arose in Mexico over the eighteenth century. Religious reform, however, proved only partially successful by the end of the colonial period, for the baroque faithful and reformers continually contested proper forms of worship. My analysis relies heavily on last wills and testaments written by the faithful of Mexico City over the Bourbon period as well as contemporary devotional literature and ecclesiastical documentation to uncover changing devotions and religious sensibilities in New Spain's capital.

Baroque and Reformed Catholicism

Although baroque Catholicism did not consist of a stable or codified set of practices, it was primarily a religion of outward gesture and ritual observance. This does not mean that Catholics who participated in baroque devotions did so in an empty or formulaic way or that they could not worship God through contemplation and inward exercises. But much of the devotional practice of baroque Catholicism was exterior, and Catholics who engaged in baroque devotions often demonstrated interior states with outward expressions. Baroque Catholics outwardly venerated images of saints: making pilgrimages to their shrines, lavishing gifts of wax and precious items upon them, touching and kissing them, and parading them through villages and cities in times of crisis or celebration. They practiced many of the same external devotions to the eucharist, the wafer of bread that contained Christ's true bodily presence. Catholics cast adoring gazes upon it as the priest elevated it at the moment of consecration during the mass, accompanied it with prayers and song as it was magnificently displayed on altars during special devotions, marched along with it in Corpus Christi and numerous other processions, and on occasion consumed it. The faithful also sought to honor God and the saints through the adornment of sacred space and the enhancement of liturgical rites with gifts of light (in the form of wax and oil) and precious items. Furthermore, they often orchestrated their own bodily gestures in symbolic ways to forge "unions" with Christ and the saints, for instance, fasting and practicing self-flagellation to recall Christ's passion and death.[3]

The faithful did these things for several reasons, but primarily because the sacred for baroque Catholics was immanent. In other words, the sacred could inhere within the physical world and thus was proximate and palpable. God and the saints manifested themselves physically in three ways. First, certain objects were sacredly charged. For example, images of saints made the essence of the saints they depicted present in the world. The eucharist, the central mystery of Catholicism, really contained Christ's corporeal presence. Because these physical objects truly manifested the sacred within the world, they demanded human care and devotion. Catholics venerated and sought contact with images and the eucharist not out of a mechanical sense of piety, but because these items bridged the gap between the sacred and the profane and introduced the holy into the physical world. Second, baroque Catholics conjured sacred manifestations within the world through ritual action. By performing symbolic gestures that mimicked events from salvation history, human actors invoked the sacred's mystical but real presence. The practitioner par excellence of sacredly efficacious symbolic gesture was the priest. The priest at the altar, symbolically attired in cassock, alb, surplice, and stole, and performing a set of symbolic motions and utterances, truly recreated Christ's passion and death and their salvific effect. But the priesthood did not monopolize religiously effective symbolic gesture. The faithful of any estate could orchestrate symbolic gestures to forge "unions" with Christ and the saints that mystically but effectively made them present in the world and allowed the actor to participate in their grace. Just as the ritual of the mass collapsed time between the present and Christ's historic acts and truly recreated their salvific efficacy, so symbolically crafted gestures abolished time, linked the performer with the event or figure represented, and imbued the performer with salvific grace. For this reason I refer to both types of ritual action as liturgical gesture.[4] Last, Catholics gave gifts to adorn sacred space and enhance the liturgy because church interiors were microcosms of the heavenly kingdom that mystically situated Catholics within the divine realm. Since baroque Catholics primarily conceived of heaven as a celestial court, with God as king, the Virgin as queen, and the hosts of angels and saints as courtiers, church interiors that sought to recreate the celestial court on earth must necessarily resemble the splendor of their heavenly prototype. Therefore, churches had to be elaborately designed and decorated so as to make present the celestial kingdom.

Catholics bestowed gifts on churches and images for other reasons as well. Engaged in a religion of ritual and outward expression, baroque Catholics felt compelled to express inward states with outward gestures. Baroque Catholics bestowed precious objects on churches, chapels, and images to manifest their devotions to the saints and God. Much as an image manifested the essence of a saint, so a gift to an image manifested the faithful's devotion. Linked with this compulsion, baroque Catholics were especially concerned with materially dignifying worship. A scantily adorned church reflected poorly on the community's devotional zeal. Last, the splendor and drama of sacred space and ritual were intended to awe spectators and impress upon them the might and glory of God. As the archbishop of Mexico, Alonso Núñez de Haro y Peralta, stated, splendor "suspends or forcefully strikes [*suspende o hiere con viveza*] the senses."[5] In essence, richly adorned sacred space induced a corporeal experience of the sacred's awesome presence in Catholics and fomented a deeply felt, affective adoration for God and the saints. Splendor and drama were integral components of baroque Catholicism that manifested the divine kingdom, demonstrated devotion, and inspired religious fervor all at the same time.

The experience of God's real presence within the world and the baroque religious practices based on it were founded on an epistemology that united the sign and signified. Baroque Catholics did not sharply distinguish between the symbol and the thing it symbolized; rather, the symbol contained the essence of or made present the thing symbolized. For example, the eucharist did not simply stand for or symbolize Christ; it truly was him. Likewise, the image of a saint, the liturgical gestures of the faithful, and symbolically designed and decorated church interiors did not merely bring God, the saints, or the heavenly kingdom to mind; they made them present within the world.

The ability of the sacred to inhere within the world in turn accounts for the corporeal nature of much baroque piety. Baroque Catholic practice in large measure consisted of establishing a bodily connection with divinity. Baroque believers literally touched the sacred when they caressed and kissed holy images, and they consumed the divine when they received the eucharist. They invoked the sacred through their bodies when they performed symbolic gestures and they felt the divine through their senses when they worshipped in ornate churches. Furthermore, baroque Catholics often utilized the body as a co-participant with the mind in prayer. Among other practices, they often prayed with their arms outstretched in the form of a cross or walking on their knees to enhance the experience and the effectiveness of prayer. In many ways then, the baroque body served as a religiously charged vehicle for encountering the sacred.

Not only a religion of sacred real presence, baroque Catholicism privileged collective devotions. Of course, baroque Catholics could and often did worship individually, but the rites and institutions of baroque Catholicism fostered a collective subjectivity. The mass and other aspects of the liturgy were designed to bring diverse segments of the social hierarchy together at one moment in one act and foster a sense of community by suspending social divisions and tensions that divided the congregation.[6] In cities, where the population's size prevented the entire community from gathering as one for the liturgy, parishes and confraternities, or religious brotherhoods dedicated to the veneration of a saint, structured microcommunities of the faithful. Even salvation was not left entirely to the lone Catholic. The larger community aided the soul's passage through purgatory with prayers, indulgences, and masses. The baroque Catholic never stood entirely alone before God. This spiritual and ritual interdependence stemmed from and fostered a horizontally structured community, one in which bonds between Catholics defined the church as the body of the faithful.

Catholic reformers of the second half of the eighteenth century advocated a new religious practice. They sought to interiorize and simplify piety. For them, God was eminently spiritual and thus largely incapable of being confined within the physical world. This spiritualization of the sacred necessitated new forms of religious engagement. Rather than seeking physical contact with a proximate and palpable God, reformers encouraged Catholics to offer God an inner tribute. This largely consisted of close attention to the meaning of the mass as it was performed; contemplation of God's eminence, goodness, and justice in mental prayer; and reflection on his word as recorded in scripture. This new form of religious practice was largely interior. It required mental concentration and the development of a personal relationship with God.

To promote the new piety, reformers attacked the practices of baroque Catholicism, which they viewed as obstacles to true worship. Because they conceived of God as spiritual, they repudiated forms of worship predicated on an immanent conception of the sacred. They downplayed veneration of images and relics. Instead, they asked Catholics to honor saints by imitating their Christian virtues. Rather than celestial powerbrokers, saints for reformed Catholics were models for moral living. Reformers likewise undermined lay liturgical gesture and performative piety. The body now no longer served as a way to invoke the sacred into the world or as a vehicle for the sensual experience of the divine. It at best was religiously inert; at worst, an obstacle that hindered the mind from prayer and contemplation of the goodness and greatness of God. Hence, reformers encouraged the faithful to minimize bodily gesture during religious ceremonies and act in a decorous and dignified manner. Last, reformed Catholics discouraged the lavish decoration of sacred space and the embellishment of the liturgy. Rather than incentives to piety and means to experience the felt presence of God, they distracted the faithful from prayer and were inducements to irreligion. Therefore, reformers sought to simplify church architecture and adornment and curb the spectacle of ritual performance.

Although never articulated by them in this way, reformers worked within a new epistemology. They ruptured the close connection between sign and signified. For them, the sign only stood for, but did not make present, the signified. This theory of signs sundered the multitudinous links between this world and the sacred. God became physically distant from the world as the avenues of contact between the sacred and mundane were spiritualized. This allowed reformers to reinterpret proper forms of worship. As orthodox Catholics, they would never challenge the doctrine of Christ's corporeal presence in the eucharist, the veneration of venerable images and relics, or the use of priestly liturgical gesture within the confines of the sacraments. But they denigrated the excessive devotion to saints, the use of liturgical gesture by the laity, and the splendor and dramatic flare of traditional religious ceremony. In short, they sought to redefine the balance in Catholic practice between ritual action and pious contemplation in favor of the latter.

At the same time, reformers implicitly redefined Catholic community. Instead of seeking God in human sociability, they sought him in individual contemplation. The Christian community became a set of individuals who had reference to the same deity and who shared the same understanding of his word, rather than a group of people who worshipped together. Of course, reformed Catholics continued to participate in the sacraments, and these rites still possessed the capacity to structure and reconcile community. Reformed Catholics were after all still Catholics, and the doctrine of the bodily presence of Christ in the consecrated host vitiated the tendency of reformers toward a purely cognitive and individual experience of God. Nonetheless, reformed Catholicism de-emphasized communal piety and thus gave greater weight to the individual.

Religion, the Colonial Mexican Church, and Historians

My understanding of religion is strongly influenced by the works of Clifford Geertz and Pierre Bourdieu. Although admittedly not novel, Geertz cogently links religion with other social arenas and, more importantly, highlights the role of ritual in religion. Geertz links religious belief and practice to other sociocultural systems in two ways. First, he argues that religion creates a conception of the "really real," or a meta-understanding of the world and its workings, that simultaneously functions as a "model for" and a "model of" society.[7] In other words, religious beliefs and practices are intimately and dialectically connected to social, political, and economic realms because conceptions of the really real both mirror the organization of human society and mold it. Therefore, understanding conceptions of the really real illuminates other realms of human experience. More important for this book, understanding changing conceptions of the really real clarifies transformations occurring in those other realms. I do not assert that changes in eighteenth-century Mexican religion caused transformations in other sociocultural practices, but I do argue that changing conceptions of the really real in Mexico shaped and, in turn, were shaped by those broader transformations.

Second, Geertz contends that religion authenticates the really real through ritual, which encourages believers to think, feel, and act in ways consistent with their prevailing conceptions of a religiously imbued world. The logical circularity of religion reinforces it as a cultural system because conceptions of the really real inspire human actions and motivations consistent with those conceptions that in turn confirm them.[8] Here, Geertz lays bare the power of religion to motivate social action, for human beings act in ways consistent with their understanding of the really real. Therefore, if we want to understand the cultural practices of colonial Mexicans—some of which may appear bizarre to modern readers, like self-flagellation and gift giving to images—we would do well to examine colonial Mexican conceptions of the really real and the devotions consistent with them.

Although I take Geertz's definition of religion as an analytical starting point, my understanding of religion and its connection with broader cultural practice incorporates other perspectives as well. Geertz has been critiqued for his overly harmonious view of culture, his lack of attention to issues of power and contestation in struggles to shape cultural understanding, his emphasis on the shared meanings of cultural symbols, and his neglect of cultural change over time.[9] I view culture not as a shared set of meanings, but rather as a shared argument over meanings, conceptions, and practices. Not all eighteenth-century Mexicans shared a common understanding of Catholic practice, but they did share an argument about proper forms of worship and conceptions of divinity. These arguments became particularly pronounced in the second half of the century. Furthermore, power plays a central role in changing understandings of religion in eighteenth-century Mexico City. Many bishops, ecclesiastics, and some members of the laity who had access to formal institutions of power attempted to reform the religious culture of the laity (and other

ecclesiastics) who by and large did not. In short, the history of religious
change in late colonial Mexico is largely a story of how groups with differential access to power negotiated cultural change over time. Finally,
although I examine the many possible meanings of religious symbols and
practices of eighteenth-century Mexicans, I do not presume that they fully
comprehended those meanings or held them present in mind when they
performed their devotions. The depth of their understanding of their own
pious practices certainly ranged depending on their own zeal and training.
Some must have possessed a sophisticated understanding of the rich and
multiple meanings of their devotions. Others must have had only a vague
sense of their meanings and must have performed them more out of habit
than profound understanding.

Here, Pierre Bourdieu's concepts of the "habitus" and "practice" become
helpful. Bourdieu contends that much cultural practice is not necessarily conscious or meaningful, but rather consists of embodied habits. For
instance, believers in colonial Mexico might not have been able to articu-
late their reasons for lavishing gifts upon images or prostrating themselves
before them.[10] They nonetheless performed these rites out of cultural habit
ingrained within them at an unconscious (embodied) level. In short, the religious practices of many eighteenth-century Mexicans went without saying
because they came without saying. We can expand Bourdieu's insight from
the realm of practice to the sphere of thought and conception. Not only did
the pious practices of many Mexicans go without saying; to borrow a phrase
from William Taylor, so did their "habits of conceiving the sacred."[11] It was
precisely these embodied habits of practice and, at a deeper level, unconscious habits of conception that religious reformers sought to transform in
late Bourbon Mexico.

This book then examines the forms, meanings, and embodied practices
of baroque Catholicism, the attempt by religious reformers to transform
them, and the piety the faithful and reformers negotiated within the changing sociocultural context of Bourbon Mexico City. At the same time, it seeks
to balance and reinterpret trends within the historiography of the church and
religion in colonial Mexico.

The study of the Catholic church in colonial Mexico has occupied historians for some time. Much of the historiography treats institutional aspects
of the church[12] and the religious practices of rural, indigenous populations
and their complex process of "conversion."[13] More recently, scholars have

focused on the understudied subject of urban and Spanish religion in New Spain. Many of these studies focus on the religious experience of mystics or the celebration of grand religious festivals.[14] Other works have examined sundry aspects of religious culture, primarily various local practices for the veneration of saints and their meanings.[15]

This book contributes to this new historiography on urban and Spanish religiosity. But it investigates the religious sensibilities and practices of the everyday faithful rather than religious specialists who experienced mystical states. More important, this work emphasizes the profound role the Catholic liturgy played in shaping the faithful's understanding of death and salvation. Despite the central role the liturgy played in the lives of the faithful, it has not been studied in the Latin American context.[16] This is all the more surprising given the centrality of the liturgy in traditional Catholic practice. Baroque Catholicism, as stated earlier, was a religion of ritual observance. The faithful by and large attended mass regularly, received communion at least once a year and probably more frequently, and took part in the other sacraments of the universal church at significant turning points in their lives. Their frequent participation in liturgical ritual gave meaning to the world and human relationships within it. The liturgy narrated salvation history and influenced how the devout understood the ultimate questions of death, judgment, and redemption. This book focuses precisely on these ultimate questions, on how the Spanish population of Mexico City conceived of the sacred and how Spaniards sought to engage it and thus gain salvation. Catholics in the eighteenth century were highly concerned with questions of sin and redemption. It is my goal to analyze the strategies that Spanish Catholics in Mexico City employed to win salvation and how these strategies changed over the eighteenth century.

This book also seeks to reinterpret the eighteenth-century project of religious reform in Mexico.[17] In a probing and multifaceted work, Pamela Voekel investigates the course of religious reform in Mexico City and Veracruz by examining campaigns to eliminate church burials and move cemeteries to the outskirts of urban areas for religious and sanitary reasons. She contends that reformed piety, because it promoted the individual Christian's relationship with God and denigrated saintly and churchly mediation between believers and divinity, laid the groundwork for Mexican modernity in the nineteenth century. She argues that a self-conscious group formed from the middling and elite sectors of society promoted reformed religiosity in part because it furthered their own social interests. They derided baroque Catholicism's exuberant display because it encoded social distinctions that inhibited their quest for social advancement. They viewed their fellow Catholics' penchant for lavish ceremony and display as a sign of moral weakness and a sure indicator that God had not illuminated their hearts. In place of ostentation, reformed Catholics practiced decorum and self-restraint. They believed that this self-composure constituted true Christian virtue and thus justified their social ascent and bestowed upon them the authority to rule. Voekel sees this group as the vanguard of liberal political ideals, especially the notion of the republic as a sovereign community of individuals that would come into prominence in Mexico after independence.[18] Voekel's study offers the first cultural history of religious reform in Mexico and cogently explains the social logic of some advocates of reformed piety.

Although her overarching argument about the religious origins of Mexican modernity rings true—in fact, evidence from the wills used in this study reveals the decline of corporate identity as an individual sense of self rose over the eighteenth century—Voekel overestimates the appeal of reformed Catholicism and misreads its intellectual foundations. Moreover, given her focus on the rise of reformed Catholicism and its influence on postindependence Mexican politics, she only briefly analyzes baroque Catholicism. She asserts that a renewed debate first argued by St. Augustine and Pelagius about the source of grace for salvation lay at the heart of reformed Catholicism. Reformers adopted the Augustinian approach, which downplayed human efficacy in earning grace and viewed salvation as a gift from God. A reading of literature produced by reformed-minded ecclesiastics, however, shows little evidence of concern over sources of grace. Rather, the very nature of the divine preoccupied them. The fact that they viewed God as a spiritual being who could not be contained within physical objects served as the intellectual foundation of reformed Catholicism. This shift in habits of conceiving the very nature of the sacred, as stated above, rested upon a deeper and, at the time, unarticulated transformation in epistemology and the function of signs. Moreover, a sustained investigation of baroque Catholicism reveals its vibrancy and enduring popularity throughout the colonial period. Although reformed Catholicism gained many adherents by the end of the colonial period, it remained a minority religious practice even among the elite.

Reformed Catholicism and Modernity

Voekel's study raises the issue of the relationship between Catholicism and modernity. Modernity is a multifaceted concept. I have chosen to examine three of its aspects, ones that are sometimes conflated in scholarly analysis. They are the emergence of the bounded individual, the movement toward economic rationality, and the trend toward the disciplining of human bodies to make them efficient producers of wealth.[19] Catholicism in Bourbon Mexico City impinged on each of these processes, and concepts about the very nature of God lay at the heart of the intersection of faith and modernity in late colonial Mexico.

It was long believed that Catholicism hindered the emergence of modernity.[20] Certainly, confraternities promoted collective identities at the expense of individualism. And early modern devotions, such as pilgrimages and the elaborate adornment of churches, ran counter to economic rationality. Believers who saw collective devotions as necessary for salvation and who disrupted work routines with daily devotions, disciplined their bodies with mortifications, and spent wealth on religious feasts hardly provided examples of individual autonomy, industry, and thrift.

Recently, scholars have contested this view of Catholicism's inhibitive effect on modernity. Historians of early modern Europe have argued that changes within eighteenth-century Catholicism helped birth modern republics by undermining the sacral status of monarchs.[21] In the case of Mexico, Pamela Voekel has deepened this historiography on the religious origins of republican states and argued that reformed Catholicism fostered the birth of the republic's primary component: the modern, bounded individual. Evidence from the wills for this study corroborates her general argument, though it also modifies the particulars.

The debate over religion's impact on economic rationality has a longer history. The subject of religion's connection with economic rationality has generally occurred as part of larger discussions of Christianity's influence on the rise of capitalism. Max Weber began the debate almost a century ago. In his classic study, *The Protestant Ethic and the Spirit of Capitalism*, he argues that ascetic forms of Protestantism, particularly Puritanism in New England, gave birth to the capitalist spirit, or the rational accumulation and reinvestment of wealth in profit-seeking endeavors. Implicit in Weber's thesis is the argument that Catholicism and less ascetic forms of Protestantism played no role in, or may even have hindered, the development of economic rationality.[22] Scholars have critiqued Weber's work since its publication. Most recently, Rodney Stark has argued that Christianity's promotion of capitalism predated the Reformation. He contends that the medieval Christian emphasis on rational theology as a complement to divine revelation as recorded in scripture allowed Christians to critique tradition and modify religious practice. This privileging of reason and freedom to improvise were eventually applied to production and commerce, promoting the rational management of industry and wealth and fostering the rise of capitalism in medieval Europe.[23] Although I have no intention of entering the debate over the religious origins of capitalism, it is clear that reformed Catholicism in Mexico facilitated the evolution of economic rationality. By discouraging the splendor of baroque worship, reformed Catholicism allowed believers to economize on religious expenditures and thus opened the possibility of redirecting wealth toward productive ends.

Unlike Catholicism's role in fostering the autonomous individual and economic rationality, the impact of religion on the disciplining of bodies has not been studied.[24] Michel Foucault in his revisionary works on the Enlightenment argues that the body became a site of reform in the eighteenth century. Institutions of power began to individuate, observe, and exert control over the once labile human body in an attempt to instill self-discipline and rationality of gesture within it. This disciplining promoted self-observation and self-regulation to render bodies more pliant to authority and more efficient in production. Foucault's analysis, however, elides the question of religion's impact on bodily comportment.[25] I argue that religion played a vital role in opening a space for the disciplining of the body. Baroque Catholicism promoted the use of the body as a means to invoke and experience the sacred. The baroque body was religiously charged, and its pious performances impeded its modern, rationalized use for efficient production. Religious reform's negation of the body's religious capacity thus facilitated disciplining and participated in the emergence of the modern self-regulated, efficient body.

At the heart of reformed Catholicism's participation in modernity in eighteenth-century Mexico lay its conception of the very nature of God. The immanential nature of the baroque sacred promoted practices counter to modernity. Baroque manifestations of God and the saints in the world commanded the community's devotion and the dedication of its financial resources and bodily energies to them. The physicality of the sacred required a material reverence and privileged an ostentatious and corporeal worship. In contrast, the spiritual conception of divinity promoted by reformed Catholicism distanced the sacred from the physical world and thus allowed Catholics to worship simply and still their religiously charged bodies. In short, reformed Catholicism's redefinition of the very nature of God opened the possibility for Catholics to redirect their resources and energies away from materially honoring God and the saints so that they could be focused on other, more mundane ends.

Reformed Catholicism participated in the rise of modernity in Mexico, but it did not birth it. At best, the new way of conceptualizing the divine opened the possibility of a modernizing project. This religious transformation, though an essential precondition of modernity, did not itself lead to economic rationality and disciplined bodies. Economic resources and corporeal energies saved through simplified devotions and religiously calmed bodies were not necessarily directed toward capital accumulation and production. Nonetheless, religious reform helped establish the conditions for modernity in eighteenth-century Mexico.

Religious reform, as we will see, did not occur within a vacuum; rather it simultaneously responded to and reinforced broader sociocultural transformations aimed at promoting modernity in Bourbon Mexico. At the same time that Mexican prelates attempted to remake religious culture, the Spanish crown and viceregal state implemented myriad reforms intended to discipline the populace and promote prosperity. The secular reform project stemmed from the same new epistemology and subjectivity that underlay religious reform, and thus these two projects tended to support one another. This mutual support was not necessarily intentional. In fact, religious and secular reform often did not share ultimate goals. Nonetheless, because they emerged from the same deep cultural roots, their intermediate goals often overlapped and both projects promoted modernity in late colonial Mexico.

We can thus view the late eighteenth century in Mexico as a time of emerging conditions for modernity. These conditions rested on a new epistemology and subjectivity that undermined the unity of sign and signified, the labile nature of human bodies, and the collective sense of personhood that underlay baroque sociocultural practice. In their different ways, both religious and secular reformers advocated these deep cultural transformations. We must remember, however, that often goals and results do not coincide. This was certainly the case for religious reform in Bourbon Mexico

City. Some of the faithful wholly adopted reformed Catholicism, even anticipating ecclesiastically advocated reform by half a century. But despite their
bishops' admonitions, many Spanish Catholics in Mexico City continued to
practice liturgical gesture and to adorn sacred space lavishly into the early
nineteenth century. Clearly, reformers had not entirely broken the close connection between sign and signified. But the Spanish Catholics of Mexico City,
even those who continued to worship an immanent God, engaged in a more
individual piety by the end of the eighteenth century. The bounded individual emerged over this period, but the new individual continued to seek
the divine in its physical manifestations and to invoke its mystical presence
through the crafting of lay liturgical gestures. In short, religious reform did
not succeed in unequivocally establishing the conditions for modernity in
Bourbon Mexico.

Perhaps focusing on Catholicism's relationship to modernity obfuscates
as much as it enlightens. It certainly represents and reinforces a post-
Enlightenment view of religion that diminishes its cultural weight and significance. Although this book analyzes Catholicism in relation to other
sociocultural patterns, we would do well to remember that religion held
great importance for the residents of eighteenth-century Mexico City in
its own right. It gave meaning to existence, human relations, and death.
Moreover and most important for Christians, proper religious observance
ensured eternal life, the unquestioned ultimate goal of the vast majority of
Spanish Catholics in New Spain. Therefore, disputes about proper forms of
worship and, by implication, how to attain salvation in themselves greatly
mattered to believers. The eighteenth century in New Spain was an age
of faith, and religious reformers confronted Catholics with a repudiation
of time-honored methods of worshipping God and achieving redemption.
Because the radically new conception of the sacred inherent in reformed
Catholicism cast doubt on traditional devotions and strategies for salvation, it at best met a mixed fate.

The Will as a Source

The last wills and testaments written by the population of Mexico City
over the long eighteenth century constitute a major source for this study.
The will reveals much about piety and religious sensibilities because during the early modern it was as much a religious as a secular document.[26]

Testators employed it as much to prepare for God's judgment as to arrange their earthly affairs. In the last days and weeks before death, in the midst of numerous other rites of dying, those who had property to distribute called a notary to their bedsides to redact their final wishes. In addition to distributing property to their heirs, testators included pious clauses in their wills to gain grace for their souls and improve their standing before God. They ordered masses, proclaimed their membership in confraternities, arranged their funerals, funded liturgical celebrations, and donated gifts to religious institutions and the poor. These religious directives allow for the investigation into past pious practices and their meanings. But these directives must be analyzed with care.

I have read and sampled wills differently than have others who have studied piety. Historians who have used wills have largely been content to quantify a limited range of pious directives. Most commonly, they count requests for masses, the number of masses requested, and/or gifts to ecclesiastical or charitable institutions.[27] Although valuable, this methodology misses much. I have chosen to examine a wider range of pious directives and also to analyze religious clauses qualitatively. I thus try to capture the rich and revealing detail contained in wills that was previously ignored. For instance, I distinguish between a testator who merely requested twenty-five masses for her soul and one who commissioned thirty-three masses in honor of the number of years that Christ lived as man.[28] Likewise, I distinguish between the testator who bequeathed one hundred pesos to the poor in general, the one who gave money only to the shamefaced poor, and the one who gave twelve pesos to twelve poor people on holy Thursday in honor of the last supper. The meanings of these directives differ markedly, but simple quantification masks them. Because my methodology marks this type of detail, it allows for a finer-grained analysis. Moreover, I examine a broad range of pious activities rather than focusing on one type of directive, such as mass requests or charitable bequests, to provide a more complete picture of how religious change occurred in a variety of arenas.

This finer analysis of pious directives necessitates careful attention to the factors that accounted for their presence in the will. Certainly, testators recorded their general pious desires in their testaments, but it was the notary who actually wrote the will. In fact, notaries often took notes while testators dictated their wills and then composed the will later. Only afterwards did notaries read the will back to testators for their signatures. Given this procedure, notaries obviously exercised significant influence over the form and style of the will. How then is it possible to distinguish what the notary and the testator contributed to any given will? How is it possible to disentangle the testator's words from those of the notary? Although the relations between notary and testator that account for a will can never be fully documented, we can gain insight into the relational process of will writing by using an appropriate sampling technique.

I chose to read all wills written during seven sample years that stretch from the very late seventeenth to the early nineteenth centuries, a period roughly contemporaneous with Bourbon rule in New Spain[29] (see Table 1). I originally sampled four plague years—1696, 1737, 1779, and 1813—because high mortality rates translated into an unusually large number of wills for those years.[30] This in turn created a high ratio of wills per notary, which permitted an examination of notarial influence on will writing. Any repetitive wording or directives found in the wills proved by the same notary probably occurred because of his influence. On the other hand, unique gestures and wording must have occurred from the relational process of will writing that included the notary, testators, and other people present at the redaction of the will, such as witnesses and family members. We cannot attribute these unique phrases and gestures solely to testators, but they must have significantly influenced if not absolutely determined their inclusion.

I added three additional years—1717, 1758, and 1796—in which epidemics did not afflict Mexico City. I did so for three reasons. First, I used non-plague years as a control to examine if pandemics measurably affected patterns of pious activity recorded in the wills. As I show later in the book, they did not. Second, the addition of three sample years allowed for more precise dating of changes in pious activity. Last, I determined that, even in non-plague years, most notaries wrote enough wills to test for notarial influence on pious gestures. Except for a few cases noted in later chapters, notaries exerted little influence over testators' inclusion of pious directives or their specific design.

TABLE 1 Number of Wills and Notaries in Sample

	1696*	1717	1737*	1758	1779*	1796	1813*
Number of wills in sample	344	171	324	189	222	202	270
Number of notaries in sample	40	35	56	48	44	43	34

* Indicates Plague Years

I also adopted this sampling technique because it includes a large number of notaries in each of the selected years (see Table 1). This is important because notaries worked within microcommunities in Mexico City and developed particular clientele networks. Therefore, wills from many notaries are needed to obtain a truly representative sample. I decided to include all notaries who attested wills in each sample year to eliminate the possibility of mistaking differences in notarial clientele for changes in pious activity, a possibility that haunts random sampling techniques. Although it was impossible to reconstruct the particular sociocultural milieu within which notaries worked or the precise nature of their clientele networks, it is clear that the residents of Mexico City did not choose their notaries at random. For example, some testators wrote multiple wills and almost always utilized the same notary for their documents. Cristóbal Leonel Hurtado de Mendoza y Castilla wrote two wills in 1696, one by himself when ill and a joint will with his wife after he had recuperated, before the same notary, José Anaya y Bonillo.[31] Members of the same family also tended to use the same notary. A brother and sister, Antonio Marcos de Mendieta and Antonia de Mendieta, both dictated their wills to Juan de Condarco y Cárceres within the same week in 1696. A day after Antonia had given her will, her husband, Felipe de Rivas Ángulo, redacted his testament before the same notary.[32] If both a husband and a wife gave separate wills, they almost always did so before the same notary.

Clientele networks of notaries spread beyond family units. In 1737 Juan Moredo gave his will before Juan Francisco Benítez Trigueros and named José Comelles as his executor. On the same day, José dictated his testament before the same notary.[33] Likewise, in 1779 Francisco Palacio Castillo gave his will before Andrés Delgado Camargo and named Father Manuel de Bolea, a priest who belonged to the Oratory of San Felipe Neri, as one of his executors. Within three weeks, Father Bolea also wrote his will before the same notary.[34] This type of connection between various clients of a single notary was relatively common in the wills, indicating that notaries were part of community networks in Mexico City. What formed the basis of these communities is difficult to determine. Until a historian thoroughly investigates notarial practice in Mexico City, little more can be said about notaries' clientele networks.[35]

Careful sampling techniques, however, cannot overcome some inherent limitations of the will as a source. Certain populations were more likely to write wills than others, resulting in the overrepresentation of some social groups and the underrepresentation of others. But almost all social groups, except the destitute, are represented to some extent. Most testators were Spanish (creole or peninsular) or passed as Spanish. Notaries otherwise listed the testator's racial category. Less than 3 percent of the entire testator population was non-Spanish, with Indians making up the largest section of this tiny minority. Men wrote almost twice as many wills as women. Although Hispanic law allowed women to dispose of their property freely in wills, patterns of deference to men must have inhibited many from composing a testament. Many professional groups are represented in the sample, but some more than others. Merchants form the single largest block, accounting for 15 percent of all wills. Varying levels of wealth hide under the label "merchant." Notaries described wholesalers who traded goods from Europe and China, retailers who owned stalls in the *zócolo*, and peddlers who hawked inexpensive goods all as "del comercio" of Mexico City. In many cases it is impossible to discern what type of merchant redacted a particular will. Priests comprise the second largest professional group, followed by artisans, bureaucrats, and soldiers. Members of the liberal professions, such as lawyers, administrators, notaries, physicians, and teachers, also wrote wills, as did rural land owners like *hacendados* and *rancheros*.[36] No profession was listed or could be inferred for over 40 percent of the testator population. For some unknown reason, notaries simply failed to mark the occupational status of some testators.

Testator wealth is difficult to measure. Most wills do not contain an appraisal of the testator's goods at the time the instrument was written. Moreover, most testators did not enumerate their goods or only listed their most cherished items. They usually stated that they had communicated the extent of their belongings to their spouses or executors. Rather than attempt to quantify testator wealth on the basis of patchy data, I have decided to rely on impressionistic evidence when necessary. Most testators possessed some wealth—a few possessed enormous wealth—but the poor also wrote wills. Some testators specifically requested a simple funeral or a pauper's burial because they had nothing with which to pay parish fees.

The corpus of wills used in this book reflects the testamentary practice of the populace of Mexico City. Therefore, analysis is largely restricted to the non-destitute Spanish population. This social group, however, composed a significant segment of the population and, thus, an analysis of wills can reveal much about the changing nature of piety in Bourbon Mexico City.

Structure of this Study

Part I of this book examines the forms and meanings of baroque Catholicism. Chapter 1 briefly introduces the social and economic context of early eighteenth-century Mexico City. Each of the four following chapters of this section examines one aspect of baroque piety: Chapter 2, sacred immanence, or the ability of the sacred to inhere in physical objects; Chapter 3, the performative and liturgical nature of many baroque devotions; Chapter 4, the baroque penchant to adorn sacred space and embellish the liturgy; and Chapter 5, the collective nature of much baroque Catholic practice. This section relies heavily on the analysis of contemporary devotional literature and various pious directives contained in the wills written in Bourbon Mexico City.

Part II examines the project of religious reform. Chapter 6 sets the stage by examining the changing socioeconomic context of Mexico City in the second half of the eighteenth century. Chapter 7 employs ecclesiastical literature to investigate the episcopal attempt to transform religious culture and the intellectual rationale that lay behind it. The next two chapters analyze the changing nature of religious practice in Mexico City in the late eighteenth and early nineteenth centuries. Both rely heavily on numeric analysis of pious directives contained in the corpus of 1,722 wills used in this study. Chapter 8 examines continuities and changes in the religious practices associated with sacred immanence, performative and liturgical piety, and the decoration of sacred space. Chapter 9 investigates transformations in Catholic community and the decline of collective devotions.

The eighteenth century was a period of remarkable stability and flux in the religious culture of Mexico. Many practices of baroque Catholicism remained eminently popular and diffuse among the population. But by the end of the century many Catholics turned to the practices of reformed religiosity. As Mexicans moved into the nineteenth century, no single pious practice dominated religious culture in Mexico City.

PART I

Baroque Catholicism

CHAPTER 1

Baroque Mexico City

✦ MEXICO CITY, THE POLITICAL, FINANCIAL, AND ECCLESIASTICAL HEART of Spain's wealthiest American colony, proved particularly suited to support the florescence of baroque Catholicism. Founded in 1521 by Hernán Cortés on the ruins of the Aztec capital, Mexico City was the largest urban center in the Americas in the eighteenth century. By midcentury, it had a population of about one hundred thousand. Although periodic epidemics ravaged the city, immigration continued to swell its population, raising the total number of inhabitants to an estimated 124,000 by 1813.[1] This large urban populace was racially diverse. In the early nineteenth century, Spaniards (peninsular and creole) accounted for just over half of the city's population, Indians just over a quarter, and *castas* (blacks and people of mixed race) the rest.[2]

As the capital of New Spain, Mexico City concentrated wealth and power that fueled baroque ostentation. It was home to the viceroy, the *audiencia* (high court), and an expanding imperial bureaucracy. It also functioned as the commercial and financial hub of New Spain. For much of the eighteenth century virtually all the colony's wealthy wholesale merchants who controlled international trade lived and worked near the *plaza mayor*, or the city's central square. Lesser merchants who shunted goods from the capital to the provinces and numerous well-off retailers who plied their wares in the capital's various markets, shops, and street corners likewise resided in the city. Moreover, other members of the financial elite called Mexico City home. Many mine owners who held claims in the northern reaches of the colony preferred to live in the luxury of the capital rather than in the isolation of provincial cities or the squalor of mining camps. And almost all those who owned *haciendas* in the capital's hinterland chose to reside in the city.[3] This pattern of residence funneled wealth into Mexico City. Virtually all the wealthiest individuals and families in New Spain were rooted in the capital, and their pious donations financed the baroque religiosity of the city.[4]

The size and wealth of Mexico City supported a large ecclesiastical foundation, which in turn provided the religious venues and personnel necessary for baroque piety. Much of the Mexican hierarchy, including the archbishop of Mexico, his staff, and prelates of the Mexico City cathedral chapter, resided there. Members of the lower clergy likewise congregated in the capital. Although Mexico City possessed only thirteen parishes by the end of the eighteenth century, the number of secular priests who lived there far outnumbered the parish positions available. In 1790, 517 secular priests who did not serve in a parish resided in the city. They supported themselves by reciting masses for the dead, working in the church or civil bureaucracies, engaging in secular enterprises, or combining all three activities.[5] Apart from the secular clergy, Mexico City housed numerous male and female religious orders, including the Franciscans, Dominicans, Augustinians, Mercedarians, Jesuits, Carmelites, Capuchins, Conceptionists, Benedictines, Hieronymites, the order of St. Mary, the order of St. Bernard, and various hospital orders.[6] In fact, members of the religious orders far outnumbered the secular clergy. In 1790, 867 monks and friars and 923 nuns lived in the capital, whereas only 602 secular clerics, including members of the cathedral chapter, parish priests, and nonbeneficed priests, resided in the city.[7] These various ecclesiastical bodies administered a total of eighty-five churches.[8]

Although wealth and power were concentrated in Mexico City, poverty was widespread. The majority of the capital's population lived hand to mouth working as petty retailers, minor functionaries, artisans, servants, and unskilled laborers. These people lived in tenement buildings or the workshops, stables, homes, or offices in which they worked, and spent most of their waking, nonworking hours in the streets, plazas, and other public areas of the city. Earning a livelihood was difficult. Many simply could not find work and had to resort to begging.[9] The destitute, sometimes clad only in blankets, lived in the streets and plazas and pleaded for alms in the city's churches, at its monasteries and convents, and at the homes of its wealthy.

Rising prices of basic staples and declining real wages only made matters worse in the second half of the century.[10] Mexico City was a city of stark social contrasts: the wealthy paraded through the city on horseback or in carriages to raise themselves above the plebeians and poor who crowded the ill-paved, muddy streets contaminated with refuse and human waste. This social distance, however, provided the opportunity for the countless acts of personalized almsgiving so important in baroque piety.

CHAPTER 2

Sacred Immanence

✤ IN OCTOBER 1779 MARÍA MANUELA DE JESÚS CADENA GALINDO, A mestiza nurse who worked in the Hospital Real de los Naturales (Royal Indian Hospital) of Mexico City, called the notary Francisco Juan de Velasco to her bed to write her will. She was ill and probably feared that death was near. She asked to be buried in her parish church and requested a humble funeral because of her poverty. She stated that she had been married twice and had two married children, but that she was now a widow. María Manuela then listed her belongings: a small house next to the new Capuchin convent of Corpus Christi and images of St. Raphael, Mary Magdalene, St. Anne, St. John, and of Our Ladies of Guadalupe and Sorrows. She also claimed membership in five confraternities and ordered that masses be celebrated for her soul and those of her parents, paying for them with the proceeds from the sale of her goods. After requesting masses, she included an unusual clause in her will. María Manuela declared that she had rescued an image of Ecce Homo located in the Hospital Real from neglect and dedicated herself to its care. She asked her children to continue her endeavors and "burn as many candles as they can [*hasta donde ellos puedan*] to him so that, not lacking light, he may communicate his [light] to us and use his mercies with our souls and those of purgatory."[1] In this clause, María Manuela clearly revealed her understanding that honoring images of holy figures and performing acts of devotion, like burning candles, before them functioned as a powerful suffrage. For her, the image of a tortured Christ was not simply a reminder of the passion or a spur to prayer. More than a mere inanimate object, it served as a conduit that passed her act of lighting candles to Christ and called upon him to reciprocate by shedding his light upon her soul and those of others. But the clause's wording suggests more than this. It created a shared identity between the image of Ecce Homo and Christ. The essence that received the lighted candles (the image) was one and the same with the one that communicated his lights and used his mercies with her soul and those of purgatory (Christ). In some way, the image and Christ shared an identity, making Christ present and approachable in the world.

María Manuela thus illuminates for us a fundamental aspect of baroque Catholicism: sacred immanence. Immanence refers to the ability of the sacred to inhere within physical objects. A statue of Ecce Homo is not merely sculpted wood, a painting of Our Lady of Guadalupe is not merely a painted canvas, and the eucharist is not merely a disk of unleavened bread and a cup of wine. Each of these objects contains sacred power, though in different ways. According to Catholic theology during the early modern period, the bread and wine of the eucharist were in their essence truly the body and blood of Christ. On the other hand, holy images, according to learned Catholic thought, did not share the same essence with the holy figures they represented. Images were still ontologically wood, canvas, and paint. But images shared a likeness with their prototypes, and this likeness opened a direct channel between image and prototype. Not all Catholics, however, made such fine distinctions, as the example of María Manuela's pious directive shows. For some, the image and the holy figure shared an identity, so that reference to an image naturally included the holy person it represented. In either case, images, like the eucharist, manifested the sacred within the world.

This chapter relates the history of sacred immanence in Christianity and examines pious practices of eighteenth-century Mexicans that revolved around the ability of the divine to inhere in physical objects. Mexican Catholics frequently honored physical instantiations of the sacred and sought to harness their celestial power by bestowing gifts upon and making physical contact with them. Like other baroque Catholic practices that we will examine in following chapters, sacred immanence rested on an epistemology that united the sign and the signified, thus allowing distinct objects to share the same substance.

The History and Theology of Sacred Immanence

The origins of Christian belief in sacred immanence lie deep in the medieval past. The concept that the divine could inhere in physical objects held currency among Christians by the fifth century. By that time in the Latin West the faithful venerated the relics, the physical remains, of earlier Christian martyrs. Relics served as objects of sacred immanence because they were the saint, or what physically remained of him or her after death, and maintained a link to the saint's spirit in heaven. Christians esteemed them for their miraculous powers. They built shrines on the tombs of martyrs and constructed reliquaries, containers often made from precious materials and adorned elaborately, to house relics. Shrines became sites for the celebration of the liturgy and destinations for local pilgrimages. There, believers used relics to cure disease, cast out demons, and call for divine aid. They even demanded burial close to them to gain saintly aid for salvation.[2]

In the Eastern church, the icon functioned as an object of sacred immanence by the sixth century. Paintings of Christ and the Virgin proliferated in churches. Believers viewed them not merely as representations that called Jesus and Mary to mind, but venerated them by performing acts of devotion before them. This practice, however, was not universally accepted. Some opposed the veneration of icons, basing their opposition on God's commandment to Moses that forbade the production of "graven images." The Council of Nicaea (787 A.D.), in reaction to a campaign by Eastern emperors in the first half of the eighth century to eradicate icons from churches, upheld the orthodoxy of images, promoted the placement of icons in churches, and defended the veneration of these likenesses. The council based its defense on the theology of St. John Damascene (675–749 A.D.) and St. Theodore of Studios (759–826 A.D.). They argued that, although images do not share in the essence of holy figures, they nonetheless share a likeness of form with their prototypes. This likeness links icon and prototype, thus allowing devotions performed before an icon to pass on to the holy person it represents.[3]

Veneration of images in the Latin West took longer to develop. While the East elaborated a sophisticated theology of icons, Western theologians for much of the medieval period viewed them merely as didactic tools, a way to teach the illiterate stories from salvation history. By the eleventh century, however, Western Christians venerated images as well. This perhaps occurred because of the new practice in the tenth-century West of fashioning reliquaries in the form of saints. Devotions to relics may then have become confused with veneration of images.[4] Whatever the origin of the Western devotion, the cult of images spread rapidly.

By the late medieval period in the Latin West, relics and images manifested sacred immanence and served as central features in Christian devotions. The faithful made pilgrimages to the shrines of saints and sought to touch their earthly remains or artistic likenesses to cure ailments, plead for aid in times of distress, and gain salvific grace. They paraded images and relics through villages and cities in public religious celebrations—celebrations that often times possessed a fair-like quality and included feasting, merriment, dances, and other forms of entertainment. And in times of need, they swore vows before them, and bestowed gifts of wax, clothing, and precious objects on them to win their favor and celestial intercession.[5]

In addition to relics and images, the eucharist made the sacred present within the world. In fact, the eucharist was the site of sacred immanence par excellence even though the theology that underlay it developed well after that which supported images. For much of the medieval period, the doctrine of the eucharist remained uncodified. The church never endorsed a precise position on the exact nature of Christ's presence in the host or how that presence, whatever it may have been, occurred during the mass. In the eleventh century, though, Christian thinkers started to argue over the nature of the eucharist. Berengarius of Tours (ca. 999–1088) refuted the notion developed by a ninth-century theologian that Christ resided bodily in the bread and wine. He argued that, if Christ had died and ascended bodily into heaven, he could not be present corporeally in the eucharist. Instead, Berengarius argued that the eucharist contained only Christ's spiritual presence. This assertion provoked counterarguments. Other theologians contended that the celebrant of the mass truly transformed the eucharistic species, the bread and wine used during the mass, into the body and blood of Christ. In substance, the eucharist was Christ, though its accidents, or its appearance to the human senses, remained those of bread and wine. After the consecration, Christ resided bodily in a wafer of bread and cup of wine. The church endorsed this doctrine, now known as transubstantiation, at the Fourth Lateran Council in 1215.[6] By the end of thirteenth century, the church had widely disseminated this understanding of the eucharist. The feast of Corpus Christi, the church's joyous summer celebration of the corporeal presence of Christ in the eucharist, arose at that time and became popular throughout Europe during the next century. Around the same time, Christians began to venerate the consecrated host as a relic. They prayed to it and used it in paraliturgical ceremonies much as they did with the relics and images of saints.[7]

Thus for late-medieval Christians the sacred was proximate, palpable, and approachable. It infused mundane objects and could be seen, touched, dressed, possessed, or ingested. God and the saints manifested themselves physically and so blurred the distinction between the sacred and worldly. Believers could resort to sites of sacred immanence to set things right in times of danger and disorder—hence the recourse to relics, images, and the eucharist during times of illness, drought, and plague. Because the sacred resided in certain objects, the faithful approached them hoping to access their miraculous power. In the late middle ages Christians did not perceive miracles as out of the ordinary; rather, they expected them.[8]

Sacred immanence remained a central feature of Christian practice until the Protestant Reformation of the sixteenth century. Even Erasmus of Rotterdam (ca. 1466–1536), an early reformer who remained within the Catholic fold, ridiculed the veneration of saints and devotions to relics and images. Erasmus, however, never publicly discounted the doctrine of Christ's bodily presence in the eucharist. Martin Luther (1483–1546), the first Protestant reformer, agreed with Erasmus's critique of the cult of saints but also questioned the doctrine of transubstantiation, preferring instead the notion of consubstantiation. He asserted that, although Christ resided bodily in the host after its consecration, the substance of the species remained. Thus the host contained both the substances of Christ and of the bread and wine.[9] John Calvin (1509–64), the reformer from Geneva who penned the most thorough and systematic critiques of Catholic doctrine, proved the most ardent critic of sacred immanence. He labeled images and relics idols and insisted that they were inducements to false religion. He impugned the notion of Christ's bodily presence in the eucharist, declaring that God could not be confined within bread and wine, or any other physical object. Calvin denigrated sacred immanence and the devotions dedicated to relics, images, and the eucharist because he viewed God as radically spiritual. This spiritual divinity, he contended, was entirely distinct from the physical world and incapable of being bound within it. Because God was spirit, Calvin insisted that the only proper method for approaching him was through the spirit or its expression, the rational mind. Therefore, he sought to strip churches of images, extirpate veneration of images and relics, and teach his followers to seek understanding of God's will through the study of scripture. For Calvin and his followers, the age of miracles and sacred immanence had begun to close.[10]

As Protestantism spread in Europe during the sixteenth and seventeenth centuries and curtailed manifestations of the sacred within the world, Catholics took a different path.[11] At the Council of Trent (1545–63), the general church council called to battle the growth of Protestantism, the church reaffirmed late-medieval religious practices. During its thirteenth session (October 1551), the council affirmed the traditional understanding of the eucharist:

> First of all, the holy council teaches and openly and plainly professes that after the consecration of bread and wine, our Lord Jesus Christ, true God and true man, is truly, really and substantially contained in the august sacrament of the Holy Eucharist under the appearance of those sensible things.[12]

Catholic scholars at Trent, however, did not entirely ignore the reformers' critiques. At the same time as they upheld the doctrine of real presence, they condemned "superstitious" practices and abuses that surrounded them. For instance, in the twenty-second session (1562), the council warned priests to celebrate the mass only at approved times and to employ only those prayers and rites officially sanctioned by the church. It also ordered priests to abandon "the practice of any fixed number of masses and candles, which has its origin in superstitious worship rather than in true religion."[13] The theologians at Trent upheld the central mystery of the sacramental presence of Christ's body in the eucharist, but they sought to extirpate those practices that they saw as superstitious accretions that dangerously distracted the faithful from the profound and true miracle of the consecration.

Trent followed a similar course when dealing with the cult of saints in its twenty-fifth session (1563). The council explicitly stated that it was good for Christians to invoke the saints in time of need and to make pilgrimages to their shrines. Moreover, it declared that through the practice of prostrating oneself before and kissing images and relics, Catholics honored the saints and through them, God. The council then immediately established regulations for correct veneration. It first clearly stated that images did not contain the essence of the saints they represented. Nonetheless, images, through their resemblance to the holy person, "referred" the devotions practiced before and on them to their "prototypes." In other words, images do not make saints present in the physical word, but they act as conduits, transmitting human acts of veneration to the saints in heaven. This does not mean that the council denied the sacred power of images. Catholics could still approach them for miraculous cures and the mitigation of plagues and drought. The council, however, instructed the faithful that these miracles were not the work of the saints themselves, but acts of God. The saints only served as intercessors for humans before the divine throne. It was God who performed miraculous deeds through relics and images. Next, the council ordered all profane activities abolished from the veneration of saints. In the eyes of prelates and theologians, saints' festivals were no longer appropriate occasions for boisterous celebrations, drink, and other secular entertainments. Last, the council mandated that no "unusual" image be placed in churches or any new miracle or relic be recognized without the local bishop's approval.[14]

The council upheld the notion that the sacred inhered in certain objects of the world, but it tried to circumscribe its manifestations to the eucharist and approved relics and images. It also announced its opposition to practices now considered superstitious or irreligious. The council deemed such acts not simply superfluous, but affronts to the dignity of the divine. Although Catholic ecclesiastics did not proclaim God to be radically spiritual, like Protestant reformers they sought to separate the sacred from the profane.

Not only did the Tridentine church refute Protestant critiques of sacred immanence, it deliberately sought to invigorate pious practices dedicated to ecclesiastically approved sites of immanence—the host and reputable relics and images—in the face of Protestant challenges. For example, in response to Calvin's attack on the doctrine of transubstantiation, the church redoubled the expense and pomp of Corpus Christi processions. It also sponsored a new form of worship for the eucharist: the forty hours' devotion. As its name suggests, for three days practitioners of this devotion accompanied the consecrated host displayed in a monstrance, a highly ornate portable display stand, without interruption (except for the closing of the church at night). (See Figure 1.) It began in Italy after the sack of Rome by the troops of Charles V as a propitiatory measure, but soon spread and became an elaborate production. The church often staged it during carnival to draw Christians away from secular revelry and focus them on religious concerns, but the devotion could be performed at almost any time of the liturgical year.[15]

FIGURE 1. Gilded silver monstrance, baroque style. Artist unknown. Cast, chiseled, embossed, and gilded silver with precious stones. New Spain, 18th century. Photograph by Jorge Vértiz. Reproduced by permission of the Museo Franz Mayer.

The Tridentine church likewise promoted devotion to the saints and pilgrimage. Philip Soergel has argued that the church in Bavaria used miracle stories of the Virgin as propaganda to combat Protestant attacks on the cult of saints. The stories worked. The incidence of pilgrimage exploded during the seventeenth century and far exceeded that of the fifteenth century, often considered the age of pilgrimage. Soergel therefore concludes that pilgrimage is a largely modern, not medieval, phenomenon.[16] Likewise, devotion to saints increased dramatically in Spain during the seventeenth and eighteenth centuries. William Christian notes a doubling in images drawing special devotion in Castilian towns that responded to questionnaires issued in 1580 and 1780. New devotions to Christ and Mary accounted for the entire increase.[17] In short, sacred immanence remained a central feature of Catholic practice in early modern Europe despite Protestant critiques.

Sacred Immanence in Colonial Mexico

Colonial Mexicans, although shielded by the Atlantic from the intense contestations between the Catholic and Protestant churches in Europe, practiced their faith in an environment shaped by the Reformation and the Council of Trent. In fact, the Mexican church, like other Catholic kingdoms in Europe, held provincial councils to adopt Tridentine reforms locally. In New Spain this task fell to the Third Mexican Provincial Council convoked by Archbishop Pedro Moya de Contreras in 1585. The decrees of the Mexican Provincial Council echoed the tenor and language of Trent.[18] In fact, some of the wording in sections concerning the eucharist and saints mimics Tridentine decrees. The Mexican council, however, tended to be more specific. This stemmed from the fact that, as a provincial council, it had the task of interpreting, adjusting, and expanding upon Tridentine decrees to suit local conditions. Despite this greater specificity, the Third Mexican Provincial Council in no way contravened the spirit of Trent.

The Mexican council devoted much attention to the cult of saints and issued numerous directives concerning proper veneration. It explicitly forbade "profane dances, representations and songs even on the day of the nativity of the Lord, on the feast of Corpus and other similar [feasts]."[19] It further instructed bishops to examine and determine the authenticity of all relics open to public view, not simply newly acquired ones as Trent had mandated. The Mexican prelates also ordered destroyed all paintings and images that represented apocryphal saints or portrayed approved ones in indecent attire or poses. Furthermore, they placed restrictions on artists who produced images and required that local bishops test their orthodoxy and religious knowledge before approving them for such work.[20] Last, they instructed artisans to sculpt only full statues of saints, rather than affixing the saint's head and hands to a frame covered with clothes so as to give the impression of a complete image. They directed artisans to paint the statues they produced so that they would not require clothing or jewelry as adornment and stated that all clothing and other items worn by an image were to become its inalienable property.[21] In essence, the council sought to undermine the custom of dressing and adorning images without prohibiting it outright. Its decrees demonstrate that some Catholics loaned clothes and jewelry to images and later reclaimed them.[22] Perhaps these individuals did so to attire an image with great splendor on its feast day or other special festivity. Or then again, maybe they did so to possess an item that had been placed in sustained and intimate contact with an image and therefore imbued with its sacred power. By banning the temporary donation of items to images, the council sought to limit the circulation of sacred objects among the laity. In this way, the council promoted the larger Tridentine project of diminishing ecclesiastically unsupervised access to the sacred and of sacramentalizing Catholic religious practice at the expense of paraliturgical activities. But the Mexican Council, like Trent, never discouraged veneration of relics and images or adoration of the host. In fact, it labeled such acts of devotion a "pious and laudable custom."[23] The Mexican church, just like the church in Europe, sought to extinguish only pious practices that crossed the newly demarcated line of religious propriety.

Colonial Mexican Catholics engaged in a religious milieu that encouraged devotion to the host, relics, and images.[24] Just like their counterparts in Europe, they participated in church-sanctioned liturgical celebrations of the eucharist and saints. Every year since 1539 when it became an annual event in Mexico City, the Mexican faithful honored the eucharist during the celebration of Corpus Christi. To show their devotion, Mexicans spent lavishly on the joyous procession of the eucharist through the streets of Mexico City and participated in the revelry that accompanied it. By the end of the sixteenth century, the city council paid for theater troupes, musicians, dancers, and fireworks. Contravening the decrees of the Third Mexican Provincial Council, the Count of Monterrey, a viceroy in the early seventeenth century, added mock jousting and three days of bullfights to the celebration.[25] Mexicans also participated in holy week processions, some parading images of the passion through the streets while others whipped themselves in commemoration of Christ's suffering and death. In addition, believers took part in less elaborate processions at other times during the year, particularly on saints' feast days or in times of crisis.[26]

As if the numerous yearly processions failed to encourage enough devotion, spiritual tracts written in Mexico over the colonial period celebrated
Mexico's store of miraculous images and promoted their veneration. In the
seventeenth century, Francisco de Florencia began work on a catalogue of
New Spain's most famous Marian images, a project brought to fruition only
after his death by Juan Antonio de Oviedo, a Jesuit priest from Mexico
City. Their *Zodiaco Mariano* (Marian Zodiac), finally published in 1755,
provides sacred histories and miracle stories for the selected images. It not
only celebrated the special favor with which they believed the Virgin had
blessed Mexico, but also promoted veneration of and recourse to her many
images.[27] Other devotional works likewise encouraged veneration of images
and often instructed readers to perform specific pious acts before them.
Juan de Abreu, a Franciscan priest from Mexico City, published a book of
spiritual exercises dedicated to Our Lady of Sorrows in 1726; because of its
great popularity it was reprinted numerous times over the eighteenth century. Abreu instructed readers to present gifts of "lights . . . silver, flowers,
and incense" (*olores*) to images of the crucified Christ or the Virgin Mary
during the days that they performed the spiritual exercises described in
his book.[28] Another devotional treatise, dedicated to the sacred heart of
Jesus, encouraged the faithful to procure an image of the sacred heart and
"kiss it often, as if you did so with the very divine heart [of Jesus]" (*besarla
muchas veces, como si se hiciese con el mismo Deifico Corazon*).[29] This same
work directed readers to visit the eucharist with frequency, "to reverence
the images of Our Lady," and "to adorn the altars and images of the Virgin
with flowers or in another manner."[30] Certainly, pious literature in colonial
Mexico encouraged the faithful to dedicate themselves to honoring the host
and holy images.

Sacred Immanence in Wills

The faithful of Mexico City needed little prompting to display their devotion. Apart from participating in the numerous processions that sanctified
the city and reverencing the host and holy images in unrecorded routine acts
of devotion that are lost to the historian, they frequently honored the eucharist and images in the wills they wrote. Over the course of the eighteenth
century, testators in Mexico City bequeathed many gifts to the eucharist
and images and, on occasion, asked for burial before a saint's altar (above

which the image stood) or image. These pious directives demonstrate that the Catholics of colonial Mexico City fully participated in a religion of sacred immanence.

The gifts that testators bequeathed to the eucharist and images mostly fell into three categories: wax, candles, or oil for illumination; clothing or jewelry; and money to purchase adornments. The most common specified gift—almost one-third of all those donated by testators sampled for this study—was light, either in the form of wax, candles, candle holders, lamps, or oil for lamps.[31] Gifts for illumination were popular for three primary reasons. First, although relatively costly, most people could afford wax and oil. Second, illumination served any type of image—paintings, prints, and statues—equally well. Last, unlike clothing and jewelry, testators could give light to the host. In fact, of the thirty gifts that testators bequeathed to the eucharist over the seven years sampled in this study, all but eight were made to illuminate the sacrament.[32] The following bequests typified such gifts. In her 1696 will María de Cobarrubias, the wife of a tailor, gave two pounds of wax to Our Lady of the Assumption and another pound to St. Blaze, both of whose images were located in the church of Santa María la Redonda.[33] In the same year Juan Mudarra, a cleric in minor orders, gave six pesos to be spent on oil "that burns in front of Christ at the Column," an image housed in the parish of Santa Catarina Mártir,[34] and in 1737 Catarina Páez de la Cadena, a widow, bequeathed three hundred pesos to serve as a capital fund whose interest was to be used to purchase oil for the lamp that "burns in front of Our Lady of the Unprotected" (*Desamparados*) and the blessed sacrament in a parish in her native city of Seville. She also gave to images in Mexico City: four hundred pesos for wax to the "miraculous image of Our Lady of Guadalupe" in her sanctuary in Tepeyac and two hundred pesos for wax to the "image of Our Lady of la Merced" venerated in the monastery of same name.[35] (For examples of Mexican baroque lamps and candlesticks, see Figures 2 and 3.)

Gifts of wax, candles, and oil served multiple functions and could have various meanings for the testators who bestowed them. Artificial illumination was a practical necessity for church buildings constructed with few and small windows. But the number of candles and lamps that burned in most churches far exceeded that necessary to dispel darkness. As with other forms of churchly ornamentation during the baroque era, the more numerous the candles and more brilliant the display of light, the better. Light also served

FIGURE 2. Embossed, engraved silver lamp with chain. José Joaquín Pérez Calderón? Cast, hammered, embossed, chiseled, and engraved silver. New Spain, 18th century. Photograph by Jorge Vértiz. Reproduced by permission of the Museo Franz Mayer.

FIGURE 3. Pair of silver candlesticks. Manuel Barrientos Lomerín. Cast, chiseled silver. Mexico City, New Spain, 18th century. Photograph by Jorge Vértiz. Reproduced by permission of the Museo Franz Mayer.

symbolic functions. It represented divinity and marked its presence. In learned medieval discourse, the beeswax candle—the type used in almost all liturgical functions—symbolized Christ. This association stemmed from the belief in the virginity of bees; as Mary conceived Christ as a virgin, so bees produced wax in a state of purity. The beeswax represented Christ's flesh, the wick his soul, and the flame, his godhead that outshone and consumed both.[36] In a sense, the lighted candle recalled Christ. Blurred with this function was the use of light to mark the presence of divinity or the sacred. It was no coincidence that the placement of lighted candles on the altar during mass began in the twelfth century, when theologians began to develop the doctrine of Christ's corporeal presence in the eucharist.[37] Because light marked manifestations of divinity, at least one lamp, and ideally many more, should burn continuously before the tabernacle, the sanctuary in which Christ resided in the host.[38] The only time the lamp was extinguished lasted from the end of the prayer service held on Good Friday to the lighting of the new paschal candle during the Easter vigil, the liturgical period that recalled the time from Christ's death to resurrection during which the tabernacle stood bare.[39] Just as light denoted Christ's presence, it also marked the presence of saints. The candle or lamp placed before the image of the saint functioned like those located in front of the tabernacle. By donating oil and wax, testators proclaimed the sacred immanence that images manifested and honored the saints whom they made present within the world.

The bequest of wax and oil, as revealed by a handful of testators, could simultaneously serve other purposes as well. The consumption of these materials by flame could act as a sacrificial offering and as a suffrage to gain grace for one's soul. Mariana Josefa Sálazar, a *doncella* who voluntarily lived within the Conceptionist convent of San Bernardo, inscribed this meaning upon her gift of wax to the Virgin in 1813. She set aside three hundred pesos for the annual celebration on Holy Tuesday of seven masses to the Virgin of Sorrows and "the holocaust of three pounds of wax until its consumption before the sovereign image" located in the convent where she resided.[40] The sacrificial element in the word "holocaust" suggests that, beyond honoring the Virgin, Mariana gave her gift to atone for sin and receive God's cleansing grace. Religious writers of the time often referred to Christ's historic self-sacrifice on the cross and its reiteration during the mass as a "holocaust."[41] According to Christian theology, Christ's crucifixion had repaid humankind's debt to God incurred by Adam and Eve's disobedience and opened the path to salvation. The sacramental sacrifice of the altar likewise placated God's ire and bestowed grace on the community of believers. Therefore, it is likely that Mariana used her yearly gift of three pounds of wax as a means to repent for an offense she had committed against the Virgin. Whether an act of repentance or not, Mariana's sacrificial gift certainly served as a suffrage for her soul. In a similar act, Juan Ángel de Puras, who planned to sail back to his native Castile in 1758, explicitly stated that he viewed his gift of wax as a way to attain salvific grace. He ordered a chapel built in his home town and images of St. Victores and St. Joseph placed in it. He separately called for the establishment of a capital foundation to pay in perpetuity for the candles used during the celebration of the mass in his chapel and implored that this foundation not fail because "it is a suffrage for my soul and those of purgatory."[42]

The use of lights before saints had other possible meanings in late colonial Mexico. As revealed by the gift of wax to the image of Ecce Homo by María Manuela de Jesús Cadena Galindo, whose unusual bequest opened this chapter, the ephemeral and wavering light produced by candles and lamps in this world could represent and call forth the eternal, unchanging light of glory. One other testator, Nicolás Cayetano Abrego, made a similar statement. He believed that his gift of oil to the Virgin would aid the souls of purgatory by showering heavenly light upon them. In his 1737 will he recorded the establishment of a capital fund of 250 pesos as a lien on his home so that its annual interest of twelve and half pesos would purchase oil for a lamp that burned in front of the "most holy Virgin of Loreto" in the Franciscan convent of San Juan de la Penitencia and "illuminate such a great Queen." At the end of this clause, he added that the abbess of the convent should intervene in the reimposition of the capital fund if a future owner of his home decided to pay off the lien "so that the light of said lamp may continue, by way of which the great lady illuminates the blessed souls of purgatory with the lights of glory."[43] Like María Manuela, Nicolás exchanged mundane light for sacred light. The candles and oil they purchased to illuminate their chosen images redounded to the benefit of their souls and to those in purgatory. They both understood that the earthly light flickering before an image called on the illuminated saint to shower the light of glory upon them and the hosts of purgatory. Their symbolic actions in this world triggered a similar and reciprocal action in the next.

A gift of wax or oil, like any other item, to the host or an image could also function as a payment to Christ or a saint for earthly benefits they had granted the testator. In effect, this type of gift was a utilitarian bargaining chip offered by the faithful to curry favor with Christ or the saints or to pay for services rendered. The practice of striking bargains with saints and promising them remuneration if they performed a service was common in eighteenth-century Mexico. María Manuela Villavicencio concretely stated the terms of her bargain in her 1779 will. She asked that her executors fulfill "a promise that I owe to Our Lady of Guadalupe that I promised when

I was ill with rheumatism. It was a communion and two pounds of wax."[44] In exchange for curing her ailment, María had promised the Virgin wax. Antonio de Ruilova y Villegas, a native of Burgos but resident of Mexico City, offers another example of a contract with saints in his 1717 will. In one of his numerous religious clauses, he stated that he had formed a partnership *(compañia)* with St. Anne and that she was his "partner [*compañera*] in . . . five percent of the profits from the principle of my goods." In short, Antonio declared that he had struck a bargain with St. Anne to give her five percent of all his profits if she aided him in his business endeavors. St. Anne must have agreed. To repay her, Antonio bequeathed one hundred pesos to buy oil for the lamp that "continuously illuminates . . . said lady, St. Anne," financed an altar dedicated to her, and paid for her feast day celebration in Burgos.[45] Such bargains were in no way unorthodox. Christians had offered gifts to saints as an enticement to action or repayment for services rendered since the early middle ages.[46] The above bequests show that Catholics in Mexico continued to do so throughout the eighteenth century.

Less common than the gift of light, testators bequeathed articles of clothing to objects of sacred immanence.[47] Perhaps the faithful bequeathed fewer gifts of clothing because such donations contravened the spirit if not the letter of the decrees of the Third Mexican Provincial Council. Or maybe clothing, which could honor only statues, was simply less versatile than light. The gift offered by Rosalía de Aguirre, the wife of a merchant, exemplifies this practice. In 1779 she bequeathed her embroidered petticoat to Our Lady of the Angels to serve as "adornment for the most holy lady."[48] Somewhat uncommonly, she bequeathed an article of her personal attire—though most likely the finest piece of her trousseau—to an image. Testators usually had specific pieces of dress tailored for an image. For instance, Cristóbal Martínez de Cepeda, a priest and financial administrator of the Conceptionist convent of Balbanera, bequeathed a new pair of embroidered gloves to the image of St. Bernard that was housed in the convent that bore his name. Cristóbal included one unusual directive in this bequest. He ordered that the nuns of the convent place the gloves on St. Bernard's image only on his feast day and not to use them for any other purpose.[49]

Gifts of attire, beyond simply honoring a holy figure, could have symbolic significances. Clothing protects the body from the elements; it warms and comforts it despite cold, wind, and rain. The gift of clothing to an image was intended to offer this same protection and comfort in the hope that the saint so honored would reciprocate by lending protection, solace, and comfort to the benefactor's soul as it stood before God and passed through the trials of purgatory. The gift of a cloak to an image of the Virgin especially resonated with this meaning. Often portrayed in the iconography of the late middle ages and the early modern period holding her cloak around her devotees or the souls of purgatory, Mary sheltered those who called upon her.[50] She cloaked the devout from the just wrath of God and eternal damnation. In 1758 Manuel Paulin, a native of Castile and a merchant in Mexico City, likely sought such refuge with the donation of a cloak of "medium quality cloth [*tela moderada*] to Our Lady of Balvanera" that resided in the Benedictine convent in his home province of Rioja. If the bequest proved too difficult to fulfill, however, his executors could bestow the garment on any image of Our Lady of Balvanera located in the churches of Mexico City.[51]

Jewelry was another common gift to images, particularly to those of the Virgin.[52] María Mariana de la Encarnación y Lorenzana, a free *mulata*, bequeathed a typical gift in her 1696 will. Unlike most testators, however, she explained the purpose of her offering:

> Because of the great devotion that I have always had and have for her and through whose intercession I hope for the salvation of my soul, I order to Our Lady of the Rosary that is in her chapel in the royal monastery of Santo Domingo of this city some enameled gold and pearl earrings and each one with four red stones so that they may serve her in the adornment of her dress.[53]

María bestowed her gift on the Virgin for three specific reasons: to demonstrate her long-term devotion to Our Lady of the Rosary, specifically the image housed in Mexico City's Dominican monastery; to beseech the Virgin to intercede and win salvation for her; and to adorn the image and contribute to its majesty. As her bequest reveals, a gift to an image could perform many functions at once. María's gift, however, was relatively modest. Other testators gave highly precious items. For example, in 1813 Juana María de Quintanar, a doncella older than twenty-five, donated "a thick string of pearls composed of thirty gems [*granos*] and a round pendant [*calabacilla*] of diamonds, and the matching earrings" to Our Lady of the Rosary of the pueblo of San Juan del Río; "six strings of pearls without pendant" to Our

Lady of Sorrows also in the pueblo of San Juan del Río; "four strings" to the image of the Dormition of Our Lady (*del tránsito*) in the Royal Indian Hospital; "four strings of pearls with the pendant of diamonds" to Our Lady of Sorrows in the same hospital; "four strings" to Our Lady of Sorrows in an unspecified *beaterio,* or house of devout women who had not taken solemn monastic vows; "three strings of pearls with pendent" to Our Lady of La Merced; and "two small belts [*cintillos*] of diamonds" to Our Lady of Solitude in the parish of Santa Cruz y Soledad.[54] The value of Juana's gifts must have totaled thousands of pesos, a considerable fortune at that time. The expense of such gifts confined the practice of giving jewelry to the wealthy or relatively well off. Only a few testators bequeathed jewelry of lesser value to images.

One reason testators avoided the bequest of low-value jewelry to images was because of the symbolic connotations attached to such gifts. Catholics in colonial Mexico often conceived of heaven as a reflection of and model for an earthly royal court. God, like a monarch, ruled the heavenly kingdom; the Virgin, upon her bodily assumption into the divine kingdom, had been crowned its queen; and the choirs of angels and saints functioned as servants and courtiers. In fact, notaries often referred to the communion of saints as the "celestial court" in the invocation structure of will preambles.[55] Like earthly courtiers—and in the case of the Virgin, like an earthly queen— the saints deserved and required sumptuous dress and ornamentation to discharge their exalted station and activities properly. The desire to adorn images with precious objects recognized the heavenly status of the saints they represented.

Gifts of money to the eucharist and images of saints for the purpose of enhancing their ornamentation constituted the most common bequeathals.[56] No specific instructions typically accompanied these gifts, other than that they should add to the material splendor of worship owed to the eucharist or veneration due the saints. For instance, Juan Agustín de Esquivel y Maldonado, an owner of a hacienda worth 26,000 pesos in Chalco just southeast of Mexico City, claimed in his 1696 will that he had placed a lien worth two thousand pesos on his land. With the one hundred pesos annually produced from the lien, he had financed masses for the deceased members of the Third Order of St. Francis to which he belonged and gifts to adorn the altar of Our Lady of Piety. He instructed his heirs to continue this pious work because he had "received many blessings through [the intercession] of

Our Lady, and I confide in the divine majesty that there will be more in the future" (*haver tenido mediantte la señora muy buenos sucesos y que confío en su Divina Mag^d los hara en lo de adelantte*).[57] Similarly, Pedro Rodríguez, a merchant from Galicia who lived in Mexico City, established a capital fund worth two thousand pesos in his 1758 will. He directed that the annual proceeds of one hundred pesos be used for the "veneration [*culto*] and adornments" of Our Lady of Loreto in the Colegio of San Gregorio "to whom I owe many and special favors from the divine majesty [gained] through her pious supplications."[58] Clearly, such testators sought to honor Christ and the saints by enriching the splendor of their material adoration and veneration. Why did these testators not specify a use for their monetary donations? Most likely they believed that any gift that added to the magnificence of the host and holy images functioned equally well to honor, remunerate, or beseech Christ and the saints and so left the decision about the nature of the offering to others. Those charged with the care of the host and images likely used this money to purchase oil, candles, clothing, flowers, incense, or other precious objects regularly employed to adorn them as they stood on their altars or were paraded in processions.

Some testators left no indication at all about the purpose of their monetary donations.[59] They simply donated a sum to an image with no further explanation. Manuel Gutiérrez de la Concha, an unmarried merchant from Galicia who lived in Mexico City, provides a good example of this type of unspecific gift. In his 1758 will he bequeathed fifty pesos to the "sovereign image" of Our Lady of Soto housed in the Franciscan monastery of the same advocation and fifty pesos to the image of Our Lady of Caldas in the Dominican monastery of the same name, both of which were located in his diocese of origin in Galicia. He then offered one hundred pesos to an unspecified image of the Virgin and fifty pesos to St. Joseph, both located in Guanajuato. Last, he offered two hundred pesos for the image of Our Lady of the Rosary in his home town and fifty pesos to the image of Our Lady of la Bien Aparecida also in Galicia. Apart from specifying that the two hundred pesos intended for Our Lady of the Rosary should be used for her material veneration (*culto*), Manuel gave no other instruction for his gifts. Apparently, he intended to let those charged with the care of these images decide the best use for his donation.

Although most gifts to the eucharist and images consisted of light, clothing, or money, a small number of testators donated uncommon items.

These included an altar cloth, reliquaries, panes of glass, a rosary, a quilt, silver pedestals, land, and livestock. One of the oddest gifts granted to an image, however, was donated by Francisco de Algarra y Sánchez, a native of Murcia and a knight of the military order of Calatrava. In his 1717 will he bequeathed his slave, "a black man named Juan Joseph," to the "most sacred image" of Our Lady of the Rosary that stood in her own chapel in the monastery of Santo Domingo.[60] Francisco stipulated that Juan Joseph could never be sold. If those charged with the care of the image sought to do so, the monastery of Nuestra Señora del Carmen was to take possession of him. Francisco never indicated exactly what Juan Joseph should do once he became the property of the Our Lady of the Rosary. Most likely, he was to serve as the image's caretaker, helping to dress it and clean its altar and chapel.

Whatever their form, gifts to the eucharist and images shared common functions. All honored Christ and the saints by adding to the glory and material richness of their worship and veneration. Moreover, a gift physically demonstrated a testator's devotion to a particular image or advocation of Christ. They could function as a symbolic call for Christ or the saints to lend their mercies, grace, celestial lights and protection. They could serve as an incentive to Christ and the saints to reward their devotees with material blessings, cures, and aid. Last, they could act as a suffrage to aid the soul's salvation. In the minds of testators, their gifts probably performed many if not all of these functions simultaneously. Regardless of their intended purpose, every gift to the eucharist and images represented an immanential understanding of the sacred.

Similarly, burial in proximity to an image demonstrated sacred immanence. Testators in Mexico City had the freedom to select their burial site. Just over half left this decision to their executors, but the rest chose specific churches in which to inter their corpses.[61] A small portion of testators asked for burial close to sites of sacred immanence, either indicating a specific altar upon which an image stood or an image itself.[62] The request for such a burial was universally laconic. For example, in 1696 Mariana Núñez de Rojas simply requested that her corpse be buried "in the church of Santísima Trinidad under the altar of the Holy Christ of the Blacks" (*Santo Cristo de los Pardos*), giving no explanation for her choice.[63] Similarly, Antonia de Sosa Altamirano in 1717 requested burial by "the altar of Our Lady of Pardon" in the Cathedral of Mexico City, and Francisco Martínez, a master painter and guilder, in 1758 asked for interment by "the altar of Our Lady of Aid in the church where, on the occasion [of my death], there may be one."[64]

Only on rare occasions did testators provide more information about their choice of burial close to an image. For instance, Diego de Arellano, a bakery owner, claimed membership in the Third Order of St. Francis in his 1696 will. Because of this, he requested burial in the Third Order's Chapel in the monastery of San Francisco "in front of the altar of Our Lady of Remedies and St. Roach."[65] Diego's membership certainly did not determine his choice of burial altar, for the Third Order's chapel contained more than one. It did, however, narrow his options. Selecting her burial site for a different reason, the widow María Catarina Celis in 1796 asked for burial in the monastery of Nuestra Señora de la Merced "in front of the privileged altar that is named Santo Cristo."[66] Privileged altars possessed special indulgences granted by the Catholic hierarchy that endowed masses celebrated on them with great efficacy in aiding agonized souls in purgatory. María probably assumed that burial by the altar of Santo Cristo would thus tremendously benefit her soul as it languished in purgatory awaiting admittance into heaven.

A testator's devotion to a particular advocation of Christ or a saint constituted the most likely reason for burial close to an image. For instance, in 1758 José de Cevallos Quevedo, a priest and a lawyer for the Audiencia, explicitly requested interment before an "altar of any church where there is found the most beautiful [*bellissima*] image of Our Lady of Guadalupe."[67] The fact that José's only instruction referenced the image of Our Lady of Guadalupe, without stipulating a church for burial, indicates that he primarily revered the image. His choice of the word "most beautiful" in connection with the image only reinforces this conclusion. Like most testators who indicated an altar or image for their burial, he must have felt a strong connection to his chosen advocation.

Those requesting burial near images must have understood on some level that those representations made the saints' essences present within the world or that they channeled devotions to their prototypes in heaven. Burial in proximity to images called on saints to protect the earthly remains of their devotees and act as their advocates before God. The prolonged presence of the corpse near the image was intended to prompt the saint into advocacy and thus significantly reduce the time the devotees' souls languished in purgatory. Images of a saint could thus aid the faithful even after death.

Conclusion

Testators in Mexico City, in their gifts to images and the eucharist and in their requests for burials in proximity to them, demonstrate the importance of sacred immanence in baroque Catholicism. Although the faithful could attribute different meanings to their gifts and desire for burial close to their favored advocations, these devotions only make sense in a religious culture in which the sacred inheres within concrete objects. Because the sacred physically inhabited discrete sites in the world, the faithful could confidently approach them to demonstrate their devotion, honor the divine, plead for aid, and in all cases literarily touch the sacred. In such a religion, physically approaching a site of sacred immanence could be spiritually and materially efficacious. The eucharist and images did not simply call to mind Christian holy figures; they manifested their sacred power within the world and, therefore, acted as sources of spiritual grace and worldly miracles.

This belief in sacred immanence, which rested on the unification of the sign and signified, comprised one of the central elements of baroque Catholicism. In the following three chapters, we will examine other elements of baroque piety.

CHAPTER 3

Performative and Liturgical Piety

✢ ON FEBRUARY 16, 1696, INÉS VELARDE, WIDOW OF THE LATE CAPITAN Don Miguel de Vera, a former notary of the Mexico City *cabildo* (city council), redacted her will before Juan de Condarco y Cáceres. Despite the typhus (matlazáhuatl) epidemic that ravaged the city, Inés was in good health. She had carefully prepared for the pious act of will writing, issuing over thirty meticulously designed religious directives in her testament. Two directives in particular reveal much about colonial Mexican religious sensibilities. In the thirty-seventh clause of her twenty-page will, she founded a perpetual act of charity with three thousand pesos. She requested that priests from the parish of Santa Catarina Mártir use the annual proceeds of 150 pesos from this foundation to clothe twelve "virtuous" poor people every year on Holy Thursday "in reverence of the institution of the most holy sacrament of the eucharist and the washing of the twelve apostles' feet [*labaritorio*] that our Lord Jesus Christ did at his last supper [*santa cena*]." In an earlier clause, Inés established a chantry, a perpetual mass foundation, worth three thousand pesos. She insisted that the friars of the monastery of San Francisco celebrate thirty-three masses yearly for her soul and those of her parents, deceased husband, children, and siblings "in memory and reverence of the thirty-three years that our redeemer and savior my Lord Jesus Christ lived and suffered in this world."[1] In both of these highly Christocentric clauses, Inés employed numeric and temporal symbolism—the twelve poor to represent the twelve apostles, thirty-three masses to represent Christ's thirty-three years as man, and Holy Thursday to commemorate the institution of the eucharist—to link her devotions to Christ's life and passion.

Inés's symbolic devotions—devotions that may seem odd to the modern reader—reveal another aspect of baroque Catholicism. They demonstrate that colonial Mexican Catholics participated in a largely performative religious culture that was highly influenced by the Catholic liturgy. In other words, the faithful of New Spain practiced activity-based devotions as a means of religious engagement and expression. Performative piety includes such acts as those detailed in the previous chapter—pilgrimage, procession, and the physical manipulation (e.g., touching, caressing, and kissing) of saints' images—but also incorporates choreographed bodily dispositions and movement during prayer and what I term "liturgical gesture." Liturgical gesture refers to symbolic actions performed by the faithful that recalled the life and death of Christ or the saints and therefore forged "unions" with them.[2] Liturgical gesture showered the grace of the holy figure imitated upon the performer, who thus accrued spiritual merit necessary for salvation. I label these symbolic performances "liturgical" because their religious efficacy rested on a fundamentally liturgical understanding of how humans invoked the sacred into the physical world. This insight in turn reveals that the rites and rituals of the universal church established much of the basic language of devotions, even informing many of those performed outside the confines of formally liturgical celebrations, namely the mass and the other six sacraments of the Catholic church.[3] The liturgy's decisive role in shaping religious practice in colonial Mexico is logical. The mass was by far the most common religious activity in which colonial Mexican Catholics participated.[4] Simply counting Sundays and feasts days of obligation, days on which Catholics were required to attend mass, reveals that most of the faithful witnessed about ninety masses a year.[5] Many probably attended more.

The highest form of liturgical gesture was the celebration of the eucharist. According to Catholic theology first defined at the Fourth Lateran Council (1215) and later expanded and reaffirmed by the Council of Trent (1545–63), the priest at the altar, symbolically attired in cassock, alb, surplice, and stole, performed a set of symbolic motions and utterances that truly recreated the passion and death of Christ and their salvific efficacy.[6] I argue that liturgical gesture spilled beyond the confines of the eucharistic celebration and the purview of the clergy. Catholics of any estate could orchestrate symbolic gestures to forge mystical "unions" with Christ and the saints.[7] Common forms of nonsacramental liturgical gesture included penitential rites like self-flagellation and fasting, both of which recalled the agony of Christ's passion and death, the sign of the cross, and numeric and temporal symbolism in religious activities. Just as the ritual of the mass collapsed time between the present and Christ's historic acts and truly recreated their salvific efficacy, so symbolically crafted gestures abolished time, linked the performer with the event or figure represented, and imbued the performer with sacred grace. The eucharistic celebration and nonsacramental liturgical gesture, however, were not identical. The difference between the two was a matter of degree. The priest at the altar truly consecrated the bread and wine, making Christ corporeally present in the world. Other forms of liturgical gesture constructed "unions" with holy figures and formed a mystical identity between actor and holy figure, but did not make the holy figure physically present within the world.

The sacred efficacy of liturgical gesture so prominent in late colonial Spanish Catholicism rested on an epistemology that united sign and signified. Celebrating the eucharist or practicing self-flagellation did not simply bring Christ's passion and death to mind; they sacramentally or mystically recreated those historic acts and allowed contemporary actors to participate in salvation history. This epistemology allowed for the true presence of divinity in the world. Liturgical gesture and other religious symbols—particularly images of saints and the host—manifested the sacred either mystically or physically, but in both cases truly, within the world.[8] These divine manifestations demanded attention from the faithful and in large measure accounted for the common practice of penitential rites, pilgrimages, and processions of and gift giving to images.[9] Baroque Catholicism was largely a religion of performance and ritual, but not in an empty or mechanical way. In fact, the key to salvation for late colonial Spanish Catholics lay precisely in making contact with the sacred through performance of religious rites.

Baroque Catholics regularly made this contact with the sacred in and through their bodies. On pilgrimages and in churches, believers literally touched the sacred when they caressed and kissed images. They also connected bodily with divinity by orchestrating their own gestures liturgically. By symbolically arranging their bodily movements—for instance engaging in self-flagellation or performing the sign of the cross—the faithful created an identity with holy figures and thus invoked them into the world.

Furthermore, they often employed certain bodily dispositions, such as kneeling, genuflecting, and bowing during prayer to enhance the religious performance. In each of these ways, baroque Catholics deployed their bodies as vehicles for experiencing the sacred. In short, they accumulated much of the grace necessary for salvation through bodily performance of religious rites.

The History and Theology of Performative and Liturgical Piety

The intellectual rationale that supported the sacred efficacy of liturgical gesture derived from Catholic theology, especially doctrine concerning the central mystery of the faith. As shown in the previous chapter, the Fourth Lateran Council first defined the doctrine of transubstantiation and the Council of Trent subsequently endorsed it. More important to the current discussion is how this transformation of bread and wine into the body and blood of Christ took place. The Fourth Lateran Council merely stated that only ordained priests could perform the sacrament of the altar, suggesting that this had not been the case beforehand. After Lateran, liturgists precisely elaborated the actions priests must perform during the mass and particularly during the canon or consecration of the host.[10] In the sixteenth century Trent reaffirmed Lateran's understanding of the eucharist and restrictions on its performance. Trent, however, more fully developed Catholic theology of the eucharistic celebration. It decreed that transubstantiation occurred because the priest at the altar represented Christ and, through his symbolic performance of the last supper and Christ's passion and death, truly recreated, not simply commemorated, Christ's historic sacrifice. At its twenty-second session (1562), Trent decreed:

> the divine sacrifice which is celebrated in the mass is contained
> and immolated in an unbloody manner the same Christ who once
> offered Himself in a bloody manner on the altar of the cross.[11]

In other words, the council confirmed as dogma the belief that priests during the celebration of the mass liturgically recreated Christ's sacrifice, reiterated its salvific efficacy, and made God physically present within the world in a wafer of bread and cup of wine.

Because Trent imbued this symbolic performance with such religious power, it sought to regulate it closely. It mandated the publication of a text that would prescribe in minute detail every symbolic action and utterance of the mass and the precise order in which the priest must perform them. This text, finally published in 1570 and known as the Tridentine Missal, eventually served to standardize the practice of the sacraments, which local custom and priestly proclivities had previously rendered a diverse pastiche.[12] Henceforth, the mass was ideally to follow the same regimented formula in all Catholic territories so that Catholics in regions as geographically and culturally distant as New Spain and Bavaria experienced the same eucharistic celebration.[13]

The Council of Trent culminated the long process begun by the Fourth Lateran Council of restricting the celebration of the eucharist to ordained priests and highlighting their identification with Christ.[14] Despite the fact that the church succeeded in limiting the performance of the mass to the clergy during the late middle ages, it did not restrict the laity's use of other, lesser symbolic gestures that linked the performer with Christ or the saints. Caroline Walker Bynum, in her classic study of women's corporeal practices of eucharistic piety during the late middle ages, argues that female mystics, nuns, and saints practiced devotions in which they linked their own gestures symbolically with the life and passion of Christ. As he had sacrificed himself on the cross and continued to do so in the eucharist at every mass, medieval women offered up their bodies to God. Through asceticism and the scourging of their flesh, they reenacted Christ's agony and thus made present and participated in his salvific act. As he had suffered and died to redeem humankind, they deprived, humiliated, and flagellated their bodies to redeem their own souls and those of others.[15]

Penitential piety, however, was not restricted to saintly women.[16] Men and women of all estates employed symbolic bodily gesture as a vehicle of religious engagement and redemption. The rise of penitential piety, especially the founding and popularity of flagellant confraternities, attests to the depth of gestural religiosity in late medieval Christendom. The early history of self-flagellation is uncertain, but monks in the Iberian Peninsula practiced it as early as the seventh century. Self-scourging spread beyond the cloister to the laity by the thirteenth century, when public processions of lay flagellants were first recorded in Italy. These penitential processions were largely spontaneous and the result of fiery sermons. This penitential movement spread throughout Europe, including the kingdoms of Spain, in the following century as the Black Death encouraged intense self-mortification as people sought personal and public expiation of sin. Organized confraternities of flagellants soon formed, again first in Italy, to institutionalize public self-mortification. These organizations participated regularly in feast-day processions.[17] In Spain, confraternities of the Holy Cross typically practiced flagellation. Although brotherhoods under this advocation existed in Spain during the fifteenth century, the first documented case of a flagellant confraternity of the Holy Cross appears in 1520. Whatever their early history, these penitential confraternities grew greatly in number and membership during the next two centuries and became a common sight at Holy Thursday and Good Friday processions throughout the Iberian Peninsula.[18]

Performative and Liturgical Piety in Colonial Mexico

Penitential piety featured prominently in colonial Mexican Catholic practice. As demonstrated by a decree of the Third Mexican Provincial Council of 1585, self-flagellation was commonly practiced in the sixteenth century and processions of flagellants drew crowds of the devout. The council recommended that the faithful visit churches to accompany the blessed sacrament on Holy Thursday, the anniversary of its institution by Christ at the last supper. Few people had been performing this pious act, drawn instead to "the procession of the *penitentes*." The council did not condemn the practice of self-flagellation or the penitential processions of holy week. It simply encouraged the faithful also to attend to the eucharist.[19] Over fifty years later Juan de Palafox y Mendoza, the bishop of Puebla renowned for his conflict with the Jesuits over payment of the tithe, advocated and practiced a strict regimen of penance. Among other disciplines, he fasted three times a week, wore hair shirts, and whipped himself three times a day. He encouraged the Indians of his diocese to venerate the Virgin of Ocotlán and led a procession to her shrine on a hill above Tlaxcala walking barefoot and carrying a cross.[20]

Devotional treatises published in New Spain likewise promoted acts of penitence. One work, *Gritos del purgatorio y medios para callarlos* (Shouts from Purgatory and Methods to Quiet Them) by José Boneta y Laplana (1638–1714) on the horrors of purgatory and methods to reduce the soul's time there presented the nun "Francisca" as a model for pious Christians. She covered her body with "beads and medals" and counted every step she took. She offered up her steps to Christ every time she reached the number thirty-three in honor of the number of years he had resided on earth. She fasted on bread and water, disciplined her flesh until it bled, and wore hair shirts. The author later encouraged his readers to practice penances such as "fasts, disciplining, [wearing of] cilices, [and] praying with arms outstretched in the form of a cross [*rezar en cruz*], etc."[21] Boneta's advice to readers was in no way unusual.

Other devotional writers similarly encouraged readers to practice mortification. Cayetano de Cabrera y Quintero (d. 1775), a priest from the Archdiocese of Mexico, first published in 1734 his book of spiritual exercises practiced over twenty-one days and designed to placate the ire of the holy trinity. He instructed readers to employ "prudent mortifications" of the flesh, including fasts, silence, hair shirts, and self-flagellation.[22] Another author, José Vicente de Ochoa Villaseñor, a priest from New Spain, published a book of daily meditations and spiritual exercises in 1793. He told readers that "mortification is . . . necessary to make us pleasing to Jesus Christ" and that

> mortification is the patrimony of true Christians. It is the truth that characterizes all of God's chosen. Resolve yourself to put it into practice from today, considering that without a cross there is no entrance into heaven.[23]

Although it is not known how widespread penitential devotions were among colonial Mexicans, devotional literature and decrees of the Third Mexican Provincial Council suggest that the faithful of New Spain, like their late medieval counterparts, engaged in self-mortification frequently.[24] They reenacted Christ's agonies on their own flesh to link their suffering with his and merit the grace he won for all Christians through his self-sacrifice.

Liturgical gesture was not limited to penitential acts. Many Mexican Catholics regularly employed diverse types of symbolic actions that recalled the life and death of Christ and the saints to invoke and participate in their sacred power. Liturgical gestures could be as flamboyant as public self-flagellation or as commonplace as the sign of the cross. The catechism written by Gerónimo de Ripalda (ca. 1536–1618), a Spanish Jesuit, reveals the liturgical nature of this simple action for colonial Catholics. First published in Spanish in 1591 and subsequently translated into indigenous tongues, it served as the instrument of choice for catechization in colonial Mexico.[25] Ripalda opened it with rhymed instructions on how to cross oneself properly.

Todo fiel christiano / está muy obligado / a tener devoción / de todo corazón, con la Santa Cruz, / de Jesu-Christo nuestra luz; / pues en ella quiso morir, por nos redimir / de nuestro pecado, / y del enemigo malo. Y por tanto /te has de acostumbrar / a signar y santiguar, haciendo tres cruces. / La primera en la frente, porque nos libre Dios de los malos pensamientos. / La sengunda en la boca, / porque nos libre Dios de las malas palabras. / La tercera en los pechos, / porque nos libre Dios de las malas obras. / Diciendo así: / Por la señal / de la Santa Cruz, de nuestros enemigos / libranos, Señor, / Dios Nuestro. En el nombre del Padre, / y del Hijo, / y del Espíritu Santo. / Amén Jesus.[26]

By giving these instructions primacy of place at the opening of his catechism, Ripalda signaled that the sign of the cross surpassed in importance all other prayers, articles of faith, and rules of behavior. Furthermore, it was more than a doctrine that a good Catholic must know. It was an action one could perform in times of danger and temptation. By tracing three crosses on the body, at the forehead, mouth, and breast, the Catholic called on God to liberate him or her from the snares of the "evil enemy," bringing his divine power to bear on situations in this world.

The sign of the cross functioned as a powerful tool because, through its performance, the actor created a mimetic link to the true cross upon which Christ had sacrificed himself. Ripalda made this connection between the sign of the cross and the historical cross explicit. He stated that frequently signing oneself was an act of devotion to the holy cross on which "Jesus Christ, our light," had died and insisted that all Christians were "obliged" to make the sign of the cross in honor of the true cross. By doing so, the actor recalled Christ's redemptive act and made its power present. Later in the same work Ripalda remarked that the sign of the cross functioned as a protective action because Christ defeated our enemies "with his death on it [i.e., the real cross]."[27] Just as fragments of the true cross and certain miraculous crucifixes manifested the sacred because of their physical contact with Christ or their likeness to the true cross, the ephemeral crosses performed on the body by fleeting human action contained divine power.

Numeric symbolism that referenced the life of Christ and the saints in prayers and other devotions likewise functioned as religiously efficacious performances. Above, we encountered the example of the nun Francisca who counted her steps and, when she reached thirty-three, offered them to Christ in memory of his life on earth. Although the activity Francisca performed—walking—as a devotional exercise was atypical, her employment of numeric symbolism to link her life with Christ's was by no means unusual. Many devotional tracts published in Mexico during the colonial period enjoined readers to include numeric symbolism in their pious endeavors. Juan de Abreu, a Franciscan friar from New Spain, first published in 1726 a remarkably popular book of spiritual exercises dedicated to the Virgin and designed to be practiced for twenty days. Each day of the exercise consisted of a morning and evening meditation on the nativity and passion of Christ coupled with other pious actions, including self-flagellation, wearing of hair shirts, fasting, silence, reception of the eucharist, and rounds of prayer. Abreu often included numeric symbolism in these prayer sequences to commemorate the Virgin and Christ. For example, on the evening of the second day, he instructed readers to recite "thirty-three Creeds in reverence of Jesus's labors"; on the morning of the fifth day, "seven Creeds to the seven words that the Lord spoke on the cross and the [seven] sorrows of his mother"; on the evening of the fifteenth day, "nine Salves to the nine months that the Word was in the womb of his mother"; and on the morning of the seventeenth day, "five Creeds . . . to the [five] wounds of Jesus."[28] In fact, Abreu devised the entire spiritual exercise as a form of numeric symbolism dedicated to the Virgin. In the book's introduction, he ruminated on his decision to extend the spiritual exercises over twenty days. He admitted that, in fact, the exercises should last seventy-two days to correspond with the number of years, according to Christian tradition, that the Virgin had lived before her assumption into heaven. But he realized that such a period was too long. He then reminded readers that the Virgin suffered "forty hours of . . . desolation and solitude" during her son's passion. Because each day of the spiritual exercise consisted of both morning and evening devotions, its total of forty spiritual activities corresponded to the "forty hours of [her] agonies."[29]

Other devotional works regularly included numeric symbolism in prayer rounds, and in some cases, virtually any aspect of salvation history could be commemorated numerically. For example, one anonymous devotional work published in Mexico in 1774 frequently used numeric symbolism in its daily devotions to the nativity of Christ. Its spiritual exercises lasted thirty-three days, the number of years Christ lived in the world. During the exercises, practitioners were to flagellate themselves, wear hair shirts, fast, and pray. The author employed common forms of numeric symbolism, for instance, "twelve Hail Maries to the twelve virtues [*excelencias*] with which God adorned Mary" and "nine Our Fathers and nine Hail Maries to the nine choirs of Angels." But he also included symbolic numbers whose referents were quite obscure. On the fifth day of the exercise, he instructed readers to pray "fifteen Salves to the fifteen steps that the most holy Mary ascended to prepare herself for these sovereign mysteries [i.e., the annunciation]"; on the fourteenth day, "nine Salves . . . in reverence of the nine leagues" that the Virgin walked after the annunciation to visit her cousin Elizabeth; and on the nineteenth day "twenty-seven Our Fathers and Hail Maries" to Joseph and the Virgin in honor of the "twenty-seven leagues in the mountains" that they walked after departing from the house of Elizabeth.[30] In short, the liturgical performative piety of the period allowed the devout to forge symbolic "unions" with almost any quantifiable aspect of salvation history.

In addition to numeric symbolism, temporal symbolism could forge liturgical unions with Christ and the saints. The liturgical calendar, with its numerous special feast days to commemorate sacred days in salvation history or the death of saints, provided the rationale. But temporal symbolism could be more specific. Certain days of the weeks were inscribed with symbolic significance: Monday with the souls in purgatory, Thursday with Christ's institution of the eucharist, Friday with Christ's passion and death, Saturday with the Virgin, and Sunday with Christ's resurrection.[31] Even certain hours resonated symbolically. Every day at three o'clock in the afternoon bells tolled throughout New Spain to commemorate the hour that Christ died.[32] In baroque religious culture, the faithful could perform special devotions at other hours as well. Juan de Abreu, for instance, asked his readers to have special devotion to seven o'clock in the evening because that was when Christ ended the last supper and withdrew with his mother for prayer.[33] Another devotional work, published in 1805 and dedicated to the sacred heart of Jesus, instructed devotees to pray one hour every week from midnight Thursday to one in the morning on Friday, "accompanying the divine savior in the garden [of Gethsemane]."[34] Clearly, Mexican Catholics could use many hours of the day and days of the year to practice liturgical piety.

Many performative devotions were symbolic and therefore liturgical in nature, but performative piety also includes nonsymbolic gestures and bodily comportment during prayer. Devotional works sometimes instructed readers to pray the prescribed number of prayers while moving or holding their bodies in particular ways. Most commonly they directed the faithful to recite prayers while kneeling, genuflecting, laying prostrate on the ground, bowing, touching their heads to the ground, or standing with arms outstretched in the form of the cross. Sometimes gestures were more elaborate. Juan de Abreu, for example, instructed readers to demonstrate their repentance by performing the following devotion: "in your room [*retiro*] with a cross on your shoulder you will kiss the ground thirty-three times, [while] walking on your knees."[35] Likewise the anonymous author of the devotional treatise dedicated to the nativity of Jesus directed readers to recite "three Creeds in the form of the cross and standing on one leg."[36] These bodily dispositions and movements were intended to make the body a co-participant with the mind during devotions, intensify the faithful's emotional commitment, and thus enhance the effectiveness of prayer.

Liturgical Piety in Wills

Unfortunately for historians, Catholics in New Spain (and elsewhere during the early modern period) left few sources for the study of their performative religious practices. We simply cannot know how many practiced self-flagellation, how long they fasted, how often they crossed themselves, or how many times they genuflected or prostrated themselves during prayer. But the faithful did leave indications of their performative piety, particularly those devotions of a liturgical nature, in their wills. In them they choreographed their funerals, gave gifts to the church and to the poor, and purchased masses for their souls in symbolic ways that resonated with events from salvation history. These pious directives reveal the deeply liturgical nature of baroque Catholicism in Mexico.

Funerals were prime occasions for orchestrating liturgical gestures. Many testators symbolically designed their funeral corteges, the corpse's procession from home to church. In 1696 Antonio Marcos de Mendieta, a well-off merchant, requested that thirty-three poor people attend his funeral and burial. Each was to receive a candle weighing one-quarter pound. Contradicting protocol, Antonio asked that the poor precede his coffin rather than follow it as was customary for the laity. He also requested that they commend his soul to God. In return for their act of mercy each was to receive four reales as alms.[37] Antonio's particular arrangement made two overt symbolic connections with Christ's life. First, he requested poor people to attend his funeral. In traditional Christian discourse on poverty, the poor represented Christ. For, as Christ had lived poorly and humbly, so did they. Antonio revealed his understanding of the poor's special status by stipulating that they precede his corpse in procession, the space usually reserved for clerics and confraternities. Second, the specific request for thirty-three poor people made reference to the number of years that Christ lived as man. Each poor person represented one year of Christ's life and as a whole recalled his entire earthly existence. Other testators similarly designed their corteges to invoke Christ's presence. In 1717 Francisco del Castillo, a master tailor, requested that twelve "shamefaced poor people" accompany his body to the monastery of San Francisco for burial. He asked that they recite the rosary as they preceded his body in the procession. In return, he offered two reales to each of the twelve attendants.[38] The number twelve recalled the apostles. It created a highly charged symbolic connection because it directly linked the testator's body with Christ's. As the apostles accompanied Christ during his ministry, so the twelve poor accompanied the body of the testator. Thus, the testator and Christ symbolically became one.

Symbolic numbers in corteges did not always reference Christ. In 1779, Josefa Rodríguez de Pinillos, the sister of the Marquis of Selvanevada, stipulated that seven poor people attend her funeral and recite the "crown" (corona) to the Virgin of Sorrows.[39] The crown was a series of repeated prayers, much like the rosary. But it consisted of seven sets of ten "Hail Marys," not five as in the modern rosary. Each set of ten prayers represented one of the seven pains that the Virgin experienced in her life on account of her divine son.[40] Josefa's recurrent use of the number seven linked her to the Virgin, the most influential advocate for the souls of the dead.

Apart from funerals, testators employed liturgical gestures in acts of charity. On occasion, testators engaged in what Maureen Flynn dubs "sacred charity," or charitable acts symbolically designed to recall Christ or the saints.[41] Testators crafted liturgical gestures in bequests to charitable institutions and to the poor in general. Sacred charity to the poor in general could consist of numeric or temporal symbolism, as demonstrated by Inés Velarde's directive to clothe twelve poor people on Holy Thursday that opened this chapter. On the other hand, Diego José Ramírez del Corral, a merchant, only included numeric symbolism in his bequest to the poor in 1758. He asked his executors to distribute fifty pesos to fifty poor people on the day of his death. He requested that in return each of them recite the rosary.[42] In this pious directive, fifty became a sacred number because it referred to the rosary, a devotion that consists of praying five sets of ten Hail Marys. In contrast, sacred charity to hospitals in Mexico City only entailed temporal symbolism: the distribution of the proffered gift on a particular feast day. For instance, José Francisco de Urbina, a wholesale merchant (*mercader alma-zenero*), established a capital fund worth two thousand pesos in his 1717 will. He stipulated that the one hundred pesos of interest that it produced annually be used to purchase cloth for clothes and sheets for the hospital of San Juan de Dios. This gift was to be given each year in perpetuity on the eve of the feast of San Juan de Dios.[43] This type of bequest to hospitals, however, was infrequent and restricted to the first half of the eighteenth century.[44] The practice of sacred charity in gifts to the poor was more common than in bequests to hospitals and occurred throughout the century. Nonetheless it was never widespread.

Requests for masses proved the most common venue for liturgical gesture in wills. Testators used symbolic numbers—most often three, seven, twelve, and thirteen—and symbolic days—primarily saints feast days—to forge links between the masses they ordered on behalf of their souls on the one hand and Christ, the trinity, and a range of saintly intercessors on the other. The symbolic numbers and days they used created "unions" with these celestial entities and mystically invoked their presence at the celebration of the masses or spurred them into advocacy in heaven. In either case the use of numeric or temporal symbolism heightened the salvific effect of the mass and accelerated the soul's progress through purgatory.

The symbolic numbers testators employed in their arrangement of masses had no set meanings, and different testators could use the same charged number to speak to different holy entities or events. The number three offers an example of this polyvalence. Three obviously recalled the trinity, but its range of meanings was much wider. By tradition, Christ's active ministry on earth lasted three years, he fell three times as he bore his own cross to Calvary, he suffered for three hours on the cross, he died at three o'clock in the afternoon, and he spent three days in the tomb. Liturgists recognized the importance of the number three and incorporated it into Catholic practice. During the canon of the mass, when the celebrant transformed the bread and wine into the body and blood of Christ, the priest murmured prayers only audible to himself three times. The three secrets, as these prayers were known, represented the three days Christ spent in the tomb.[45] Moreover, the invocation of the *Ecce agnus dei* (This is the lamb of God) that closed the canon was thrice repeated. Other uses of the number three abounded in the liturgy: triple genuflections, triple aspersions with holy water, and triple incensings.[46]

Although Catholics may not have understood the full symbolic significances of the number three, they apprehended its sacred power and deployed it to their benefit. Many testators commissioned cycles of three masses, but gave different meanings to the number. Some used the number to honor the trinity. In 1758, Jacinto del Conal y Rozo commissioned three masses to do precisely that. He stated:

> It is my will that three low masses to the most holy trinity be said for my soul, those of my parents and the rest of my obligation for the alms of three pesos for each one.[47]

Other testators commissioned three masses to recall Christ's three days in the tomb. In 1737, Francisco José Ponce de León Enrríquez, ordered his executors

> to give alms of one hundred pesos as soon as I die to the monastery of Nuestra Señora del Carmen of this city with the obligation that they then say for me three sung [*sic*] masses with their vigils and offices in the three days after my burial.[48]

With this particular arrangement, Francisco José linked his death and burial with Christ's, apparently in hope of spiritual resurrection at the end of three days' time. Another testator, José Domingo de la Peña, combined these two meanings. He ordered:

> as soon as I die, in the three following days, one low mass be said on each day . . . for my soul and intention on the altar and in the chapel of the most holy trinity that is venerated in the hospital of Señor San Pedro.[49]

The number three could have other meanings as well. María Antonia Luján y Quiroz requested three masses "to the blessed sacrament"[50]; and

Marcelo Ignacio Flores, a merchant, asked for three masses each year on three Fridays during Lent "in memory of the passion of our Lord Jesus Christ."[51] Other testators simply used the number three without ascribing a particular meaning to it. For instance, Juan de Mata Barbosa, asked that:

> as soon as I die, three masses be ordered . . . one of which is to be applied to Our Lady of Sorrows, another to Our Lady of Remedies, and the other to Our Lady of Guadalupe.[52]

Juan's understanding of the symbolic significance of the number three is not apparent from this passage. The number is not linked with the Marian lore associated with any of the advocations he honored with masses. But the fact that he specifically requested three masses, instead of one or some round number, indicates that it held at least a vague significance for him. Because the number three pervaded the liturgy, Juan probably understood on an unconscious, embodied level that it possessed sacred power. But perhaps he did not fully comprehend its many significations. In whatever manner he understood the number, he knew it exercised power within the economy of salvation and employed it for his eschatological benefit.

Seven was another commonly used symbolic number. Seven, though not associated with the liturgy itself, was used in many ecclesiastically sanctioned models, including the seven sacraments, the seven deadly sins, the seven gifts of the holy spirit, the seven archangels who attended the divine throne, and the seven sorrows of Mary. As mentioned in the discussion of funeral corteges, some testators associated the number seven with the Virgin in her advocation of the Lady of Sorrows, often represented in art with seven swords piercing her heart. But the number seven was hardly confined to associations with the Virgin. In fact, testators used it as a generally symbolic number that spoke equally well to all the saints. Domingo Antonio Gil y Fernández provides a good example of the flexible use of the number seven. In his 1779 will, he commissioned seven masses to honor each of the following saints—St. Joseph, Our Lady of Sorrows, St. Dominic, St. Francis, Our Lady of Carmel, Our Lady of Guadalupe, and Our Lady of the Rosary—for a total of forty-nine (seven times seven) masses.[53]

The number twelve was the most commonly used of all symbolic numbers and recalled the apostles who accompanied Christ during his earthly ministry. This is precisely the meaning with which José Núñez de Azebedo invested

the number when he commissioned twelve masses "to the most blessed sacrament" in 1696.[54] Núñez's twelve masses were to accompany Christ in the
eucharist just as his apostles had followed him during his ministry in the
holy land. Most testators, however, used twelve as a generally sacred number
that communicated equally well with any celestial being or functioned on
its own merit to increase the efficacy of suffrages. For instance, José Antonio
Rodríguez in his 1813 will commissioned twelve masses "to the most holy
trinity, another twelve to the most holy Mary, and another twelve to Señor
St. Joseph."[55] More often than not, testators simply requested twelve masses
for their souls or twelve annual masses for their perpetual mass foundations
without reference to the eucharist or saints.

The testators of Mexico City used the number thirteen to refer to Christ
and his twelve apostles. Using thirteen to represent Christ and his disciples
had a basis in the liturgy. In a decree he issued on the proper care of the oil
and chrism used in the sacraments of baptism and extreme unction, the
bishop of Puebla, Francisco Fabián y Fuero remarked on the special symbolism involved in the consecration of these substances. The oils and chrism
were always blessed at a special mass held on Holy Thursday, the day commemorating the last supper and was performed by a bishop assisted by twelve
priests. The bishop stated that in this particular arrangement of celebrant
and assistants "the twelve priests and the prelate [acted] in representation
of the twelve apostles and of God made man."[56] The presence of the bishop
among twelve priests was essential to create this mimetic connection. The
arrangement of thirteen ministers of equal status would not serve to represent the preeminence of Christ and separate him from his disciples. The
testators who used the sacred number thirteen almost always preserved the
eminence of Christ in their mass requests. For instance, Francisco Galindo
y Quiñones, a knight of the order of Santiago and prosecutor (*fiscal*) for the
royal court (*real sala de crimen*), asked that his executors forego the customary obsequies performed on the third, seventh, and thirtieth days after death
and, in their place, commission the celebration of one sung requiem mass
along with twelve low masses in the Carmelite monastery of Mexico City.[57] In
this arrangement the sung high mass represented Christ, whereas the twelve
low ones his apostles.

Less commonly used symbolic numbers were five, nine, and thirty-
three. The few mass requests that employed the number five either made
reference to the five wounds of Christ, the five persons of the holy family

(Christ, Joseph, Mary, and Mary's parents St. Joaquin and St. Anne) or the Virgin.[58] Testators who used the number five in reference to Mary probably had a strong devotion either to the "five great sorrows" of Mary or to the rosary.[59] The rosary consisted of the recitation of five sets of ten "Hail Marys," and devotees were instructed to meditate on the three sets of five mysteries— sorrowful, joyful, and glorious—that properly accompanied its recitation. Nine, of course, was the number of masses contained in a novena, or a pious exercise that usually included masses, prayers, litanies, and mortification of the flesh that lasted nine days. The few testators who arranged series of nine masses must have used the novena as a model.[60] As for thirty-three, it represented the number of years that Christ lived as a man. The celebration of thirty-three masses was doubly symbolic. Not only did each mass consecrate the host, but the performance of thirty-three of them invoked Christ's historic human presence during the mass cycle.

Catholics in Bourbon Mexico City used another form of numeric symbolism to invoke the mystical presence of Christ and the saints. Testators commonly struck symbolic connections between the number of masses they requested and the date of a saint's feast day. For instance, not all who used the number thirteen utilized it in reference to Christ and his apostles. Thirteen also referred to St. Anthony of Padua, and a few testators specifically employed it to this end. For example, the widow María Teresa de Montemayor, requested thirteen masses to St. Anthony and gave him thirteen pounds of wax in her 1737 will.[61] St. Anthony was associated with the number thirteen because his feast day falls on June 13. Similarly in 1779, María Josefa del Niño Jesús, a novice in the Conceptionist convent of Jesús María, established a perpetual mass foundation in her convent centered on the feast day of the Virgin's Assumption, August 15. She requested that fifteen masses be celebrated on the fifteen days preceding the feast, three on the feast, and seven in the seven remaining days of the octave.[62] Although María commissioned twenty-five masses in all, the fifteen to be celebrated in anticipation of the feast resonated with its date. María Dolores de la Cruz Saravia constructed a less ambiguous connection in her 1813 will between masses and a saint's feast day. She founded a chantry in her will to honor the death (*tránsito*) of St. Joseph, which falls on July 20. She stipulated that the chaplain of the chantry order twenty annual masses for her soul, twelve of which were to be celebrated on the 20th day of each month. The remaining eight masses were to be performed during the eight days preceding the feast of St. Joseph, forming a novena to him in July.[63] María's chantry was a circle of numeric and temporal symbolism specifically designed to maximize the sacred power that resided in the symbolic connections she made.

Apart from using symbolic numbers to forge links with God, Christ, and the saints, testators commonly requested the performance of their masses on feast days or other days that resonated with symbolic meaning. The stipulation that masses be celebrated on symbolic days was largely a characteristic of perpetual mass foundations. For instance, Francisca García del Valle and Baltazar de Vidaurre, a wife and husband who wrote a joint will in 1779, established a foundation worth 2,500 pesos with the requirement of twenty-five annual masses. They requested masses on the feast days of St. Joseph, Our Lady of Light (*de la Luz*), Epiphany, St. Francis de Salle, St. Anne, Mary Magdalene, and the other nineteen in the Octave of All Souls.[64] Most testators who founded perpetual masses and who stipulated the days of celebration did not assign all their masses to certain days. For example, Josefa Joaquina Ramírez established a chaplaincy with the requirement of fifty annual masses, but she only assigned twenty-two of them to feast days.[65] Feast days, though the most common special days chosen by testators, were not the only ones singled out as symbolic. Testators also chose Mondays, Fridays, Saturdays, and Sundays with some frequency. The symbolism of Friday and Sunday is obvious; they were the days of Christ's death and resurrection. The significance of Monday and Saturday lies in the liturgical calendar of the late medieval and early modern periods. The performance of the divine office on Mondays was dedicated to the souls of purgatory and on Saturdays to the Virgin. To requests masses on these days was to pay honor to the blessed souls and Mary.

Conclusion

As the symbolic pious directives testators included in their wills show, liturgical gesture permeated religious practice in eighteenth-century Mexico City. Due to the scanty nature of historical documentation, we will never know how often the devout of Mexico City practiced the various pious performances that baroque Catholicism made available to them. But it is clear that colonial Mexican Catholics engaged in penitential rites and other religiously symbolic actions and used numeric and temporal symbolism in their daily lives, funerals, acts of charity, and mass requests to forge mystical "unions" with holy figures and thus obtain grace necessary for salvation. These symbolic performative devotions collapsed time and invoked the mystical but real presence of the holy figures imitated. These performances, although perhaps bizarre to the modern reader, were orthodox at the time. In fact, the central mystery of the Catholic faith, the eucharist, depended on the notion that symbolic human performances could invoke God into the world. Although the laity of New Spain could not consecrate the host, they, like priests during the mass, could avail themselves of symbolic performances to create unions with the holy figures they sought to honor. The effectiveness of liturgical gesture rested on the very same notion that supported sacred immanence. In both cases, similarity, either in the shared likeness of image and prototype or the congruence between symbolic performance and event in salvation history, established an identity between the worldly and the sacred. This identity created by similarity opened the way for the real presence of the sacred within the world. This real presence was physically approachable, and baroque Catholics often made contact with it in and through their bodies. They could touch manifestations of the sacred with their hands or invoke its mystical presence through their symbolically arranged gestures. And as we will see in the next chapter, they could feel the divine presence through their senses. Not only a religion of immanence and ritual performance, baroque Catholicism privileged the bodily experience of divinity.

CHAPTER 4

The Splendor of Worship

✢ IN SEPTEMBER 1717 MARÍA JOSEFA DE ABENDAÑO Y ORDUÑA, an unmarried woman of considerable wealth, wrote a remarkable will in which she issued sixty-four pious directives. She was healthy at the time and called upon Juan Clemente Guerrero to serve as her notary. Because María Josefa had no heirs, she was free to distribute her wealth as she saw fit. She dedicated her entire estate, valued at 48,000 pesos, to religious ends, minus two thousand pesos she assigned to her executors for their work. Although María Josefa distributed her wealth widely among various pious works, she used many of her gifts to enhance the splendor of Catholic worship and adorn sacred spaces in Mexico City. She founded seventeen liturgical feast-day celebrations to fifteen advocations of Christ and the saints. In total, these gifts valued 19,000 pesos. For instance, she established a capital foundation of one thousand pesos so that its annual interest of fifty pesos could be used for the "solemnity and feast" of "my protector and advocate señor St. Joseph" in the convent of La Purísima Concepción. The nuns were to use the funds every year on March 19, the feast day of St. Joseph, to celebrate that day's liturgy with magnificence, certainly including a high mass, music, flowers, incense, and much light from candles, "in jubilation of whom we all have certain faith of our salvation." Likewise, María Josefa established a capital fund worth one thousand pesos to celebrate the feast day of St. Barbara in the church of Santo Calvario. She asked that the celebrations occur with "all brilliance, piety, and veneration [*todo lucimiento culto y veneracion*] so that devotion to said glorious saint extends among the Christian faithful."

Beyond her many foundations to support lavish feast-day celebrations, María Josefa donated numerous items from her home to decorate the churches of Mexico City. For example, to the hospital of Espíritu Santo she gave thirteen paintings, each with a gilded frame depicting the life of the Virgin; two tortoiseshell and mother of pearl desks, one with an image of St. Augustine and the other with an image of St. Thomas; three embroidered calfskin leather chairs; a rainbow-colored rug; and an image of the Christ child with a pedestal, silver cross, and blanket (*velillo*) for the "adornment" of the hospital church. She showered gifts even more lavishly on the parish church of San Miguel. From her private oratory, or home chapel, she donated four paintings—Our Lady of Guadalupe, Our Lady of Populo, Our Lady of Piety, and St. Michael—an ivory image of Christ, and forty-six engravings (*laminas*) with images of saints. In addition to these items from her oratory, María Josefa donated nineteen more paintings of saints including Christ and the twelve apostles, eleven other engravings with depictions of saints, four mirrors, and four large ceramic vases (*tibores*) from China all for the "adornment" of the church.[1] Although María Josefa was not as generous in her gifts to other religious institutions, in total she bequeathed items to thirteen churches in Mexico City to enhance their ornamentation. Her bequests demonstrate yet another, and certainly the most visible, component of baroque Catholicism: the penchant to adorn sacred space ornately and prolifically and to heighten the drama and splendor of religious ritual.

Over the seventeenth and eighteenth centuries, Mexican Catholics spent freely to construct and adorn churches. Church interiors became ornate staging grounds for the liturgy as Mexicans poured wealth into ornamentation of sacred space. Altarscreens—the gilded wooden structures that towered behind altars and that bore images of saints and numerous candles—proliferated and served as elaborate backdrops for the mass (see, for example, Figures 4 and 5). Many church walls, ceilings, and columns were painted in vivid colors or, in some cases, covered with silver and gold leaf (see, for example, Figure 6). Images, either paintings or statues, abounded on altarscreens, on walls, and in the aisles of churches. Influenced by an artistic movement toward naturalism, especially after the mid-seventeenth century, artists crafted these images as lifelike representations that often depicted dramatic scenes from the lives of Christ and the saints. Images

FIGURE 4. Altar of Our Lady of Covadonga. Church of Santo Domingo, Mexico City. Photograph by Jorge Pérez de Lara.

FIGURE 5. Collateral altar. Church of San Francisco, Mexico City. Photograph by Jorge Pérez de Lara.

FIGURE 6. Church of La Enseñanza, Mexico City. Photograph by Jorge Pérez de Lara.

of Christ regularly highlighted the passion and portrayed Christ as broken and tortured. He bled from wounds caused by the scourging, the crown of thorns, and the nails of the cross, and he emoted intense agony. Images of saints expressed sorrow, movement, the agony of martyrdom, or the ecstasy of union with God. Copious candles and lamps cast a dancing light on the sacred images and gilded surfaces of the church.

This splendorous space served as the setting for the drama of the liturgy. Many priests performed private masses for the souls of the dead almost continuously during the morning hours in the multiple side chapels and collateral altars of most urban churches. The low murmur of the celebrants filled the church, and the faithful of Mexico City could see the host elevated at the moment of consecration numerous times a day simply by visiting one of the over eighty churches in the city.[2] Beyond the multiplicity of private masses, the clergy performed at least one public mass every day at the main altar of most churches. On Sundays and feast days, these public masses were celebrated as high masses, requiring the full drama of the liturgy. High masses included multiple priestly participants, repeated incensing of the altar, music, and a sermon. To heighten the drama of the liturgical performance, priests donned colorful liturgical garb often made of silk and intricately embroidered with floral designs or scenes from salvation history. They also utilized precious objects, such as gold and silver chalices, patens, cruets, and incense boats (see, for example, Figure 7). In short, every aspect of the liturgy, from the setting, lighting, sound, and scent, was designed meticulously to contribute to the splendor of worship and materially demonstrate reverence for God.

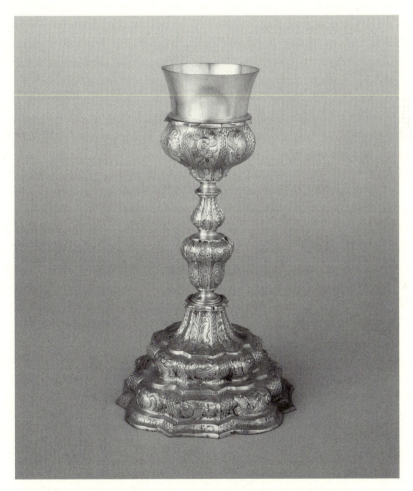

FIGURE 7. Embossed, engraved, gilded silver chalice, rococo style. Artist unknown. Cast, chiseled, embossed, gilded, and stamped silver. New Spain, 18th century. Photograph by Jorge Vértiz. Reproduced by permission of the Museo Franz Mayer.

Why did Mexican Catholics devote so much wealth to ornament their churches and fund the magnificence of the liturgy? Certainly, they did so to manifest their faith publicly and to display their wealth and social status in competition with others. But the display of precious objects and the elaborate staging of the liturgy in baroque Catholicism were more than that. They simultaneously served a higher religious function. Splendor was intended to trigger pious sentiments and thoughts among spectators, to alter the consciousness and elevate it toward the sacred. But more than a mere catalyst for devotional musings, magnificent ornamentation of church interiors recalled and mystically situated Catholics within the heavenly kingdom. Ornate church interiors represented the divine kingdom and symbolically located the faithful among the choirs of angels and the celestial court of saints. Based on the same epistemology that united sign and signified that underlay sacred immanence and liturgical piety, baroque churches and liturgy created sites of heaven on earth, places where divinity resided with especially dense presence. In these heavenly microcosms, the devout connected with the sacred through their bodies. In addition to mimicking the magnificence of the divine realm, splendor stunned the senses of the faithful and induced within them a corporeal experience of divinity. Within ornate church interiors, believers felt God through their senses. The sacred for colonial Mexican Catholics was not distant or abstract. On the contrary, baroque Catholicism privileged the sensuous, immediate, and physical apprehension of God.[3]

The History and Theology of Splendor

Although the medieval church had used splendor in religious architecture and ritual, not until the late sixteenth century did its employment become systematic and nearly universal. The concerted effort by the church to enhance the splendor of worship started in the late sixteenth century and was in part a reaction to the Protestant Reformation. As they had critiqued the notion of sacred immanence and performative piety, Protestant reformers criticized the decoration of sacred space and the dramatic performance of the liturgy. They saw ornate decoration, particularly sacred images, as a dangerous medieval invention that deviated from the simplicity of the early church. Splendor, they contended, distracted Christians from attention to the word of God and, in the case of images, offered incentive to idolatry.

Because of this understanding, Protestants generally simplified their places of worship, stripping churches of most images and other ornaments.[4]

The Catholic church, as it had done in the case of sacred immanence and performative piety, endorsed traditional practice in the face of Protestant critiques and defended the decoration of sacred space and dramatic staging of the liturgy. In 1562 in its twenty-second session, the Council of Trent stated:

> And since the nature of man is such that he cannot without external means be raised easily to meditation on divine things, holy mother Church has instituted certain rites, namely, that some things in the mass be pronounced in a low tone and others in a louder tone. She has likewise, in accordance with apostolic discipline and tradition, made use of ceremonies, such as mystical blessings, lights, incense, vestments, and many other things of this kind, whereby both *the majesty of so great a sacrifice might be emphasized and the minds of the faithful excited by those visible signs of religion and piety to the contemplation of those most sublime things which are hidden in this sacrifice.* [emphasis mine][5]

In short, the church justified the proliferation of ornate adornment and the use of precious objects in ritual because they heightened the magnificence of the sacred and because these physical accouterments moved the soul toward contemplation of divinity.

Girded with Trent's proclamation and the later support of the Tridentine church, Catholic architects and artists soon developed a new artistic style, subsequently labeled baroque, that celebrated profusion of detail and ornate design. Henceforth, Catholic architecture and ornamentation would become highly elaborate and ornate. The use of the altarscreen spread and the screen itself became more exuberant. Golden, spiraling pillars on the screens framed paintings, statues, and the priests who celebrated the mass. Images, which had been largely hieratic during the medieval period, became more lifelike.[6] Apart from art and architecture, other elements of the liturgy become more elaborate. Polyphonic music, first introduced in the fifteenth century, gradually replaced plainsong. In many collegiate churches the ancient duty of chapter members to chant the hours of the divine office devolved upon professional choirs and orchestras.[7]

The Baroque in Colonial Mexico

The baroque as an architectural and artistic style arrived in Mexico over half a century after it had begun in Europe. It emerged in Rome in the 1580s in church construction sponsored by the papacy. It soon spread to other parts of Catholic Europe, where architects and artists adapted the style to local sensibilities.[8] From Spain the baroque arrived in Mexico by the mid-seventeenth century. As in Europe, Mexican architects and artists modified the style. Even in New Spain, baroque style was far from static and varied from place to place. Over time, architects and artists, often influenced by trends in Europe, transformed the Mexican baroque, usually moving toward greater exuberance in design and coloration.

In Mexican churches, the baroque style is most manifest in the design of altarscreens and facades. In the seventeenth and early eighteenth centuries, baroque architects emphasized horizontal segmentation that broke altarscreens and facades into clearly tiered levels. Moreover, they compartmentalized their works, distinctly framing each image that composed the screen or facade (see, for example, Figure 8). By the 1730s, a new baroque architectural style arose called churrigueresque or ultrabaroque. It highlighted verticality, raising attention toward the heights of the church, and played with depth. Whereas the altarscreens and facades of the earlier baroque were relatively flat, churrigueresque works utilized intensely three-dimensional highlights. Altarscreens three meters or more in depth were not uncommon. Furthermore, the ultrabaroque favored profuse ornamentation, leaving almost no surface within the church undecorated. It left no spot for the eye to rest. The style accentuated undulation and movement intended to dizzy the viewer as the eye continuously moved from one ornamental flourish to the next.[9]

The numerous churches of Mexico City, because they were built over long periods, often contain elements of various architectural styles. The cathedral of Mexico City, begun in 1573 but not finished until the nineteenth century, was designed as a solidly Renaissance structure. But it was one of the first churches in New Spain to receive baroque touches. The facade of the main entrance includes an early baroque stone carving of the Assumption of Mary completed in the 1680s. The cathedral also contains fourteen collateral chapels and even more collateral altars. Each of these chapels and altars stylistically reflects the period in which it was constructed. The Altar of Our Lady of Pardon (see Figure 9), begun in 1718, combines elements of the early

FIGURE 8. Chapel of the Angels, Metropolitan Cathedral, Mexico City.
Photograph by Jorge Pérez de Lara.

FIGURE 9. Altar of Our Lady of Pardon, Metropolitan Cathedral, Mexico City. Photograph by Jorge Pérez de Lara.

and the ultrabaroque, and the Altar of the Kings (see Figure 10), finished in 1737, is considered one of the best examples of a churrigueresque altarscreen in Mexico.[10] Like the cathedral, most churches in Mexico City contain stylistically mixed elements.[11]

The baroque, however, transcended architectural and artistic style. It was a broader culture of religious practice as well—one that valued decorative exuberance and dramatic presentation. It is precisely this broader culture of religious practice, rather than formal elements of architecture and art, that is of significance here. This religious culture of ornamental accumulation and dramatic flourish was not an empty celebration of the external. As a whole, baroque religious practice was designed to tantalize the senses for the purpose of inciting devotional fervor. Ornamentation dazzled the eyes, music sounded in the ears, the smells of incense and flowers filled the nostrils, the kissing and touching of relics and images awakened the body, and the occasional consumption of the host overwhelmed the mouth. All were staged to heighten religious engagement and induce a felt experience of God's presence.

The colonial Mexican church fully endorsed baroque exuberance. Ecclesiastical authorities themselves commissioned baroque altarscreens,

FIGURE 10. Altar of the Kings, Metropolitan Cathedral, Mexico City. Photograph by Jorge Pérez de Lara.

precious liturgical utensils, and saintly images. At provincial councils, even
before the arrival of baroque architectural and artistic style in New Spain,
the bishops and prelates of Mexico concluded that true piety required ornamentation of sacred space. At the First Mexican Provincial Council in 1555,
ecclesiastical leaders insisted that only those churches necessary for the
propagation of the faith be built and that any church that lacked the "necessary decency and ornamentation" be closed.[12] Thirty years later, the Third
Mexican Provincial Council issued a similar decree. It instructed pastors to
ensure "the greatest splendor and ornamentation" of their churches and of
the liturgy.[13] Not surprisingly, this official inclination to ornament sacred
space and enhance the splendor the liturgy continued into the eighteenth
century, the height of baroque style. In an instruction he left for the priests
of his diocese upon his death, Juan José de Escanlona y Calatayud, the bishop
of Michoacán (d. 1737), encouraged pastors to increase the splendor of their
churches by obtaining the finest clothes for the altar, maintaining the clean-
liness of the sanctuary, and augmenting the silver ornaments of the church.
The instruction stated that such work was necessary because "God visits us
according to how we reverence him."[14] During the colonial period decoration of sacred space was not an optional matter of taste, but a requirement
for proper worship. Churches that lacked "decency and ornamentation"
were unsuitable sites for the performance of the liturgy and the adoration
of God. At worst the lack of proper adornment offended God. At best bare
churches did not please him, so the faithful who worshipped in them could
little expect his favor. Not surprisingly, New Spain's ecclesiastics sought diligently to multiply the ornamentation of church interiors.

Splendor in Wills

The faithful of New Spain enthusiastically aided the church in decorating
sacred space and fully participated in the culture of baroque Catholicism.
In their wills they bestowed numerous gifts on Mexico City's religious institutions—churches, religious orders, and confraternities—to heighten the
splendor of public worship. Although they gave gifts to religious institutions for various reasons, the desire to adorn sacred space motivated many
donations.[15] In addition to gifts to religious institutions, testators commonly
established capital funds to sponsor the liturgy on the feast days of favored
advocations. These funds were qualitatively different from chaplaincies and

chantries, other types of foundations designed to support the celebration of masses.[16] Chantries and chaplaincies set aside capital for the perpetual celebration of private masses to aid the soul of the benefactor who established the fund and usually the souls of his or her family members. Funds for feast-day celebrations supplied money for the perpetual performance of lavish public high masses on special days of devotion. Feast-day foundations thus participated in the baroque inclination to promote the magnificence of the liturgy in a way that chaplaincies and chantries did not.

Testators could enhance the ornamentation of church interiors through the donation of money or gifts in kind. Of the two, monetary gifts were more common.[17] Testators who bestowed monetary gifts usually did not specify the exact purpose of their gifts beyond the desire to ornament sacred space. For example, Juan Mudarra, a cleric in minor orders, bequeathed 120 pesos in his 1696 will to the parish of Santa Catarina Mártir for "ornaments" without further specifying the type of adornment.[18] In the same year Francisco Martínez, a Mexico City merchant, donated fifty pesos to the confraternity of San Nicolás housed in the monastery of Santo Domingo simply for the "adornment" of its chapel.[19] Few testators, however, revealed the prevailing desire to adorn churches and chapels to increase the magnificence of worship better than Juan de Iraizos, a native of Spain's Basque territories and a clerk in a Mexico City confectioner's shop. In 1737 he bequeathed fifty pesos to the Capuchin convent of Mexico City to be used in the "worship [*culto*] and adornment of its church" and donated another fifty pesos to the Third Order of St. Dominic to be spent on the "worship and adornment" of its chapel. He also left one-third of all his belongings to the parish church of his native town for the purchase of "precious silver objects [*alhajas de plata*] . . . such as chalices, patens, cruets, servers, thuribles, incense boats [*navetas*], or a lamp."[20] In his bequests, Juan demonstrated the deep association between splendor, ornamentation, and the use of precious objects on the one hand and proper religious practice on the other. By linking the words "worship" [*culto*] and "adornment" [*adorno*], he highlighted the necessary relationship between worship and splendor.[21] To worship God or venerate the saints properly required magnificence in outward practice, and he was willing to donate much of his personal fortune to that end.

Although most testators who gave gifts to religious institutions to enhance the splendor of worship failed to specify exactly how they wished their donation to be used, a handful precisely stipulated the ends to which their donations were to be employed. All of these specific bequests concerned the liturgy. As we have already seen, Juan de Iraizos donated one-third of his fortune to purchase items used in the mass. Tomás Díaz de Vargas, a wealthy widower, likewise bequeathed fifty pesos in 1779 to the parish of Santa Catarina Mártir to pay for altar cloths.[22] And in 1796 María Josefa del Niño Jesús, a novice about to profess in the convent of San Jerónimo, donated three thousand pesos to establish a capital fund in favor of the monastery of Nuestra Señora del Carmen. The Carmelite friars were to use the interest from the fund to purchase liturgical items, "especially . . . corporals, purifiers, and tabernacle curtains."[23]

Although most gifts given to religious institutions were bequests of money or items convertible into cash, a minority of gifts, all of which were directed toward the enhancement of liturgical and paraliturgical activities, were made in kind. Clerics were the most likely group to donate such gifts. Gonzalo de Cervantes, an unbeneficed priest in Mexico City, made a gift in 1696 of an altar cloth and canopy to the sanctuary of Nuestra Señora de Guadalupe to serve as accessories to the liturgy at the main altar and two silver candleholders for the sanctuary of Nuestra Señora de Remedios.[24] Similarly, Miguel Ramón de Cruz, a novice about to profess in the monastery of San Juan de Dios and a son of a master goldsmith, donated a silver chalice and paten to the novice chapel of his monastic house in his 1737 will.[25] Priests also donated their own ecclesiastical vestments to embellish the liturgy. Manuel Ordóñez y Aguilar, a pastor in Ciudad Real in Chiapas but residing in Mexico City in 1779, left his three "best, most expensive, and splendorous [lusidos]" pieces of his personal liturgical attire to three separate churches in the city of San Cristóbal.[26] Similarly, Marcos Reinel Hernández, the pastor in Iztapalapa just to the south of Mexico City, donated his alb and chasuble (singulo) to his parish church.[27] Not surprisingly, gifts in kind to aid the liturgy were the domain of ecclesiastical testators; except for a few who maintained private oratories in their homes, members of the laity had no reason to own liturgical items.

In terms of gifts in kind, the laity almost exclusively donated images of saints. Donating an image was relatively common, suggesting that the possession of images in the home for private devotion was prevalent in eighteenth-century Mexico City.[28] Many people forged close emotional connections with their private images and lavished gifts upon them.[29] The veneration of saints was not an exclusively public devotion reserved for communal vows and paraliturgical practices; it entered the confines of the home and absorbed the individual energies and finances of early modern Catholics.[30]

Testators bestowed statues, paintings, and prints on churches. María Josefa de Abendaño y Orduña, the testator whose splendorous gifts opened this chapter, gave all three types of images to both the hospital of Espíritu Santo and the parish of San Miguel. Similarly, María Francisca Sáenz de Rosas, the widow of an accountant in the mercury monopoly, in 1779 donated statues of Our Lady of the Assumption, Our Lady of Guadalupe, and St. Anthony, paintings of St. Joseph, St. Rosalia, and Our Lady of las Caldas, and a print of Our Lady of the Rosary to the Capuchin convent of Mexico City to be placed either in its church or cloister.[31]

In many cases, the gift of an image included more than the representation of the saint itself. Many testators gave the jewelry and ornaments that they had lavished on the statue or (more rarely) painting as a sign of devotion to and method of honoring and compensating the saint for favors gained through his or her intercession. In her 1696 will Melcora Montejo, for example, gave a sculpted image of Our Lady of the Immaculate Conception along with "her gilded pedestal and four silk dresses and crown of silver" to the Conceptionist convent of Jesús María to serve as an altarpiece for the main altar of its church.[32] In comparison to the fineries some testators bestowed upon their images, the accouterments Melcora gave to her statue of the Virgin appear modest. Some people must have spent thousands of pesos to adorn their favored saints. Baltazar de Vidaurre and Francisca García del Valle, a husband and wife who wrote a joint will in 1779, are a case in point. They left five images to the Carmelite convent of Santa Teresa la Antigua. The bequest included a sculpted image of Our Lady of Light with her "choker [*ahogador*] of diamonds and belt of gold, with her display case [*nicho*] and table, and in said belt an emerald in the center"; two cherubs (*angelitos*) with crowns of silver; an image of Our Lady of Sorrows with "a hallow of silver, two rings with pearls, and earrings of gold with rubies"; another of Our Lady of Loreto with "her tiara of silver, her earrings, and necklace of pearls"; another of St. John Nepomucene "with his quill of silver, display case, and table"; and a painting of Our Lady of the Immaculate Conception "with its glass pane."[33] Splendor not only formed a vital component of public worship in churches and chapels, it characterized private devotions in the home as well.

The fact that many testators gave saints laden with precious items to religious institutions indicates that an important motive behind their donations was to increase the ornamentation of churches. Both the images themselves and the fineries adorning them added to the opulence of the recipient churches and chapels, which represented and attempted to recreate the brilliance and magnificence of the heavenly kingdom and its celestial court.

Testators also donated images to public places of worship to foment veneration of their favored saints. A number of testators stated this motivation in their wills. In 1779 Cristóbal Mariano de Leon donated a statue of Our Lady of Sorrows along with its "adornment" to the Capuchin convent of Mexico City so that "it may have the adoration and veneration [*culto*] that it merits."[34] In the same vein and in the same year, Teresa del Rivero y Zúñiga, the widow of a master pharmacist, donated her images of Our Lady of Sorrows and John the Evangelist to an unspecified "poor church" so that they "may achieve the veneration [*culto y veneracion*] that my just devotion and cordial affection desires [*sic*]."[35] By spreading devotion to their images, these testators honored their favored patrons and sought to intensify the pious sentiments of fellow Christians. Both actions redounded to the benefit of their souls. In return for this act of devotion, the honored saints escalated their intercession on behalf of their devotees. Furthermore, God rewarded those who increased his glory by promoting the cult of saints. The donation of an image in this sense was a double suffrage. Not only did benefactors receive merit because they bestowed alms upon the church; they also gained continual grace as long as their images attracted devotees and prompted the faithful to acts of devotion.

Not all donations of images, however, specifically sought to promote devotions to favored saints. A few testators who must have possessed especially intimate bonds with their images and the saints they represented bequeathed images to the churches in which they planned to be buried. In essence, they sought to preserve a physical connection to their images in perpetuity and, thus, maintain the close relations with their saints that they had cultivated during life. For instance, Josefa de Salcedo, the widow of a cobbler, bestowed her image of Our Lady of the Immaculate Conception "with her string of fine pearls, hoop earrings [*sarcillos*] of gold, and crown of silver" upon the chapel of Espíritu Santo in the barrio of San Lázaro "where my body is to be buried."[36] In her 1737 will María Ana González de Valdeosera, an unmarried and probably young woman, was more explicit about her bonds of affection and devotion to her image. She wrote that she owned a baby Jesus from Naples, in his glass case [*urna*] with various precious items of pearls, gold, [and] fine necklaces [*bejuquillos*] that my devotion and affection [*cariño*] has placed upon him, for I have placed all my heart, affection, and will in my little lord [*señorito*] which has been mine since my childhood. [I ask] that he be carried to the [monastic] house or college where I will be buried for my consolation and be put [in a place] at the disposition of the reverend father abbot [*padre prepósito*] or rector and its care [*aseo*] will be at the disposition of my parents, my executors.[37]

María's emotional bond with her image of the Christ child is evident. In life, she showered her devotion and attention on it as shown by her numerous gifts of precious objects to adorn it; now, in death, she desired to preserve those bonds of affection. The proximity of the image to her corpse would continue to offer her "consolation." María's bequest betrays no desire to increase devotion to the infant Christ; rather, she spoke of ties of affection and psychological support between person and image fostered over a lifetime of intimate interactions. Nevertheless, as she no doubt appreciated, the gift of her image with all of its fineries certainly added to the splendor of the church where she was to be interred.

Images and liturgical items comprised the majority of gifts in kind to religious institutions, but the rare testator bequeathed other objects. For example, Cayetano Elías de Arávallo, a landowner in Coyoacán, donated to the Franciscan monastery and missionary college of San Fernando "a holy cross that I have in its glass display case [*nicho*] which appeared to my father of which there is testimony."[38] Like many testators who gave images to religious institutions, Cayetano made his gift to promote devotion to his mysterious cross. In the same manner, Felipe Betancur, an unbeneficed priest, bequeathed a reliquary "with a bone from the body of señor St. Lawrence" to the Augustinian convent dedicated to that saint in Mexico City.[39] Other rare gifts included carpets, chairs, desks, cushions, panes of glass, holy water receptacles, and a clock. Even these less common gifts shared the same basic purpose as bequests of images, liturgical utensils, and monetary gifts for the adornment of churches and chapels. All were designed to heighten the splendor, intensity, and dramatic impact of worship.

A few testators went beyond the mere desire to decorate sacred space and elected to finance the construction and adornment of chapels and collateral altars.[40] José Miguel de Reyna, a master pharmacist, recorded in his 1737 will that he had already built a chapel next to the Franciscan convent of Santa Clara. He dedicated it to Our Lady of the Immaculate Conception and placed an image of her there. He stated that he had "adorned" the chapel with "mirrors, sculptures, and paintings" and asked that a caretaker be named so that devotion to the Virgin "increases and that the precious objects [alajas] [of the chapel] do not deteriorate."[41] In the same year Juana de Arriaga Mendizaval Mexía de Vera, a wealthy widow, dedicated four thousand pesos for the construction of a collateral altar in the (at that time) unfinished Franciscan church of San Fernando. She wanted it dedicated to St. Joseph and stipulated the precise order of images for the altarscreen. Images of St. John the Baptist and St. Francis of Assisi were to occupy the bottom section. Juana indicated that the "large image of the crucified lord that I have and have venerated and venerate in the oratory in the house of my residence" was to have precedence of place in the center of the altarscreen. Images of St. Teresa de Jesus and St. Gertrude were to flank the crucifix on either side.[42] As both José's and Juana's bequests reveal, sacred space was not complete without ornamentation, particularly the presence of saintly images. A single image, however, hardly sufficed. In the baroque culture of the era, sacred space required a profusion of images and ideally other ornaments as well.

Gifts to enhance the ostentation of already splendidly ornamented churches helped set the stage for the performance of the liturgy. The ornate decoration of sacred space symbolized the majesty of God and represented the splendors of heaven, thus inducing a sense of awe within the faithful. This intense feeling was intended to move the mind to contemplate and reverence the sacred and also primed worshippers to feel God's presence. This experience ideally occurred during the mass, when the priest—framed by a glittering backdrop of altarscreen and images, costumed in resplendent symbolic vestments, and manipulating liturgical utensils crafted of precious materials—consecrated the host and made Christ corporeally present within the world. The setting of the mass was splendid. But its performance was the essential feature of churchly practice. Just like the ornamentation of sacred space, the more lavish and splendid the public performance of the mass, the better.

The faithful of Mexico City certainly apprehended the necessity for splendid celebration of the eucharist. They spent lavishly in their wills to endow extravagant public performance of the mass on holy days throughout the liturgical year. In their endowments for feast-day liturgies, they often explicitly stated how the mass they commissioned should be embellished. In 1717 Beatriz de Figueroa, an elderly doncella, set aside one thousand pesos as a capital fund to support the feast-day liturgy in honor of Our Lady of Remedies in the Franciscan convent of Santa Clara. She wanted the nuns to use the fifty pesos of annual interest to finance the celebration with a "mass, wax, flowers, perfumes [*olores*] and additional things for the just brilliance" of the performance.[43] Similarly, María de Jesús, a novice about to swear her solemn vows as a nun in 1796, set aside two thousand pesos to serve as a capital fund to finance the "solemn" feast-day liturgy for St. Luis Gonzaga on every June 21. The interest from her fund was destined to pay for incense, a mass with a sermon, and "the most decent music that . . . good voices and instruments can produce [*formen*]." She also asked for "that number of lights that corresponds to the pomp of such a festivity."[44]

A small minority of testators designed their feast-day celebrations in a highly specific manner. María Guadalupe Marín del Castillo, a widow of a *governador* (district governor) and, at the time she wrote her will in 1813, a resident in the convent of San José de Gracia, offers a good example of an ultra-detailed feast foundation. She set aside 5,700 pesos, or 285 pesos annually, to fund a solemn mass in the convent in which she lived on the nineteenth of every month "in honor and glory" of St. Joseph. She chose this date because the feast of St. Joseph falls on March 19. Each month, twenty-three pesos and six reales were to be spent on one "sung mass with three ministers," the money to be divided as follows:

> two pesos to the priest who sings the mass, one to each one of the ministers who help to officiate it, three reales to each one of the three acolytes who should assist at the mass and deposition, four pesos to the musicians so that they sing at the mass and the deposition [of the eucharist publicly displayed in a monstrance], eleven pesos and one real for the wax that is to burn all day from the mass until the deposition, four reales to the sacristan for the work that he occasions in this, and three pesos that are to be distributed to six poor people of the convent, whether they be nuns, lay residents [*seculares*], or servants, at the rate of four reales [for] each one, with the obligation that two by two they are to accompany the blessed sacrament [*señor sacrementado*] from twelve until three in the afternoon.[45]

The expenses María incurred for the ministers, acolytes, music, and wax were common to all feast foundations. In fact, other testators probably spent more on these expenses, considering that the average capital fund of a feast foundation provided almost twice as much money per mass as María's did. María's bequest is unusual because of her liturgically symbolic request that the eucharist be exhibited for the entire day of the celebration and that at least six people accompany it from noon to three, the hours Christ agonized on the cross. In fact, her feast-day foundation was the only one that included a symbolically performative directive. It is unknown if feast-day celebrations normally included this type of liturgical piety. Perhaps María's inclusion of temporal symbolism simply resulted from the unusual specificity of her instructions.

On rare occasions, testators indicated that the celebration of a saint's feast day spilled beyond the liturgical activities that occurred within the confines of a church. Colonial Mexicans often engaged in merriment and feasting on holy days in addition to participating in religious processions and attending mass. These festivities, as Fernando García de Rojas, a hacendado from Nueva Galicia, reveals in his 1737 will, often lasted into the evening. Fernando established a capital fund worth six thousand pesos to honor the feast of St. Anthony in the Franciscan monastery in his home town. The friars were to use the three hundred pesos of annual interest to stage the feast with "a solemn mass with a deacon and subdeacon, sermon, [and] adornment of the altar." In addition, they were to spend the yearly income on "wax and the other expressions of solemnity." According to Fernando, these expressions included "fireworks [*fuegos*] and festive lights [*luminarias*] as is customary."[46] For Fernando and many other Mexicans, honoring a saint's feast day did not consist solely of the liturgy, but also included joyous festivities that marked the day as extraordinary.

In addition to feast-day celebrations, a few testators funded other liturgical events that contributed to the splendor of worship. For example, Margarita Josefa de la Concepción, a novice about to profess her solemn vows in the convent of La Purísima Concepción in 1737, donated 1,500 pesos to her religious house to finance the customary "Salves" sung to the Virgin as part of the office of Our Lady performed on Saturdays throughout the year.[47] In 1758 Francisco Ignacio de Gojendola, a resident of Pázcuaro, gave six hundred pesos to fund the Holy Friday "celebration of the three hours that Christ our

Lord was on the holy cross" in the sanctuary of Our Lady of Guadalupe in his home town.[48] Similarly, in 1813 Francisco Reyes, an unbeneficed priest of the archdiocese, left 5,500 pesos as a capital fund to the convent of La Enseñanza. He stipulated that the fund's annual interest of 275 pesos finance the convent's Thursday masses of renovation—the liturgy during which the celebrant consecrated enough hosts for use as the viaticum during the coming week and consumed the surplus eucharistic wafers not distributed during the previous one—and its Saturday masses celebrated in honor of the Virgin. Francisco stipulated that seventy-five pesos annually be spent on wax used during the masses he funded.[49] Although not as lavish as the feast-day endowments established by many testators, the support for other liturgical activities fulfilled the same function of embellishing Catholic ritual and emotionally engaging the faithful with dramatic religious performance. Hence, these less common liturgical foundations likewise participated in the baroque pious culture of the time.

Conclusion

Splendor was not a mere accessory to piety in colonial Mexico City; it was an essential component of baroque Catholic practice. Both the clergy and laity sought to heighten the decorative appeal of church interiors and the dramatic impact of liturgical performance. The Catholic hierarchy, in opposition to the attacks by Protestant reformers, defended the use of images and ornaments in sacred space and the lavish celebration of the mass. In fact, the Council of Trent labeled these externals "stimulants to piety."[50] The church encouraged the profusion of decoration by commissioning new baroque church buildings that demonstrated the church's resurgence and defiance of Protestantism. In New Spain the church embraced the baroque by the mid-seventeenth century. The faithful wholly participated in the baroque religious culture of the age. In Mexico City they bequeathed numerous gifts in their wills to increase the brilliance of church decoration and the drama of the liturgy.

The gift of a precious object to a church or the foundation of a lavish feast day celebration functioned on various levels. Such gifts attested to the devotion of the testator and pleased the saints and God. Equally important, such gifts enhanced the splendor of church interiors and the performance of the liturgy. Ornate churches served as earthly models of the heavenly kingdom and gave the faithful a glimpse of the joys of the afterlife. Moreover, in the baroque aesthetic, splendor had the capacity to stun the senses, to awe spectators, and thus induce in Catholics a felt sense of God's might and presence. The use of sculpted and glittering altarscreens, the profusion of images, the sumptuousness of ecclesiastical dress, the glint of silver and golden sacred vessels, the multitude of flickering candles and lamps, the strains of music from the choir, the ringing of bells, the smell of incense and flowers, the taste of the eucharist, the contact of images pressed against lips and caressed by hands, and the feel of holy water sprinkled on the body aroused the senses and created a palpable experience of God. To increase the splendor of worship, then, was to ensure and heighten the experience of God among the faithful. In short, splendid churches and lavish liturgy created sites of heaven on earth where the faithful could communicate with the sacred through prayer and their bodies.

CHAPTER 5

Charity, Confraternities, and Community

✝ IN NOVEMBER 1737 JOSÉ DE ARCE Y CARRIEDO, THE OWNER OF A hacienda in Cuernavaca and a butcher shop in Mexico City, called the notary Manuel de Benjumea Jiménez to his home to redact his will. José, ill and confined to bed, included eight pious clauses in his testament. Just after the preamble and the disposition of his funeral, he claimed membership in at least six pious brotherhoods in Mexico City including the Third Order of St. Francis, the lay branches of the hospital orders of San Juan de Dios and the Bethlehemites, and "other confraternities," all of which could be confirmed by the patents, or certificates of membership, that he possessed. He then turned to masses, ordering four hundred for his soul, and to charity. Although José was a widower without offspring, he had raised three orphans, a category in colonial Mexico that included both children whose parents had died and children whose parents had abandoned them. Two of them were women—Micaela Francisca de los Dolores y Arce, who was nineteen years old, and Inés Francisca de Sales y Arce, who was thirteen. According to José, they had been "exposed at the house of my residence" (*expuestas en la casa de mi morada*), that is, abandoned by their birth parents at his home when they were young, probably just infants. To each of these women, he gave one thousand pesos to help her take the "state [either married or religious] that God gives her." Because José's mother still lived at the time he wrote his will, he could freely dispose of only one-third of his estate, and the remainder by law passed to her. He stipulated, however, that if he outlived his mother, he wished to give an additional two thousand pesos to each of his two female orphans. José was less generous with the male orphan, Nicolás de Loreto, age seven, whom he had also raised. He bequeathed only two hundred pesos to Nicolás, to be given to him only after he had left home to learn a trade. José's charity did not stop with the orphans he raised. He gave two hundred pesos each to the hospital of San Juan de Dios of the order of the same name and the hospital of Convalesencia of the Bethlehemite order for whatever purpose the rectors of these institutions deemed appropriate. Finally, he donated an additional two hundred pesos to each hospital for the establishment of capital funds. He stipulated that the ten pesos of annual interest from each fund were to be used to purchase food for the sick in each hospital. In the hospital of San Juan de Dios the food was to be distributed on the feast day of St. Joseph, and in the hospital of Convalesencia on Pentecost.[1] Apart from requests for masses, all of José's pious clauses involved confraternities, or pious brotherhoods, and charity. The importance José placed on membership in confraternities and charitable giving reveals the last aspect of baroque Catholicism for our consideration.

In addition to sacred immanence, liturgical gesture, and ornamentation of sacred space, baroque Catholic practice emphasized community in Christ through charity and collective devotions. Although baroque Catholics performed individual devotions to God and the saints, much of their religious practice was communal. For instance, in early modern Spain villagers often made communal vows to saints and, as an entire village, honored their chosen patrons by collectively celebrating their feast days.[2] Spaniards in New Spain performed similar practices. The clearest expression of this communal piety in urban areas consisted of collective participation in processions on feast days or other special occasions. On high feast days like Corpus Christi the members of Mexico City's important corporate entities—guilds, confraternities, religious orders, the secular clergy, the city council, and the viceregal court—paraded through the capital, sanctifying its streets and plazas. These large-scale processions simultaneously demonstrated hierarchy, for the most socially prominent entities marched at the end of the procession nearest the host or the saintly image on parade, and ideally displayed social cohesion, for all social groups from the lowliest to the highest participated together to honor and beseech Christ and the saints.[3] Collective city-wide processions occurred for other reasons, such as to plead before God and the saints for the end of earthquakes, floods, and, most commonly, plagues.[4] On a smaller scale, individual parishes and monastic communities often held neighborhood processions before the celebration of solemn masses or on the feast days of parish and monastic patron saints. In these smaller processions, all members of the neighborhood community could participate. In large or small processions, participants acted collectively to honor God and the saints, to call upon them for aid in times of crisis, or to repent publicly for the community's sins. The collective nature of the devotions forged and reinforced a sense of Christian community, uniting believers through a common devotional practice. Moreover, parading in unison amplified the tribute or the petition aimed at God and the saints by the mere fact that many members of the community joined their voices, prayers, and performances in one pious act.

In addition to processions, baroque Catholics forged and maintained community through other mechanisms. The central mystery of the Catholic faith, the celebration of the eucharist, was a public act designed to suspend enmity in the community and unite the faithful regardless of social rank or kin divisions—at least for the duration of the ceremony. Almsgiving and participation in confraternities also structured and expressed community. The personal distribution of alms united the rich and poor and mediated the social distance between them, whereas participation in pious brotherhoods linked one member's struggle for salvation with that of the entire confraternity.

While social cohesion was the ideal, it was not always realized. The social distance inherent in acts of charity certainly could cause rancor toward the wealthy on the part of the poor. Furthermore, the distribution of alms could reinforce social distinctions, for the act of giving money to the poor clearly displayed the social positions of both the benefactor and recipient. Likewise, membership in confraternities could induce rifts in Christian community, especially when these pious organizations vied with each other for precedence of place in processions on feast days. Despite the fact that baroque Catholic practices could not entirely prevent social friction and in some cases outright conflict, personalized acts of charity and membership in confraternities, among other baroque practices, aimed toward the ideal of Christian fellowship. Colonial Mexican Catholics, as they engaged in collective devotions and encountered each other in personalized acts of charity, sought to forge, if never entirely successfully, Christian community.

Two fundamental principles underlay baroque Catholic community. First, it was ideally structured through intimate connections that linked members of the faithful together in Christ. Face-to-face interactions, such as the kiss of peace during the mass, the personal distribution of alms, and the cheek-by-jowl closeness of processional participation, bridged spatial and social distance, if only temporarily, and united diverse Catholics in common cause. Second, Catholic community mediated the individual's relationship with God and the quest for salvation. Although each Catholic must face God at individual judgment soon after death, he or she did not stand entirely alone. Salvation was a collective affair in which members of the Catholic community could aid the individual soul with prayers, masses, and other suffrages. One's own merits did not wholly determine one's eternal fate. The lone Catholic could always utilize grace accumulated by the community of the faithful through the celebration of the mass and performance of good works to enhance the possibility of a favorable judgment by God and acceler-ate the soul's passage through purgatory.

In the language of contemporary Catholic writers, all Catholics par-ticipated in the mystical body of Christ and the community of saints. The entirety of the faithful composed the mystical body of Christ, with Christ as the head and the rest of the faithful the remainder of the body. As mem-bers of the mystical body, all Catholics enjoyed access to the salvific merits earned by Christ's crucifixion and possessed an intimate and (metaphori-cally) organic connection to all the members of the faithful. As members of the community of saints, Catholics were linked with the faithful, both living and dead, in the collective quest for salvation. An individual Catholic could resort to the merits earned by the saints, the church, and the other faithful to help ensure salvation. These two concepts explain how the church could endorse the recourse to suffrages such as masses, indulgences, and prayers to aid souls as they languished in purgatory.[5]

Baroque Catholic community rested upon a subjectivity, or sense of per-sonhood, in which the self was not a bounded, impermeable entity. On the contrary, the baroque sense of self was porous, open to outside influence, and subsumed under a larger, collective identity. The pioneering work of a handful of European historians reveals that the sense that modern Western individuals have of being one autonomous, wholly integrated personality throughout a lifetime emerged to varying degrees throughout the West in the late medieval and early modern eras, the period during which Europe colonized the Americas.[6] Prior to this time, Europeans in both the Old and New Worlds perceived themselves primarily as part of larger groups, such as families, lineages, guilds, estates, and religious communities that were situated within a hierarchical yet integrative social order. This open and porous sense of personhood did not merely allow for collective devotions and the communal quest for salvation, but rather necessitated collective piety. Porous individuals depended on other members of the community for self-definition.[7] One's acts, identity, and fate were not entirely or, in some cases, even mostly self-determined. In such a cultural environment collective religious practices helped ensure the community's and the individual's proper relationship with God.

The Theology and Practice of Charity in Colonial Mexico

Granting alms to the poor constituted one way Catholics could promote community cohesion and thus strengthen their relationship with God. In fact, all Catholics of means were obliged to give alms to the poor in order to ensure their own salvation. The catechism issued by the Fourth Mexican Provincial Council, held in 1771, spelled out this obligation unambiguously. It stated that "men who omit acts of mercy are condemned to eternal pain . . . and to those who do these works are promised eternal life."[8] The "acts of mercy" referred to in this passage are the seven corporeal and seven spiritual acts taught in every catechism.[9] The church did not expect each Christian to perform all these acts, but more generally to aid those in need through the distribution of alms and bequests to institutions charged with the care of the destitute and ill.

The Tridentine church emphasized good works to counter Protestant theology that dismissed charity as unnecessary for salvation.[10] The Catholic obligation to perform acts of charity, however, was not a mere basic requirement for salvation. Like the mass, almsgiving was an efficacious suffrage that won grace for the benefactor and improved his or her standing before God. The more alms one gave, the more merit one gained and the less time one spent in purgatory atoning for past sins. In fact, in the hierarchy of suffrages, learned opinion classified gifts to the poor among the most efficacious of acts, second only to the celebration of masses for the soul.[11] The gift of alms was so beneficial because it was actually a double suffrage. The benefactor not only received grace for the act itself, but also gained merit when the recipients of his or her largesse commended him or her to God in their prayers. Moreover, almsgiving provided the recipient with the opportunity to obtain grace. The poor person who humbly and graciously accepted alms exercised Christian virtue and increased his or her own store of merit. Therefore, Catholics had good reason to distribute wealth in charitable acts. Every peso given as alms to the poor who populated this world redounded doubly to the giver's benefit in the next and aided the salvation of others.

Although the distribution of alms could certainly be a mercenary transaction in which one exchanged earthly goods for heavenly rewards, we should be wary of characterizing it as necessarily so. Almsgiving in a religion of sacred immanence was itself a sacred act. Like symbolically charged liturgical gestures, the granting of alms invoked Christ into the world. The basis for such an understanding came from the Gospel of Matthew, specifically the passage on which the seven corporeal acts of mercy were based.

> For I was hungry and you gave me food, I was thirsty and you gave me drink. I was a stranger and you welcomed me, naked and you clothed me. I was ill and you comforted me, in prison and you came to visit me. Then the just will ask him: "Lord, when did we see you hungry and feed you or see you thirsty and give you drink? When did we welcome you away from home or clothe you in your naked-ness? When did we visit you when you were ill or in prison?" The king will answer them: "I assure you, as often as you did it for one of my least brothers, you did it for me."[12]

The poor represented Christ and received alms in his name. In fact, in traditional Catholic discourse, the poor held a special spiritual status because their destitution reflected Christ's own earthy poverty. Because of this similarity, the poor were considered Christlike. Therefore, the gift of alms was not a casual act in traditional Catholic practice, but a ceremony intended to communicate one's adoration and devotion to Christ.

Moreover, in traditional Catholic practice the bequest of alms to the poor participated in the larger realm of charity. In late medieval and, for a time, in early modern parlance, charity referred to a state of amicable relations among Christians and between Christians and God, not solely to an act of beneficence toward the poor. John Bossy, in his cogent history of Christianity in this period of transformation, argues that the creation and extension of charity was the primary goal of traditional Catholicism. All religious activity, and especially the mass, was intended to induce a sense of *comunitas*, or a state of fellowship unmarred by distinctions of social group or the animosity of kin rivalries, among participants. In essence, through performance of liturgical and paraliturgical activities, late medieval and early modern Christians sought to suspend tension and participate in the mystical body of Christ.[13] The bequest of alms to the poor did not simply aid the unfortunate in their trials; it also mediated social distinctions as it incorporated both the benefactor and recipient into Christ's mystical body.

In Europe during the early modern period, however, learned discourse on charity began to change. The poor were no longer regularly portrayed as symbols of Christ within the world. They were divided into two categories: the deserving and undeserving. The deserving poor included the ill, the infirm, and the shamefaced poor (*pobres vergonzantes*) who hid their poverty and did not beg publicly, along with other categories such as widows and virtuous unmarried women (doncellas). On the other hand, the undeserving poor consisted of the able bodied and in many cases the mendicant poor (*pobres mendigos*), or those who begged publicly in the streets and plazas or went door-to-door asking for aid. During the sixteenth century and afterwards, this latter group was frequently represented as a source of contagion, crime, and disorder. For these reasons, ecclesiastical and royal authorities sought to limit their number and regulate their activities by allowing only those who possessed official licenses to beg within a certain parish or secular jurisdiction. Over the early modern period in Europe, in the elite's estimation, the poor dropped in status from symbols of Christ within the world to vile elements who threatened the established order. The elite, however, were not entirely successful in disseminating the new discourse on poverty and charity. The faithful of Spain, for instance, continued to practice traditional forms of charity and almsgiving throughout the seventeenth century.[14]

In New Spain, like Europe, divergent discourses on poverty and charity competed. The traditional understanding of charity as a state of amicable relations in the Christian community persisted.[15] In an instruction he left upon his death for the priests in his diocese, Juan José de Escalona y Calatayud (d. 1737), the bishop of Michoacán, discussed Christian charity through a parable. He related the story of the enmity between two women, one well off and the other poor. A parish priest refused to give the eucharist to the well-off woman until she pardoned her enemy. She did so and received the host. But upon leaving the church, she encountered the poor woman who thanked her for the pardon. But the well-off woman then recanted her act, stating "I do not pardon you; before [I do] that I'll see myself on the gallows." Immediately, the woman choked and died. The eucharist, however, sailed from her mouth through the air until the priest recovered it and placed it in the tabernacle. He then ordered the woman's cadaver thrown to the dogs. The story's message is clear. Christ, who is present in the eucharist, resides only among those who live in Christian charity. Rancor and animosity fracture the community, thereby banishing him. Furthermore, those who bear grudges and refuse to reconcile with their neighbors risk irreparably rupturing their relationship with God and dying without Christ's consolation. Bishop Escalona y Calatayud explicitly stated the moral of this parable when he wrote: "The blessing of God is not present [*no cabe*] where all are not one through charity."[16]

Other pious literature produced in colonial Mexico likewise operated within a traditional understanding of poverty and charity. Mexican devotional writers often marked the special religious status of the poor when directing readers to perform acts of charity. An anonymous book of spiritual exercises dedicated to the nativity of Christ clearly exalts the sacral status of the poor. Published in 1774, these devotional exercises to the Christ child span thirty-three days and end on Christmas. The devotional work called on readers to engage in many acts of charity. Among others, it instructed readers on one day to "wash the feet of a poor person." In this instance, the author certainly makes reference to the gospel story in which Christ, on the day of the last supper, washed the feet of his twelve apostles. The poor person who received this symbolic pious act thus was associated with Christ's closest companions. On Christmas day, the final day of the exercises, the author directed the faithful in memory of Jesus, Mary, and Joseph and their journey to Bethlehem for Christ's birth to "bring [*meteras*] three poor people into your home, making intention to lodge *through them* [emphasis mine] the three divine pilgrims, and give them food this first day of Christmas [*Pasqua*] without vanity, from the sweat of your brow. Serve them with humility, love, and reverence."[17] In this case the three poor people represented the holy family. The practitioner honored the real holy family through lodging, feeding, and reverencing the poor. According to many religious writers in colonial Mexico, the poor clearly possessed a special religious character. Like Christ, the apostles, and the holy family, they were also poor and so in some measure participated in their sacred nature. Devotional writers recognized this special status and instructed the faithful to honor the poor with alms and other acts of charity.

Despite the persistence of traditional notions of charity as harmony within the Christian community and the special sacral status of the poor, the poor of New Spain suffered the same deflation in status in learned discourse as their counterparts across the Atlantic. The Catholic hierarchy in Mexico classified the destitute as deserving or undeserving from an early date. It began to regulate begging, the principle means for the face-to-face exchanges between rich and poor that bridged social distance, reinforced Christian community, and accrued divine grace for the wealthy and poor alike. Church leaders sought to restrict begging, particularly in and around church buildings, the physical heart of Christian community. Eventually, as we will see in Chapter 7, the church in the late eighteenth century attempted to remove the mendicant poor from public view and confine them in workhouses.

The first steps in classifying the poor as worthy or unworthy and to restrict begging in church buildings occurred early in the colonial period. In 1584 the cathedral chapter of Mexico City issued a set of rules to govern begging. These regulations allowed the "shamefaced poor" to ask for alms on any day of the year in any church in the city. They did not explicitly reference the mendicant poor, but the cathedral chapter's use of the term "shamefaced poor" indicates that its members distinguished between the deserving and undeserving poor. Apparently, the mendicant poor were not approved to beg within churches. The cathedral chapter's regulations did, however, specifically mention "professional" beggars, or those who collected alms for hospitals, schools, mendicant orders, and other pious institutions. The chapter restricted them to asking for donations on certain days of the year and to particular churches. Some almoners were even limited to collecting at church doors and not allowed to beg within church buildings.[18] This decree simultaneously participated in both the traditional and new discourses on poverty: it divided the poor into categories but approved begging by the deserving poor in church interiors.

One year later the Third Mexican Provincial Council increased restrictions on begging. The Council encouraged bishops to promote the distribution of alms, but stipulated that pastors not allow unknown mendicants to beg within their parishes unless they possessed episcopal licenses. Thus the council granted priests the right to regulate acts of charity, officially

approve each poor person to request alms, and to prohibit the unsanc-
tioned poor from begging in their communities. Furthermore, the council
restricted begging within church buildings, although it did not entirely forbid it. The council henceforth prohibited the poor from begging in church
during the daily high mass and from "restlessly and noisily" asking for
alms from people attending private masses.[19] Here, we see the restriction
of begging within church buildings in an attempt to halt disruptions during the mass. But this decree did not entirely ban begging in churches. The
church was still open to the poor throughout the day, except for the hour
or so that it took to sing the day's solemn mass. This restriction was not
intended to displace the acts that forged bonds of human community from
the church. It simply sought to focus the faithful solely on God, and thus
away from their neighbors, during the most solemn act of Catholic worship.
Nonetheless, these two decrees by the Third Mexican Provincial Council
represent a growing wariness toward the poor and an increasing desire to
regulate begging and charity.

Charity in Wills

The faithful of Mexico City practiced charity within this contested and
changing discourse on poverty. In their wills they performed acts of charity
largely in three ways: by declaring that they had raised orphans and bequeathing gifts to them, by granting alms to the poor, and by donating money to
charitable institutions, usually hospitals that cared for the sick, infirm, and
destitute. All these pious directives structured and maintained religious
community, though in different ways, and each testified to the Catholic precept that those endowed with wealth by God must perform acts of charity
toward the poor to gain the grace necessary for salvation. Charitable gifts,
then, had a double function. They ideally united the faithful and opened the
gates of heaven.

The rearing of orphans and the bestowal of gifts upon them was the most
intimate form of charity practiced by the faithful of Mexico City. Neither
church nor state mediated the relationship between orphan and caretaker,
and years of caring for abandoned children often engendered affection. This
highly personal act was the ideal type of charity in baroque Catholicism,
for it forged an enduring relationship that involved repeated occasions for
face-to-face charity including most of the formal acts of mercy. Moreover,

the raising of orphans literally expanded community as families welcomed strangers into their midst and in many cases incorporated them within familial structures.

Bequests to orphans in the wills from eighteenth-century Mexico City were remarkably similar in nature. They almost universally consisted of simple gifts of money, though on occasion a testator bequeathed land, a house, household items, or an image of a saint to an orphan. In most cases, testators had raised or were raising the orphan to whom they bequeathed their gift. Most commonly, the orphan had been unknown to the testator before he or she had been left as an infant at the testator's doorstep. If the orphaned child had not yet reached the age of majority, the testator usually entrusted the gift to a family member or associate with the stipulation that the holder pay an annual return of five percent on the sum so that the interest could be used to support the child as he or she grew. In most cases, girls did not receive their gifts until they married or entered a convent. In fact, most testators included a phrase in the bequest specifying that the gift was intended as a dowry to help the girl "take a state." In contrast, boys were given their gifts without reference to marriage or religious vocation, usually at an undefined age. Testators bestowed gifts on girls more often than boys, by a factor of almost two to one.[20] They also tended to bequeath larger sums to girls than to boys.[21] Both of these situations suggest that testators expected boys to work and pay their own way in life, whereas they expected girls to marry well with the aid of a dowry.

Bequests to orphans often reveal the bonds of affection that grew between adult and child over a lifetime of care. For instance, Antonio de Nebro, a petty merchant, recorded in 1696 that he was raising "Juan José, a Spanish child one year and ten months old" who had been abandoned at his home. Antonio also stated that he did not know who the boy's parents were. Then, "because of the affection that raising [a child] engenders and [because] I look on him as a son," he bestowed one-fifth of his property on the boy. This is a particularly telling gift because Antonio had four biological daughters. He thus gave Juan José the same share of his wealth as he bestowed on each of his daughters.[22] Just over one-third of all testators who bestowed gifts on orphans made similar protestations of love and affection for the children they raised. This suggests that many who cared for orphans incorporated these children into their families and treated them more or less the same as their own offspring.

Even some testators who did not insert phrases of endearment in clauses about the orphans they raised clearly viewed them as their children. Francisco Antonio Narváez y Sánchez, a childless widower and provincial merchant from Texcoco, provides a case in point. In 1813, he claimed to have raised two abandoned "little orphans" (*huerfanitos*), Luiz Gonzaga Sánchez, age eight, and María de la Concepción, age twenty-two. Having no mandatory heirs by law, Francisco was free to grant his estate to any person, institution, or cause. He named Luis and María, his two "adoptive children," as his only heirs.[23] If affection can be measured by inheritance, Francisco clearly saw the two orphans as his children.

Not all testators, however, incorporated orphans into their families on an equal footing with their own offspring. In fact, as seen in the case of José de Arce y Carriedo, whose will opened this chapter, not all testators treated the orphans they raised equitably. Antonio Ruíz Morandiel and María Gonzáles de Celisco, a husband and wife who wrote a joint will in 1696, provide another example of this differential treatment. Antonio and María owned a hacienda in Xochimilco and had five offspring. They also raised seven orphans and bequeathed gifts to each of them. To Juana de la Asención, a mestiza and age ten, they gave one hundred pesos for when she took a state. They gave Juan, age five, and José, age nine, fifty pesos a piece and asked their executors to ensure that they learned to read and write. They were only to receive the fifty pesos after they had taken a profession (*oficio*). Last, Antonio and María gave twenty-five pesos a piece to Isidro de los Santos, age nine; Sebastiana Catarina, age seven; Bernarda Manuela, age four; and Francisco Bernardo, age two. These four orphans were to receive their sums only upon taking a state or reaching the age of majority.[24] Because Antonio and María had offspring of their own, the law allowed them to bequeath only up to one-fifth of their property to people other than their biological children. This inheritance law ensured Antonio's and María's seven orphans did not share equally with their children in their estate. But it is also clear, if monetary value can stand as a proxy for affection, that Antonio and María placed more value or hope in some orphans than in others. The criteria they used for this valuation remains unclear. Age, sex, and race all fail to explain why they bequeathed four times as much money to Juana de la Asención as to four of their other orphans. Nonetheless, Antonio and María, just like José de Arce y Carriedo, must have esteemed some of their orphans more than others.

Although not as intimate as the raising of orphans, gifts to the poor in general often constituted a personalized form of charitable activity that shaped and supported Christian community. Testators themselves obviously did not distribute the bequests to the poor they included in their wills. But their executors or others they stipulated probably dispersed the sums on a face-to-face basis. Most likely, bequests to the poor in general followed patterns of pious giving that testators had established in life. Even in death, the faithful of Mexico City continued to contribute in a personalized way to community formation.

A bequest to the poor in general was a traditional method testators employed to aid their less fortunate neighbors.[25] For the most part, testators bequeathed money or a portion of their estates convertible into cash to the poor. They never specified how the poor were to use the alms they received, and only a few explicitly requested some sort of reciprocity for the gift, usually prayers for their souls.[26] Bequests to the poor in general were always made to anonymous recipients.[27] In the majority of cases, testators simply bequeathed a specified cash sum to "the poor," without further elaboration. Others stipulated that their gifts be given to a specific segment of the poor, usually widows, unmarried women of virtue, or the shamefaced poor. Just over one-third of the gifts granted to the poor carried restrictions about recipients.[28] This suggests that the populace of Mexico City was divided over the practice promoted by the ecclesiastical elite of granting alms exclusively to the deserving poor.

More than half of those who gave to the poor either ignored the issue of deserving versus undeserving poor or consciously rejected the restrictive view that only the shamefaced or deserving poor should receive alms. Most of these testators simply sidestepped the question by refusing to specify the type of poor who would receive alms. For instance, Fernando Zorrila, a merchant, instructed his executors in 1758 to distribute one thousand pesos among the "needy," giving each poor person between one and four pesos depending on their judgment. In return for this gift, Fernando asked the recipients to commend his soul to God.[29] A few testators explicitly resisted favoritism in charity. Juan Ángel de Urra, a moderately wealthy merchant, left 4,333 pesos to both the "shamefaced and mendicant poor" in his 1737 will. He also asked that his clothes be given simply to the "poor" without distinguishing between deserving and undeserving recipients.[30]

In contrast, others specifically destined their alms for the deserving poor.

For example, Francisco José Ponce de Leon Enrríquez Ladrón de Guevara, a native of Seville and son of the Count of Campo, bequeathed two gifts to the poor in 1737. He asked his executors to distribute two hundred pesos "among poor women—widows and wives who prove to them [his executors] to have bad or absent husbands, the shamefaced or official poor who being burdened with children do not have enough to maintain themselves with their work." Francisco also instructed his executors to distribute his clothes among the shamefaced poor "who usually are more needy than the mendicant poor."[31] In a similar vein, Pedro Gordillo, a merchant who inserted three gifts to the poor in his 1758 will, restricted the reach of his charity. He gave his bedding to the "solemn poor" (*pobres de solemnidad*), fifty pesos to "shamefaced poor families," and the remainder of the third of his estate to "shamefaced poor families, unmarried women of virtue, and widows."[32] As these examples show, the diverse testator population of Mexico City appropriated the discourse on charity that marginalized the mendicant poor in varying ways. Some adopted it, many rejected it, and most probably fell somewhere in between. In short, there existed no single understanding of the appropriate recipient of charity in eighteenth-century Mexico.

After selecting the recipient for acts of charity, testators had to concern themselves about the mechanics of distributing alms. A minority of testators left their gifts to religious institutions—confraternities, parishes, religious orders, and the archdiocese—so that they in turn could distribute them to the poor.[33] This was an effective method of granting alms. Most parishes and religious orders and some confraternities regularly dispensed food and clothing to the poor.[34] Entrusting alms to religious institutions not only aided the poor who ultimately received the gift, but also demonstrated a testator's devotion to a particular parish, order, or confraternity and the charitable work it performed. Most testators, however, left the distribution of alms to the discretion of their executors.[35] For instance, Pedro Gordillo, one of the above testators who bequeathed alms solely to the shamefaced poor, asked that his executors distribute his bequests. He, like most testators who used executors to disperse alms, left the selection of specific recipients to their executors' discretion. Somewhat unusually, Juan Ángel de Urra, the above testator who donated over four thousand pesos to both the shamefaced and mendicant poor, deliberately selected two friars whom he knew, one a Franciscan and the other a Bethlehemite, to distribute his charity. The deliberate selection of executors or others to bestow alms suggests that testators expected them to distribute their gifts in face-to-face acts of charity. Even in death, the testators of Mexico City sought to forge and maintain Christian community through personalized gifts to the poor.

The practice of distributing alms to the poor in return for their participation in funeral corteges likewise reveals the personalized nature of charitable bequests and the special religious status the poor possessed in eighteenth-century Mexico City. Although it was common for the poor to march in funeral corteges, few testators explicitly requested their presence in their wills. This was probably because testators and notaries normally gave short shrift to the funeral clause, usually just recording the testator's preferred burial site and stating that the testator left all other decisions about the funeral to the executor's discretion. The presence of the poor at funerals was so commonplace that most testators must have seen no reason to mention it. The few who do mention the poor, however, clearly believed that the poor were an essential component of the funeral, for the presence and prayers of the Christ-like poor served as particularly effective suffrages for their souls and gave testators another opportunity to practice works of charity within the living Christian community. Juan de la Vega y Vela and Francisca de Puga y Villanueva, a husband and wife who wrote a joint will in 1758, designed their funeral clause carefully so that they could perform one last act of highly personalized, face-to-face charity. They requested that four mendicant poor carry their corpses during their funeral corteges. In recompense for their labor, Juan and Francisca ordered that each be given a shirt, cape, hat, underwear, stockings, and shoes.[36] They literally sought to perform one of the corporeal acts of mercy: clothing the naked. Similarly, Francisco del Castillo, a master tailor, requested the presence of the poor at his funeral in his 1717 will. He asked that twelve shamefaced poor people attend. Rather than carry his corpse, however, Francisco asked that they precede it, "honoring my body . . . [and] praying the rosary of Our Lady." In remuneration, they were to receive two reales a piece.[37] Francisco obviously deemed at least the shamefaced poor of great religious status, for he employed twelve of them to represent the apostles and believed that their recitation of the rosary would benefit his soul. And like Juan and Francisca, he used the proximity his funeral procession created between his corpse and its accompaniment to structure a last act of personalized charity.

Of the three major ways the faithful of Mexico City performed acts of charity in their wills, bequests to charitable institutions constituted the least personalized. Testators gave the vast majority of these institutional gifts to hospitals.[38] We must remember that the word "hospital" in early modern usage included a wider range of meanings than its modern equivalent. Early modern hospitals not only catered to the ill, but also sheltered travelers, the old, poor students, orphans, or the poor. Most hospitals specialized in one type of beneficence or in the care of one kind of illness. For instance, the hospital order of San Hipólito administered two hospitals in Mexico City. One was the hospital of San Hipólito, which treated all patients but was especially known for care of the mentally ill. The other was the Casa de Misericordia (House of Mercy), which housed students, priests, and the elderly. In fact, out of Mexico City's eleven hospitals that functioned in the eighteenth century, only three, San Juan de Dios, Jesús Nazareno (also known as La Concepción), and, in the last decades of the century, San Andrés served as general hospitals open to the entire population of the ill and infirm.[39] Specialized religious orders, known as hospital orders, often administered these institutions, but lay benefactors and the crown also funded and supervised hospitals. The patronage of Mexico City's hospitals was almost equally divided between orders on the one hand and lay philanthropists and the monarchy on the other.

Bequests to hospitals followed a basic pattern. They were almost universally made in cash, though a few testators bequeathed their entire estates to individual institutions. Furthermore, testators usually did not stipulate a specific use for their gifts, instead allowing hospital administrators to determine the best use of their donation. José Freyre, an unwed and childless merchant who wrote his will in 1758, gave many such gifts to hospitals. He ordered his executors to give 150 pesos each to the "innocent poor" in the hospital of San Hipólito, which cared for the mentally ill, and to the "sick" in the hospital of San Lázaro, an institution that specialized in the treatment of lepers. José also gave 150 pesos to the "ill poor" in the hospital of San Juan de Dios as "aid for their necessities" and one hundred pesos to the "poor demented women" housed in the Casa del Salvador, a hospital that treated women with mental illness, to be used for the "emergencies and necessities" of the hospital. Last, he gave one hundred pesos to the hospital of Convalesencia as "aid for the convalescing sick who are sheltered there."[40] The wording of all but the last bequest suggests that José intended to give alms directly to the patients housed in these hospitals. But this makes little sense, especially given the fact that he donated money to two hospitals that treated the mentally ill and one hospital that cared for lepers. It is highly unlikely that caregivers would have allowed these patients to handle sums of money on their own. More probable, José worded his gifts in this way to emphasize the ultimate recipients of his bequests without expecting his executors to distribute them to individual patients. Thus, José emphasized the personal nature of his charitable giving even though institutions mediated the exchange between testator and patient.

Although testators normally did not indicate a particular end for their donations, a few specifically earmarked their donations to fund an individual bed, to purchase bedclothes, or to provision a hospital with food. In most of these cases, this type of charitable giving included temporal symbolism that marked the gift as a liturgical gesture. Pedro de Borja Altamirano y Reynoso, a priest of the Archdiocese of Mexico, made two such specific bequests to hospitals in his 1737 will. He set aside two hundred pesos to serve as a capital fund in favor of the hospital of San Juan de Dios and asked the prior of the hospital to use the ten pesos of annual interest to finance the cost of one of the hospital's beds on the feast day of St. Joseph, a pious practice he had performed for many years. In return, he asked that the hospital order commend him to God. Pedro also donated two hundred additional pesos to establish another capital fund. He asked that the interest from this fund be used to provide food on the feast day of St. Augustine for the ill priests housed in the hospital of Santísima Trinidad also known as the hospital of San Pedro, which catered exclusively to ecclesiastics.[41]

Testators in eighteenth-century Mexico City practiced charity in the form of rearing and bestowing gifts upon orphans, granting alms to the poor, and donating money to hospitals. In these ways they accrued grace for their souls and strengthened Christian community. Many of them certainly used their wills to continue good works in death that they had performed in life. Their directives reveal that many testators valued personalized forms of pious giving. But now executors completed the face-to-face acts of charity that testators had practiced while alive. Though testators could no longer perform the intimate giving so valued in baroque Catholicism, their bequests carried out by proxies participated in the formation and maintenance of community cohesion.

Confraternities and Community in Colonial Mexico City

In addition to acts of charity, the faithful of Mexico City engaged in religious community formation through membership in confraternities. Confraternities structured community through the promotion of collective devotions by people of disparate social backgrounds. Although some placed social restrictions on membership, such as racial, natal, or occupational requirements, most were open to a wide social range.[42] Confraternities brought together different segments of the faithful into a cohesive group to perform numerous collective acts of devotion over the liturgical year. They distributed charity, sponsored religious festivals and processions, and promoted the cult of saints. Most importantly, however, they participated in the rites of death and dying and memorialized the dead. In fact, membership in a confraternity was a form of spiritual charity and reciprocity. By becoming a confrere, a member of a confraternity, one pledged to perform suffrages for all members of the organization living and dead. Of course, one also received the grace from suffrages practiced by other confreres. In this way, confraternities linked in perpetuity all members in a spiritual reciprocity society designed to foster group identity in the collective quest for salvation. In and through this practice of mutual spiritual aid, as well as through their other devotional activities, confraternities cultivated a sense of Christian unity and fellowship among their diverse memberships.

Confraternities arose in Europe during the twelfth and thirteenth centuries, increased rapidly in number, and became an important feature of late medieval piety.[43] In the fifteenth and sixteenth centuries they witnessed a period of accelerated expansion, at first in response to incipient stirrings of Catholic reform and later to the church's advocacy of these fraternal organizations to counter Protestant assaults on Catholic doctrine.[44] Of course, lay enthusiasm was a necessary ingredient for the rapid growth of confraternities. The laity founded, joined, and participated in numerous new confraternities on their own initiative and under the clergy's aegis.

The conquistadors and other early Spanish immigrants quickly established confraternities in Mexico. Hernán Cortés founded the first confraternity, the Knights of the Cross (Cabelleros de la Cruz), in the chapel of Santa Veracruz in 1526, just five years after the capture of Tenochtitlán, the Aztec capital and site of Mexico City. Other settlers soon followed suit. Apparently, they founded many of these congregations in Mexico City on their own initiative because in 1555 the First Mexican Provincial Council observed that some people, "moved by well intentioned zeal," established confraternities but never obtained episcopal approbation of their statutes and constitutions, a situation that led to "many troubles" (*inconvenientes*).[45] The tension that existed between communal lay religiosity as expressed and formed by confraternities and the growing desire of the Catholic hierarchy, especially after the Council of Trent, to regulate all aspects of religious practice remained a constant problem in colonial Mexico City but never seems to have provoked a general crisis. Although the Council of Trent had mandated close episcopal supervision of confraternal governance and finance, the archbishops of Mexico generally allowed these institutions to function independently, only occasionally monitoring internal confraternal elections or auditing accounts.[46]

The confraternities of colonial Mexico City, like those in Europe, were largely concerned with death, burial, and the memorialization of the dead. Although not all of them provided aid for deceased members, many specified in their governing constitutions that confreres must attend the funerals of and perform other suffrages for fallen brothers and sisters. For example, confreres of the confraternity of Our Lady of Sorrows founded in the parish of Santa Catarina Mártir in the late seventeenth century had the obligation to provide a bier with twelve candles for the funerals of deceased members. They also were required to pay for a requiem mass with a catafalque, a funerary monument usually consisting of a wooden frame draped in black cloth and adorned with numerous candles, every year during the octave of All Souls as a suffrage for all dead members.[47] The confraternity of St. Benedict, founded in the monastery of San Francisco, offered members the option of having the friars from the community carry their cadaver in formal procession to the monastery church for a solemn requiem mass and burial or alternatively receiving seventeen pesos for burial in a parish church. Beyond this, the confraternity promised an annual anniversary requiem mass for the souls of all departed members.[48] Confreres, then, could count on the aid of their brothers and sisters during their final passage, for most confraternities arranged funerals and burials and prayed for the souls of the departed as they faced judgment and the purifying flames of purgatory.

Confraternities participated in a wide range of pious activities apart from memorializing the dead. Funded by pious donations and membership fees, they performed acts of charity to gain merit for both living and deceased members. They engaged in such acts as founding and administering hospitals for the care of the ill and lodging of pilgrims, the granting of dowries to poor or orphaned girls so they could marry honorably, the visitation of prisoners, and the distribution of alms to the poor. For example, the Congregation of the Immaculate Conception in Mexico City donated over 1,700 pesos annually to the hospital of San Hipólito. Most of these funds went to provide food and clothing for the hospital's wards. Likewise, the congregation earmarked lesser funds to feed the ill in the hospital of Espíritu Santo and the inmates of Mexico City's three jails.[49]

Just as importantly, confraternities encouraged the veneration of their patron saints and Catholic worship in general through processions, sponsorship of feast-day liturgies, construction of chapels, adornment of churches with religious art, and the purchase of liturgical and paraliturgical items for religious ceremony. The confraternity of the Precious Blood of Christ, founded in the parish of Santa Catarina Mártir of Mexico City, hired a chaplain to collect alms every day for the upkeep and adornment of its chapel in the parish church. It also sponsored masses every Friday in its chapel to honor the crucified Christ and a mass and procession every Thursday to commemorate Christ's first celebration of the eucharist at the last supper. Furthermore, it patronized a lavish annual solemn mass on the feast of the Transfiguration of Christ in November, paying up to fifty-five pesos for the priests, choir, musicians, wax, and fireworks necessary for the celebration. Last, it hired a preacher "of great reputation" (de mas fama) to deliver a sermon from the door of its chapel every Thursday during Lent.[50]

In all of their activities, confraternities promoted sacred sociability between members both living and dead. As living institutions designed to unite diverse groups of Christians, confraternities sought to establish the mystical body of Christ on earth and invoke his presence among members. The most evident expression of this function, other than the regular services to memorialize the dead, was the confraternal feast that usually followed liturgical services on select holy days throughout the year. The sharing of food in a ritual context encouraged conviviality and recalled the central tenet of the mass, the communal consumption of Christ's body and blood in the form of bread and wine, and the early Christian ritual meal, or agape, that constituted an integral part of the liturgy in antiquity. The confraternal banquet was more than a simple secular affair; it sought both to express and induce the Christian virtue of charity—charity as understood as love of God and love of neighbor.[51]

Confraternal Community in Wills

Many testators in Mexico City voiced their understanding of confraternities as sacral societies dedicated to spiritual reciprocity in the wills they wrote. Testators often declared membership in confraternities and asked executors to notify confraternal leaders of their deaths so that the brotherhoods fulfilled their spiritual obligations to pray for the deceased confreres, participate in their funerals, and offer masses for their souls. Although the traditional understanding of the confraternity's purpose would later change, most testators in the first half of the eighteenth century called on confraternities to attend their funerals and perform other acts of spiritual charity for their souls. For instance, Felix Vela de Castillo, a physician, stated in his 1696 will:

> I am a confrere of señor St. Peter and on account of having as all confreres [of this congregation] have the obligation to say for my soul the masses that are said for each confrere after they die, I leave no other masses for my soul.[52]

At the end of his will, just before signing it, Felix added:

> I am a brother of San Diego, St. Michael, and of others . . . Likewise [I am] a confrere of Our Lady of Antigua, and this confraternity has the obligation of attending my burial with acolytes [*monacillos*], processional cross, and choir [*capilla*].[53]

Felix revealed many aspects of confraternal practice in these clauses. First, he belonged to at least six confraternities. Most people who mentioned membership in brotherhoods belonged to more than one. It is impossible, however, to count accurately the number of confraternities to which confreres belonged because most listed only the one or two most prestigious ones in which they were members. Afterwards they simply stated that they belonged to others without naming them. Even Felix listed only four confraternities by name but indicated that he belonged to more with the phrase, "I am a brother . . . of others." Second, confraternities provided various suffrages for the deceased. The congregation of St. Peter, a brotherhood composed mainly of the archdiocese's secular clergy but which also invited the laity to join for an entrance fee of five hundred pesos,[54] required each member to say or commission three masses for each confrere who died. The total number of masses said for each departed confrere must have been large for Felix to desist from requesting other masses for his soul. On the other hand, the confraternity of Our Lady of Antigua, whose chapel was located in the cathedral, participated in an extraordinary manner in the funeral and burial rites of confreres, providing acolytes and a choir to enhance the solemnity of these ceremonies. The fact that the confraternity furnished a processional cross suggests that its members also marched in the funeral procession from the deceased's home to the church where the requiem mass and burial took place. Confraternal participation in these processions must have been common, for the manual for priests written by Fray Miguel Venegas in the early eighteenth century specifically mentioned the presence and precise placement of confreres in describing the proper arrangement and activities of funeral corteges.[55] Felix remained silent about the obligations of the other confraternities to which he belonged, suggesting that their duties were more standard: participation in the funeral cortege, payment of funeral dues, and collective commemoration of the dead with masses and prayers.

Antonio de Aguilar, a priest and administrator of the Conceptionist nunnery of La Concepción, likewise dictated a telling confraternity clause in 1696. He stated that he belonged to the congregation of St. Peter and faithfully fulfilled his obligation to say three masses for each departed confrere "within a week" of his or her death. But he lamented that since he had begun his work as administrator of La Concepción, "I do not attend the burials and suffrages of the said my brothers as I used to." In recompense for his breach of this sacred obligation, Antonio said that he had given ten pesos a year to a hospital the confraternity had founded for the care of ill clerics to pay for food on the feast of St. Joseph. He then asked that twelve members of the congregation carry his corpse during his funeral procession and asked his fellow confreres to each say or commission one mass for his soul on the day of his funeral. Antonio's admitted absence from the funerals and commemorative services of the congregation reveals that the participation of individual confreres in these rituals was not necessarily certain. Nonetheless, they were not obligations dismissed lightly. Antonio felt compelled to make restitution to the confraternity for his dereliction of service by endowing the hospital it administered. In a separate clause, he stated that he belonged to at least five other confraternities and requested that the members of each of them "commend me to God and fulfill what may be of their obligation as I do for all [of them]."[56] In this phrase Antonio encapsulated the basic logic of confraternities, mutual obligation between members to aid each other in the quest for salvation.

Most testators wrote less revealing confraternity clauses in their wills, but almost all of them in the first half of the eighteenth century made some reference to the obligation of members to perform suffrages for the souls of the departed. For instance, Felipa Juárez de Sálazar spoke only in general terms of the spiritual obligations of the confraternities to which she belonged in her 1696 will. She stated that

> I am a confrere of the confraternities of the Blessed Sacrament, of the Rosary, of the most Holy Trinity, of St. Cajetan, of Jesus the Nazarene, and of other confraternities that are made known by their patents. I order that notice of my death be given to them so that they do the good for my soul that they are obligated to do.[57]

Even in these less revealing clauses, it is evident that confraternities were obliged to perform suffrages of some kind on behalf of the deceased. Although Felipa did not specify the precise nature of these pious acts, she and her fellow confreres certainly knew what suffrages their confraternal memberships entailed. Confraternal charters and in some cases confraternal patents clearly listed the spiritual obligations of confreres upon the death of one of their fellows, and confreres performed these rites repeatedly during their lives as their spiritual brothers and sisters passed away. Each time they performed the prescribed suffrages for their deceased fellows, they enacted the Christian virtue of charity and accrued for others the merit needed for salvation.

Conclusion

The suffrages confraternities performed for deceased members were efficacious because confreres participated in the community of saints. The soul of each confrere was not a bounded entity entirely separate from the rest of the faithful. It was subsumed in the mystical body of Christ and the community of saints and thus could benefit from good works the living performed on its behalf. In this way, confraternities joined the living and the dead in an ongoing, ever-expanding religious community. Apart from these mutual suffrages, confraternities promoted Christian community among the living through their sponsorship of collective devotions. Communal participation in charitable activities, processions, ritual feasting, and the eucharistic celebration was designed to unite confreres in a common religious experience and forge a sense of collective identity among them.

Like confraternal membership, charitable giving structured and maintained Christian community in baroque Catholicism. Catholics of means not only aided the poor in their need when they sheltered orphans, distributed alms to the poor, and donated money to hospitals. They also bridged social distance, especially when performing personal acts of charity. Many testators revealed their preference for such face-to-face charitable acts in their wills, the most intimate of which was the rearing of orphans. The wills from eighteenth-century Mexico City also reveal that the faithful were divided in their response to the new discourse on the poor that arose in sixteenth-century Europe. Although some testators earmarked their bequests strictly for the deserving poor, more refused to distinguish between the shamefaced and mendicant poor. It is clear, moreover, that the poor still possessed a sacral status in the eyes of many of the faithful in the eighteenth century. The poor then were important members of the Christian community and deserved aid and attention from the faithful of means.

Baroque Catholicism privileged social cohesion among diverse segments of the faithful. Collective devotions and reciprocal spiritual obligations structured by confraternities brought disparate social groups together to honor Christ and the saints and to seek salvation communally. Likewise, the gift of alms united rich and poor, ideally in personal encounters, in a sacral act that recalled Christ. Moreover, distribution of alms established unity through the mutual obligation of the wealthy to care for the poor and the poor to pray for their benefactors. Of course, social cohesion was the ideal and at best was a temporary state. Confreres could argue with each other over the election of confraternal officials or expenditures for religious duties. Individual confreres might even ignore statutes and fail to participate in confraternal activities. Certainly, confraternities contested each other for the right of precedence in processions. Furthermore, alms could only reduce social distance partially and temporarily, and acts of charity never aimed at complete social leveling. The rich remained rich, and the poor continued to live precariously from the wealthy's voluntary largesse. Such a social state certainly engendered resentment. Nonetheless, baroque Catholicism sought to ameliorate these tensions through face-to-face interactions of spiritual reciprocity among all the faithful. This ideal, as we will see, faded as the eighteenth century wore on.

PART II

Religious Reform

CHAPTER 6

Reforming Mexico City

✦ THE WEALTH AND PRESTIGE OF MEXICO CITY MADE IT AN IMPORTANT
site for reform, both religious and secular, during the second half of the eighteenth century. The Bourbon monarchs, particularly Charles III (1759–88),
sought to revive Spain's military and political stature after the final collapse
of the Spanish Habsburgs' continental empire at the beginning of the century. Influenced by Enlightenment thought, the Bourbons sought to increase
the prosperity of their realms so that the state could then tax the additional
wealth and strengthen its own position. To foment prosperity in New Spain,
the Bourbons stimulated the economy and removed barriers to economic
growth. Furthermore, they attempted to instill habits of self-restraint, order,
and economy within the Mexican populace so that it would work efficiently
to create the wealth that would ideally fund Spain's geopolitical resurrection.
At the same time, like other absolutist rulers in Europe, the monarchy tried
to rationalize government and concentrate power within the royal bureaucracy at the expense of corporate interests like the church. In all, the reforms
were designed to discipline the population, subordinate autonomous institutions, and heighten the power and financial resources of the state in the name
of national revival.[1] Although not necessarily their objective, these measures
helped undermine baroque piety and aid religious reform.

The Bourbon economic and fiscal reforms generally destabilized the econ-
omies of Mexico City's elite families and drained wealth from the colony, which

in turn potentially decreased support for baroque piety. The Bourbon program to create prosperity sought to stimulate especially profitable sectors of the economy. The Bourbons subsidized the flagging silver mining sector, the motor that had driven the early colonization of central Mexico and had partially funded Habsburg might. Crown stimulus combined with new mining techniques paid off. The average yearly silver output from Mexican mines rose fivefold over the eighteenth century.[2] Similarly, though later in the century, the crown encouraged greater mercantile links between New Spain and the mother country by ending the rigid fleet system. In 1778 it established free trade, allowing ships sailing from any port in Spain to trade with Mexico. Again, the reform had the intended effect. The number of ships crossing the Atlantic increased tenfold.[3]

Although these measures at first blush would appear to have multiplied wealth in Mexico City, they resulted in greater economic uncertainty for the capital's elite. Clearly, some mine owners accumulated vast fortunes from mining revival. But other elite sectors of Mexico City's population saw their positions destabilized. The great wholesalers who dominated international trade earned substantial profits during the first four-fifths of the century. In fact, complaints lodged against them and their guild, the *consulado*, were one reason for the institution of free trade. As more ships docked in Veracruz after 1778, European goods flooded the Mexican market, and profits dropped significantly. In another blow to the Mexico City merchants' control of trade, the crown authorized the establishment of consulados in the port of Veracruz and the provincial city of Guadalajara in 1795. The merchants of Mexico City now faced intense competition. Due to these conditions, many great merchant families in Mexico City shifted their capital from commerce to mining in the 1780s. Mining, however, was a precarious investment. More mines failed than succeeded.[4] Many families must have lost fortunes pouring capital into expensive but ultimately barren claims. On the other hand, those who struck silver may have increased their revenues substantially. Whether free trade drained money from Mexico City or indirectly channeled greater resources into it through greater investment in mining is impossible to say at present. It is clear, however, that economic activity for the Mexico City merchant elite became much riskier after 1778.

Bourbon economic policy, whatever its effects on the elite of Mexico City, failed to produce the crown's promised prosperity. Economic expansion in New Spain was only nominal. Demographic expansion and inflation matched the growth in the value of economic output.[5] In fact, the lives of the poor and middling groups grew more precarious during the last decades of the eighteenth century as real wages declined and prices of basic foodstuffs soared.[6]

Exacerbating the greater economic instability of the late eighteenth century, the Bourbon monarchy vastly increased tax revenue from New Spain, draining wealth from the colony—wealth that could have financed baroque piety. The crown raised and invented numerous taxes, created state-controlled monopolies, and levied extraordinary forced loans on corporate bodies and the wealthy. Tax revenues rose exponentially, outpacing inflation and population growth. In 1712 royal tax receipts from Mexico totaled about three million pesos; by the end of the eighteenth century, yearly taxes from New Spain amounted to about twenty million pesos.[7]

Bourbon social and cultural reforms likewise tended to undercut baroque Catholicism. The main objective of these projects was to mold self-composed, economically efficient subjects who, imbued with a work ethic, would produce prosperity. To this end, the royal officials targeted the vast population of Mexico City's poor for reform. They instituted new security forces to police the poor, repeatedly outlawed begging, and founded the Hospicio de Pobres, or workhouse, to intern mendicants. All these projects served to impose order on the city to facilitate commerce and, as Pamela Voekel has argued, to discipline the poor and inculcate within them habits of self-restraint and industry.[8] At the same time, they subtly undermined the baroque penchant for personalized acts of charity. As targets of state-sponsored reform, the poor were no longer deemed worthy recipients of individual largesse.

The Bourbon program of sculpting prosperous, self-composed individuals more directly affected baroque religious practice when the crown sought to eliminate obstacles to economy and efficiency. The state banned practices it deemed useless and prodigal, primarily "excessive" religious celebrations that impeded work schedules and squandered resources in boisterous and profane activities. Though not the only religious festival singled out for reform, Corpus Christi celebrations attracted much attention because of their particular gaiety and splendor.[9] Mexico City had celebrated the feast of Corpus Christi, the exultant summer celebration of Christ's corporeal presence in the eucharist, since the early sixteenth century. The town council supported the feast by festooning buildings with banners, crafting portable altars for images of saints, commissioning dances and religious plays, and paying for fireworks, bullfights, jousts, and a post-processional feast. All orders of the capital participated in the culmination of the celebration, a procession that wound its way through the city's major streets. The poor led the procession along with festive giants representing all the peoples of the world and a dragon symbolizing sin defeated by the eucharist. The capital's confraternities, religious orders, other ecclesiastical institutions, and secular authorities all participated. They were followed by the host triumphantly displayed in a splendid monstrance shaded by a canopy carried by the city's dignitaries.[10] Bourbon authorities, although they never attempted to ban Corpus celebrations, sought to make them more solemn, restrained, and less expensive affairs. The city council stopped contracting dancers and, under orders from José de Gálvez, the crown inspector who toured Mexico from 1765 to 1771, precipitously reduced its expenditures for the celebration. Other regulations removed food stalls and vendors from the processional route and forbade drinking during the festival. And in 1790, Viceroy Revillagigedo banned the poor, Indian dancers, giant images, and dragon from the parade.[11] The celebration of Corpus continued, but Bourbon officials reduced it to a decorous occasion that did not deplete the municipal budget—a budget needed to support new secular projects aimed at cleaning, ordering, and disciplining the city. By curbing the exuberance of public religious festivities in the cause of economic growth, the monarchy directly attacked the rites of baroque Catholicism and supported religious reform.

The Bourbon project to subordinate autonomous institutions, particularly the church, to state authority also impinged on the vitality of baroque Catholicism. During the Habsburg dynasty, the various bodies of the Catholic church had wielded significant judicial, economic, and moral influence over the population and enjoyed a large measure of autonomy from the crown. In fact, the Habsburgs had generally viewed the church as a junior partner in the governance of New Spain. The Bourbons, on the other hand, abhorred ecclesiastical independence and diligently labored to undermine the wealth and power of church bodies. Because religious orders enjoyed more autonomy from the crown than the secular clergy, the Bourbons strove to curtail them.[12] They turned over rural, Indian parishes administered by the orders to the secular clergy and began a policy of inspecting monastic houses to impose greater discipline within them and to reduce their membership. These projects weakened the orders and, according to David Brading, led to a crisis in some as fewer candidates entered the novitiate and friars petitioned for release from their monastic vows.[13] The crown's boldest move against the religious orders, however, targeted the Jesuits. In 1767 the Bourbons expelled the Society of Jesus from all of its realms.[14]

In addition to undermining the regular clergy to consolidate its power, the monarchy also wrested great wealth from the Mexican church. In particular, Charles IV (1788–1808) levied new taxes on ecclesiastical institutions. Most important, he ordered the Consolidation of Royal Bonds in 1804.[15] This law mandated the alienation of the principal funds of chantries and chaplaincies, foundations for the perpetual celebration of masses for the dead, and their remittance to the royal treasury. It forced ecclesiastical corporations in New Spain to call in the loans they had made with the principal from these foundations or to require the payment of the liens established to erect them.[16] Because thousands of chaplaincies and chantries existed in Mexico at the time, the law burdened the church and wealthy Mexicans who benefited from ecclesiastical financing.[17] The Consolidation ultimately undermined pious foundations that supported much of the non-beneficed lower secular clergy.[18] In short, Bourbon ecclesiastical policy as a whole served to undermine the prestige and financial independence of the Mexican church and reduce the number of clerics available for the performance of religious rites.

These policies, along with other Bourbon reforms, created resentment among various segments of New Spain's population and in part explain the independence insurgency that began in rural Mexico in 1810.[19] Mexico City, however, never openly rebelled against the crown. Despite a few minor conspiracies, its population remained quiescent even as independence movements broke out in much of New Spain from 1810 to 1821. Nonetheless, the insurrection affected Mexico City in a number of ways. The insurgent armies threatened the capital militarily in 1810 and 1812, but never invaded the city. Beyond direct military challenges, the rebels often closed roads leading into Mexico City, depriving the capital of supplies. Shortages of basic commodities, an influx of rural immigrants fleeing the war, and "mysterious fevers" that scourged the capital combined in 1813 to make it a particularly devastating year. Public charities were overwhelmed and could not raise funds among the elite who had been financially drained by the Consolidation of Royal Bonds, other taxes, and forced loans.[20] As the colonial order came to a close, both the wealthy and poor of Mexico City faced financial hardship and the church suffered institutional decline and instability. These conditions, although not all directly related to the Bourbon reforms, combined with religious reform to make the continued support of lavish baroque piety more problematic by the early nineteenth century.

CHAPTER 7

The Reformers' Program

✝ IN THE MID-EIGHTEENTH CENTURY A NEW PIETY EMERGED IN SPAIN AND
its territories that challenged baroque Catholicism. Adherents to this new
piety, in part influenced by currents of the Enlightenment that were spreading in Europe and the Americas at the time, stressed the need for individual,
quiet, and inward forms of devotion and rejected ostentatious display, resort
to miraculous relics and images, and dramatic forms of symbolic piety characteristic of baroque Catholicism.[1] In Mexico a segment of the episcopate
strongly promoted the new piety after midcentury. The reform-minded bishops of the late colonial period derided many baroque practices as "puerile"
and "superstitious" and sought to eliminate the "excesses" and "abuses" of
traditional Catholicism that offended their Enlightenment sensibilities. In
place of contact with or experience of the sacred, the promoters of religious
reform encouraged contemplation of God and the study of his word. They
sought to still symbolically charged bodies, reduce the many earthly manifestations of the sacred to the ecclesiastically controlled context of the eucharist, and achieve simplicity and decorum in sacred space and ceremonies.
Moreover, they sought to undermine the collective religious responsibilities
that underlay baroque Catholicism. The piety they advocated restricted the
physical manifestations of the sacred within the world and rendered religious
practice more "spiritual" and "interior."

Reformed Catholicism rested on a different understanding of the nature of the sacred than baroque Catholicism. Whereas the sacred in baroque Catholicism was highly immanential, in reformed Catholicism it was much more transcendent. In baroque Catholicism, the sacred could inhere easily within the physical world. Reformed Catholics on the other hand conceived of the sacred as much more spiritual and much less likely to reside within physical objects. Consequently, reformed Catholics questioned baroque practices based on sacred immanence and those designed to make contact with physical manifestations of the sacred within the world. In short, reformed Catholicism separated the sacred from the profane more clearly than had baroque practice. Moreover, the spiritual nature of the sacred required a spiritual type of worship. Reformed Catholics therefore devalued much of the performative and gestural piety encouraged in baroque Catholicism and critiqued the lavish ornamentation of sacred space. They considered these practices "external" and not worthy of a spiritual deity. The mind rather than the body became the primary vehicle for correct worship and veneration. Although not articulated by religious reformers in this way, their conception of the sacred and their project to transform religious culture rested on an epistemology that sundered the close relationship between sign and signified. Likeness in all but a few cases would no longer serve to create a shared identity or forge unions between sacred images or symbolic performances and the holy figures they resembled.

Reformed Catholicism also rested on a different conception of community than baroque Catholicism. The latter emphasized a horizontal understanding of community; baroque Catholics sought to maintain intimate connections with their neighbors through personal interactions. Moreover, baroque Catholicism privileged communal devotions and the collective endeavor for salvation. Reformed Catholicism, on the other hand, encouraged a more vertical conception of religious community. All the faithful were united because they worshipped the same divinity more than because they aided each other corporeally and spiritually. Although religious reformers never denied the importance of charity and confraternities, they subtly undermined baroque means of community formation. Probably unknown by reformers themselves, this project rested on a broader cultural shift in subjectivity that emphasized individualism at the expense of communal identity and obligations.

Although reformers sought to remake religious culture in late colonial Mexico, it would be incorrect to view them as proposing a radical break with traditional religious practices. They were orthodox Catholics shaped and constrained by doctrines concerning the eucharist, sacred images, and ritual piety codified at the Council of Trent. They never advocated a radically spiritual understanding of divinity and devotions as had the Protestant reformer John Calvin. Rather, they proposed a shift in emphasis. They downplayed and, in some cases, lampooned the immanential and somatic tendencies of baroque Catholicism, but almost never rejected them outright. Instead, they highlighted God's spiritual nature and advocated mental prayer and contemplation, practices that had certainly existed in baroque Catholicism but that had been overshadowed by more performative and flamboyant devotions. In sum, Catholic reformers in late eighteenth-century Mexico never rejected traditional Catholic practices, but chose to deemphasize and work around them as they sought to transform religious culture in New Spain.

Religious reform unfolded within, responded to, and, in turn, reinforced and shaped broader social and cultural changes. The second half of the eighteenth century was a time of widespread reform in Spain and its American colonies. In this period the Bourbon monarchy sought to centralize political power in its hands at the expense of nobles and the church, stimulate economic activity such as mining and trade, police and discipline its subjects more systematically, and increase royal tax receipts through expansion and professionalization of government bureaucracy. In all, the Bourbon project aimed at creating prosperity so that the crown could boost tax revenue, which in turn could be used to bolster the authority of the centralizing state. Although not directly conditioned by broader Bourbon political and economic reforms, religious reform occurred in the same milieu and responded to and participated in some of the underlining principles of broader reform. For instance, both reforming projects sought to still bodies: the Bourbons to render them more efficient producers and the reforming bishops to undermine the efficacy of lay liturgical piety. Similarly, the Bourbons sought to stimulate the economy. At the same time reforming bishops attempted to decrease baroque splendor. Religious reformers did not necessarily have increased prosperity in mind when they advocated simple and sedate ceremony and sacred space, but wealth not sunk into sacred ornamentation could be invested in other, perhaps economically productive, activities. The rationales were different, but the two reforming projects shared intermediate if not ultimate goals. In this way, both reforming projects supported each other. Religious reform was not an epiphenomenon of the broader Bourbon reforms, but attempts to transform Catholicism emerged from and responded to the same larger sociocultural shifts from which the broader Bourbon program arose.

The Very Nature of God: Reforming Immanence, Liturgical Piety, and Splendor

Three prelates, bishop of Puebla Francisco Fabián y Fuero (1765–73), archbishop of Mexico Francisco Antonio Lorenzana (1766–72), and his successor as archbishop, Alonso Núñez de Haro y Peralta (1772–1800), all born and educated in Spain, were the most ardent advocates of religious reform in Mexico. They used a number of strategies to implement their reforms. First, Archbishop Lorenzana convoked the Fourth Mexican Provincial Council in 1771 to update church governance and pastoral care. It was the first general council of the Mexican church since the Third Mexican Provincial Council held almost two hundred years earlier. The decrees of the council, though not promulgated until the nineteenth century, reflected many of the reformers' intentions and must have influenced ecclesiastical work despite the delay in promulgation. Second, the bishops published episcopal edicts to regulate religion and issued less formal instructions to parish priests throughout their dioceses advocating changes in pious activities. Third, they visited parishes and inspected schools and ecclesiastical institutions. Finally, and perhaps most importantly, they communicated directly to their flocks through pastoral letters and sermons. Especially through frequent sermons, they sought to persuade the faithful to adopt reformed pious practices.

Reformed Catholicism at its intellectual base rested upon a spiritual conception of God's nature. Of the three prelates, Archbishop Núñez de Haro most emphatically represented God as spirit in his homilies. He warned his flock against the practice of conceiving the first and third persons of the trinity, God the father and God the holy spirit, under the image of "corporeal" forms, such as an "infinite light," because this could lead to the danger of "forming an idol, believing God to be like these images." Archbishop Núñez de Haro's choice of the word "idol" to describe a corporeal image of God is telling. An idol is not a product of superstition, but a false god. It is something that must be torn down and destroyed to preserve the purity of religious practice and commitment. With this word he laid his program bare; imagining God as a physical substance ran the risk of perdition. In place of physical conceptions of the divine, he asked his listeners to imagine God as "truth, wisdom, and justice . . . for these ideas are the most spiritual and the most distant from corporeal ideas."[2] A spiritual divinity, as a corollary, requires different devotional practices than a proximate and palpable one. The archbishop explained this logic cogently to the faithful: "All purely corporeal worship is unworthy of God and, thus, you are to unite [to it] a spiritual worship in order to please God."[3]

Archbishop Núñez de Haro ruminated frequently on the theme of true and false worship in his sermons and writings. He always equated spiritual worship with true worship and scorned external (ritual) worship, in itself, as empty and meaningless. Moreover, purely external worship offended God. He declared in one sermon: "And if your worship and adorations are exterior and are not . . . in spirit and truth, your works will be poorer every day and more disagreeable in the eyes of God."[4] One passage from a pastoral letter the archbishop issued in July 1777 is particularly telling and deserves extensive quotation:

> Now then, as Jesus Christ expressly told us, adoration only pleases God when it is sincere, when it is offered to him in spirit and truth, because worship in the law of grace is true and spiritual worship. Its perfection consists in knowing and loving God. Without this, exterior worship is absolutely worthless. Therefore, we are obligated to make acts of love toward God frequently so that our worship, adoration and prayers directed to the Lord, may not be in vain and full of superstition or hypocrisy. We cannot adore God in spirit without knowing him and loving him. Nor can we adore him in truth, according to what St. Thomas tells us, if we do not adore him with sincere faith, purified of all error and superstition, born in the depths of our heart and out of a love of observing his divine precepts. This is, Jesus Christ himself tells us, the adoration that the heavenly father looks for and wants . . . The prophet Isaiah says: all peoples who only offer honor and glory to God our Lord with their lips, having his divine majesty distant from the heart, are abominable people, hypocrites, and abhorred by God. Therefore, in the opinion of St. Jerome, it is expressly and positively added and assured: "My soul abhors your calends and solemnities."

Take note, my beloved children, that these solemnities abhorred
by the Lord and which he refused to recognize as his own, were festivities of the ancient chosen people, in whom nothing was lacking
concerning the magnificence of worship and exterior ceremonies.
As the same holy doctor [St. Thomas] makes known, interior worship, contrite and humble hearts that thought about a swift and serious conversion so that their devotions would not be full of hypocrisy
was all that was desired of them. And as the Pharisees in the time of
our Redeemer Jesus Christ were dedicated to exterior worship, had
a worldly, corrupted, and execrable heart, the Lord harshly repri-
manded them and told them: "Hypocrites! How well Isaiah proph-
esied of you, saying: this people honors me with its lips, but its heart
is most distant from me."[5]

Archbishop Núñez de Haro's vehemence in this passage is striking. He compared Christians who practiced exterior piety without a contrite heart to
Jews and Pharisees (whom Christ had emphatically rebuked in the temple).
The anti-Semitic nature of these comparisons was intended as a particularly
sharp condemnation of external worship. Despite the waning of inquisito-
rial persecution of Jews after the 1730s in Spain and Mexico, Spaniards still
considered Jews the ultimate heretics because of their refusal to recognize
the divinity of Christ. To be compared to a Jew was an insult to Spanish
Christians, and Archbishop Núñez de Haro likely employed the comparison
precisely for that effect.

He also claimed that ritual piety, in itself, was "absolutely worthless."
With this phrase the archbishop repudiated a millennium of Christian religious practice. He attributed little value to the splendor of worship, to the
images of saints, and to performative piety. In essence, he sought to close off
lay contact with the divine. He even undermined the Tridentine justification
for the use of external apparatus to stimulate piety by raising the souls of the
faithful to the contemplation of the divine through excitement of the senses.
For Archbishop Núñez de Haro, external cult had no function. It neither
made the divine present nor turned the thoughts of the faithful to celestial things. At best it was merely an epiphenomenon of interior worship, an
apparently unnecessary sign of an inward state. Nonetheless, he never condemned external worship outright. He was confined by centuries of Catholic
tradition. Clearly, the archbishop did not recollect or chose to ignore the

baroque value of ritual piety. But if the church had advocated these forms of worship in the past, he could not uproot them. He faced a conundrum. His solution was to fulminate against ritual piety's limitations as a devotion to a spiritual God and to promote a "spiritual and true" piety to undergird it.

Spiritual piety, as Archbishop Núñez de Haro stated, consisted of knowing and loving God. The emphasis the archbishop placed on love of God would seem to indicate that he proposed a highly affective relationship between the individual believer and God. His recurrent use of the word "heart" (mentioned five times in the above passage) and his association of the heart with the source of true devotion also seem to imply a religion of emotion. Arriving at this conclusion, however, rests on a misreading of the historic meanings of the words "love" and "heart." While the heart is the seat of emotion, particularly passion, longing, and affection in modern parlance, it had other connotations during the eighteenth century. In the late middle ages, the heart was conceived of as the seat of the rational soul, or the intellect. The brain at that time was thought of as an organ that merely received and registered sensory perceptions. Any rational processes—thought, reason, logic—were the domain of the soul, which resided in the heart. In fact, death was recognized as the moment the heart ceased to beat: the moment when the soul that animated the body departed from the heart.[6] Although in the eighteenth century both the older conception of the heart as the organ that thinks and the newer one of the organ that feels were in use, Archbishop Núñez de Haro spoke within the parameters of the older discourse. He also worked within an older discourse on love. Before the nineteenth century, the Thomistic conception of love dominated Hispanic discourse on the subject. In the philosophy of St. Thomas, love existed as an expression of the will, and the will was one of the faculties (along with reason and memory) of the rational soul. Love, then, was not a passionate loss of self in another. It was a regulated state of affection bound within the constraints of the intellect.[7] These understandings clarify seemingly incongruous associations Archbishop Núñez de Haro constructed in his pastoral letter. When referring to the lack of spiritual devotion among the ancient Jews, he insisted that God desired from them "hearts . . . that *thought* [*pensasen*]) [emphasis mine] about a swift and serious conversion." Only the heart that houses the rational soul has the capacity to think and ponder. The archbishop also declared that spiritual piety requires a "sincere faith, purified of all error and superstition, born in the depths of our heart." Faith was an act of belief that was a judgment of the will, and the will was a faculty of the rational soul. A faith that has been purified of misconceptions, "error and superstition," is a self-reflexive one that has been schooled and consists of a body of conscious beliefs concerning the nature of God. Archbishop Núñez de Haro, then, proposed a religion governed by the intellect and understanding. In essence, to know God was to love him.

The emphasis on knowing God necessitated an effort to instruct believers about him. The catechism was the central pillar of this project of Christian indoctrination.[8] The church had employed the catechism since the sixteenth century, and the Council of Trent in its twenty-fourth session in 1563 ordered bishops to ensure that pastors and their assistants teach the rudiments of the faith to children on every Sunday and feast day.[9] The Third Mexican Provincial Council of 1585 enthusiastically endorsed and expanded upon the Tridentine decree. It ordered all pastors in New Spain to hold an hour of catechism classes on Sundays and feast days for the children, servants, and slaves of their parishes. To ensure attendance, the council recommended that pastors carry out a census of their parishes to identify those required to participate in the catechization and to fine parents and masters who neglected to send children and servants to the parish church for instruction. The council also stipulated that confessors examine penitents on the tenets of faith during the sacrament of penance and that pastors only marry those couples who demonstrated a mastery of their prayers and precepts of the church.[10]

Although the Tridentine church encouraged the use of the catechism, the content of the lessons contained in these works changed over time. The catechism written by Gerónimo Ripalda, whose opening passages we examined in Chapter 3, formed the basis for the classes prescribed by the Third Mexican Provincial Council. Recall that this work, first published in 1591, opens with instructions for proper performance of the sign of the cross, thus revealing the vital importance of performing this simple but symbolically charged gesture. Performative piety preceded matters of doctrine and careful exposition of points of the faith. Thus, the catechism well represented the theology of baroque Catholicism.

This emphasis on performance was absent from the next major catechism published and disseminated in Mexico, the catechism commissioned by the reform-oriented Fourth Mexican Provincial Council.[11] The council's catechism immediately opens with an in-depth explication of the Creed. It glosses the entire prayer, commenting on the meaning of each phrase. It takes almost thirty pages to explain this statement of faith as it moves through the meaning of "Almighty" in reference to God the father to the "Communion of Saints."[12] The difference between this and the Ripalda catechism is striking. The Ripalda catechism begins with what Christians should do and how to do it properly. In contrast, the council catechism opens with what the faithful should believe. In fact, the performance of the sign of the cross, so prominent in the Ripalda catechism, is buried in the council's work. It does not appear until the last hundred pages of this voluminous (over five hundred pages) book. Clearly, the clerics who authored the later catechism deemed performative piety much less important than Ripalda. Understanding was now the primary concern.[13]

Focused now on deepening the laity's understanding of the Catholic faith, the reforming prelates of the mid-eighteenth century reinvigorated and transformed the program for the instruction of the faithful. William Taylor in his study of parish priests in rural Mexico during the eighteenth century argues that after 1760 teaching became the primary function of pastors.[14] Questions of indoctrination certainly figured prominently in the proceedings of the Fourth Mexican Provincial Council. Although the bishops and theologians of the council largely reiterated the decrees of Third Mexican Provincial Council, they indicated the supreme importance of catechization by placing the decrees concerning it at the opening of the council's proceedings before any other issue.[15]

The reform-minded bishops also reemphasized preaching to complement catechization. Preaching was not new. Trent and the Third Mexican Provincial Council had both required pastors to deliver sermons on Sundays and feast days,[16] but these councils had never specified a method of delivery or subject matter for the weekly homily. The Fourth Mexican Provincial Council sought to regulate preaching in a more detailed manner. It mandated that all pastors preach a sermon "for the space of a half hour" on Sundays and feast days and that all sermons concern a point of doctrine or an article of faith. It also advised preachers to adopt a simple rhetorical style, avoid "pure ceremony," and employ gentle persuasion rather than recrimination in their sermons.[17]

The reformed emphasis on understanding God's word and church doctrine necessitated a new mode of lay attendance at liturgical events. To impart religious instruction effectively, priests required an attentive audience. Archbishop Núñez de Haro repeatedly spoke on the theme of the proper manner of lay presence at mass. Ignoring the Fourth Mexican Provincial

Council's advice to persuade flocks gently, he excoriated the faithful who acted the same way in church as they did in the

> plazas or stores, in discussing and dealing with their temporal
> affairs, who do not offer to God the same attention that they give
> to whomever they speak; who only kneel for appearances, and after
> a thousand postures and movements that declare their distraction
> and their disgust [with the mass] exit church without knowing why
> they came.[18]

At first sight, the archbishop in this passage seems to condemn those who came to church to fulfill the precept to hear mass on Sundays and feast days but who spent their time occupied in profane thoughts, chafing until the mass ended. His admonition, however, may have encompassed more than the nondevout. As we saw in Chapter 3, authors of devotional tracts encouraged the faithful of New Spain to move while in prayer. The faithful commonly rocked their bodies, held their arms outstretched in the form of a cross, prostrated themselves on the ground, or repeatedly genuflected during prayer to increase the efficacy of their orations. Movement was an integral part of the mass and prayer in another way. Many of the faithful approached, touched, and kissed relics and images housed in churches during and outside the celebration of the eucharist.[19] With this in mind, the archbishop's use of the phrase "a thousand postures and movements" likely included as a target of his condemnation those who employed exterior techniques in prayer.

In place of a "thousand postures and movements," Archbishop Núñez de Haro advocated a piety in which the body remained still and the Christian maintained interior "attention" to the sacred rites priests performed and to the sermons they pronounced. In another homily the archbishop reiterated this message by castigating those gathered to hear mass because they lacked the "concentration [*recogimiento*] and interior attention" necessary to profit from the truths he spoke.[20] This emphasis contrasted with earlier practices of prayer. At least as early as the fifteenth century theologians viewed inattention during prayer as an acceptable, even desirable, state as long as the Christian began with the intention of keeping God in mind. Prayer was equated to an arrow. The initial intention gave it its velocity and carried it to its destination. Even in the eighteenth century, devotional writers in the Hispanic world endorsed this view, stating that the initial intention imbued the rest of the pious act with "virtual" attention even if the Christian was involuntarily distracted.[21] Even the catechism issued by the Fourth Mexican Provincial Council supported this doctrine to some extent. It stated that those involuntarily distracted during the mass still fulfilled the church's precept to attend the sacred rite, but added that those who were distracted, even if not by an act of their will, committed a venial sin.[22] Over the course of three centuries, distraction during prayer had changed from a desirable state to a mild sin. Archbishop Núñez de Haro, in opposition to more moderate thinkers, simply rejected this older view. He condemned as "absolutely worthless" acts of worship without interior attention. Concentrating on the meaning of prayers and sacraments was his necessary requirement for "true and spiritual" worship.

As reformers made God spiritual and proclaimed understanding and interior attention the marks of true worship, they de-emphasized or dismissed practices designed for a religion of sacred immanence. They first sought to limit the frequency with which Catholics had traditionally been able to encounter the divine in its physical manifestations. The public and ostentatious exposition of the eucharist had become common in Mexico City by the eighteenth century. A decree issued by the cathedral chapter in 1756 reveals that the host was exhibited every third day in one church of the city. The ceremony rotated among the parishes, convents, and monasteries in such a way that each church displayed the host in magnificence twice a year.[23] Parishes, convents, and monasteries also displayed the host in a splendid monstrance on their main altars on the feast days of their patron saints and other special saintly benefactors. The reforming bishops reacted strongly against this practice, which they considered an excessive display of the most sacred mystery of the church. In 1768 Archbishop Lorenzana rebuked those who "seek the exposition of the blessed [sacrament] for any reason" and decreed that henceforth episcopal approval would be necessary for public display of the eucharist.[24] Three years later, the Fourth Mexican Provincial Council issued a similar statement. It lamented the "great excess" in the exposition of the sacrament because this constant display decreased its majesty, making it "ordinary and common."[25] The council's justification for limiting public display of the eucharist is intriguing. It sought to preserve its dignity and magnificence, for the host remained the most perfect site of God's physical presence within the world. But it sought to remove it from public view. As the church tried to limit manifestations of the divine within the world to the eucharist, it placed a heightened value on the consecrated host. The laity could no longer easily or frequently access Christ as he was exhibited on the altar. The restrictions, beyond being part of a project to remove the sacred from the world, were an attempt to structure hierarchy, to exult the clergy, who still retained access to the consecrated host, over the laity, who were bereft of this avenue for approaching God. Reformed Catholicism, more than baroque Catholicism before it, sought to elevate priests above parishioners.[26]

As part of the project to limit sites of sacred immanence, the reformers also tried to redefine the role of saints in Catholic practice. At least since the sixteenth century, some Catholic thinkers had tried to transform devotion to saints—to move the faithful away from approaching saints for miracles and aid in this world to viewing them as paragons of virtue worthy of imitation. The saint would be less a celestial power broker and more an example for Christian life. During the baroque era, Catholics still looked to saints as miracle workers (although it is difficult to know to what extent Catholics of the seventeenth century also viewed saints as exemplars). Reformed Catholic discourse elided the saints' intercessory function and emphasized their humanity, portraying their lives as worthy and capable, though perhaps imperfectly, of imitation. Archbishop Núñez de Haro delivered several sermons commemorating the lives of saints. Not once did he mention a miracle performed by any of them. Rather, he depicted even the greatest saints in their humanity. In a sermon on St. Joseph, the archbishop recalled the human weaknesses of the putative father of Christ. He portrayed Joseph as a man plagued by doubt concerning Mary's conception of a child and about his worthiness to act as Christ's guardian. He then argued that despite these gnawing questions, Joseph trusted the visions revealed to him by angels and never contravened God's will. In another sermon the archbishop emphasized the Virgin's virtue and humility in her unquestioning acceptance of God's decision for her to bear Christ. He explicitly called on the faithful to look to Mary's humility as a model: "imitation is the homage that the Lady [Virgin] awaits, the true worship that pleases her, and the greater glory that creates affection in her toward men."[27] By emphasizing the humanity and virtue of saints, the archbishop implicitly undermined their function as divine power brokers. In fact, the saint who acted as a model of morality no longer required the use of relics and images, those physical objects that manifested their heavenly power, for proper devotion.

Despite their effort to redefine the purpose of saints, the reforming prelates were bound by centuries of Catholic practice and officially codified doctrine. At times they even resorted to traditional practices. Archbishop Lorenzana defended questionable relics housed in the cathedral in Mexico City from an attempt by a member of the cathedral chapter to remove them. He even upheld the validity of relics whose authenticity could not be documented but that supposedly were those of a nameless saint. He argued that "it was not new to celebrate a martyr whose name is unknown." In fact, he condemned critics who sought to remove apocryphal saints from the canon because these men were "highly open to error."[28] Furthermore, in 1768 when Mexico City suffered a series of earthquakes, Archbishop Lorenzana proposed that the cathedral chapter organize three processions in which the faithful would parade an image of St. Joseph around the city's central square on three successive Sundays.[29] Likewise, Archbishop Núñez de Haro, the most persistent advocate of reform, even made an occasional concession to traditional forms of piety. Before being named archbishop of Mexico, he delivered a sermon in Spain on the feast of the Assumption and commented that veneration of Mary "should be exterior and public," with processions of her images to demonstrate Christian joy. But he immediately added that veneration of Mary, and by extension that offered to God and all saints, must also be "interior and spiritual." He stated that, without establishing the "reign [of the Virgin] in our hearts," public and external forms of veneration "are vain and simple ceremonies."[30]

As they sought to limit and regulate sacred immanence, the reforming bishops simultaneously attempted to reduce the lavish physical apparatus of baroque worship and veneration. Bishop Fabián y Fuero was the first to order a curtailment of baroque splendor. In 1767 he issued an edict in which he mandated the simplification of all music performed in the cathedral of Puebla. He condemned the "addition and multiplication of notes" that characterized baroque music because they hindered the true purpose of music, which was to move the soul with its beauty and convey the "meaning of the words and of the sentences" sung by the choir to the spirit of the listener. The bishop argued that elaborate scores moved the mind to concupiscence and the contemplation of worldly things, whereas "grave and sonorous" music that imitated the simplicity of nature excited the soul to thoughts of the divine.[31] Bishop Fabián y Fuero's decree interests us beyond the fact that in it he began a movement in Mexico to reduce the splendor of Catholic worship. In it he also twisted the baroque understanding of the use of sensuous display in sacred ritual. The church employed the physical, in this case music, as a method to excite Catholics to devotion. The sight of images, the touch of relics, and the rhythm of music moved the soul to contemplate divinity. In his edict Bishop Fabián y Fuero stated that it was not music in itself that moved the soul, but rather the "meaning of the words and of the sentences." Here, the bishop signaled a fundamental shift in Catholic thought. In the eyes of the reformers, Catholicism, though it still employed the external in worship, was now a religion of the word and understanding, not the image (or the musical note) and the sensuous. Archbishop Lorenzana worked within the same framework. In 1769 he issued a decree on Indian religious practices forbidding religious dances and live representations of Christ's passion. Besides his distaste for the external nature of these devotions, he also denied their capacity to move those who watched them. Although he conceded that visual display aided the conversion of the indigenous peoples of New Spain during the early colonial period, he dismissed those who argued that these visual representations were of continued value. He denied that now, more than two centuries after the conquest, "the faith enters them [the Indians] more easily through sight than through the ear."[32] In other words, Archbishop Lorenzana, like Bishop Fabián y Fuero, privileged the word over the image (or sensual). This denigration of the sensuous was part of the movement from a religion in which the faithful sought contact with God through his physical manifestations to one in which they contemplated and attempted to comprehend his word.

Emphasizing the word facilitated the simplification of baroque devotional practices, which ideally allowed for greater economy in religious expenditures. Money and energy spent on the physical apparatus of worship could be redirected to other needs. Archbishop Lorenzana encouraged the monasteries and convents of the viceregal capital to economize on their expenditures for wax. Rather than invest huge sums on candles, he called on them to spend moderately and devote the savings to the workhouse he hoped to build to house, train, and discipline the city's beggars. Charity, Lorenzana argued, was a better use of money than expenditures on external worship, for the poor were "living temples of God." Referring to the teachings of St. Jerome and St. Ambrose, he argued that the ornaments of the church used in worship were in fact simply a form of deposit to be sold to aid the poor in times of need.[33]

Despite his desire to reduce the splendor of worship, Archbishop Lorenzana refused to diminish the pomp owed to the eucharist during public displays. He insisted that because the consecrated host truly contained the body of Christ, it deserved "the most special worship" and "magnificence" in its display: a decent accompaniment of candles, "the continual vigil of priests, [the singing of] canticles and psalms, and other circumstance."[34] Although he promoted splendor in the exposition of the eucharist, at the same time, as we have seen, he attempted to limit the frequency with which it was displayed. He argued that the majesty of the exhibited host would move the faithful to greater veneration if the event were uncommon.

Even the eucharist, however, could forego the splendor owed to it in special circumstances. Most Catholics received the viaticum on their deathbeds. A priest, accompanied by others who carried torches and candles, took the host in full procession to the home of the dying so that they might receive communion one last time before death. Bishop Fabián y Fuero, in an edict issued to the clergy of his diocese in 1769, exhorted priests in cases of necessity to omit the procession and accompaniment of lights rather than deny the viaticum to the dying. He insisted that they continue to employ the traditional external rites whenever possible, but also stated that the solemnities established by the church were dispensable when they conflicted with the needs of the faithful.[35] Like Archbishop Lorenzana, Bishop Fabián y Fuero took the middle ground; both tried to reduce external worship when appropriate, but never wholly repudiated it.

Once again, Archbishop Núñez de Haro proved the most ardent critic of traditional forms of piety—in this case baroque splendor. In one of the first sermons he delivered as archbishop of Mexico, he castigated the Mexican church for its commitment to splendor. He sardonically exclaimed:

> What height of felicity! What lovable repose! And I rejoice, my beloved children, upon seeing in this New World the magnificence of the temples, the prodigious multitude of gold, silver, pearls, and precious stones that you have offered and consecrated to the worship of the Lord. I am stunned [*me embeleso*] to see the devotion, the apparatus, the brilliance of lights [*incendio de luces*], the precious ornaments with which, apparently, God is offered all the worship possible in the world.[36]

All this splendor, the archbishop continued, did not signal true devotion, but rather invited distraction: "And in the midst of so many marvels, your spirit, distracted, flees; your imagination, inconstant, flies; and you entertain your-self with a thousand frivolous, and perhaps criminal, objects."[37] In this pas-sage Archbishop Núñez de Haro turned baroque epistemology on its head. Splendid objects were at best "frivolous," at worst "criminal." Splendor did not move the soul toward God; it did just the opposite. It distracted the spirit from attention to the mass and to God and led to irreligion.

In place of splendor, the prelates stressed humility. Archbishop Núñez de Haro rebuked his listeners because, in his opinion, they considered splen-dor, which "suspends or forcefully strikes [*hiere con viveza*] the senses," as the only true signs of greatness and power. To his mind, the multiplication of pomp instead revealed inner debility; ostentation simply hid weakness behind a blusterous facade. True greatness had no need for extravagance or show.[38] In a sermon on the annunciation to the Virgin, the archbishop told his audience to look for sublime greatness not in splendorous things but in the "depths of humility." He then proclaimed that God had chosen Mary to bear and rear Christ only on account of her great humility. Mary, he stated, "was humble in her purity, humble in her faith, humble in her obedience."[39]

This shift from splendor to the topos of humility included representa-tions of Christ. The reforming bishops emphasized Christ's earthly life, his saving act, and his manner of presence in the eucharist as signs of humility. Bishop Fabián y Fuero commented that Christ's incarnation was the supreme act of humility. By becoming human, he eschewed signs of might and power and "dressed himself in humility."[40] Archbishop Núñez de Haro in a ser-mon on the transfiguration remarked that the only path to salvation was the faithful imitation of Christ. He then stated that as Christ was humble, poor, and despised, so only the humble who refused to entrap themselves with the riches and delights of the world could follow him.[41] Christ's passion and death on the cross were considered particularly ignominious. For this reason, Archbishop Núñez de Haro labeled the crucifix the sign of "humil-ity and dejection" that called Christians to embrace humility, penitence, and poverty.[42] According to Bishop Fabián y Fuero, Christ even presented him-self humbly and dejectedly in the eucharist, for in it he hid the fact that he was God and humbly exposed himself to the insults, indevotion, and the sacrilege of Protestants and heretics.[43] The message of these statements was clear. If Christ had chosen to live, die, and present himself in the host humbly, without fanfare and the visible signs of majesty, Christians must follow his example and practice their religion in the same way.

As Mexican prelates sought to replace splendor with humility in religious practice, they also attempted to substitute a modest and stilled body for an active and symbolically charged one. Decorum, or bodily restraint, became the proper disposition for participation in sacred rites. The Fourth Mexican Provincial Council ordered all who attended Corpus Christi processions to participate with "gravity, decency, and modesty."[44] No excess of movement that may have struck symbolic resonances was to be permitted in religious activities. Likewise, Archbishop Núñez de Haro sermonized that the Catholic should present a "modest and respectful exterior" while in church.[45] The bishops emphasized modest comportment to sunder the relationship between lay symbolic gesture and the sacred that characterized baroque Catholic practice. But modesty fulfilled another function. A disciplined and modest body liberated the soul to contemplate God without distraction. The stilled body was a prerequisite for the rationally oriented piety of the reforming bishops.

A corollary to stilling the body was the delegitimization of penitential piety. Mexican bishops banned public acts of self-flagellation.[46] The Fourth Mexican Provincial Council ordered that penitentes, those who scourged themselves publicly while marching in religious celebrations, refrain from participating in holy week processions. The council commented:

> the penitences that should be agreeable to God are a cause of mockery and laughter because certain *castas* of vice-ridden [*viciosos*] and drunk men whip themselves with barbed whips [*pelotillas*], gird themselves with swords, and do other acts of mortification that are more a proof of their barbarity than of devotion.[47]

This passage is pregnant with meaning. Obviously, the bishops no longer viewed self-flagellation as a means of imitating the passion of Christ and, thus, liturgically make his salvific act present in real time. Self-flagellation and intense bodily mortification indicated "barbarity," not devotion. Moreover, penitential acts undermined true religion because they opened Catholicism to ridicule. They were the worst excesses of dramatic public display that Protestants and Enlightenment thinkers so easily, sardonically—and apparently in the minds of the Mexican prelates, correctly—mocked. This mockery stemmed not merely from the "barbarity" of these mortifications, but also from the category of person who practiced them. According to the bishops of the council, flagellants were immoral drunkards. The fact that the council described them as "castas" suggests that they belonged to the growing mixed-blood population of Mexico City. Although this may be true, it is not certain. The fact that Archbishop Núñez de Haro would later insult Catholics who advocated baroque splendor and display by comparing them to the ancient Jews (see above) should warn us about the reliability of the bishops' ascription of social status to the penitentes. They obviously considered flagellants repugnant, but their social ascription may have been more an effort to marginalize them rather than to classify them objectively. Although we have no evidence of the social composition of the penitentes in Mexico City in the eighteenth century, we have seen that devotional tracts encouraged the literate faithful to practice self-flagellation. This situation suggests that public self-disciplining was a more socially diffuse practice than the decree of the Fourth Mexican Provincial Council indicates.[48]

The bishops, however, never issued a blanket condemnation of mortification, simply its most dramatic forms. They recommended that the flagellants march in the processions with "a rope around their necks, a crown on their heads, and a candle in their hands" all as a "sign of mortification." In this case, the "sign" testified to an interior state of penitence in the participant, but did not create a mimetic link with the passion of Christ. The council even conceded that penitents could continue to practice self-flagellation, but only in the secrecy of their homes and only if they practiced it without excessive zeal and "cruelty."[49]

Although the reforming prelates condoned mild mortifications, they by and large no longer understood or chose to ignore the historic meaning of acts of penitence. Mortification served only as an external sign of an inward state or, as the history of fasting in the eighteenth century reveals, it disciplined the flesh and subjected it to the spirit. Fasting was a practice recommended by the gospel story of Christ's forty days of abstinence from food before beginning his ministry and was an ancient discipline of the church. The early history of fasting and its significations are beyond our scope here. Suffice it to say that by the late medieval period, Christians practiced food deprivation as a mortification to construct a symbolic relationship between themselves and the sufferings of Christ. Like self-flagellation, fasting allowed the faithful to participate in salvation history and mystically invoke the presence of Christ through symbolic human performance.[50] The Council of Trent endorsed fasting as a pious act and ordered that existing customs and laws regulating the times for fasting be followed, recommendations that the Third Mexican Provincial Council reiterated.[51] As early as the late sixteenth century, official church discourse ignored the symbolic aspect of fasting. The decree of the Third Mexican Provincial Council concerning the efficacy of food abstinence simply stated that by fasting "we restrain the impetuses of our rebel flesh . . . [and] subject it to the direction of the spirit."[52] The Fourth Mexican Provincial Council said essentially the same.[53] But a symbolic understanding of fasting persisted in official ecclesiastical discourse into the eighteenth century. In an edict on the necessity of abstaining from food during Lent, Bishop Fabián y Fuero commented that fasting creates a "union and company with the mortification and cross of Christ" and that through this act "let us do something . . . that our redeemer suffered for us."[54] But in a later episcopal decree, Bishop Fabián y Fuero elided this justification and insisted that God had instituted abstinence and mortification to discipline the flesh.[55] Why the bishop retreated from his earlier comments is unclear. It is evident, however, that both Archbishop Lorenzana and Archbishop Núñez de Haro never shared Bishop Fabián y Fuero's earlier view. Archbishop Lorenzana stated that through fasting Christians' battle against the concupiscence of the flesh and signal an interior state of repentance.[56] Archbishop Núñez de Haro on the other hand denied the efficacy of fasting as a pious act in itself. He recommended that the faithful "seek to accompany fasting, so that it may be fruitful, with prayer, [the giving of] alms, and the exercise of the acts of mercy."[57] Only with the addition of other pious acts did fasting take on merit. As learned ecclesiastics began to suppress or forget the symbolic underpinnings and meanings of this penitential practice, they recommended it less. Beginning in the mid-eighteenth century, they began to relax the rules of abstinence regarding certain foods until by the beginning of the nineteenth century the faithful could eat any foods indiscriminately on many days of abstention.[58] Essentially, this symbolic practice lost its efficacy as a suffrage over the course of the early modern period as lay performative piety was devalued.

The Rise of the Individual: Reforming Christian Community

As God became spirit, the source of community formation among Christians also changed. In baroque Catholicism, sociability and charity among the faithful expressed and invoked Christ's mystical body. In other words, baroque Catholic practice emphasized horizontal bonds of community between human beings. In the eighteenth century, the reforming bishops conceived of a more vertically structured community. They tried to forge a community of individuals who related primarily to God and only secondarily to each other. Sociability in this model was based on individuals having reference to the same deity, not on a community participating in the mystical body of Christ through spiritual reciprocity. Although religious practices structured community in both cases, sociability in baroque Catholicism was a religious act in itself, whereas in reformed Catholicism it was a product of shared religious belief.

The reforming bishops' regulation of charity and discourse on the poor reveal their new definition of Christian community. As noted in Chapter 5, many Catholics began to distinguish between the deserving and undeserving poor as early as the sixteenth century, and some began to view the poor with distaste and suspicion rather than as Christ-like figures who shared his poverty. Also beginning in the sixteenth century, the church in Mexico began to restrict begging, especially in churches, but did not ban it outright. Church buildings, the very heart of Christian community, still functioned as places, outside the performance of the high mass, to forge horizontal bonds between the faithful through the distribution and reception of alms. The reforming bishops of late colonial Mexico, however, moved to strip church buildings of that function.

Each of the three reforming bishops in the eighteenth century issued decrees prohibiting the poor from begging within church buildings. Bishop Fabián y Fuero was the first. In 1765 he ordered all beggars to remain at the church doors so that "the faithful are not interrupted in their attention to the mass and other pious exercises for which they come to the church [*templo*]." Churches, according to the bishop, were uniquely for worship, and worship demanded inner concentration.[59] In 1767 Archbishop Lorenzana reiterated the gist of Bishop Fabián y Fuero's decree. He ordered that a table be set up at the door of churches where the poor could solicit charity. At no time were they to beg in church, for this would disrupt the "attention" of those gathered and break the silence one should observe there.[60] The Fourth Mexican Provincial Council, at which Archbishop Lorenzana presided, extended this prohibition to all churches in New Spain. The council completely prohibited begging in church buildings because a "church was made for praying to and supplicating God, and it is against [this] precept to disturb the faithful when they hear mass or the divine office."[61] Archbishop Núñez de Haro simply called begging in churches a profanation. But unlike the other prelates, he also castigated those who gave alms in church for their "immodesty and worldly vanity."[62] With these decrees, the reforming bishops abolished acts that structured and expressed human community from the sacred space of the church. In their minds, the church building was the location for individuals, in silence and separated from one another, to construct their personal relationships with a spiritual God. The church no longer functioned to build and reflect ties of human sociability.

The removal of beggars from churches resulted not only from a redefinition of Catholic community, but also from an intensification of the crisis of image suffered by the poor during the eighteenth century. Of the episcopal reformers, Archbishop Lorenzana proved the most vehement critic of the poor. Although he conceded that there existed people truly in need of charity, "the honorable, impeded . . . old women, widows . . . [and] unmarried women of virtue [*doncellas*],"[63] he argued that the majority of the poor were simply "lazy." It was the lazy poor, he stated, who "inundated the land [*los pueblos*]," resorted to monasteries and convents for food, harassed the wealthy for money, and frequented taverns.[64] Archbishop Lorenzana heaped invective on the poor because he perceived them as a threat to civil and religious order. "The lazy person," he argued,

> is a sponge that receives in itself all poison, a pump that attracts all filth, a toadstool where all serpents are harbored, wax in which is impressed and sealed all bad judgment . . . nocturnal bird that is blinded by the light of day and supports itself with theft in the night, rotted member of the republic that infects and sickens [*cancera*] the whole body . . . Catholic without religion, Christian in name, and ultimately an obstacle to human life, bothersome to all, useful to none, harmful to himself. He lives mechanically, without aim in his steps, without plan [*modelo*] in his activities, and without rationality in his speech.[65]

The symbolic association between the poor and Christ (which rested on the unity of the sign and signified) had withered in elite discourse. According to the archbishop, the mendicant at best was an aimless and irreligious rogue who never benefited "the republic"; at worst, he was an element that poisoned and infested the community. In his view, the mendicant poor posed two great dangers to the community. First, their indolence nullified the work of others and even threatened "to annihilate the authority of the prince, which consists in the wealth and industry of his vassals." Second, the slanders they uttered promoted sedition and unrest among the populace and rendered others unwilling "to obey their superiors."[66] In short, the poor imperiled the wealth of the republic, the finances of the crown, and patterns of deference and obedience to authority.

Archbishop Núñez de Haro was more ambiguous than his predecessor regarding almsgiving and the poor. In a sermon delivered on the necessity of granting alms to the poor, he mixed traditional and new notions of charity. He stated:

> The rich, through charity, enter into communion with the privileges of the poor, and conserve over them all the preeminence of their wealth. If the poor man, by [his] need, is similar to the savior, the rich man, by his generosity resembles God. If the poor man, by his patience and suffering is like the savior, the rich man, with his largesse, exchanges his goods for the riches of God. The humble and virtuous poor man (although there are few of these) is a true imitation of Christ; the truly charitable rich man (although there are fewer of these) is certainly a benefactor of God himself. . . . The poor man, in his suffering finds the means to exercise patience and the subject of his penance; the virtuous and meritorious rich man, erases and redeems with his alms the insuperable defects of indulgent [*lisonjera*] abundance. The poor man prays to God for his benefactors, and his prayer has influence in heaven that his credit lacks on earth; the rich man supports his prayers on these very prayers and plaints of the poor. The poor man dies without having to bear goods that he does not possess; the merciful rich man awaits death with confidence because he has passed his alms over to the other life with a return [*usura*] of a hundred to one.[67]

Archbishop Núñez de Haro still placed almsgiving squarely in the economy of salvation. The gift to the poor gained merit for the benefactor, and the poor exercised the Christian virtues of patience and humility in their need. Considering his vehement rejection of other forms of symbolic religious practice, he surprisingly retained the traditional image of the poor as representations of Christ on earth. But he did not fully preserve traditional notions of charity. His comment that few truly "humble and virtuous" poor existed shows that he accepted the classification of the poor into worthy and unworthy groups.[68] Moreover, he did not simply equate the poor with Christ. He constructed a full analogy: the poor are to Christ as the rich are to God the father. In this analogy social distinction is preserved. The rich and poor are not reconciled in the mystical body of Christ through the sacred act of charity. The rich always remain separate from the poor and retain their preeminence over them. In essence, the act of charity had become a method to preserve and strengthen social distinction and hierarchy at the expense of a more horizontal practice of Catholic community.

The darkening image of the poor as sources of disorder and contagion prompted Catholic reformers to attempt to confine them. They sought to instill within the poor respect for authority and a work ethic. Not surprisingly, Archbishop Lorenzana, the most vehement critic of the poor, dedicated the greatest effort toward confinement. He supported construction of a poorhouse in Mexico City known as the Hospicio de Pobres. But the poorhouse did not open until 1774, two years after Archbishop Lorenzana had departed Mexico to become archbishop of Toledo. The stated purpose of the Hospicio was to remove beggars from the streets and plazas of the capital and compel them to work for their livelihood. The archbishop touted the benefits of such a foundation to the community. He promised that the sequestration of beggars would curtail epidemics, reduce homicides and robberies, and prompt plebeians to seek work. Moreover, it would benefit the inmates themselves by teaching them Christian doctrine and trades and instilling in them a work discipline.[69] He encouraged benefactors to support the Hospicio and even went so far as to order the diversion of all bequests made in wills in favor of the poor in general to this institution.[70]

The foundation of the workhouse in Mexico City was part of a movement toward greater institutionalization of charity apparent in the early modern era. Hospitals, workhouses, and orphanages were established and promoted because some believed that they could distribute alms and provide for the ill, poor, and dispossessed more efficiently than thousands of individual benefactors who bestowed their largesse in a multitude of face-to-face encounters with the poor. Furthermore, the proponents of institutional charity held that the confinement of beggars, mandatory instruction in trade skills, and imposed patterns of personal industry would ameliorate poverty by encouraging the "lazy" poor to be productive. They equated idleness solely with personal choice and ignored other factors that led to destitution. Archbishop Lorenzana, in his decree requesting financial support for his new foundation, declared that it was time to "establish a good method of policy and order in charity." Aware that at least some of the capital's residents would resist the institutionalization of beneficence because it would deny the wealthy the opportunity to practice sacred acts of charity, the archbishop stated that bequests to the Hospicio, in which the benefactor never came into direct contact with the poor, would accrue just as much grace to the giver as personal acts of almsgiving. In fact, the more anonymous bequest to the workhouse could prove more beneficial in terms of divine rewards because it eliminated the temptations of pride and vanity that could accompany face-to-face gifts to the poor. Furthermore, he argued that donations to the Hospicio would better aid the souls of benefactors because they served the interests of the larger community, whereas gifts to individual beggars did not.[71] Institutionalized charity thus not only economized on alms to the poor; it offered unsurpassed merit to benefactors.

The movement toward institutionalized charity also accounted for Archbishop Lorenzana's foundation of an orphanage known as the Cuna de Huérfanos (Cradle of Orphans) in Mexico City.[72] The archbishop justified its establishment by arguing that, although in the past individual Christians had cared for orphans, by the mid-eighteenth century this charitable practice had declined. The Cuna, according to Archbishop Lorenzana, filled a gap in the capital's system of beneficence. Moreover, like the Hospicio de Pobres, it would further the causes of public order and economic activity. Not only would the Cuna feed, clothe, and shelter orphans; it would instruct them in Christian doctrine and teach them trades. The pedagogical activities of the orphanage would instill in its charges "ordered . . . customs" and render them "useful to the republic."[73] The archbishop curried support for the orphanage by appealing to the guilty consciences of the population of Mexico City. He warned potential benefactors, who in his mind were entirely men, that with bequests to religious institutions for the construction of "sumptuous buildings and altarscreens you will not repair the damage of fornication [*estupro*] with a girl [*doncella*] already dead or married, adultery with a married woman . . . [or] incest with a dishonored kinswoman."[74] A gift of alms to the orphanage, however, provided the best method to pay restitution for these offenses, for it aided the offspring of these illicit encounters. The Cuna thus benefited the orphans of Mexico City, the general public, and sinners who transgressed Christian sexual morality.

The institutionalization of charity in Mexico during the second half of the eighteenth century was intended to have the same dampening effect on horizontal community formation as the removal of beggars from church buildings. It segregated the wealthy from the poor and restricted charitable interactions between them. The anonymous bequest to a workhouse, orphanage, or hospital prevented benefactors and recipients of charity from forging personal ties through the sacred act of almsgiving. Henceforth, the institution would mediate contact between two increasingly distant segments of the population and thus preserve social distinctions in an act that had once served to dissolve them with the incorporation of social unequals in the mystical body of Christ.

The church's institutionalization of charity shared the same underlying principles evident in the Bourbon state's foray into public welfare and urban planning in the late eighteenth century. Both church and state responded to (and promoted) the breakdown in patron-client relationships as the population of Mexico City swelled at the end of the century. But their motives were not entirely altruistic. Not merely a response to the growing anonymity of the urban arena, the institutionalization of charity reflected new techniques of power designed to redefine social relationships and simultaneously create and mold the individual.

The new method of charity reflected and shaped a process of disciplining human bodies and ordering the physical environment begun in much of the West during the eighteenth century. Michel Foucault, in his numerous revisionist studies of the Enlightenment, has argued that as intellectual discourse freed itself from strictures of Christianity and recourse to traditional authority, an amorphous project that targeted the autonomy of the body arose. New methods of pedagogy, military training, medical examination, and penal reform sought to still labile bodies and impress upon them an economy of gesture. These techniques were aimed at rendering the body more pliant to authority and molding it into an efficient tool of action.[75] At the same time that religious reformers sought to still symbolically charged bodies and confine the poor to workhouses, urban reform projects, like the one begun by Viceroy Revillagigedo in Mexico City, restructured urban landscapes. They opened wide avenues to ease transit and commerce, ordered streets and addresses to facilitate the location and observation of individuals, and introduced new police agencies to maintain public tranquility, preserve authority, and defend capital.[76] Archbishop Lorenzana justified the establishment of the Hospicio de Pobres and Cuna de Huérfanos by emphasizing that they would impress habits of work and obeisance to authority on the mendicant poor and dispossessed. The poor, left to their own devices, endangered the established authority of crown and church and undermined prosperity. But if disciplined and transformed into "useful" members of the republic, they could enhance the prosperity of the realm and become a stable part of the social order. Both the Hospicio de Pobres and the Cuna de Huérfanos were designed precisely to achieve these ends.

The reforming bishops of New Spain certainly attempted to break horizontal bonds of community in the realm of charity, but they spoke and acted much less forcefully concerning confraternities, those pious brotherhoods that forged Christian sociability through collective devotions and shared spiritual obligations. Despite much criticism from lay thinkers in Spain during the late eighteenth century about the wasteful nature of confraternal expenditures on wax and ornaments for worship, the Mexican prelates, including Archbishop Núñez de Haro, never attempted to undermine the urban confraternity. The bishops amalgamated some economically struggling confraternities into more stable ones and dissolved some defunct congregations, but they never systematically sought to reduce their number or membership.[77] They may have refrained from assaulting confraternities because the Spanish crown took the lead in regulating them and because they saw the brotherhoods as potentially useful tools to support parish finances and liturgical activities.

The first sustained project to monitor the confraternities of New Spain came late in the colonial period, not from the church hierarchy, but from the Spanish crown. The monarchy had a financial interest in them. It viewed these organizations as reservoirs of untapped revenue and denigrated what it considered their wasteful expenditures on paraliturgical items for the celebration of an excessive number of feast days. Using an early seventeenth-century law that ordered all confraternities to obtain royal approval of their constitutions, the crown in 1776 commissioned a report on their state and number in Mexico. The initial surveys focused solely on rural confraternities. The viceroy did not order an examination of urban confraternities in Mexico until 1787, when he charged Archbishop Núñez de Haro to conduct it.[78]

Ecclesiastical participation in the effort to monitor and regulate confraternities was not reluctant. The reforming bishops of Mexico disapproved of many confraternal practices. Bishop Fabián y Fuero condemned their "profane expenses, ostentation and gluttonous dissipation [of funds]."[79] His counterpart, Archbishop Lorenzana issued a more extensive castigation in an edict published in 1769:

> Confraternities, brotherhoods, and congregations are founded only so that the faithful may partake, as brothers closely united together, in sacred functions and not for profane expenses, ostentation, or to provide incentives to gluttony. Even the gentiles venerated with great respect the places destined for the false worship of their gods and held graves as religious. Then should not we Christians [do the same] in our cemeteries, in which are deposited some bodies whose souls we piously believe are in God's presence [*gozando de Dios*] and [that] are to revive united [with their souls] from that sleep of the earth for the eternity of heaven?[80]

He continued:

> We exhort all pastors of our diocese, particularly those of this city, that they take care that on feast days and other ecclesiastical solemnities that no one sell edible things nor beverages in the cemeteries of churches under the pretext of gatherings at them, nor that the brothers of any confraternity, brotherhood, or congregation hold lunches, suppers, refreshments, or other excesses with the motive or as a result of their processions, festivities, and meetings, especially during holy week.[81]

In this passage, the archbishop revealed his distaste for the traditional activities of confraternities. He dismissed their paraliturgical functions designed to praise, thank, and promote veneration of their patron saints and increase the splendor of holy days as "profane expenses" and "ostentation." Rather than view confraternal banquets as mechanisms to promote Christian unity and participate in the mystical body of Christ, he condemned them as "incentives to gluttony." Moreover, he sought to distance these organizations from their close association with death and aid for the souls of deceased members in purgatory by banning confraternal functions from cemeteries. Confraternities traditionally held their meetings, commemoration ceremonies, and feasts close to grave sites precisely to emphasize the intimate connection between the living and dead. Proximity to their earthly remains also increased the merit of suffrages performed on behalf of the departed. By declaring cemeteries off limits, the archbishop undermined the traditional *raison d'être* of confraternities.

The reform-minded Mexican prelates, however, never disbanded these organizations. They believed that confraternities could be useful in the dissemination of doctrine if they were properly regulated, participated appropriately in solemn religious practices, and contributed resources to parish expenses. In fact, during the eighteenth century the hierarchy promoted the foundation of confraternities dedicated to the blessed sacrament in each parish of Mexico City. The bishops believed that these confraternities would conform to prescriptions concerning ecclesiastical supervision and act more as adjuncts to the parish than independent organizations for lay religious practice.[82] Archbishop Núñez de Haro enlarged the blessed sacrament confraternities when he finally acted on the surveys he had commissioned at the insistence of the viceroy.

After completing the survey of Mexico City's confraternities in 1794, Archbishop Núñez de Haro suppressed many urban brotherhoods but left the majority of them intact. The surveys of rural and urban confraternities revealed 991 of them in the Archdiocese of Mexico. Archbishop Núñez de Haro ordered the dissolution of over 450 of these organizations, most of them rural, because of mismanagement of funds or precarious finances. In Mexico City there existed 152 confraternities. The archbishop suppressed at least forty of them either totally or by amalgamating them with other, more vibrant ones, often confraternities of the blessed sacrament.[83] In this way, the hierarchy sought to extend its influence and authority over lay devotions. Nonetheless, well over one hundred confraternities remained active in late colonial Mexico City, serving as centers for communal lay religiosity. The reforming bishops, despite their objections to some traditional confraternal practices, considered confraternities potentially useful religious organizations and so promoted them as they simultaneously sought to regulate them more closely. This stance left intact an important source of horizontal community formation in Mexico City.

Conclusion

The early modern period was a time in which the Catholic church attempted to restrict the manifestations of the divine in the world to the sacrament of the eucharist and certain officially approved images and relics. This process of separating the sacred from the profane began in the sixteenth century and was approved and promoted by the Council of Trent. Catholic bishops of eighteenth-century Mexico maneuvered within the parameters of Trent. They never denied the possibility of God's physical presence within the world and never questioned the doctrine of transubstantiation. Nonetheless, these prelates, especially Archbishop Núñez de Haro, reconceived God and worship in a manner that went beyond the Tridentine program. They worked to reduce the laity's contact with the eucharist, reinterpret the function of saints away from their traditional role as divine power brokers, devalue the use of splendorous display as a means to excite devotion in the faithful, and undermine the use of lay liturgical gesture to forge "unions" with Christ and the saints. In essence, they ruptured the unity of the sign and signified in all but very special cases and thus sundered the many and dense connections that bridged the divide between the mundane and sacred. They reconceived God as spirit and therefore demanded different devotions from Catholics so that they might worship their new spiritual deity properly. Although they never directly attacked the communal enterprise of salvation that underlay baroque Catholicism, their reform of charity undermined horizontal bonds of unity among the faithful and subtly delegitimized the collective subjectivity that supported baroque communal piety. In short, the reforming bishops desacralized the physical world by removing manifestations of the divine from it and created new spiritual devotions to replace "exterior," performative ones. Furthermore, they desocialized religious practice and redirected believers toward individual contemplation of God.

The reforms initiated by the bishops participated in a larger realm of social, economic, and cultural reform. Although not directly inspired by the Bourbon project to mold productive, well-ordered, self-regulating subjects or the Bourbon desire to foment economic growth, both projects bubbled from the same wellspring and shared intermediate goals. Like secular reformers, the bishops demanded calm bodies, a populace that respected industry and authority, and a reduction of expenditures for religious ceremonies. Religious reformers were not necessarily inspired by the same ultimate ends as their secular counterparts, but their projects coincided in some cases, mutually reinforcing and sustaining each other.

How did the bishops' attempts to transform piety affect religious practice in late colonial Mexico City? It is precisely to this question that we now turn.

CHAPTER 8

Immanence, Splendor, and Liturgical Piety in the Age of Reform

✝ IN DECEMBER 1813 JOSÉ BUENAVENTURA SANTA MARÍA Y LIPARZA, A prebendary of the Mexico City cathedral chapter wrote his will with the aid of the notary Juan Manuel Pozo. Although not infected by the "mysterious fevers" that plagued Mexico City that year, José suffered from unspecified chronic ailments (*achaques*) that sapped his vigor. José devoted an unusual amount of his will to the design of his funeral. Like a growing number of testators in Mexico City during the latter half of the eighteenth and early nineteenth centuries, José requested moderation in the celebration of his funeral and burial. He asked that, once dead, his cadaver "be removed from his bed and thrown on the bare ground [*haz de la tierra*], without a mat [*tapete*], rug, or shroud [*paño de difunto*]." Moreover, he asked that his executors "not invite anyone of dignity or position [*en dignidad o cargo*], neither the rich nor merchants" to his funeral, for he stated that only those people who "spontaneously want to exercise the act of mercy of burying the dead" should attend. José also insisted that no catafalque, a decorated wooden structure illuminated by candles that held the coffin during the funeral or represented the dead in funerary rites performed after burial, be erected for his obsequies and that the cathedral's bells not toll during the ceremonies as was customary for members of the cathedral chapter. His desire to minimize the pomp of his funeral reflected a growing trend in late colonial Mexico City to reduce the extravagant orchestration of funerals that had characterized baroque Catholicism. In this way, José seems to have rejected baroque practices and adopted the tenets of reformed Catholicism promoted by reforming bishops.[1]

But after choreographing his funeral, José issued other pious directives, many of them baroque in nature. He clearly wished to enhance the splendor of Catholic worship and held images, those sites of sacred immanence, in high esteem. He donated 150 pesos to the parish church of the pueblo of Matatán, where he had served as a pastor before his appointment to the cathedral chapter, to be used for churchly "ornaments." He also gave his personal image of Our Lady of Sorrows "with all her corresponding dresses and ornaments" to the parish church of San Pedro de Chametla. Furthermore, he ordered that his executors commission a "cloak of the best cloth" for the image of the Virgin of Quila, a cloak for Our Lady of Cacalotán, and a "satin habit of the best quality" for an image of St. Nicholas in the pueblo of Chametla. Likewise, he recorded in his will that he had earlier founded two feast-day celebrations, one to the holy trinity and the other to the precious blood of Christ, in the parish church of Chametla. Last, José included a liturgical gesture in his will when he established a perpetual mass foundation worth one thousand pesos. He stipulated that each year on the anniversary of his death, thirteen masses, one solemn sung mass and twelve private masses, be celebrated over thirteen days for his soul.[2] José certainly intended this mass clause to resonate symbolically with Christ and the twelve apostles. These pious directives reveal a continuing attachment to baroque sensibilities and seem to contradict José's desire for funerary simplicity. These contradictions in José's will testify to the complex nature of religious reform and its multifaceted effect on religious practice in late colonial Mexico.

Scholars who have investigated religious culture in New Spain have argued that religion changed in the late colonial period. They suggest a growing disillusionment, particularly among the elite, with the baroque and a greater desire for simplicity in pious practices. Furthermore, they argue that this movement represented a greater interiorization of religion and less reliance on external stimuli for pious engagement.[3] They point to the downturn in construction of new churches, the declining extravagance of public processions, a greater focus on contemplation rather than performative piety in devotional literature, a turn away from the miraculous in sermons, and mounting requests for simplicity in funerary rites as indicators of this profound transformation in religious culture. It is true that religion did change in the late colonial period. But a nuanced reading of last wills and testaments reveals that the impact of religious reform was more shallow and restricted than once thought and that religious change was far from straightforward.

Religious reform certainly affected pious practice. Testators in late colonial Mexico City increasingly preferred simplicity in funerary rites—a trend that must have stemmed in part from the religious reformers' project. In fact, Pamela Voekel in her study of cemetery reform argues that the significant spread of the simple funeral indicates that reformers largely succeeded in disseminating anti-baroque sensibilities among the Mexican elite by the end of the colonial period.[4] But evidence also reveals that the trend toward simplicity in funerals began long before reformers advocated religious change. Religious reformers undeniably intensified this trend in Mexico City, but they did not begin it. Rather, they fostered a pious current already in limited practice as early as the late seventeenth century. Furthermore, the request for a simple funeral did not have one set meaning. Some testators opted for funerary simplicity for other reasons than adherence to reformed Catholicism. In other words, a simple funeral is hardly an unambiguous indicator of a rejection of baroque Catholicism and acceptance of reformed piety.

Although religious culture underwent change in the late eighteenth century, baroque piety continued to guide religious practice for much of the faithful at least until the close of the colonial period. Evidence from the wills indicates that more testators maintained baroque practices than adopted the tenets of reformed Catholicism even in 1813. Although many testators were willing to forgo baroque extravagance in their own funerals, they were unwilling to practice a simplified piety in regard to the ornamentation of sacred space, the drama of the liturgy, the honor due to images and the eucharist, and the choreography of symbolic performances to forge unions between themselves and salvation history. In short, sacred immanence, liturgical gesture, and lavish staging of religious rites continued to dominate religious practice until at least the end of the colonial period.

The Persistence of Baroque Catholicism

The persistence of baroque sensibilities among the faithful of Mexico City is evident in Table 2. This table aggregates the prevalence of baroque pious directives in the wills written by the testator population of New Spain's capital in the seven sample years that span from the late seventeenth to the early nineteenth centuries. I have designated five types of pious directive as baroque in nature. The first gesture is gifts of wax, oil, precious objects, or money to honor images and the eucharist. The second is a request for burial in proximity to an image or an altar that housed an image. These directives indicate that the testator sought to make contact with the sacred through physical objects that manifested their immanence. The third type of pious directive I have coded as baroque is the arrangement of liturgical performances, the use of symbolic numbers, hours, days, or penitential actions, in requests for masses, the distribution of charity, and the arrangement of funerals. The use of liturgical gesture reveals how symbolic action performed by human beings could invoke the presence of the sacred by forging mimetic links with the life, passion, and death of Christ or the saints. The fourth type of directive is gifts of objects or money to churches, orders, or confraternities to ornament sacred space. This and the fifth type, the foundation of lavish feast-day celebrations or donations to enhance the drama of liturgical functions, testify to the notion that magnificence and dramatic display in sacred spaces or in liturgical or paraliturgical contexts properly honored God and the saints. They also reveal that splendor could stun the senses and induce a corporeal experience of the sacred among the faithful.

The table shows the percentage of testators in the seven sample years who issued baroque pious directives in their wills. The table also lists the average number of each type of baroque pious directive made by testators who included that type of directive in their wills (with the exception of requests for burial next to an image). For example, each testator who composed the 5.2 percent of testators who gave gifts to images or the eucharist in 1696 gave an average of 1.6 such gifts. Last, the table reveals the percentage of testators who included at least one baroque directive in their wills in each of the seven sample years. This global percentage is not a sum of the other five figures. An individual testator may have included anywhere from one to all five types of baroque directive in his or her will. Therefore, a single testator may be counted more than once in the table if he or she issued more than one type of baroque directive, but is counted only once, regardless of the number of baroque directives issued in his or her will, in the global percentage of testators who included at least one baroque directive in their wills.

Immediately apparent is the high percentage of testators who issued baroque directives. Between roughly one-quarter and one-third of testators, depending on the year, commissioned at least one of the five acts coded as

TABLE 2 Baroque Pious Directives

	1696	1717	1737
Testators who gave gifts to images or the eucharist	5.2% (n = 18)	11.1% (n = 19)	5.9% (n = 19)
Average number of such gifts	1.6	1.9	2.5
Testators who requested burial by an image, altar, or special site	8.1% (n = 28)	3.5% (n = 6)	4.0% (n = 13)
Testators who used numeric or temporal symbolism in pious directives	12.5% (n = 43)	20.5% (n = 35)	17.6% (n = 57)
Average number of such requests	2.4	3.3	2.3
Testators who gave gifts to religious institutions to ornament sacred space	6.7% (n = 23)	10.5% (n = 18)	9.9% (n = 32)
Average number of such gifts	1.9	2.7	1.7
Testators who founded feast-day liturgical celebrations	3.8% (n = 13)	6.4% (n = 11)	6.5% (n = 21)
Average number of such foundations	1.5	3.2	1.6
Testators who included at least one baroque directive in their wills	23.3% (n = 80)	32.2% (n = 55)	27.5% (n = 89)

baroque. In other words, baroque religious practice was highly diffuse among the testator population of Mexico City and, most likely, among the rest of the urban populace as well. This should not surprise us. The fact that the reforming prelates of Mexico vociferously and repeatedly denigrated symbolic practices and splendorous ceremonial in their pastoral letters and edicts suggests a widespread participation in the practices of baroque Catholicism on the part of their flocks.

Table 2 also demonstrates the limited success the reforming bishops had in their efforts to undermine baroque religious culture in Mexico. During the years of episcopal-led reform (1765–1800), the percentage of testators who issued at least one baroque pious directive remained high. In fact, 1779 and 1796 represented two of the three most intensely baroque years, with 30.6 percent and 31.2 percent of testators, respectively, issuing at least one baroque directive. In reality, however, these percentages do not differ much from those of the other three sample years within the eighteenth century.

1758	1779	1796	1813	Total
5.3% (n = 10)	11.7% (n = 26)	6.9% (n = 14)	5.2% (n = 14)	7.0% (n = 120)
1.6	1.2	1.7	2.1	1.8
1.6% (n = 3)	5.0% (n = 11)	9.4% (n = 19)	4.8% (n = 13)	5.4% (n = 93)
22.2% (n = 42)	17.1% (n = 38)	20.3% (n = 41)	13.0% (n = 35)	16.9% (n = 291)
2.0	2.5	1.7	2.6	2.4
9.5% (n = 18)	8.6% (n = 19)	9.9% (n = 20)	5.6% (n = 15)	8.4% (n = 145)
1.7	1.6	2.0	2.1	1.9
5.3% (n = 10)	7.7% (n = 17)	7.9% (n = 16)	4.4% (n = 12)	5.8% (n = 100)
1.5	1.9	1.1	2.0	1.8
29.6% (n = 56)	30.6% (n = 68)	31.2% (n = 63)	21.9% (n = 59)	27.3% (n = 470)

The two sample years with relatively low percentages of testators who issued at least one baroque pious directive bookend the period under study. The fact that only 23.3 percent of testators in 1696 issued baroque pious directives indicates that the eighteenth century proper is truly the age of the baroque in Mexico. In fact, the height of the baroque in Mexico lasted until the end of the eighteenth century, longer than historians have previously suggested. Certainly, varied and complex factors accounted for this sustained intensity of the baroque. The revitalization of silver mining and Atlantic trade during the eighteenth century increased profits for miners, merchants, and their dependents.[5] These groups may have bestowed more of their growing wealth on their favored churches and saints. Also, as the population of the colony doubled in the eighteenth century, subsistence crises multiplied and plagues became more numerous.[6] Testators may have spent much of their personal fortunes on pious causes in an attempt to accrue merit for their souls at a time when God's ire appeared to have been severely piqued. Of course, the increased devotions could simply reflect a greater sense of religious zeal at the time. Whatever its causes, the persistence of baroque directives in the wills of eighteenth-century Mexico City shows that baroque Catholicism remained prominent among the faithful despite the efforts of the reforming episcopate to instill a new religious sensibility.

The reforming bishops, however, enjoyed some success. Although their efforts bore little fruit among their contemporaries, the bishops certainly influenced the next generation of testators, the cohort that wrote their wills in 1813. By that time baroque Catholicism appears to have been in decline. In 1813 only 21.9 percent of testators issued at least one baroque directive in their wills, the lowest percentage of all seven sample years. But the bishops could not claim unmitigated success in the long run. The percentage of testators who issued at least one baroque directive in 1813 was not significantly lower than that of 1696. The project to reform religious culture reigned in baroque Catholicism from the heights it had reached during most of the eighteenth century, but had not substantially undermined it. Virtually the same percentage of testators openly practiced baroque pious activities in the early nineteenth century as in the late seventeenth century, a period when the church in Mexico strongly supported baroque Catholicism. Moreover, the decline in baroque directives in 1813 may not have been entirely due to religious reform. By that year, New Spain had experienced three years of bloody and costly insurgency as rebels fought for independence from Spain. The colony had also suffered years of economic hardship as the bankrupt Spanish crown imposed a series of new taxes and one-time financial extractions on its American territories. The Consolidation of Royal Bonds from 1804 to 1809 proved particularly onerous, draining much liquid capital from New Spain. It is likely that the political and economic instability of Mexico in the early nineteenth century in some part conditioned the decline in baroque pious directives in 1813. For, as testators faced mounting economic difficulties, they likely had less free capital to sink into pious endeavors.

Many reasons account for the at best moderate success of the reforming project. For one, reformers had to balance their promotion of new pious sensibilities and practices with faithful adherence to centuries of Catholic tradition and Catholic doctrines codified at the Council of Trent. As we saw in the previous chapter, the reforming bishops criticized many baroque practices and advocated new forms of piety, but they could not disregard or ban traditional religious activities. Archbishop Lorenzana defended anonymous relics in the cathedral and advocated processions of the image of St. Joseph to end earthquakes that rattled Mexico City. He also encouraged splendor in the display of the eucharist. Even Archbishop Núñez de Haro stated that veneration of the Virgin should include external practices to reflect an internal devotion. The reforming bishops, constrained by the orthodoxy of traditional practices, had to make fine distinctions that may have been lost on their flocks or simply confused them. In practice much of the faithful, already wedded to the practices of baroque Catholicism, could easily have conflated defense of particular relics with the defense of sacred immanence in general. They may have also understood the promotion of external rites as signs of an interior state of devotion simply as the promotion of external forms of piety. In this way, orthodox Catholic tradition impeded the progress of religious reform.

Mediators like priests and devotional literature likewise played a role in the fate of the reforming project. Mexico's reforming bishops possessed a number of means to influence their flocks. They visited and inspected parishes and other religious institutions, issued decrees, wrote pastoral letters, and delivered sermons. But the number of Catholics who directly encountered these means of persuasion, either by reading edicts or letters or by hearing or reading sermons authored by the reforming bishops, must have been small. Of course, much of the faithful would have been affected by episcopal decrees that regulated religious practice, but only if the decrees were enforced at the local level. Furthermore, even if enforced, those affected may well not have known the rationale for the decree's promulgation. Most of the faithful would have encountered the tenets of reformed Catholicism through the mediation of priests with whom they interacted and, if literate, the devotional tracts they read. These mediators, however, were far from perfect conduits for the dissemination of reformed Catholicism.

Catholics who read devotional literature published after the mideighteenth century could choose between works that adhered to a baroque conception of religious practice or those that promoted new pious sensibilities. It is true that much pious literature written in the late colonial period reflected shifts in religious discourse. Antonio Rubial García, in his study of the endeavors to convince the papacy to canonize Mexican holy figures as saints, writes that by the late eighteenth century hagiographies of these beatos focused less on their rigorous and flamboyant acts of penitence and the miracles they performed and more on their verifiable histories and Christian virtues.[7] Other devotional literature published in Mexico City at the end of the colonial period also reveals a new focus on the precepts of reformed Catholicism. Fernando Martagon, a Franciscan friar in New Spain, first published a book of devotional exercises devoted to Our Lady of Sorrows in 1802 that strongly emphasized many tenets of reformed piety. The exercises consisted of twenty days' meditation on the passion of Christ and the sorrows of the Virgin. But unlike earlier exercises, Martagon's work did not focus on numeric and temporal symbolism, performative piety, or repeated acts of self-flagellation. Martagon asked his readers to forge an emotional connection with the Virgin and to repent for their sins. The friar insisted that the faithful most offended the Virgin when they participated in religious rites without the proper solemnity and decorum and without the proper heartfelt engagement. Like Archbishop Núñez de Haro, he rejected the baroque justification for exuberant ornamentation of sacred space and criticized his readers for "entertaining yourselves with the adornment of the altars and recreating your material senses with the harmony of the music or with the variety of the objects" that proliferated in the baroque church interiors of Mexico and decried "purely exterior acts" of worship and veneration.[8] He scolded his readers for "adorning images and altars with much brilliance" when their hearts and minds were more concerned with earthly vanity than with praising God and the saints.[9] And like the reforming bishops, he viewed church buildings as sites mainly for individual Catholics to construct their personal relationships with God rather than as meeting places for the Christian community. Martagon emphasized that the faithful must attend fully to the performance of the mass while in church and avoid distractions. He even insisted that the faithful not bring small children to church, for they "distract priests at the time of the sacrifice [i.e., the canon of the mass] and preachers at that of the word of God [i.e., the sermon] with their impertinences and restlessness."[10] Although Martagon encouraged his readers to perform some acts of corporeal penitence and included some instructions for numerically symbolic prayer cycles, the emphasis of his work differs greatly from that of earlier pious exercises.[11]

Other devotional writers of the late colonial period wrote less explicitly about proper forms of worship and veneration, but the principles of reformed Catholicism guided their works. For instance, an anonymously authored novena to St. Anthony of Padua published in 1821 shows the influence of reformed piety. The author follows the standard pattern for novenas, asking readers to meditate on the life of St. Anthony over nine days. But this tract includes no instructions for fasting, self-mortification, or honoring of images of St. Anthony with gifts and performative devotions so common in earlier devotionals. Furthermore, the author, like the reforming bishops when they spoke of saints, focused on St. Anthony's human virtues rather than his status as miracle worker. Although he did devote one day's meditation to St. Anthony's miracles, the others centered on his prayerfulness, knowledge of sacred doctrine, sexual purity, and his pastoral activities among heretics.[12] This and other devotional tracts like it promoted the reformed conception of saints: sources of spiritual inspiration and models for Christian living rather than celestial powerbrokers to whom the faithful could turn for miracles.

Not all new devotional literature, however, advocated the practices of reformed Catholicism. In 1793 José Vicente de Ochoa Villaseñor, a parish priest in rural Mexico and an official of the Holy Office of the Inquisition, published a work that provided a spiritual meditation for each day of the week. Although Ochoa included little numeric or temporal symbolism in his work, he highlighted the importance of self-mortification for salvation. He instructed readers to fast, "to macerate the flesh with hair shirts and whips," and to deprive themselves regularly of even licit pleasures. He insisted that these forms of self-mortification imitated Christ, strongly indicating that he viewed them not only as means to discipline the flesh but also as efficacious forms of lay liturgical gesture. He summed up the need for intense mortification by commenting that the faithful could either "now suffer the sweet works and light pains of this briefest life, or burn in hell for all eternity."[13] This work was certainly no manifesto of reformed religiosity.

In addition to the publication of new devotional literature that promoted baroque practices, many older baroque devotional tracts were repeatedly reprinted despite the project of religious reform. Cayetano de Cabrara y Quintero's work in honor of the trinity, which we examined previously, remained remarkably popular in late colonial Mexico. Recall that this text advocated performative and penitential piety and the use of lay liturgical gesture. First published in 1734, it was reprinted in 1745, 1769, 1778, 1815, and 1818. Likewise, the baroque devotional treatise written by the Franciscan Juan de Abreu dedicated to Our Lady of Sorrows and means to atone for sins against her was reprinted eight times over the eighteenth century.[14] The sustained popularity of this devotional literature attests to the continuing appeal of baroque religious practices among the faithful of Mexico into the nineteenth century.

Apart from devotional literature, the faithful of Mexico City encountered the tenets of reformed Catholicism through their contacts with their parish and other local priests. In fact, given limited literacy rates (though the testator population was highly literate if judged by the ability to sign their names), local priests must have served as the primary mediators between most Mexican Catholics and the project of religious reform. These local priests celebrated the masses most of the faithful of Mexico City attended, preached the sermons they heard, listened to the confessions they made, and performed the other sacraments they received. Local priests consisted of both secular and regular clergy, for religious orders celebrated public masses and processions regularly and many members of the regular clergy aided diocesan priests as confessors and preachers.[15] By the late eighteenth century, these local priests, especially the diocesan clergy, were well trained to disseminate religious doctrine and regulate the religious practices of their flocks. William Taylor in his study of the rural parish clergy of New Spain in the eighteenth century notes the years of education and training priests had to undergo before ordination. Moreover, as their role as judges and authorities in civil matters declined under the Bourbon program to consolidate power in the royal bureaucracy at the expense of the church, teaching became priests' primary role. Although Taylor's study focuses on rural priests, these conclusions apply equally to the urban clergy. In fact, the urban parish clergy undertook more years of education than rural priests. Because wealthy urban parishes attracted great competition when vacancies occurred, bishops had the luxury of appointing highly educated and qualified priests to them.[16]

Although the history of the urban parish clergy in New Spain remains to be written, it is evident that many local urban priests proved ardent supporters of religious reform. Pamela Voekel states that in the city of Veracruz a mulatto parish priest, Laso de la Vega, served as the staunchest promoter of reformed Catholicism.[17] In Mexico City local priests similarly advocated reformed piety. José Ruíz de Conejares, a canon on the cathedral chapter of Mexico City, delivered a sermon on the merits of reformed Catholicism when he addressed the members of a blessed sacrament confraternity in the parish of San Sebastián in 1793. He focused his sermon on the proper method of adoring the eucharist. Like Archbishop Núñez de Haro, who presided as head of the Mexican church at that time, Conejares emphatically portrayed

God as spirit and stated that this spiritual deity required a spiritual worship. He warned his listeners that external actions like prostrating themselves in front of the eucharist or muttering prayers to it without engaging their under-standing and their hearts in adoration was merely "vain and sterile worship." He insisted that purely exterior piety failed to serve and honor God. In the end, he asked those gathered the following question: "And will a God, who is essentially spirit and truth, be content with an ostentatious apparatus of acts of thanks and praises that do not leave our mouths with more soul, with more spirit than the ringing of a bell [*que sale la voz de una campana*]?"[18] The faithful of Mexico City must have heard numerous sermons like this one that exhorted them to place less faith in the baroque externals of worship and veneration and instead focus on an internal and intellectual piety to honor God and the saints.

Although elements of the local clergy promoted reformed Catholicism, not all priests conformed to the new piety. In fact, many local priests con-tinued to promote traditional devotions in the face of the reforming pro-gram. William Taylor has studied the case of Francisco Antonio de la Rosa Figueroa, a Franciscan friar who acted as pastor to the parish of Nativitas Tepetlatcingo, just a few miles south of Mexico City. In the last years of his life in the 1770s, de la Rosa authored a devotional tract about the miracles performed by the Marian image of Our Lady of Intercession in the parish of Nativitas. The thirty-five miracles he included in his text included quite mundane acts, such as timely provision of building materials for a church and protection of workers from near accidents on the construction site. De la Rosa's account was never published, probably because his promotion of the image and his broad definition of the miraculous contradicted the reformed religiosity promoted by the hierarchy at the time. Nonetheless, his long-time advocacy for the image and his account reveal that "parish priests were not just disembodied voices of official doctrine, orthodoxy, and institutional order."[19] Priests, like all the other faithful of Mexico, had been shaped in a baroque religious culture, and many were reluctant, despite years of educa-tion and indoctrination, to abandon cherished traditions.

The case of Joaquín Ladrón de Guevara, a canon on the cathedral chap-ter of Mexico City, further illustrates clerical promotion of baroque practices despite episcopal attempts to transform religious culture. Sometime between 1801 and 1803, Ladrón de Guevara was commissioned to collect alms to pur-sue the canonization case in Rome of San Felipe de Jesús, a sixteenth-century

Mexican friar, missionary to Japan, and Christian martyr.[20] In 1804 Francisco
Sosa, who did not identify his social position, petitioned the king to have
Ladrón de Guevara removed from his post. Echoing the language of secular
Spanish thinkers on religion, Sosa complained that the canon's excessive zeal
in promoting the canonization caused economic hardship for the faithful
of Mexico City. Sosa related that Ladrón de Guevara obligated members of
artisan guilds to march in processions honoring San Felipe de Jesús and that
competition among guilds pressured members to spend funds on candles for
the processions—funds that could have been used to purchase bread for their
families. Sosa also complained that during processions, those who marched
acted indecorously, stopped the processions at taverns, and drank. He concluded that in these disorderly processions, the faithful wasted "time and
what many apprentices, journeymen, and master [oficiales] artisans could
earn in their workshops and shops." He also lamented that many monasteries,
convents, and churches encouraged the same behavior and "make a mockery
of their processions with similar extravagances foreign to the pure discipline
of the church and sacred rites." Sosa continued by excoriating Ladrón de
Guevara for encouraging the faithful to parade many images depicting the
various life stages of San Felipe in their processions rather than carrying
just a few of the most decorous ones. He feared that the proliferation of processional images would induce religious "errors in the ignorant or vulgar
people" who participated in and witnessed the processions. At the close of his
petition, Sosa asked the king to forbid the participation of confraternities and
guilds in the San Felipe processions in order to avoid "superfluous expenses"
and reiterated his request to remove Ladrón de Guevara from his position.[21]
Sosa's letter reveals that members of the clergy, even ecclesiastical dignitaries like Ladrón de Guevara, continued to promote baroque devotions despite
efforts at religious reform. It also testifies to the tension that could occur
between advocates of traditional and reformed Catholicism. Sosa supported
the new simple piety in large measure because he believed it promoted order
and prosperity. He clearly resented Ladrón de Guevara's encouragement of
boisterous baroque processions of the common people that easily mixed the
sacred and profane, and he was willing to call upon royal authority to support his position.[22]

Because priests promoted baroque religious practices despite episcopal injunctions to the contrary, it is not surprising that they often included
baroque directives in their wills. José Buenaventura Santa María y Liparza,

the cathedral chapter prebendary whose will opened this chapter, is only a dramatic case in point. Despite their years of formal religious education, clerics issued baroque directives in their wills as commonly as any other social group. Like other social groups, priests issued baroque directives in their wills in roughly the same proportion as their representation in the overall testator population. Priests accounted for 9.9 percent of all testators and for 10.4 percent of the subset of testators who issued at least one baroque pious directive in their wills. During the years of the reforming bishops' campaign, priests continued to issue baroque pious directives in proportion to their representation in the testator population. In fact, in 1779 and 1813, they were overrepresented in the cohort of testators who issued at least one baroque directive.[23] The frequent inclusion by priests of baroque directives in their wills strongly suggests that many members of the clergy, even if they did not reject the project outright, at best served as imperfect advocates for religious reform.

That priests were drawn to a baroque conception of the sacred stands to reason. They were the practitioners of liturgical gesture par excellence. During their frequent, if not daily, celebration of the eucharist, they represented Christ and reenacted his passion and self-sacrifice. Through these symbolic gestures, they performed the greatest mystery of the Catholic religion, the transubstantiation of the human offerings of bread and wine into the body and blood of Christ. With the intonation of the canon and the elevation of the host, they invoked God and located him in a wafer of bread and a cup of wine. No other social group possessed the authority to invoke Christ's physical presence in such an unequivocal manner. The priestly inclination toward baroque religious gestures may well have stemmed from their sacramental capacities and their intense lived experience of God's bodily presence in the eucharist.

In addition to the difficulty of advocating new pious sensibilities while remaining within established Catholic orthodoxy and the mixed messages on religious reform conveyed through devotional literature and by the local clergy, the reforming bishops faced resistance and inertia when attempting to transform religious culture in Mexico. Baroque Catholicism offered the laity easy and frequent access to the sacred through its many earthly manifestations. Catholic reformers in the eighteenth century, intensifying a campaign largely initiated by the Council of Trent, sought to limit the eruptions of the sacred within the world to the eucharist and venerable images and relics and to exert priestly control over them. As we saw in the previous chapter, they depicted saints as models for Christian virtue more than as miracle workers and they restricted exhibition of the eucharist, as they claimed, to preserve its magnificence. These actions, if fully implemented, would have resulted in the severe curtailment of the laity's access to the sacred. Not surprisingly, much of the laity resisted, deflected, or ignored the episcopate's campaign. Many considered regular contact with the sacred in its physical manifestations too important in the quest for salvation and for survival in everyday life to abide by their bishops' admonitions. No evidence exists that the laity organized formal resistance to the reforming project. But in their quotidian lives much of the Mexican faithful decided, even if not fully consciously, to ignore their bishops' decrees and implorations.

The Ambiguous Simple Funeral and the Spread of Religious Reform

The population of Mexico City, however, did not uniformly reject, ignore, or misunderstand the reformed religiosity espoused by their prelates. A growing number of testators over the eighteenth century wrote wills that reflected aspects of the new piety. Unlike the five pious gestures designated as indicators of baroque religious practice, there is no range of pious directives that unambiguously point to a reformed conception of the sacred. This is in large part due to the fact that the advocates of reformed piety discounted the religious efficacy of many external actions. The more outwardly subdued and cognitive thrust of reformed piety was not conducive to expression in a will, a document primarily employed to commission pious and secular acts. Fortunately, many who embraced the new piety left one clue about their religious preferences: the explicit request that their funerals be performed humbly with moderate, minimal, or no pomp. In a sense, this was an anti-gesture, a desire to refrain from customary funeral ceremony and display.

The trend toward moderation in funerals was hardly unique to New Spain; over the eighteenth century the faithful in Europe likewise demanded simplicity in their exequies. This current, however, occurred at different times and at different rates in different regions. The arguments postulated to explain this burgeoning tendency toward more circumspect funerals have varied from scholar to scholar. They have ranged from the de-Christianization of the faithful, to the de-socialization of funerary practice as a consequence of the strengthening bonds of affection between members of nuclear families, to the advent of a purer, less external form of Christianity, to an assault on fixed hierarchies as expressed in baroque funerary practices by middling social groups in an attempt to legitimize and further their new social ascendancy.[24]

Whatever the ultimate origins of the practice, scholars have argued that testators who demanded simple funerals more or less stripped of baroque funerary paraphernalia—catafalques; numerous candles, lamps, and torches; bell ringing; music; large corteges; and the printing of invitations to increase attendance—laid bare their repudiation of traditional religious practice. For these testators, funerary pomp held little if any religious value. Splendor did not honor God or produce an experience of his presence. The light of candles and torches did not symbolize and make present the light of glory around their corpses. In their view, these gestures were empty and dispensable ceremonials. They did not aid the soul in its progress through purgatory and seemed only to encode and perpetuate social distinctions in this world. To them, baroque splendor in terms of salvific efficacy had become irrelevant at best and counterproductive at worst.

Not all testators who requested moderate funerals and burials, however, rejected a baroque conception of the divine. Many testators chose a simple funeral out of economic necessity rather than pious conviction. Furthermore, even those testators who did not claim poverty as a justification for a simple funeral did not necessarily reject baroque Catholicism. In fact, more than half of such testators in all but the last sample year (1813) commissioned other baroque gestures in their wills. For these testators, the simple funeral was not necessarily a critique of the symbolic and splendorous devotions of the baroque, but rather a statement of personal humility or a desire to recreate liturgically Christ's humble death and burial. These testators practiced personal humility, but they continued to support splendor in public worship, to honor the eucharist and images with gifts, and to design liturgical gestures to forge unions with Christ and the saints. Or they may have freely practiced both baroque and reformed devotions without a sense of contradiction. In none of these cases did the faithful directly challenge the principles of baroque piety.

From the end of the seventeenth to the beginning of the nineteenth century, the percentage of testators in Mexico City who requested simple funerals increased dramatically (see Table 3). In 1696 a total of 14 percent of testators requested simple funerals, but 6.7 percent claimed poverty as their motivation. Over the eighteenth century, the percentage of testators who asked for simple funerals without reference to poverty increased as the percentage of those who protested poverty declined. In 1813, 27.4 percent of testators stipulated in their wills that they desired simplicity in their funerary rites with less that half a percent claiming penury as a justification.

What exactly constituted a moderate or simple funeral? The response to this question varied. The most common specific request for moderation was a reduced cortege, but the actual size of the accompaniment differed from testator to testator. Bárbara Rodríguez de Velasco Jiménez, the widow of a director of the royal tobacco monopoly, specified in 1813 that only four pallbearers without any other accompaniment carry her cadaver to her parish church, where priests were to celebrate her funeral with the church doors closed, apparently to prevent the faithful who wished to perform an act of mercy by praying for her soul's repose from entering the church during her exequies.[25] Ildefonso Antonio de Iniesta Vejarano, an architect and master planner for the project to drain the lakes surrounding Mexico City, believed that a simple funeral largely consisted of a reduced attendance of priests. He asked in his 1779 will that only eight clerics accompany his body and attend his funeral in the church of Santísima Trinidad.[26] In 1796 Antonia Tenorio de la Vanda y Victoria, a childless widow, likewise asked for a moderate funeral with an ecclesiastical attendance of only twelve priests.[27] On the other hand, some testators considered much larger corteges still to be moderate. Francisco Manuel Chirlin, a lawyer for the audiencia, requested in 1737 that the cortege for his humble funeral not exceed twenty participants,[28] whereas José de Noriega asked in 1796 that only fifty residents from the Hospicio de Pobres accompany his corpse.[29]

The absence of a catafalque or a reduced number of candles and lamps marked a simple funeral for others. Juan Francisco de Segura, a butcher,

TABLE 3 Percentage of Testators Who Requested a Simple Funeral

	1696	1717	1737
Testators who requested a simple funeral because of poverty	6.7% (n = 23)	1.2% (n = 2)	3.4% (n = 11)
Testators who requested a simple funeral without reference to poverty	7.3% (n = 25)	5.3% (n = 9)	9.9% (n = 32)

directed his executors in 1779 to conduct his funeral with the "utmost moderation" and not to spend money on "anything superfluous." He specifically instructed his executors not to "erect a catafalque for me, rather only a table with four lights."[30] José Estensoro de la Peña y Cortázar, a lieutenant in the militia, wanted his funeral to be even more humble. In his 1737 will, he ordered that his corpse both in his home and in the church be placed on a straw mat (*petate*) with four lights.[31] A moderate funeral, however, did not need to be so spare. Fernando Rodríguez de Araujo simply ordered in his 1758 will that his "moderate" funeral take place with "six candles [*ciriales*]."[32]

Other testators considered music and printed invitations signs of vanity and ordered their omission from their funerals. Pedro Guerrero, a hacienda owner, stipulated in 1813 that no musical instrument be used during his exequies because it was one of the "profanities that vanity has introduced" into religious practice.[33] Similarly, Antonia Gómez Rodríguez de Pedrozo, the Marquesa of Selvanevada, requested in 1796 that her executors omit from her funeral "all pomp and vanity inappropriate to that such serious act." She specifically stated that her funeral was to occur without music.[34] Bernardo de Palacio, an elderly bachelor, likewise rejected music when he asked his executors in his 1813 testament to conduct his funeral "with the greatest moderation." He also stipulated that they not print invitations to his funeral, apparently to reduce the number of people attending.[35] Pedro Andrade Moctezuma Mellado similarly requested in 1796 that his funeral take place with only seven or eight poor people from the Hospicio de Pobres and that his executors omit invitations.[36]

A small cortege, the use of a simple bier instead of a catafalque, a reduced number of candles and other lights surrounding the corpse, the absence of instrumental music, and the omission of invitations were the specific requests testators who desired humble funerals made. Most testators, however, did not

1758	1779	1796	1813
0%	3.6%	2.5%	0.4%
(n = 0)	(n = 8)	(n = 5)	(n = 1)
10.6%	14.4%	15.3%	27.0%
(n = 20)	(n = 32)	(n = 31)	(n = 73)

indicate exactly how they wanted the funeral rite simplified, only stating that they desired a "humble" funeral or one with "moderate pomp" or "without any pomp." Testators most likely used these phrases to indicate that they wanted one or more of the above features to be incorporated into their own final rites, but this ambiguous wording could obfuscate different conceptions of what constituted a humble or moderate funeral. For instance, in 1737 Pedro de la Canadilla ordered that his funeral be celebrated "with great humility and moderation, spending only the amount of one thousand pesos."[37] Over a half century later María Bárbara Jiménez similarly requested a funeral with "moderation of pomp," but nonetheless earmarked one thousand pesos for it.[38] Considering that most laborers in late eighteenth-century Mexico City could not earn a quarter of that amount with a year's work, it is difficult to classify a funeral of one thousand pesos as "moderate."[39] Moreover, many testators who did not request funerary simplicity dedicated less or equivalent sums for their funerals. For example, Antonio de Vivanco Gutiérrez, the Marques of Vivanco, set aside one thousand pesos in his 1796 will so that his funeral could be celebrated with the "decency" (read pomp) appropriate to his social status.[40] Obviously, the actual form and splendor of funeral ceremonies that lurked behind the words "humble" and "moderate" varied greatly, and the use of these phrases in wills in some cases constituted more of a nod to a rising fashion rather than a sincere commitment to funerary moderation.

Apart from the variations in pomp that simple funerals in reality entailed, the meanings that testators ascribed to moderate funerals differed significantly. For some, even those who did not protest poverty, the request for a simple funeral must have been a financial necessity. This was probably most true in 1813. It is surprising that less than one percent of testators claimed poverty as the reason for simple funerals in the sample year when Mexico City experienced the greatest economic hardships. This situation suggests that inclusion of wording in wills indicating a testator's inability to afford funerary rites fell out of use in testamentary practice by the late colonial period. It is unlikely that the wealth of the testator population rose in that period to such an extent that almost no testator had to claim poverty to moderate funeral ceremony. Nonetheless, financial necessity did not drive most testators to request a simple funeral; rather, they elected simplicity out of religious commitment. But even for these devout testators, the simple funeral had no single meaning.

For some, the request for a simple funeral was a direct challenge to the premise of baroque Catholicism that splendor and drama acted as devotional incentives for the faithful and possessed a sacred efficacy of their own. A few testators clearly stated their conviction that pomp held no value as a suffrage, either directly or indirectly. For example, in 1696 Juana Mejía Altamirano, the wife of a field marshal (*mariscal de campo*), begged her executors to "excuse useless [*inútiles*] pomp [from her funeral] and as much as you can convert it into suffrages that aid the satisfaction that I owe to God our Lord." It is not clear exactly what type of pomp she wanted her executors to omit from her funeral, but it probably was one of the typical concerns of testators who requested simple burials. Likewise, Juana did not state what type of pious activities she considered beneficial. But an examination of the pious directives she issued in her will gives a good idea of what she meant. Juana issued three pious directives. She ordered two thousand masses celebrated for her soul, the foundation of a chantry so that masses would be celebrated for her in perpetuity, and the establishment of an annual liturgical celebration in honor of the Mexican martyr, San Felipe de Jesús.[41] Above all else, masses were useful suffrages in Juana's mind. A century later Francisco Mejía, a hacienda owner from Toluca, asked his executors to exclude pomp that "does not serve as a suffrage for the soul and only is directed to vanity and ostentation" from his funeral.[42] Similarly, in 1813 Jacinto Francisco Tesorel y Paredes, a bakery owner who asked his executors not to print invitations to his funeral, equated pomp with "superfluities nonconducive to the benefit of my soul."[43] Unfortunately, neither Francisco nor Jacinto issued pious directives in their wills, so it is impossible to know what types of religious practices they considered spiritually beneficial.

Evident in all three of these wills is a marked distinction between pomp and suffrages. All asked that pomp be omitted from their funerals so that money traditionally spent on ceremonial exuberance could be channeled into other pious works. In other words, all three believed that funerary pomp did not aid the soul in its passage through purgatory and insisted that their financial resources be used for more fruitful pious activities. This desire for effective suffrages reveals a deeply religious motivation behind the request for simplicity. Although the three rejected pomp as a truly efficacious means to gain salvific grace, none reduced the scale of their funerals on account of a disenchantment with a Christian understanding of the ultimate goal of human existence. In these three and many other cases, the simple funeral stood as a critique of the splendor of baroque Catholicism, not of the Catholic economy of salvation in general.

The case of Juana Mejía Altamirano is significant for another reason. She rejected the efficacy of pomp as a suffrage in 1696, more than half a century before the reforming bishops sought to transform religious practice in Mexico. The shift in religious sensibilities among some sectors of the Mexican population did not occur because of encouragement from above. It was a process that some segments of the laity had begun on their own accord years before the reforming prelates initiated their project. The bishops certainly reinforced and spread this movement, but they did not start it.

Not every person who requested a simple burial, however, rejected the tenets of baroque Catholicism. Like any other symbol, the humble funeral was polyvalent, and some who desired simplicity in their final rites commissioned other pious acts in their wills that were unambiguously baroque in nature. It was not uncommon for people who requested humility in their funerals to ask to be interred in front of an image of a saint or a specific altar. In 1737, Catarina Páez de la Cadena requested:

> on account of the special affection and devotion that I have toward the images that will be mentioned, it is my will that [my body] be buried either in front of the altar of the Virgin Mary Our Lady of Sorrows or that of my father St. Francis de Paul who are venerated in the church of the . . . Hospital of Convalesencia alias Nuestra Señora de Belen . . . It is my will that [the funeral] is to be executed without any pomp or vanity, but rather with all possible moderation and humility.[44]

Despite her repudiation of extravagant display during her exequies, Catarina nonetheless sought to place her body in proximity to images that manifested the divine in the world to seek their aid in the otherworldly trials that awaited her. Like Catarina, other testators who desired simple funerals requested burials near images. In 1779 María Ana Josefa de Palacio, the wife of a sugar estate owner, asked to be buried "in the crypt on the epistle side" of the chapel of Our Lady of the Rosary in the monastery of Santo Domingo or, if that was not possible, "in front of the same altar." She also gave fifty pesos for candles and "ornamentation for the most sacred image" by which her cadaver was to rest. Despite the baroque overtones of these requests, she also beseeched her executors to celebrate her funeral "without pomp or vanity, but rather with great humility."[45]

Testators who requested humility in their funerals also commonly issued pious directives to adorn sacred space, embellish the liturgy, and craft liturgical gestures. Juan de Dios de Medina y Picaso, a notary for the audiencia, requested a moderate funeral with only four pallbearers, a simple bier with only four candles, and no invitations in his 1696 will. Nonetheless, he donated two hundred pesos to the Archconfraternity of Our Lady of the Rosary to purchase a rosary for its principle devotional image and later in his will gave a diamond ring to the same image of Our Lady. He similarly bequeathed one thousand pesos to the Carmelite nunnery of Santa Teresa la Antigua to serve as a capital fund to purchase oil to illuminate the miraculous image of Christ housed in the convent's church and bestowed five hundred pesos on the Franciscan monastery of Santiago Tlaltelolco to support the annual feast-day celebration of St. Anthony of Padua, a function Juan stipulated should occur "with all solemnity." Last, he used four thousand pesos to establish a chantry in the Colegio de San Pedro y San Pablo consisting of seven (a symbolically charged number) annual sung masses for his soul and those of his family.[46] It is impossible to know exactly how Juan reconciled his desire for a simple funeral and his penchant for baroque pious directives. Clearly, Juan's request for a simple funeral did not signify a rejection of the lavish and dramatic in religious practice in general, but only in the personalized ceremony of the funeral. For Juan and other testators like him who requested simple funerals but donated gifts for the enhancement of the liturgy or adornment of sacred space, the simple funeral likely served more as a statement of personal humility than a general challenge to the splendor of baroque worship.

The growing desire for personal humility in funerals at the end of the colonial period may also have been a creative appropriation of an episcopal discourse of humility. In place of baroque splendor, the reforming bishops stressed the concept of humility in statements concerning Christ's earthly ministry, his presence in the eucharist, the lives of the saints, and Christian worship. The testators who requested simple funerals and bequeathed baroque gifts during the age of reform may have selectively adopted some aspects of their bishops' campaign while ignoring others.

Related to its use as a sign of personal humility, the simple funeral could also serve as a flamboyant form of bodily penitence, much like public self-flagellation. A few testators, all of whom requested humble funerals, asked

that their corpses be interred in particularly ignominious locations where
they would be subject to humiliation. For instance, Bernardo Juan Arias, a
miner from Nueva Viscaya and a temporary resident in Mexico City in 1779,
asked that his funeral and burial take place:

> in the chapel or oratory of the holy school of Christ in the monas-
> tery of the royal and military order of Nuestra Señora de la Merced
> in which, although unworthy, I am a disciple. [The burial] is to be
> at the entrance of said chapel so that [my body] may be stepped on
> and trampled by the people who enter it.

Bernardo also asked that his corpse be dressed in the "oldest and most miserable [*despreciable*] habit of . . . St. Francis."[47] The penitential overtones of
Bernardo's burial request are overwhelming. He wanted to locate his corpse
at a particularly humble site and he chose the "most miserable" burial dress
for his cadaver so that the humiliation it endured redounded to the benefit
of his soul.

Bernardo was not the only testator to request such an ignominious burial.
Also in 1779, Domingo Antonio López, the General Administrator of Mail in
the colony, indicated that he wanted to be buried in the yet-to-be-built chapel of Our Lady of Covadonga in the monastery of Santo Domingo "next to
the entrance step to the door of the sacristy where all may trample and step
on me."[48] Forty years later, Ignacio Herrera y Estrada, the tithe collector for
the town of Chilapa, asked for a secret funeral with a modest cortege and to
be buried "at the door of the church where all may step on me."[49] Esteban
Díaz González did not specifically state that he chose his burial site so people
would trample his grave, but his wish to be interred "under the threshold of
the principal door of the parish in which death befalls me" certainly suggests
that he likewise wanted his corpse to be humiliated.[50]

The desire for humiliation of the corpse went beyond a simple sense of
personal humility. It was an extension of dramatic penitential piety, a form
of liturgical gesture that forged a union between the penitent's and Christ's
suffering bodies, into the realm of the dead. In effect, the simple funeral for
these testators was not a rejection of the baroque, but rather a celebration of
it. They appropriated a discourse of humility propounded by the reforming
bishops and creatively redeployed it in a manner consistent with the symbolic
nature of baroque Catholicism. They flamboyantly exaggerated humility and

simplicity in an attempt, like the penitentes who marched in processions scourging their flesh, to mimic the pains and ignominy of Christ's passion and death.

The simple funeral then had many meanings in eighteenth-century Mexico. For the economically strained, it was a necessity; on the other hand, for those who earmarked substantial resources to their funerals, the request for simplicity may have merely been a half-hearted acknowledgment of a burgeoning fashion. For others, the simple funeral represented an assault on baroque Catholicism and undeniably challenged the notion that elaborate funerals acted as suffrages for the soul. For yet still others, it was a statement about personal worth that did not undermine lavish and dramatic baroque practices. And last, for some, it was a way to engage personally in Christ's ignominious passion and death through liturgical gesture. Unfortunately, many testators who requested simple funerals left no clues to their under-standing of the gesture. They may in fact not have clearly delineated between its possible meanings or fully contemplated its personal significance.

Can we determine how a particular testator understood the simple funeral? Unfortunately, we will never know for certain how most testators understood the simple funerals they requested. We can, however, attempt to determine which testators may have employed the simple funeral as a critique of baroque Catholicism, on the one hand, and which ones probably saw it as a statement of personal humility or a penitential, liturgical act on the other by separating those testators who requested a simple funeral without commissioning other baroque gestures from those who did. This is admittedly a crude measure that cannot capture the nuances of meaning contained in the request for a simple funeral. It also likely overrepresents the number of testators who employed the simple funeral as a critique of baroque Catholicism. It does so because this method assumes that a lack a baroque pious directives in a will signifies a testator's rejection of them although other reasons, such as lack of funds or the growing trend toward extra-testamentary directives (see appendix), may account for this lacuna. Many testators who requested a simple funeral and did not commission a baroque pious act in their wills may well have practiced such gestures during their lives. Last and most important, this measure assumes that the faithful of Mexico City consciously thought of themselves as adherents of either baroque or reformed Catholicism and practiced their devotions accordingly. The majority, however, probably did not make such distinctions, and some

TABLE 4 Percentage of Testators with Simple Funerals with and without Baroque Directives

	1696	1717
Testators who requested a simple funeral without reference to poverty and who issued at least one baroque directive	4.4% (n = 15)	2.3% (n = 4)
Testators who requested a simple funeral without reference to poverty and who did not include a baroque directive	2.9% (n = 10)	2.9% (n = 5)

must have practiced aspects of both baroque and reformed piety without a sense of contradiction. With these caveats about these limitations in mind, we can proceed to differentiate those testators who used the simple funeral to critique baroque Catholicism from those who did not.

For most of the period under study, the simple funeral was not an unequivocal critique of baroque Catholicism. From 1696 to 1796 the percentage of testators who asked for simple funerals but who also issued at least one baroque directive in their wills is roughly equal to that of testators who requested moderate funerals without including a baroque act (see Table 4). Only in 1813 does the percentage of testators who requested a funeral without commissioning a baroque gesture (20.4 percent) significantly outstrip the percentage of those who requested a humble funeral and issued baroque directives (6.7 percent). By the close of the colonial period it appears that the simple funeral took on anti-baroque overtones, but it did not possess a clear resonance with reformed Catholicism before the beginning of the nineteenth century. This does not mean that the simple funeral did not aid in the development and dissemination of reformed Catholicism before 1800. The mere fact that the humble funeral critiqued the use of splendor in one aspect of worship opened other devotions to question. The simple funeral was a polyvalent and transitional pious gesture. For most of the eighteenth century, it stood between baroque and reformed Catholicism. But by the early nineteenth century, it seems to have taken on a more anti-baroque connotation.

Baroque and Reformed Testators

Baroque Catholicism remained the dominant religious practice in Mexico City throughout the eighteenth century. A comparison of the figures in

1737	1758	1779	1796	1813
4.9%	5.3%	7.7%	6.4%	6.7%
(n = 16)	(n = 10)	(n = 17)	(n = 13)	(n = 18)
4.9%	5.3%	6.8%	8.9%	20.4%
(n = 16)	(n = 10)	(n = 15)	(n = 18)	(n = 55)

Table 2 and Table 4 shows that the percentage of testators who commissioned at least one baroque pious directive in their wills dwarfs the percentage of those who requested an anti-baroque simple funeral (a request for a humble funeral in a will that did not contain a baroque directive) from 1696 to 1796. Only in 1813 did these percentages rival one another and, even in that year, the percentage of testators who issued a baroque directive edged out that of testators who chose an anti-baroque funeral. Of course the percentage of testators who requested anti-baroque simple funerals, as stated earlier, is likely inflated in all cases and particularly in 1813. So, even in the early nineteenth century, reformed Catholicism was not as diffuse among the testator population of Mexico City as baroque piety.

Although reformed Catholicism never displaced traditional practices in the colonial period, it did grow significantly over the Bourbon era. The percentage of testators who opted for an anti-baroque funeral rose almost seven fold, from roughly 3 percent of all testators in 1696 to about 20 percent in 1813. The percentage of testators who requested an anti-baroque funeral grew slowly over the period until it increased dramatically between 1796 and 1813. In the mid-eighteenth century (between 1737 and 1758) roughly 5 percent of testators used a humble funeral to critique baroque practices. This small group of testators represented the vanguard of reformed Catholicism, practicing aspects of a simple piety before the reforming bishops began their campaign to transform religious culture in Mexico. During the years of episcopal-led reform, the percentage of testators who requested a simple funeral grew slowly, from 5.3 percent in 1758 to 8.9 percent in 1796. This steady but unremarkable increase indicates that the reforming bishops exercised little influence over the religious sensibilities of testators. The most striking increase occurred between 1796 and 1813, a period in which the last reforming prelate, Archbishop Núñez de Haro, passed away.[51] It is difficult to untangle the reasons behind this sudden rise. Certainly, the reforming bishops' message must have influenced their younger contemporaries, those who wrote their wills around 1813. Of course, lay initiative must also have played a role in the spread of reformed Catholicism in the early nineteenth century. Last, however, we cannot discount the dampening impact of the economic decline, the crown-led assault on religious orders, and the political instability of early nineteenth-century New Spain on baroque religious practice. All of these factors must have conditioned the decline of baroque piety and the growth of reformed Catholicism in the final years of colonial rule.

Whatever the causes of the decline in baroque Catholicism and the rise of reformed religiosity, it is clear that no one pious sensibility dominated religious culture in the early nineteenth century. By 1813 testators were divided in their religious practices. But who were these testators? Who continued to practice baroque Catholicism, and who embraced the reformed piety? Did some social groups show greater affinity for one type of religious practice than another? Did these affinities change over time? And did baroque and reformed testators form self-conscious groups set apart from each other?

One advantage of using wills to study religious behavior is that testaments reveal much about the social position of the people who wrote them. Testators often listed their occupation or social status when they identified themselves in the preamble. Just under 60 percent of all testators either so identified themselves or left substantial clues in their pious and secular clauses as to their social or occupational status. Moreover, all testators were required by law to sign their wills. Those who could not, either because illness impeded them or because they did not know how to write, cases always distinguished by the notary, had witnesses sign in their stead. Though not a perfect measurement, the ability to sign one's name relates closely to literacy. Therefore, we can measure the impact the ability to read had on religious practice. Also, a testator's first name is an unequivocal indication of his or her sex. This allows us to examine how traditional and reformed religiosity fell out along gender lines. It is to these questions of how social group, literacy, and gender intersected with religious experience that we now turn.

Baroque religious practice was equally prominent among all social groups—artisans, bureaucrats, clergy, merchants, professionals, rural landowners, and soldiers—throughout the period under study. No group was significantly overrepresented or underrepresented among those testators who included baroque pious gestures in their wills. The general diffusion of baroque gestures among all social groups of Mexico City casts doubt on Archbishop Lorenzana's portrayal of at least one type of traditional religious practice, public self-flagellation, as the preserve of the casta and other marginal populations.[52] Though we may never know the social make-up of the penitentes who marched in holy week processions, we know that traditional religious practices consistent with self-flagellation were widely popular in Mexico City and not restricted to the marginalized. Therefore, it is likely that people from diverse social, ethnic, and economic backgrounds continued to discipline themselves publicly in ritual contexts in the late eighteenth century.

On the other hand, the inclination toward reformed religiosity among social groups shows a more complex pattern. We must be careful, however, when examining data on adherence to reformed religiosity, especially during the first two-thirds of the eighteenth century. Before 1779 only a small percentage of testators requested a simple funeral without reference to poverty and without commissioning a baroque directive in their wills.[53] This limited number of cases renders numeric analysis of the social composition of reformed Catholics somewhat unreliable. Nonetheless, some trends in the data are revealing.

Only two social groups, professionals—a composite group of administrators, lawyers, notaries, physicians, and professors—and bureaucrats, consistently demonstrated an affinity with the new piety. In 1696, professionals accounted for 10.8 percent of the total testator population, but 20 percent of those testators who requested simple funerals without commissioning other traditional pious gestures in their wills; in 1737, 9.3 percent of all testators and 18.8 percent of reformed testators; and in 1779, 7.7 percent and 13.3 percent. In the other four sample years, however, professionals were neither significantly underrepresented nor overrepresented among practitioners of reformed Catholicism. Bureaucrats exhibited the strongest affinity for reformed Catholicism. They were underrepresented among the ranks of reformed Catholics in only two sample years. They accounted for 6.4 percent of all testators in 1696 and 2.1 percent in 1758, but not a single bureaucrat commissioned an anti-baroque simple funeral in those years. In the other five sample years, they were consistently overrepresented: in 1717, they accounted for 6.4 percent of all testators and 20.0 percent of anti-baroque testators; in 1737, they were 4.9 percent of the total testator population but 12.5 percent of those with anti-baroque funerals; in 1779, 7.7 percent and

13.3 percent; in 1796, 4 percent and 11.1 percent; and in 1813, 5.6 percent and 10.9 percent. One other social group, merchants, demonstrated strong but ephemeral support for the new piety. Merchants had a complex relationship with the new piety. In 1696, they comprised 10.8 percent of all testators but 30 percent of all who requested anti-baroque simple burials. Likewise, in 1717 they accounted for 9.9 percent of all testators and 20 percent of anti-baroque ones. Last, in 1779, they were 18.5 percent of all testators but 40 percent of reformed testators. In contrast to this inclination toward the new piety in these three years, they were slightly underrepresented in 1737, 1758, and 1796, and showed no inclination in favor of or opposition to the new piety in 1813. In contrast to these groups, artisans and rural landowners demonstrated a relatively consistent lack of interest in reformed religiosity. But by 1813 the representation of all social groups in the ranks of the reformed generally ran parallel to their overall representation among all testators. Only bureaucrats were overrepresented in that year.

During the first five sample years, the period when reformed religiosity was practiced only by a vanguard, it appealed to a limited range of social groups, primarily professionals, bureaucrats, and merchants. These groups may have been attracted to reformed religiosity because, as Pamela Voekel has argued, it challenged the baroque apparatus of splendorous display in religious ritual, particularly funerary rites. Display not only served as a means to honor and encounter God through a felt experience of the divine, it also encoded social distinction and status. The degree of splendor deployed in funerary rites more or less corresponded with the social status of the deceased. The splendorous funeral honored God and the deceased at the same time. Middling groups adopted, practiced, and advocated the new piety in part because it furthered their own social interests by destabilizing rigid hierarchies that excluded them from prestigious positions. The simple funeral collapsed social distinctions and undermined baroque display as a vehicle to assert status. In essence, the new piety complemented the desires of the socially ambitious.[54] By 1813, however, the new piety had spread beyond the confines of these middling groups. By that time, it had developed its own momentum, and narrow sectional interests played a smaller part in its continuing diffusion among the population at large.

Reformed piety, however, was a distinctly minority religious practice until the early nineteenth century and few people, even among vanguard social groups, practiced it. Even though professionals, bureaucrats, and merchants showed disproportionate attachment to it, the vast majority of the members of each of these social groups either engaged in traditional religious practices or demonstrated no preference for either traditional or reformed piety. For example, in 1779, merchants accounted for 40 percent of all testators who requested simple burials without commissioning other traditional religious gestures. But out of forty-one merchants who wrote wills in that year, only six asked for such a burial. On the other hand, in that same year twelve merchants included at least one baroque gesture in their wills. Although merchants were overrepresented in the ranks of adherents of the new piety, more of them continued to practice traditional devotions than adopted new ones. In short, regardless of social group, reformed piety appealed to a smaller population than traditional religiosity. It is also evident that occupational status did not determine religious sensibilities. Although members of middling groups had social incentives to adopt the reformed piety, most continued to practice baroque Catholicism.

Unlike social group, literacy had little effect on a testator's affinity for one type of piety or another. Testators who favored traditional and reformed piety were both extensively literate, as was the testator population in general. Less than 20 percent of baroque and reformed testators failed to sign their wills because they did not know how to write. This percentage more or less aligns with that of the general testator population. Reformed testators, however, demonstrated greater literacy than baroque testators from 1758 to 1813. For example, in 1796 10.9 percent of all testators did not sign their wills because they did not know how to write. In that year 14.3 percent of baroque testators but only 5.6 percent of reformed testators failed to sign their testaments because of illiteracy. Perhaps the ability to read new devotional tracts that promoted reformed piety in part explains adherence to reformed Catholicism after 1758. This conclusion is suspect, however, because both baroque and reformed tracts circulated in New Spain. Furthermore, the vast majority of both baroque and reformed testators demonstrated literacy by signing their wills.[55] The ability or lack thereof to read devotional literature, then, only marginally influenced religious preference.

Gender, however, did influence religious experience, at least by the late eighteenth century. Before that time, men and women participated in baroque religiosity almost in the exact proportion to their will-writing activity. By 1779, however, a rift in religious preference opened between the sexes, with men beginning to shun baroque practices and women embracing them. In that year, men comprised 60.8 percent of the testator population, but accounted for only 51.5 percent of those who included traditional directives in their wills. On the other hand, women comprised 35.1 percent of all testators, but accounted for 44.1 percent of those who requested at least one of the five gestures coded as baroque. After 1779, the trend became more marked. By 1813, men represented 62.6 percent of testators, but only 47.5 percent of baroque testators. In contrast, women accounted for 36.7 percent of all testators but 52.5 percent of baroque ones.

Over the entire period, with the exception of 1737, reformed religiosity appealed more to men than to women. Although the vast majority of men who showed a religious preference included baroque gestures in their wills, men were more likely to adopt reformed religious practice than women. As early as 1696, men were highly overrepresented among reformed testators. In that year, men accounted for 61 percent of the entire testator population but 80 percent of the (admittedly small) group of reformed testators. Men's overrepresentation continued throughout the period: in 1813 they accounted for 62.6 percent of all testators but 78.2 percent of reformed ones.

The division in piety among men and women that occurred by the late eighteenth century mirrored gendered understandings of the sexes in colonial Mexico. Men were generally equated with the mind and rationality, the centerpieces of the highly cognitive reformed religiosity, whereas women were linked with the body and emotion, the focuses of traditional religious practice.[56] Men's turn away from baroque Catholicism, however, began only in 1779, during the period of episcopal-led reform and when reformed religiosity started to spread beyond the vanguard that practiced and promoted it during most of the eighteenth-century. This trend is not surprising. Religious reformers, as shown by Pamela Voekel, often criticized women's adherence to external religious practices and lamented their inability to practice the more sedate and intellectual piety they promoted.[57] Their deliberate denigration of baroque practices as feminine loosened men's ties to traditional religion, a situation reflected in the growing gender divide in pious sensibilities by the late eighteenth century.

Thus, to some extent social status and gender influenced religious sensibilities. What other factors did adherents of traditional religiosity on the one hand and followers of reformed piety on the other have in common? It would seem reasonable that practitioners of both types of piety would demonstrate particular affinities for certain religious institutions. For instance, adherents of traditional piety might be expected especially to favor the Jesuits, an order intimately connected with splendorous ornamentation of sacred space, or the Capuchins, an order known for missionizing against reformed religiosity in Spain, in their pious bequests.[58] On the other hand, it would seem likely that those who practiced reformed religiosity would especially favor the capital's parishes as opposed to its monasteries in their bequests. Although reformed testators were more likely to request burial in their parish churches or in cemeteries (as opposed to church buildings), no other pattern in pious directives for either baroque or reformed testators emerges from the wills. In fact, both sets of testators dispersed gifts among a wide range of religious and charitable institutions with no particular emphasis on certain churches, orders, or hospitals.

Although testators who demonstrated an inclination to one form of piety or another did not form bonds of association around particular religious institutions, they nonetheless seem to have participated in microcommunities within Mexico City. The wills of both groups show a slight tendency to cluster in the protocols of a few notaries for each camp. For instance, testators who demonstrated strong signs of baroque piety tended to cluster in a few notaries from 1696 to 1737 and in 1813, but much less so in other years. For example, in 1737 baroque testators gave their wills in front of thirty-six notaries, but 57.3 percent of these testators wrote their wills before nine notaries whose complete count of wills accounted for only 39.3 percent of all wills written in that year.[59] But clustering is much less evident among baroque testators from 1758 to 1796. For instance, in 1779 such testators wrote their wills before twenty-nine notaries. Although seven notaries notarized 48.7 percent of all baroque wills that year (which might be considered a sign of clustering), these same seven notaries proved 43 percent of all wills written in 1779. In other words, these seven notaries simply notarized baroque wills in roughly the same proportion as they proved wills in general.[60] But even in these years in which baroque testators did not cluster, a few individual notaries exhibited marked tendencies toward baroque wills. For example, in 1796 Juan José Ramírez de Arellano notarized only five wills, but all of them contained a baroque directive. Moreover, he accounted for 7.9 percent of baroque wills in that year, but only 2.5 percent of all wills.[61] Frequent recourse to a small group of notaries suggests that testators consciously chose them to redact their wills. Unfortunately, almost nothing is known about notarial practice in colonial Mexico City: where notaries lived and worked and how they interacted with their clientele. Therefore, it is impossible to reconstruct the sociocultural milieus in which they operated. Nonetheless, it appears that piety in some way shaped their work patterns.

The notarial affiliations of adherents of reformed piety were more complex. No clustering occurred in 1696, 1717, and 1758. In those three years the twenty-five testators who requested a simple funeral without including a baroque pious directive wrote their wills before twenty-three notaries. In the other four years, some clustering occurred. For example, in 1737 sixteen testators wrote reformed wills before twelve notaries. Five of them, however, gave their wills before Juan Romo de Vera. This notary, who notarized eighteen wills in 1737, accounted for 31.3 percent of reformed wills, but only 5.6 percent of all wills in that year. Reformed testators tended to cluster around ten notaries over the entire period under study.[62] But most of these notaries also proved baroque testaments. For instance, Juan Romo de Vera notarized six wills for clients who requested baroque religious practices in 1737. In fact, nine of these ten notaries also proved baroque wills, and three of them notarized just as many or more baroque-oriented than reform-oriented wills. Only three notaries, Antonio de Casas y Orellana, who practiced in 1796, and Joaquín de Barrientos and Antonio de Vera, both of whom practiced in 1813, demonstrated an unequivocal tendency toward reformed religiosity. Casas y Orellana notarized only three wills in 1796 and all were for clients who requested a simple funeral without issuing a baroque directive. Barrientos attested seven wills in 1813. Four testators requested a simple burial without other baroque acts, and only one of his other three testators commissioned a baroque gesture. Vera notarized seven wills also. Only two requested simple burials, but no testator asked for traditional pious acts. This pattern of will writing among those testators who practiced reformed piety suggests that, although they formed conscious communities by the late eighteenth century, they did not separate themselves from the rest of the faithful as an insular faction. Rather, they interacted with Catholics who maintained a more traditional conception of the sacred. One wonders if they conceived of themselves as a community apart. Surely, many of those who practiced reformed religiosity, like the bishops who promoted it, must have scoffed at the "naive" pious gestures performed by those who retained baroque sensibilities. But they nonetheless must have considered themselves part of one Catholic community. Despite the growing divergence in religious practices in the second half of the eighteenth century, both traditional and reform-minded Catholics participated in the same sacraments of the church—sacraments that continued, but perhaps to a lesser extent, to reconcile difference and structure community.

Conclusion

The practices of baroque Catholicism, despite attempts to curb them by religious reformers, remained popular in Mexico City throughout the Bourbon period. The percentage of testators who included baroque gestures in their wills exceeded that of those who requested anti-baroque simple funerals for the entire period under study. The former disproportionately outnumbered the latter during the eighteenth century, but in the early nineteenth century reformed testators almost equaled baroque testators in number. This pattern indicates that the practices of baroque Catholicism retained popular appeal into the nineteenth century, but that reformed Catholicism, insignificant for most of the eighteenth century, began to flourish by the nineteenth. Men and women of all social ranks participated in baroque practices, but by the late eighteenth century men began to shun baroque gestures and women started to practice them more frequently. On the other hand, the practitioners of reformed Catholicism were mostly professionals, bureaucrats, and merchants until the nineteenth century, when members of all social groups began to practice the new piety. Despite their different conceptions of the divine and religious practice, baroque and reformed Catholics did not constitute separate camps in Mexico City. Apparently, collective participation in the same sacraments and membership in the same parishes vitiated divisions between them and constructed a common, if less cohesive, Catholic community.

CHAPTER 9

Charity and Confraternities
in the Age of Reform

✝ IN DECEMBER 1779 JUAN DE SIERRA URUÑUELA, A WEALTHY MERCHANT
and a *familiar*, or voluntary agent, of the Holy Office of the Inquisition, wrote
his will before the notary Diego Jacinto de Leon. Juan was in good health,
unaffected by the smallpox epidemic that swept Mexico City that year.
Perhaps inspired by the toll the plague had exacted on the urban populace,
he bequeathed much of his estate to charitable causes. He donated between
five hundred and one thousand pesos each to nine hospitals in Mexico City,
including the general hospital of San Juan de Dios and the lepers' hospital
of San Lázaro, both of which were administered by the hospital order of San
Juan de Dios; the hospital of Convalecencia run by the Bethlehemite order;
the hospitals of San Hipólito and Espíritu Santo, both of which belonged to
the order of San Hipólito; the hospital of Salvador del Mundo, which was
dedicated to the care of women with mental illness and administered by the
congregation of the same name; the hospital of San Antonio Abad run by
the eponymous hospital order; and the hospital of San Pedro dedicated to the
care of elderly and ill priests of the archdiocese. Juan also donated considerable amounts to the poor. He gave one thousand pesos to the pastor of the
parish in the mining town of Taxco in southwestern New Spain to distribute
among the "shamefaced poor" of his flock and set aside an additional two
thousand pesos to be given to the "shamefaced poor" of Mexico City. Juan
included one other charitable gift in his will. Certainly influenced by the

recent foundation of the Hospicio de Pobres in Mexico City, he bestowed an enormous sum upon the new institution to provide the poorhouse's inmates with food, clothes, and whatever else they might need. Juan considered this his most important charitable donation, for his gift aided the institution that sought to "to gather [*reclutar*] the mendicant and destitute poor." He believed that the poorhouse's mission was "such a common good and so pleasing to God [*un beneficio tan comun y tan del agrado de Dios*]" that he was willing to donate twenty thousand pesos to it, or more than double the total amount he bequeathed to nine other charitable institutions in Mexico City.[1] Clearly, he valued the institution Archbishop Lorenzana, the ardent critic of the poor, had helped to found to contain and train beggars. Juan probably shared the archbishop's distaste for the poor, for he dedicated most of his charitable giving to institutions rather than directing his executors themselves to distribute alms among the poor. Even his two noninstitutional gifts to the poor were targeted specifically at the shamefaced poor, or those who refused to beg publicly despite their economic difficulties.

As important as the charitable gifts Juan bequeathed are the silences in his will. Juan donated over thirty thousand pesos in total to charitable causes, but did not bequeath a single gift to an orphan or even mention an orphan in his will. Furthermore, although he stated that he belonged to the third order of St. Francis, he did so in an off-hand manner in his funeral clause when he asked for burial in the third order's chapel in the monastery of San Francisco. He did not mention membership in another confraternity and did not lay claim to any other spiritual benefit—masses, attendance at his funeral, or other suffrages—offered by the third order of St. Francis. In short, Juan greatly esteemed charity as a pious practice, but he did not highly value the personalized encounters fostered by face-to-face acts of charity and confraternal participation that horizontally structured community in baroque Catholicism. Rather, he was content to allow institutions to channel his remarkable generosity.

Juan's will illustrates the changing nature of charity and community in late Bourbon Mexico. Although charity remained centrally important within the economy of grace, it underwent profound changes. Charity became more exclusively defined as an act of beneficence and less commonly associated with a state of peace and unity among the faithful as the eighteenth century unfolded. The decline of confraternal membership and changing understandings of the confraternity's role in the rites of death attest to the emergence of this more restricted conception of charity. Furthermore, charity as an act of beneficence changed as well. Testators in the late eighteenth and early nineteenth centuries eschewed the most intimate act of charity, the rearing of orphans and the bequest of gifts to them, and instead favored more anonymous, institutionalized giving. Although the testators of Mexico City continued to bequeath numerous gifts to the poor, the character of these charitable donations shifted.

This shift in charity—in both senses of the word—signaled a change in subjectivity that underlay religious practice. By the end of the eighteenth century, the communal subjectivity that previously supported horizontal community formation and the collective enterprise of salvation had largely given way to a more individually oriented sense of personhood. The reforming bishops of the second half of the eighteenth century subtly fostered this transformation when they sought to desacralize the act of almsgiving—a process that had begun in the sixteenth century. They attempted to render the distribution of alms an efficient process that reformed the poor rather than a liturgical gesture that recalled Christ. Thus, they undermined the horizontal bonds that united rich and poor in the mystical body of Christ. Also, though not a process explicitly promoted by the bishops, the confraternity, the highest expression of Christian community, declined drastically in importance over the eighteenth century. By the end of the century, the organization that had once supported the collective enterprise of salvation became a proto-life-insurance policy. Although the sacraments still possessed the power to structure Catholic community and aid the soul, salvation become a more solitary process as an individual sense of selfhood emerged over the eighteenth century.

Caring for the Poor

Table 5 presents a numerical breakdown of charitable giving by the testators of Mexico City over the Bourbon period. It includes five categories of charity and shows the percentage of testators in each sample year that gave such gifts. Moreover, in the last row it shows the percentage of testators that included at least one charitable directive in their wills. This figure, however, is not a total of the previous five categories because it counts only once testators who granted more than one charitable gift in their wills. The table also presents the average number of charitable directives issued by those testators who included that type of directive in their wills. For instance, the 11.9 percent of testators who gave gifts to orphans in 1696 gave an average of 1.8 such gifts.

Immediately apparent from the table is the continuing importance of charity as a pious act in eighteenth-century Mexico. In 1696 17.2 percent of testators included at least one charitable act in their wills, and over a century later in 1813 18.5 percent did so. Charitable activity peaked from 1717 to 1758, but only modestly. Apart from this slight rise in the first half of the eighteenth, charitable activity in general remained relatively stable over the Bourbon period.

Although charitable giving in the aggregate remained steady, particular forms of charity changed substantially. The personal tending of orphans, the vast majority of whom were foundlings, declined dramatically over the eighteenth century. Care for orphans reached its height in 1717, when 17.5 percent of the testator population claimed to have reared parentless children. Furthermore, each of these testators claimed to have cared for an average of 1.6 orphans. Clearly, many testators in the first half of the eighteenth century opened their homes to foundlings and other orphans, often incorporating these children into family structures and treating them equitably with their own offspring. This openness to incorporating strangers into the household declined dramatically as the eighteenth century progressed. A slight decline occurred as early as 1758, but a precipitous drop happened between 1758 and 1779. This downward trend continued into the nineteenth century. By 1813 testators were half as likely as their counterparts from 1696 to 1737 to claim to have raised an orphan. Furthermore, the average number of orphans raised by testators declined sharply over the period under study from a high of 1.8 in 1696 and 1737 to a low of 1.3 in 1813.

Gifts to orphans naturally followed the same downward trend. In fact, the two categories—testators who reared orphans and testators who bestowed gifts upon them—largely overlap because all testators who gave gifts to orphans also claimed to have raised them and because the vast majority of testators who claimed to have reared orphans also bestowed gifts upon them.[2] In fact, in 1779 and 1796, the percentages of testators in both categories were the same. Not surprisingly then, as testators turned away from the rearing of orphans in the second half of the eighteenth century, they likewise granted fewer gifts to them. By the early nineteenth century testators were half as likely to bestow gifts upon orphans as their predecessors in the first

TABLE 5 Charitable Gifts

	1696	1717	1737
Testators who gave gifts to orphans	11.9% (n = 41)	14.6% (n = 25)	12.0% (n = 39)
Average number of such gifts	1.8	1.6	1.8
Testators who claimed an orphan (includes testators who gave gifts to orphans)	13.7% (n = 47)	17.5% (n = 30)	13.3% (n = 43)
Average number of such claims	1.8	1.6	1.8
Testators who gave gifts to hospitals	2.9% (n = 10)	7.0% (n = 12)	4.9% (n = 16)
Average number of such gifts	2.0	1.8	1.6
Testators who founded or gave gifts to schools	0% (n = 0)	1.8% (n = 3)	0.9% (n = 3)
Average number of such gifts	0.0	1.0	1.0
Testators who gave gifts to the poor	3.8% (n = 13)	4.7% (n = 8)	6.5% (n = 21)
Average number of such gifts	2.0	1.8	1.6
Testators who included at least one charitable directive in their wills	17.2% (n = 59)	23.4% (n = 40)	20.4% (n = 66)

half of the eighteenth century, and the average number of gifts they gave also dropped significantly.

What accounts for this sharp decline in care for orphans and gifts to them in the late eighteenth century? At the beginning of the period of decline, Archbishop Lorenzana justified the establishment of the Cuna de Huérfanos by arguing that Catholics no longer took orphans into their homes and that, for this reason, necessity drove the establishment of an orphanage in Mexico City. Was it true that the populace of Mexico City had begun to shun orphans by midcentury? The data from wills indicates that the testator population began to withdraw from the care of orphans by 1758, when the percentage of testators who reared orphans declined slightly from the heights of the first three sample years and the average number of orphans per testator (of those who claimed orphans) fell to 1.5. But the precipitous downturn in care for orphans did not occur until after the archbishop had established the Cuna de Huérfanos in 1766. Twelve years after its foundation, the percentage of

1758	1779	1796	1813	Total
10.6% (n = 20)	6.8% (n = 15)	8.4% (n = 17)	5.9% (n = 16)	10.0% (n = 173)
1.6	1.4	1.6	1.2	1.6
12.7% (n = 24)	6.8% (n = 15)	8.4% (n = 17)	6.7% (n = 18)	11.3% (n = 194)
1.5	1.4	1.6	1.3	1.7
4.2% (n = 8)	8.1% (n = 18)	3.5% (n = 7)	5.5% (n = 15)	5.0% (n = 86)
2.0	2.8	3.6	1.3	2.1
0.5% (n = 1)	2.3% (n = 5)	3.0% (n = 6)	1.9% (n = 5)	1.3% (n = 23)
1.0	1.0	2.0	1.4	1.3
10.1% (n = 19)	7.2% (n = 16)	9.4% (n = 19)	10.7% (n = 29)	7.3% (n = 125)
2.1	1.3	1.7	1.4	1.7
23.3% (n = 44)	18.5% (n = 41)	19.8% (n = 40)	18.5% (n = 50)	20.0% (n = 345)

testators who claimed to have raised orphans dropped almost in half from 12.7 percent in 1758 to 6.8 percent in 1779. The faithful of Mexico City continued to take orphans into their homes—albeit on a slightly diminished scale—until Archbishop Lorenzana founded the Cuna. Only after the foundation of the orphanage, did they begin to turn their backs on orphans. It appears then that the foundation of the Cuna de Huérfanos encouraged the further abandonment of foundlings.[3] Whatever the catalyst for this trend, the faithful of Mexico City began to shun charity to orphans by 1779, a pattern that persisted into the following generation. Personal care for orphans no longer figured prominently in the charitable activities of testators by the end of the eighteenth century.

While testators abandoned personal care for orphans, they began to favor charitable institutions, hospitals, and schools in their bequests. Gifts to hospitals were relatively common throughout the eighteenth century, but gifts to schools, which we did not previously examine, were largely confined to the end of the Bourbon period. An examination of the percentage of testators who bestowed gifts upon hospitals and schools reveals that giving to charitable institutions generally increased in the last forty years of the colonial period. As the most intimate form of charity diminished, nonpersonalized charity rose.

Gifts to hospitals constituted the most popular form of institutional charity throughout the eighteenth century. Only a subtle pattern of increase is evident in bequests to hospitals in the last half-century of the colonial period. Gifts to hospitals reached their height in 1779, when 8.1 percent of testators included such a gift in their wills. This percentage dropped, however, in the next two sample years. Nonetheless, in 1813 5.5 percent of testators, the third highest total, granted gifts to hospitals. The 3.5 percent of testators who bequeathed gifts to hospitals in 1796 is the second lowest percentage of all seven sample years. But in that year, the small group of testators who granted gifts to hospitals averaged 3.6 gifts a piece, by far the highest average number of gifts to hospitals in all sample years. Thus, the intensity of giving to hospitals, although not unambiguously, increased in the late colonial period.

The distribution of gifts among the hospitals of Mexico City shows a marked preference for a small number of them. Table 6 lists the number of gifts received by each hospital and, when appropriate, the religious order that administered it. Immediately apparent is the great popularity of the two hospitals administered by the order of San Juan de Dios, or Juaninos as they were called for short. Combined, they accounted for just over 40 percent of all gifts bequeathed to hospitals. The main hospital of the order, San Juan de Dios, was by far the single most popular institution throughout the century, itself accounting for almost one-third of all gifts to hospitals. Testators probably favored this hospital because it was one of only two general hospitals in Mexico City that functioned throughout the eighteenth century. It was also the largest of the general hospitals. The other general hospital, Jesús Nazareno, founded under the name of Nuestra Señora de la Concepción by Hernán Cortés in the first years after the military conquest of the Mexica, suffered a period of crisis in the 1770s and scaled back its operations by half.[4] Moreover, fire destroyed much of the hospital of San Juan de Dios in 1776, but the Juaninos soon rebuilt it.[5] The recent fire and reconstruction project must account in part for the surge of gifts bestowed upon the hospital of San Juan de Dios in 1779, when the hospital received twelve donations, the highest number granted to any hospital in a single year. But the order of San Juan de Dios and its hospitals were remarkably popular with testators throughout the period under study. This general preference for the order most likely stemmed from the fact that it was the largest hospital order in Mexico City and the fact that the other three orders, the Brothers of Charity (Hermanos de Caridad), also known as the order of San Hipólito, the Bethlehemites, and the order of San Antonio Abad all suffered serious internal crises during the eighteenth century.[6] Such troubles must have dissuaded testators from granting alms to their hospitals.

Also conspicuous in the distribution of bequests to hospitals is the surge that occurred in 1779. This remarkable increase in acts of charity toward hospitals resulted from a variety of factors. First was the relatively recent foundation of both the Hospicio de Pobres and the Cuna de Huérfanos. Archbishop Lorenzana (and other clerics and prominent members of the laity) vigorously promoted these institutions. His efforts succeeded in the short run. The Hospicio garnered six bequests and the Cuna two in 1779. Second was a short-lived reform of the Hipólitos in the 1770s. It brought an immediate increase in the number of gifts bequeathed to the hospital of San Hipólito. Third, the reconstruction of the Hospital of San Juan de Dios after fire destroyed it in 1776 prompted testators to bestow gifts upon it. The gifts granted to these four institutions, however, only accounted for a part of the increase in charity to hospitals in 1779. Nonetheless, the recent establishment of the Hospicio and Cuna, the reform of the Brothers of Charity, and the rebuilding of the hospital of San Juan de Dios created a climate that encouraged testators to give to other hospitals in Mexico City. In fact, some testators linked these hospitals with others in their wills. José Agustín de Lecumberri, a silk merchant, is a case in point. In 1779, he left two hundred pesos to each of seven hospitals: the Hospicio de Pobres, the Cuna de Huérfanos, San Hipólito, San Juan de Dios, San Lázaro, San Antonio Abad, and the Hospital Real de los Naturales.[7] In the same year, Andrés Martínez Campillo, a prebendary on the cathedral chapter, left four gifts to hospitals, one each to the Hospicio, the Cuna, San Hipólito, and Santísima Trinidad.[8] Moreover, the average number of gifts to hospitals per testator who gave to hospitals was 2.8 in 1779. In other words, charity to hospitals in 1779 was a self-promoting phenomenon; a gift to one hospital encouraged another.

Although the foundation of the Hospicio de Pobres and Cuna de Huérfanos helped spur pious giving to hospitals in 1779, testators were never

TABLE 6 Gifts to Hospitals

Hospital (Religious Order)	1696	1717	1737
Convalecencia (Betlemita)	4	2	4
Cuna de Huerfanos	0	0	0
Espíritu Santo (Hipólito)	1	2	1
Hospicio de Pobres	0	0	0
Hospital Real de los Naturales	0	0	0
Concepción/Jesús Nazareno	2	0	0
Salvador Mundi	0	1	0
San Andrés	0	0	0
San Antonio Abad (Antonio)	0	0	0
San Hipólito (Hipólito)	0	2	1
San Juan de Dios (Juanino)	6	6	9
San Lázaro (Juanino)	0	0	3
Santisima Trinidad	5	3	2
Outside Mexico City	1	2	3
Others [Not Specified]	1	4	3
Total	20	22	26

highly enthusiastic about either institution. Even in 1779, the two hospitals administered by the order of San Juan de Dios each received more bequests than the poorhouse and orphanage. Moreover, by 1796 testator enthusiasm for both institutions had cooled, and by 1813 testators almost entirely ignored them. This pattern of charitable giving indicates that, after an initial, short-lived period of support for these new institutions, the faithful of Mexico City returned to a more traditional pattern of bequeathing donations to hospitals that cared for the ill, elderly, and poor.

Although short-lived, the Hospicio de Pobres received significant support from the testators of Mexico City in the first decades after its foundation. In 1779 and 1796, testators bestowed eights gifts upon it, and about half of them were quite large. For instance, Juan de Sierra Uruñuela, the testator whose will began this chapter, gave twenty thousand pesos to the Mexico City poorhouse in 1779. In the same year, Andrés Ambrosio de Llanos, a priest, lawyer, professor of law at the Royal and Pontifical University, Rector

1758	1779	1796	1813	Total
1	3	0	0	14
0	2	1	0	3
0	1	4	0	9
0	6	2	1	9
0	0	0	1	1
0	2	1	0	5
2	1	2	0	6
0	0	1	0	1
0	4	1	0	5
4	5	2	2	16
3	12	7	11	54
2	7	4	3	19
1	4	0	0	15
3	3	0	1	13
0	0	0	1	9
16	50	25	20	179

of the college of San Juan de Letrán, and administrator of the Hospicio, bequeathed his entire fortune to it.[9] And in 1813, Policarpo Cristomo Dávila, a glass retailer, donated six thousand pesos to it.[10] Furthermore, the Hospicio received funds from the royal lottery and grants from the merchant guild (*consulado*).[11] Support for the Hospicio may have been limited, but it supplied the poorhouse adequately during its early years. The period of financial solvency for the Hospicio proved evanescent, though, as the testators of Mexico City withheld donations to it by the early nineteenth century.

The testator population's ephemeral support for the Hospicio de Pobre's mission of confining and disciplining paupers corroborates Silva Arrom's argument that the inhabitants of Mexico City undermined the stated purpose of the poorhouse. The poor themselves sought to transform the Hospicio from an institution created to contain the poor, instill discipline within them, and teach them trades in an effort to reduce begging to a charitable center that sheltered the elderly, infirm, widows, and children. Moreover, the wealthy, despite the establishment of the poorhouse and the concomitant ban on mendicancy, continued to distribute alms directly to paupers in face-to-face encounters. By its third decade of existence, the Hospicio de Pobres in Mexico City faced financial difficulties and retrenchment in its mission because the populace of Mexico City refused to support it.[12]

Perhaps equally important as the faithful's continuing resort to traditional forms of almsgiving for explaining the restricted appeal of the Hospicio was the institution's inability to fulfill its mission. The Hospicio's modest scale was woefully inadequate to confine the multitude of poor who lived and begged in the streets and plazas of New Spain's capital. Estimates suggest that one-third of Mexico City's population of over 100,000 in 1790 was unemployed or underemployed. Many of these unfortunate souls resorted to begging and the beneficence of the capital's monasteries, convents, and parishes for survival.[13] In that same year Viceroy Revillagigedo ordered a census of Mexico City; the count revealed that the Hospicio sheltered just over nine hundred indigents.[14] That was a good year for the Hospicio. From its establishment in 1774 to 1803, the Hospicio sheltered fewer than eight hundred paupers in all but two years.[15] These relatively low counts show that the Hospicio could house only a fraction of the urban poor, leaving the majority of this population to persevere as before, scratching out an existence by pleading for alms from the wealthy. Complaints about the number of the urban poor abounded well after the Hospicio had begun operating. Viceroy Iturrigaray carped in 1806 that thousands of beggars filled the streets of the capital every day and that their numbers had greatly increased over the previous two years. The rise in mendicancy noted by the viceroy stemmed from rural immigration into Mexico City caused by recent crop failures, a problem that periodically raised the number of poor seeking alms in the capital throughout the century.[16] The limited scale of the Hospicio may well have led testators to conclude that donations to it would do little to aid the multitude of the needy and, thus, led them to withhold donations to it. The *Gazeta de México* in fact made this point in 1806, when it noted a decline in the Hospicio's fortunes.[17]

Testators' aversion to the Cuna de Huérfanos is more difficult to explain. The testators of Mexico City never supported it with enthusiasm but, at the same time, they allowed fewer and fewer orphans into their homes. Orphans seem to have become pariahs during the course of the eighteenth century, neither receiving aid directly in the homes of individuals nor indirectly through bequests to the orphanage established by Archbishop Lorenzana. Perhaps the hardening of family identities over the eighteenth century shaped the disappearance of orphans from the economy of charity. Patricia Seed, in a study of marriage choice in New Spain, demonstrated that parents, influenced by a growing acceptance of acquisitiveness as the crown, church, and other reformers promoted prosperity as the wellspring of common good, began successfully to reject marriage choices by their children that they deemed inappropriate because of differences in social status between the partners. In effect, parents in late colonial Mexico successfully excluded social inferiors from the family circle.[18] Perhaps the concern to maintain the social purity and economic vitality of the familial unit likewise conditioned the rejection of orphans in the late eighteenth century. As the family became less porous, it may have refused to admit unrelated children, the offspring of an increasingly disparaged poor population, into its midst. But the sociocultural history of the family in New Spain remains to be written. Suffice it to say that the decline in giving to orphans represented a turn away from highly personalized charity during the period under study.

Bequests to schools never rivaled other forms of charitable giving. One reason for this was that schools had no pressing needs like orphans, hospitals, and the poor. Furthermore, most bequests to schools were in reality grants to found schools where none existed. The large expense entailed naturally limited who could make such a gesture. The smallest bequest to found a school totaled two thousand pesos, well beyond the means of most testators. But school foundations, despite their scarcity, were significant indicators of charitable sentiment in eighteenth-century Mexico. Education of the young and establishment of primary schools for poor children became important issues in the late eighteenth century. In 1786, the *ayuntamiento*, town council, of Mexico City became so convinced of the great utility of education that it mandated the creation of free primary schools, or *escuelas pías*, in the capital's parishes and monasteries to teach poor children Christian doctrine and reading. Despite some resistance, parishes and orders generally complied with the decree and, soon after its promulgation, they administered a total of twenty-two such schools in the capital.[19]

Like bequests to the Hospicio de Pobres and Cuna de Huérfanos, school foundations demonstrate the rise of new conceptions of charity. Like the Hospicio and Cuna, schools were designed to instill discipline into a segment of the population, in this case children, and mold it into a productive work force. The ayuntamiento of Mexico City justified its decree to found schools in exactly these terms. It stated that instruction in the rudiments of faith was necessary for the young poor "so as to free them from the laziness which inclines them to vice, and which causes them to become when adults, not only useless but dangerous to the republic."[20] Testators who bequeathed money to found schools followed suit. For example, Domingo Antonio López, the General Administrator of Mail in New Spain and a native of a town in Asturias, Spain, set aside almost half of all his property to found two separate primary schools, one for girls and the other for boys, in his home town. A priest was to teach boys Christian doctrine, reading, writing, and arithmetic, whereas a woman of "good life and customs" was to instruct girls in "Christian doctrine, reading, even writing, and the skill of sewing perfectly." Domingo described this good work designed to instruct children in the faith and instill within them "good customs" as "useful and beneficial" to his parish of origin.[21] Likewise, María Rita Yañes, a doncella over twenty-five years old, left six thousand pesos to found a school for poor boys and four thousand pesos to establish one for poor girls in the her native pueblo of Apán. The school master was charged with teaching boys "Christian doctrine, reading, and writing," the school mistress with instructing girls in "Christian doctrine, reading, and sewing." She requested that the pastor of the pueblo inspect the schools and ensure their financial stability because of the "benefit" that these good works provided the parish.[22] The "benefit" to which Domingo and María referred consisted of the fact that the schools' students would learn proper Christian decorum and work skills pertinent to them in the sexual division of labor. Schools and workhouses aimed at the same goals; they simply worked with different populations.

As care for orphans declined precipitously and the bequests to charitable institutions rose moderately over the eighteenth century, gifts to the poor in general climbed steadily. The percentage of testators who bequeathed alms to the poor more than doubled from 1696 to 1813, rising from 3.8 percent to 10.7 percent of all testators. Between 1758 and 1779 a small dip occurred in charitable giving to the poor in general. Although the reasons for this drop are not entirely clear, the foundation of the Hospicio de Pobres may have played a part. When the Hospicio was erected in 1774, secular authorities simultaneously banned begging in Mexico City.[23] This legal prohibition may have temporarily cooled testators' willingness to distribute alms among the poor. Furthermore, the faithful of Mexico City may have believed that the Hospicio would reduce mendicancy and so may have seen little need to include bequests to the poor in their wills. But as it became evident by 1796 that the Hospicio de Pobres could not fulfill its mission to clear the capital's streets of paupers and that authorities would in reality countenance begging and almsgiving, testators returned to their previous level of charitable giving.

Despite the attempts by religious and secular reformers to stigmatize and confine the poor in the late eighteenth century, testators in Mexico City did not reject almsgiving to paupers. Moreover, they did not fully embrace the distinction espoused in elite discourse between the shamefaced and the mendicant poor. As they had in the early eighteenth century, testators continued to divide their gifts to paupers almost equally between the deserving and undeserving poor. About half of all testators who gave gifts to the poor continued to place restrictions on the recipients of their gifts, usually stipulating that only the shamefaced poor, doncellas, widows, or women receive the proffered alms. But the other half refused to make such distinctions, granting their alms simply to "the poor" without further restrictions. The tepid support for the Hospicio de Pobres, the growth in charitable giving to the poor, and the continued division among testators about restricting bequests to the deserving poor all indicate that religious and secular reformers made little headway in transforming the act of almsgiving over the Bourbon period.

What does the changing nature of charitable giving in Bourbon Mexico mean? The evidence points in multiple directions. The rise in charitable giving to hospitals, schools, and the poor in general reveals a growing concern (in both senses of the word) with the rising number of the anonymous poor during the late eighteenth century who simply because of sheer numbers could not be accommodated and controlled under traditional patron-client relations. Through their charitable gifts, testators sought to confine the threatening poor, eliminate what they considered the causes of poverty through education and artisanal training, and ameliorate the severity of poverty with more frequent alms to the poor.

Despite or because of this growing concern for the poor, testators began to turn away from the highly personal charity entailed in the rearing of orphans by the mid-eighteenth century and instead gave an increasing number of gifts to charitable institutions. This transformation points to a larger ongoing change in conceptions of community. Testators started to shun the personal horizontal bonds of charity that linked them with their more unfortunate neighbors in the mystical body of Christ and replaced them, if not with a vertically structured community, then with one based on relations mediated through impersonal institutions. The rich and poor came less and less into contact with one another in personal ways as the century progressed.

Nonetheless, the faithful of Mexico City continued to bestow alms upon the poor, or had their executors do so, in face-to-face encounters. In fact, testators increased their charitable gifts to the poor in spite of prohibitions on indiscriminant almsgiving and the foundation of the Hospicio de Pobres, an institution designed to reform the poor and eliminate begging. The continued recourse to begging and the testator population's willingness to grant alms indicate that, although charity became less personalized over the eighteenth century, the faithful did not forsake all direct encounters with paupers and refused fully to endorse the disparaging discourse on the poor that permitted their removal from public view and confinement in disciplinary institutions. Changes in patterns of charity reveal that horizontal bonds of community weakened significantly over the eighteenth century, but they did not entirely disappear as charity became more institutionalized.

Confraternities

The history of confraternities in late colonial Mexico demonstrates changing notions of Christian community and the collapse of the communal quest for salvation much more unequivocally than transformations within the realm of charity as an act of beneficence. Confraternities, an essential element of Catholic practice in the early eighteenth century, declined dramatically in importance by the late decades of that period. These pious brotherhoods that had once served to foster the state of charity and forge Christian community did not disappear as the eighteenth century wore on, but they served a much diminished role in uniting believers in the mystical body of Christ. The faithful of Mexico City still joined confraternities and participated in their liturgical and paraliturgical activities at the end of the colonial period, though in lesser numbers, but their understanding of the role of these organizations changed profoundly. They no longer viewed confraternities as entities that structured pacts of reciprocal spiritual obligations between members that helped ensure the salvation of confreres both living and dead. Rather, by the end of the eighteenth century, they viewed confraternities more as financial mutual aid societies. These brotherhoods still united Christians in common purpose, but they lost the religious core that sanctified the social bonds created by the confraternities and supported the communal endeavor for salvation.

The decline of confraternities and the faithful's changing understanding of their purpose reveal a transformation in subjectivity, or sense of personhood, that occurred during the eighteenth century in New Spain. The collective identity that underlay traditional understandings of the confraternity faded as individual identity rose at the end of the colonial period. It is impossible to measure the degree to which residents of eighteenth-century Mexico City experienced their own individual sense of self. But statements about confraternity membership made by testators indicate that the bounded, autonomous self was emerging.[24] By the end of the century, Spanish testators and notaries downplayed the confraternity's responsibility for collective memorialization of the dead, revealing that the communal quest for salvation at the heart of much confraternal activity faded as the colonial era came to a close. Although individual Catholics could still rely on the sacraments of the church to mediate their relationships with God, they stood bereft of the wider Christian community's aid at judgment.

The diminished importance of confraternities in Catholic practice is evident in Table 7. This table presents the percentage of testators who claimed membership in a confraternity and the minimum average number of confraternities to which they belonged. Because testators almost always listed only the most prominent confraternities of which they were members—usually adding a phrase to the effect that they belonged to other brotherhoods after mentioning the prominent ones—it is impossible to count exactly the average number of pious brotherhoods in which the faithful participated. The table also presents the percentage of testators who bestowed gifts on confraternities and the average number of gifts this group gave.

The sharp decline in the percentage of testators who mentioned membership in a confraternity as the eighteenth century advanced strongly suggests that the populace of Mexico City increasingly viewed them as less essential than before in attaining salvation. In 1696, 25.6 percent of all testators stated that they belonged to one or more confraternities, while in 1813 only 5.6 percent claimed confraternal membership.[25] We should not, however, take these figures as a fully accurate reflection of patterns of confraternal membership over the eighteenth century in Mexico City. Changes in testamentary practice account for some portion of this decline. For some unknown reason, in

TABLE 7 Confraternity Membership and Gifts to Confraternities

	1696	1717	1737
Testators who claimed membership in a confraternity	25.6% (n = 88)	20.5% (n = 35)	19.1% (n = 62)
Minimum average number of confraternal memberships	2.6	2.7	2.3
Testators who gave gifts to confraternities	5.2% (n = 18)	4.1% (n = 7)	2.5% (n = 8)
Average number of such gifts	1.7	1.0	1.5

the latter part of the century notaries must have stopped prompting testators to list the confraternities to which they belonged. In 1813 alone, five testators asked to be buried in the chapels of various third orders, suggesting that they belonged to these organizations, but never mentioned their membership in them in their wills.[26] Other testators in the latter part of the century mentioned their membership in confraternities only in an incidental way. For example, Marcos Francisco Maldonado, a bureaucrat in the office of tribute collection, stated in his 1779 will that he was the treasurer of the confraternity of Our Lady of Loreto and that as its financial representative various people owed him money, after which he listed the sundry debts.[27] I have the impression that, if it were not for the debts owed to the confraternity through him, Maldonado would not have mentioned his association with it.

Nonetheless, the decline in references to confraternities in testaments probably did mirror, if somewhat opaquely, a growing disaffection with these organizations. A decline in membership in Mexico City's confraternities would parallel a decrease in confraternal membership and in the number of confraternities themselves that occurred in areas of Catholic Europe at the same time.[28] It would also be congruous with other evidence concerning confraternities found in the wills of Mexico City. Over the eighteenth century the percentage of testators who pledged gifts to confraternities dropped significantly, from 5.2 percent in 1696 to 1.1 percent in 1813, demonstrating a growing indifference toward them on the part of the testator population.

The waning of confraternities also helps explain Archbishop Núñez de Haro's suppression of many pious brotherhoods in Mexico City. In 1794, after completing a review of confraternities in the archdiocese ordered by the viceroy, the archbishop dissolved at least forty of the city's

1758	1779	1796	1813	Total
15.3% (n = 29)	9.9% (n = 22)	9.4% (n = 19)	5.6% (n = 15)	15.7% (n = 270)
1.7	1.9	1.7	1.3	2.2
2.6% (n = 5)	1.4% (n = 3)	3.0% (n = 6)	1.1% (n = 3)	2.9% (n = 50)
1.0	3.7	2.2	1.0	1.6

152 confraternities. Many factors contributed to this action. The reforming bishops disliked the traditional religious practices, such as processions, flamboyant self-flagellation, lavish feast-day celebrations, and ritual feasting promoted by confraternities. Furthermore, like secular reformers they believed that the funds confraternities possessed could be better employed in fruitful ends that promoted general prosperity rather than sunk into the financing of elaborate paraliturgical practices. These ideas must have played a role in Archbishop Núñez de Haro's decision to disband close to one-third of Mexico City's confraternities. But the growing indifference toward confraternities demonstrated by the testator population by the late eighteenth century suggests another reason. As the faithful withdrew from pious congregations, less popular confraternities must have diminished and faced financial insolvency. Thus, it is likely that the archbishop's dissolution of at least some of the city's brotherhoods responded to a drop in confraternal membership and fortunes.

Confraternities, however, did not disappear from Mexico City. Over one hundred of them remained active into the nineteenth century. In fact, as many old confraternities faded, the faithful of Mexico City, in an age-old practice, formed new ones. For example, responding to a petition from pious individuals in Mexico City, in 1790 King Charles IV approved the foundation of the Brothers of the Dying (Hermanos Agonizantes), a group dedicated to attending to the needs of the moribund in their last hours.[29] Despite such new foundations, the general trend in confraternal participation pointed downward.

As membership in confraternities fell and the faithful graced pious brotherhoods with fewer gifts, the perception of these institutions and of the purposes they served changed dramatically. As we have seen, at the beginning of the eighteenth century the testators of Mexico City viewed confraternities as organizations of sacred sociability in which confreres were entrusted with the care of the souls of all members, both living and dead. The basic function of most confraternities consisted of establishing bonds of spiritual reciprocity between members. Confreres had the obligation to attend the funerals of their spiritual brothers and sisters, pray for their eternal repose, and commission masses for their souls so that, in turn, the remaining members of the confraternity would perform these acts for them once they passed away. Almost all wills written by testators who declared their membership in a confraternity from 1696 to 1758 indicate such an understanding of the confraternity.

A new discourse that depicted confraternities as mutual aid societies that provided financial assistance for the costs of burial began to challenge traditional understandings of pious brotherhoods as the eighteenth century advanced. A small number of testators began to employ this new discourse by 1717. It became more common by 1758. By 1779 this new view of confraternities dominated the wills written by Mexico City. Certainly, confraternity members even in the seventeenth century looked upon confraternities as sources of material aid at death and in times of need. But the testamentary language they employed to describe their relationship to these organizations stressed its spiritual nature. The new discourse on the other hand emphasized its monetary character.

The new understanding of confraternities first appeared in wills written in 1717 as a hybrid that united both the old and new understandings of confraternities. A handful of testators in that year began to refer to confraternities as sources of both spiritual and financial assistance.[30] Bartolóme de Arellano, a resident of Mexico City and owner of a rancho in Tacuba, claimed to belong to five confraternities. He declared that as a member of the confraternity of Our Lady of Sorrows founded in the parish of Santa Catarina Mártir, he was entitled to twenty pesos "for help with my funeral." He further stated that as a confrere of the confraternity of Jesus the Nazarene founded in the church of Santísima Trinidad, he should receive one sung mass for his soul and an additional twenty pesos. Likewise, the three additional confraternities to which he belonged—Our Lady of Sorrows in the parish of Santa Veracruz, the Most Holy Cross in the church of Nuestra Señora de Belén, and St. Nicholas in the monastery and hospital of San Juan de Dios—each owed him one sung mass and a total of sixty-five pesos. Bartolóme instructed his executors to turn in his confraternal patents to the respective brotherhoods so that they "fulfill what is customary." He further stipulated that his executors spend the funds they received from the confraternities "on my burial and funeral."[31] María de Vargas, a three-time widow, like most testators, spoke less explicitly about the spiritual obligations of the confraternity to which she belonged, but also included a statement about the financial aid due her. She declared that she was a confrere of Our Lady of Sorrows in the parish of Santa Veracruz and that the confraternity had the "obligation of giving twenty pesos for her funeral and doing good for the souls of its confreres." One of the suffrages performed by this confraternity, as revealed by Bartolóme, was the celebration of one sung mass for the repose of the deceased confrere's soul. Members probably also had the obligation to attend Maria's funeral and march in her cortege, as they probably did with all their fallen confreres. María further stated that the confraternity owed her these suffrages and funds because she had "fulfilled all that has been of my obligation."[32] In these clauses both Bartólome and María combined the old and the new. The confraternity for them served as both a spiritual and financial institution.

By 1737 a small number of testators began to refer strictly to the confraternity's financial obligation to its members and elided reference to its spiritual duties. By 1758, this understanding of confraternities had become more common, and by 1779 testators referred almost exclusively to confraternities as sources of monetary aid. Almost all of these testators, however, linked the financial aid received from confraternities to costs arising from the performance of their funerals and other suffrages. The faithful still viewed confraternities as closely associated with death, but their stated obligations to members became much more restricted. For example, Josefa Rodríguez de Pinillos wrote in 1779:

> I am a confrere of the Cord [of St. Francis] from which I have twenty-five pesos and twenty for being a sister of the Holy Angels. Likewise twenty-five in the Holy Cross as is certified in their respective patents that may be found in my papers. Their sum is to be added to my goods to help pay for my funeral and burial [*para ayuda de mi funeral y entierro*].[33]

Josefa de Salcedo, the widow of a cobbler, listed the confraternities to which she belonged in the burial clause of her 1779 will, indicating their close association with death and burial rites. After stating that she wished to be interred in the chapel of Santísima Trinidad in front of an altar dedicated to Our Lady of Sorrows with the "pomp that seems fitting to my executors," she informed them that they should pay

> their [the funeral's and burial's] costs from what the confraternities of which I am a confrere should give. [The confraternities I belong to] are that of the Souls [of Purgatory] founded in the holy cathedral church, that of the most Blessed Sacrament in the parish of San Sebastián, that of St. Homobono in the church of Santísima Trinidad, that of Our Lady of Solitude in the parish of Santa Cruz, and that of the Cord of our seraphic father señor St. Francis, applying the remainder [of the money collected] that there may be so that masses may be said for my soul.[34]

Both testators still associated confraternities with death. The money received from them was specifically to be used for funeral and burial expenses and, once these had been paid, the remainder, as Josefa de Salcedo indicated, was to be used for masses for her soul. But the sacred nature of these organizations, the mutual spiritual commitments of confreres, was lost in this new discourse. Although these testators, especially Josefa de Salcedo, continued to believe that suffrages were necessary for the soul, they were no longer necessarily the obligation of confraternities. Confraternities were seen as associations that provided money for suffrages, but their actual performance was left to the testator's executors.

Only one testator sundered the close association between confraternities and death rites. Rafael de Zevallos, a single and childless man, declared in his 1758 will that he belonged to the confraternity of the archangel St. Rafael that was housed in the church and hospital of San Juan de Dios. He stipulated that his executor should claim an unspecified amount of pesos from the confraternity and use the sum to pay a debt he owed. This clause is particularly odd because Rafael was not poor. In fact, he bequeathed two thousand pesos, a considerable though not enormous sum, to his brother.[35] Thus, he had no reason to earmark the proceeds from his confraternal payment to a debt he owed. Perhaps Rafael simply realized that he possessed enough money to pay for his funeral and burial without recourse to confraternal aid and so directed it to other ends. Regardless of his reasoning, he stands as the lone testator who explicitly divorced confraternities from death, burial, and suffrages.

The most emphatic articulation of the new discourse on confraternities treated them not as human societies linked by religious purposes, but rather as possessions. Only a small group of testators referred to confraternities in this way. One of these testators was Marcos de Mendoza, a mestizo carpenter. In his 1737 will, he declared:

> I have four confraternities to which I understand I am not a debtor of any amount and in case I am it would be of very little. Understanding that said four are each worth twenty-five pesos, and independently of them, I have another worth ten pesos . . . It is my will that being dead, [these amounts] be collected and, with the sum, the costs of my burial be paid.[36]

Marcos conceived of the confraternity solely as an asset with a specific monetary value. Most likely, he was referring to the confraternal patent, the certificate that proved one's membership in a fraternity. Upon death, these certificates were returned to the issuing confraternity, which paid a specified sum to the bearer. It is noteworthy that Marcos did not conceive of the brotherhood as anything but a financial organization. He indicated that he did not owe any dues to the confraternities to which he belonged, or at most "very little." By referring to confraternities as possessions, Marcos stripped them of any and all bonds of human association. For him, the confraternity essentially represented a savings account for funeral costs rather than a congregation of the faithful. This utterly desocialized view of the confraternity remained a distinctly minority understanding among the testator population of Mexico City. Most testators, even in the late eighteenth and early nineteenth centuries, portrayed confraternities as human associations even though they elided references to the mutual spiritual obligations of confreres so prominent in earlier testamentary discourse on confraternities.

Despite the fact that testators ceased to mention them, confraternities continued to perform their traditional acts of participation in funerals and the commemoration of the departed during the last half of the eighteenth century. Archbishop Lorenzana's condemnation in 1769 of confraternal meetings and feasting in the capital's cemeteries (see Chapter 7) leaves no doubt that confraternities still practiced festive and commemorative rites during this period. Furthermore, the unique confraternity clause composed by María Manuela Jiménez de Velasco, the daughter of a royal treasury official, in 1813 shows that confraternities still practiced suffrages for their deceased members. She stated:

> I order that the patents that I have as a member of a third order [*tercera*] and the others be delivered to their corresponding confraternities so that they may apply suffrages to me. Those that should contribute some sum of reales to me, [I order] my executors to collect it and add it to my goods.[37]

María, however, was the only testator from 1779 to 1813 who mentioned the spiritual obligations of confraternities and she was quick to indicate that at least some of the confraternities to which she belonged were obligated to compensate her monetarily.

By the end of the eighteenth century in Mexico City, testators rarely spoke of the religious duties of confraternities. Although these organizations continued to exist and participate in devotions, in the minds of Mexico City's Spanish, propertied residents they no longer directly aided their fallen members with suffrages as they stood before God. Now, although the soul still received aid from the suffrages families and executors performed with funds given by the confraternities, it faced judgment without of the wider company of its fellow confreres.

Baroque and Reformed Charity and Community

Given the differing religious sensibilities of baroque and reformed Catholics, it seems likely that these two groups would have responded differently to changes in charitable giving and confraternal participation that occurred in Mexico City over the Bourbon period. Pamela Voekel, in her study of cemetery reform in Mexico at the end of the colonial period, argues that charity to the poor became a hallmark of reformed piety. Religious reformers contended that those of means should grant alms to the poor, who were "living temples of God," rather than squander their estates on the material apparatus of worship. According to Voekel, the faithful responded positively to this message. As they turned away from the exterior cult so important in baroque Catholicism, enlightened Catholics destined more and more charity to the poor.[38] This view of reformed Catholics' stance on charity corresponds well with statements by the reforming bishops. Remember that Archbishop Lorenzana called on the faithful to support the Cuna de Huérfanos and the Hospicio de Pobres instead of lavishing wealth on baroque endeavors. He even stated that the accumulated adornment of church buildings served merely as a financial deposit for the church to tap in times of need to aid the poor. Hence, it seems reasonable to expect that reformed Catholics favored charitable causes more so than their baroque counterparts.

Evidence from the wills, however, reveals that baroque testators were much more inclined to grant charitable gifts than reformed ones. Table 8 presents the percentage of baroque and reformed testators who practiced all five types of charitable donations. It also presents the percentage of testators in each group who issued at least one charitable gift. We must read this table, however, with some caveats. As stated in the previous chapter, the division between baroque and reformed testators relies on a distinction between those testators who included at least one baroque pious directive in their wills on the one hand and those testators who requested a simple funeral without reference to poverty and who did not commission a baroque directive on the other. This is an admittedly blunt distinction that is not fine enough to differentiate between various possible meanings of the simple funeral requested by testators who left no clues in their wills as to their understanding of it. Thus, this methodology probably overstates the number of reformed testators in the latter part of the Bourbon period. Furthermore, the very small number of reformed testators in the first two-thirds of the eighteenth century renders numerical analysis merely suggestive. Nonetheless, the different patterns of charitable giving among baroque and reformed testators are clear.

Baroque testators were almost twice as likely to include a charitable directive in their wills as their reformed counterparts. A total of 37.4 percent of all baroque testators, as opposed to only 20.9 percent of all reformed testators, issued at least one charitable directive in their wills. Moreover, in every category of charitable giving baroque testators gave more often than reformed ones. In fact, in almost every category in every sample year, baroque testators gave with more frequency than their reformed brethren. Furthermore, reformed testators are underrepresented in the ranks of those testators who commissioned at least one charitable directive in their wills, whereas baroque testators are slightly overrepresented. To put it concretely, 20 percent of the total testator population issued at least one charitable directive in their wills,

TABLE 8 Charitable Gifts and Confraternal Membership by Baroque and Reformed
Testators

	1696	1717	1737
Baroque testators who gave gifts to orphans	21.3% (n = 17)	25.5% (n = 14)	13.5% (n = 12)
Reformed testators who gave gifts to orphans	50.0% (n = 5)	20.0% (n = 1)	12.5% (n = 2)
Baroque testators who claimed an orphan	22.5% (n = 18)	29.1% (n = 16)	14.6% (n = 13)
Reformed testators who claimed an orphan	60.0% (n = 6)	20.0% (n = 1)	18.8% (n = 3)
Baroque testators who gave gifts to hospitals	10.0% (n = 8)	16.4% (n = 9)	14.6% (n = 13)
Reformed testators who gave gifts to hospitals	0% (n = 0)	0% (n = 0)	0% (n = 0)
Baroque testators who founded or gave gifts to schools	0% (n = 0)	3.6% (n = 2)	2.2% (n = 2)
Reformed testators who founded or gave gifts to schools	0% (n = 0)	20.0% (n = 1)	0% (n = 0)
Baroque testators who gave gifts to the poor	11.3% (n = 9)	10.9% (n = 6)	14.6% (n = 13)
Reformed testators who gave gifts to the poor	10.0% (n = 1)	20.0% (n = 1)	0% (n = 0)
Baroque testators who included at least one charitable directive	31.3% (n = 25)	41.8% (n = 23)	34.8% (n = 31)
Reformed testators who included at least one charitable directive	60.0% (n = 6)	20.0% (n = 1)	18.8% (n = 3)
Baroque testators who declared membership in a confraternity	40.0% (n = 32)	32.7% (n = 18)	30.3% (n = 27)
Reformed testators who declared membership in a confraternity	40.0% (n = 4)	0% (n = 0)	31.3% (n = 5)

but 13.2 percent of all reformed testators and 24.7 percent of all baroque testators did so. Also, within the five individual categories of charitable activity, reformed testators tended to practice charity in the same proportion as the general testator population. But baroque testators practiced each form of charitable activity with more frequency than the general testator population. To give just one example, 7.3 percent of all testators gave gifts to the poor in general. Similarly, 7.8 percent of all reformed testators gave to the poor in general. But 18.1 percent of all baroque testators did so.

1758	1779	1796	1813	Total
21.4% (n = 12)	13.3% (n = 9)	12.7% (n = 8)	8.5% (n = 5)	16.4% (n = 77)
0% (n = 0)	0% (n = 0)	5.6% (n = 1)	7.3% (n = 4)	10.1% (n = 13)
25.0% (n = 14)	13.2% (n = 9)	12.7% (n = 8)	10.2% (n = 6)	17.9% (n = 84)
10.0% (n = 1)	0% (n = 0)	5.6% (n = 1)	7.3% (n = 4)	12.4% (n = 16)
7.1% (n = 4)	14.7% (n = 10)	6.3% (n = 4)	11.9% (n = 7)	11.7% (n = 55)
0% (n = 0)	6.7% (n = 1)	5.6% (n = 1)	5.5% (n = 3)	3.9% (n = 5)
0% (n = 0)	4.4% (n = 3)	3.2% (n = 2)	8.5% (n = 5)	3.0% (n = 14)
0% (n = 0)	0% (n = 0)	5.6% (n = 1)	0% (n = 0)	1.6% (n = 2)
23.2% (n = 13)	14.7% (n = 10)	22.2% (n = 14)	33.9% (n = 20)	18.1% (n = 85)
10.0% (n = 1)	0% (n = 0)	11.1% (n = 2)	9.1% (n = 5)	7.8% (n = 10)
42.9% (n = 24)	33.8% (n = 23)	36.5% (n = 23)	45.8% (n = 27)	37.4% (n = 176)
20.0% (n = 2)	6.7% (n = 15)	16.7% (n = 3)	20.0% (n = 11)	20.9% (n = 27)
23.2% (n = 13)	16.2% (n = 11)	12.7% (n = 8)	11.9% (n = 7)	24.7% (n = 116)
20.0% (n = 2)	20.0% (n = 3)	11.1% (n = 2)	1.8% (n = 1)	13.2% (n = 17)

Reformed piety, despite the charitable proclivities of its episcopal advocates, did not spur charitable activity in late colonial Mexico. Compared with the general testator population, reformed testators were somewhat reluctant to give to charitable causes. Compared with baroque testators, they were downright miserly. Why did reformed testators contribute only reluctantly to charity? Perhaps their unwillingness stemmed from the reformers' deprecation of the poor. If the reformed faithful internalized the derogatory representation of paupers created by both secular and religious reformers, they may have declined to fund activities that succored the poor, even the deserving poor and those housed in charitable institutions. Or perhaps charitable activity among reformed testators fell victim to reformed religiosity's aversion to external acts of piety. As pious works became less important than individual contemplation of God for salvation, the reformed faithful may have turned away from charity. Or last, perhaps reformed piety's emphasis on the individual's relationship with God, which came at the expense of the individual's bonds of sociability with other Catholics, eviscerated the rationale for acts of charity. As reformed Catholics focused more on their individual standing with the sacred, they may have felt less need to aid their fellows both spiritually and corporeally.

Reformed testators participation in confraternities corroborates the conclusion that, at least by the early nineteenth century, they forged few bonds of Christian sociability with their fellows. As Table 8 shows, for most of the eighteenth century, the percentage of reformed testators who claimed membership in a confraternity remained high, usually higher than the testator population in general. By 1796, however, the percentage of reformed testators in confraternities ran more or less parallel with the total testator population, 11.9 percent and 9.4 percent, respectively. In 1813 the reformed faithful's participation in confraternities plummeted. In that year only 1.8 percent of reformed testators claimed membership in a confraternity, compared to 5.6 percent of the general testator population. By the early nineteenth century, community with fellow Christians withered among reformed Catholics.

Given baroque testators' penchant for charitable giving and the bonds of community they created, it is not surprising that they were almost twice as likely as reformed ones to join a confraternity—24.7 percent as opposed to 13.2 percent. In fact, baroque testators were more likely than the general testator population to participate in pious congregations. In almost all sample years, a greater proportion of baroque testators declared membership in confraternities than that of the general testator sample. This disproportionate representation reached its height in 1813, when 11.9 percent of baroque testators, as opposed to only 5.6 percent of all testators, declared their status as a confrere. Although the collective enterprise for salvation declined for all Catholics over the Bourbon period, the baroque faithful proved less open to the rise of individual subjectivity than reformed Catholics. Nonetheless, even baroque Catholics experienced this change in subjectivity. Baroque Catholic participation in confraternities fell from a high of 40 percent in 1696 to a low of 11.9 percent in 1813. Although not as starkly alone as their reformed counterparts, baroque Catholics by the late eighteenth century practiced their faith in a more solitary fashion than they previously had.

Conclusion

The eighteenth century in Mexico City witnessed a fundamental shift in Catholic conceptions of community. Although Catholics practiced acts that structured community horizontally and vertically throughout the eighteenth century, the balance between these types of community formation shifted over time. As the decline in personalized care for orphans, decreasing confraternal membership, and new modes of speaking about confraternal obligations reveal, testators moved away from a model of sacred community based on the incorporation of disparate individuals into the mystical body of Christ through face-to-face contact and acts of charity. Although the sacraments still possessed the capacity to reconcile social distinctions, much of Catholic practice by the end of the eighteenth century preserved social distinction more than dissolved it. As the new discourse on confraternal obligations demonstrates, community formation in general became more associational, or based on mutual, mundane interests. In the specific case of social relations between the well-to-do and the needy as expressed through acts of beneficence, it became more mediated by charitable institutions. In both cases, the traditional sacred foundation of community waned. Catholics in the late eighteenth century were less likely to invoke Christ's presence in acts of charity or religious communion. Moreover, as the decline in confraternal membership shows, Catholics deemed collective devotions less relevant for salvation. They still commissioned suffrages for their souls and so still believed God's judgment followed death. But the larger community was becoming less useful in obtaining salvation. By the early nineteenth century, Catholics sought redemption more as bounded individuals aided by the sacraments of the church than as a community of the faithful.

Conclusion

✝ ON THE DAY BEFORE CHRISTMAS IN 1813 MARÍA GUADALUPE ANTONIA
Sandoval García Bravo wrote her will before Manuel Ymaz y Cabanillas.
María, a doncella, was in good health despite the epidemic that plagued
Mexico City at the time. Although María issued other pious directives in
her will, her highly unusual funeral clause reveals much about the fate of
religious reform in Bourbon Mexico City. Apparently influenced by the simplicity encouraged by reformed Catholics, María ordered that her cadaver,
dressed in a Carmelite habit, be buried in the Carmelite convent of Santa
Teresa la Antigua "without any pomp." She further stipulated that her
"burial be done entirely in secret." She was one of only a handful of testators
who asked for a secret funeral. In other words, she wanted to be commemorated and buried without the attendance of religious orders, confraternities, the poor, and acquaintances. Most likely, only her family and closest
associates along with the officiating priests and ministers were to attend her
funeral. In this clause, María reveals the desocialization of religious practice that occurred in Mexico City over the Bourbon period. The funeral, the
public ceremony designed to gather the faithful to pray for the deceased
and speed their passage through purgatory, had become a private affair for
some by 1813. María was willing to face God's judgment alone, without the
aid of the larger Christian community. Her spare and individualist piety
suggests that her religious sensibilities aligned with reformed Catholicism.

But María continued designing her funeral, indicating that her executors should arrange it

> in such a way that at six in the evening my body be placed [*se eche*]) in the grave on account of the special devotion that I have in that hour to the burial of Our Lord Jesus Christ and the sorrows of our mother, the most holy Mary.[1]

Despite the reformed elements of her piety, María still sought to forge a mystical union with the sacred. She designed her funeral liturgically to link her death and burial with those of Christ and the sorrows suffered by the Virgin. She chose six o'clock for her burial precisely to imitate Christ's interment and must have hoped that her spiritual resurrection—the passage of her soul from purgatory to heaven—would mimic Christ's bodily resurrection after three days in the tomb.[2]

Maria's peculiar case represents the state of religious change in late colonial Mexico. Her piety combined the new and the old. She rejected baroque display in her own funeral, eschewed baroque collective devotions to shorten her soul's time in purgatory, but still utilized baroque liturgical gesture to forge a mystical union between her and Christ. María, like many Mexican Catholics in the early nineteenth century, stood betwixt and between and in this position creatively practiced a hybrid religious culture apparently without a sense of contradiction. As María's example demonstrates, reformers did not entirely succeed in remaking Catholicism in Bourbon Mexico. But at the same time, baroque religious practice did not remain static.

Baroque Catholicism dominated religious practice in New Spain's capital during the entire eighteenth century. The baroque faithful of Mexico City routinely practiced devotions to images and the eucharist. They also performed symbolic gestures that mystically linked them with the holy figures the actions represented, lavishly decorated sacred space, and sumptuously enhanced the performance of the liturgy. All these devotions were predicated on the ability of the sacred to manifest itself within the world. The sacred inhered within images and the eucharist, and the faithful, like the priest at the altar, could invoke the mystical presence of the sacred through their lay liturgical actions. Moreover, sacred space, ostentatiously adorned to resemble the heavenly kingdom, located the sacred on earth. Within splendid church interiors, the faithful encountered a proximate and palpable presence of the sacred in and through their bodies. The ability of Catholics to encounter God corporeally rested on the identity of sign and signified within the religious realm.

Baroque Catholicism also privileged communal and face-to-face devotions. The faithful participated in confraternities that incorporated diverse members into the community of saints and mystical body of Christ and preferred personalized acts of charity that fostered direct contact and a sense of *comunitas* among Christians. These devotions were predicated upon a collective sense of personhood and a horizontally structured religious community.

In the second half of the eighteenth century, a group of reforming bishops and priests attempted to remake religious culture in Mexico. Influenced by Enlightenment rationality, they attempted to undermine baroque Catholicism and instill within the faithful a restrained and interior piety. This program in many ways coincided with other secular reforms instituted by the Bourbon monarchy, though neither religious nor secular reform was predicated upon the other. The reformers eschewed devotion to most images and relics, impugned lay liturgical gesture, ridiculed the lavish adornment of sacred space, and discouraged many forms of collective devotions. Their project rested on a new way of conceiving the very nature of God and the self. For reformers God was a spiritual entity who did not inhabit physical objects, with the exception of the eucharist. They also, though less forcefully, privileged individual devotions at the expense of confraternities and face-to-face acts of charity. In short, they implicitly undermined the unity of sign and signified and the collective subjectivity that underlay many baroque devotions.

The reformers' attempt to transform religious culture in Mexico City was at best a partial success. Baroque Catholicism remained the dominant religious practice in Mexico until the very end of the eighteenth century. Far more testators included baroque pious directives in their wills than those who requested an anti-baroque simple funeral in the six sample years stretching from the late seventeenth to the late eighteenth centuries. Even in the early nineteenth century baroque testators still edged out reformed ones. Despite dogged attempts by reforming prelates and priests to remake religious culture, the faithful of Mexico City continued to perform baroque devotions until at least the end of the colonial period.

Religious reform, however, was not entirely unsuccessful. The number of testators who rejected baroque display in the personalized context of the funeral and who did not commission another baroque gesture in their wills increased over the Bourbon period. A handful of the faithful rejected such ostentation even in the early eighteenth century, anticipating religious reform by fifty years. The reforming project of the late Bourbon period accelerated this trend. The generation of testators who came of age during the intense reforming efforts of the last decades of the eighteenth century—those testators who wrote their wills in 1813—showed a marked rise in the rejection of baroque ostentation. In that year almost as many testators requested anti-baroque funerals as included baroque gestures in their wills.

Even though religious reform did not dislodge baroque sacred immanence, performative and liturgical piety, and elaborate decoration of sacred space from late colonial religious practice, the communal and face-to-face nature of baroque devotions declined over the colonial period. Claims of confraternity membership dropped dramatically in the wills, and the discourse surrounding confraternities changed. By the second half of the eighteenth century testators emphasized the economic benefits of confraternity membership over the mutual spiritual obligations of confreres that had once formed the foundation of confraternal community. At the same time, patterns of charity changed. Testators over the Bourbon period began to withdraw from the very intimate charitable practice of rearing orphans and instead granted more alms to institutions of beneficence. No longer did close personal contact between members of the faithful serve as the foundation of Christian community, nor did collective devotions speed one's passage through purgatory.

In sum, devotions in Mexico City showed both remarkable stability and change over the Bourbon period. Although religious reformers had attempted to desacralize the world by emphasizing God's spiritual nature, much of the faithful continued to live in a physical environment that regularly manifested the sacred. Nonetheless, the sense of collective subjectivity that underlay baroque, communal piety subsided over the Bourbon era. Even many baroque Catholics, like María Guadalupe Antonia Sandoval García Bravo whose will began this conclusion, practiced a desocialized piety in the early nineteenth century. Although baroque Catholicism proved resilient to the religious reformers' project, religious culture in Mexico City changed under the accumulated pressure of both religious and secular reform as well as the weight of transformations in the larger sociocultural context. By the end of the colonial period, no one type of devotion dominated religious practice in urban Mexico.

Religion and Modernity

The mixed fate of religious reform in Mexico City speaks directly to the relationship between Catholicism and modernity. As part of a larger cultural sea change that included crown efforts to discipline its subjects, promote economic efficiency, and thus produce taxable prosperity, reformed Catholicism participated in the birth of modernity in Mexico. Like their secular counterparts, religious reformers encouraged the formation of bounded, economically rational, and disciplined individuals. The reformers' desocialization of religious practice and emphasis on personal relationships with God promoted the development of a modern, individual subjectivity. Furthermore, their implicit acceptance of a modern epistemology that clearly distinguishes between the sign and signified supported economic rationality and the disciplining of bodies. Although religious reformers encouraged movement toward modernity, their lack of success in redefining the very nature of God and remaking religious culture complicated modernity's emergence in colonial Mexico.

The new subjectivity unwittingly promoted by religious reform privileged a modern, bounded, individual sense of self. As reformers deemphasized confraternities in Catholic practice, they cut the horizontal ties that bound believers together in the mystical body of Christ. Catholics could no longer count on the direct spiritual aid of their fellows as they stood before God at the moment of judgment or writhed in the cleansing torments of purgatory. Individual believers, now disassociated from the larger community of the faithful, had to rely on their own merits for salvation. This process of individualizing the quest for redemption supported the emergence of the modern, bounded individual. This new individual possessed a hardened, nonporous sense of self whose eternal (and short-term) fate could not be determined by others. The new individual, separated from larger integrative social groups, served as his or her own master.

In addition to the modern subjectivity promoted by reformed Catholicism, the new epistemology inherent within it furthered modernity in two ways. First, it allowed believers to pursue economic rationality with fewer pious restraints. Images and relics (though not the eucharist), now deemphasized in Catholic practice, no longer demanded believers' attention. Bereft of their ability to locate the sacred physically within the world, they no longer required costly gifts of light, jewelry, and clothing. Similarly, church interiors could now forgo lavish adornment because they no longer manifested heaven on earth. In these ways, Catholic reformers, like the Bourbon state, which curtailed the gaiety and expense of religious festivals, economized pious practice. They thus provided Catholics the opportunity to accumulate wealth more freely and direct it away from worship to other, more mundanely productive ends.

Second, reformed Catholicism's new epistemology aided the disciplining of bodies to render them more efficient producers. The distancing of sign and signified stripped bodies of their religious value and thus opened them to disciplinary projects. Reformed Catholicism's participation in this aspect of modernization occurred in three ways. First, reformers ridiculed lay liturgical gesture and, in its place, emphasized bodily stillness during devotions so that the mind could focus on God. Catholics could no longer forge mystical unions with holy figures through the crafting of religiously symbolic, bodily acts. Second, as church interiors lost their symbolic function to reproduce heaven on earth, reformers attacked ostentatious ornamentation of sacred space. This process in turn undermined the corporeal nature of baroque religious experience. The simplified church interiors of reformed Catholicism no longer stunned the senses of the faithful and induced a felt experience of God's presence. In short, reformers rendered bodies religiously inert. Now bodies were neither symbolically charged (thus able to invoke the sacred into the world) nor capable of registering God's presence through the senses. These two means of undermining the body's religious capacities opened the possibility for institutions of power to discipline the body to make it an efficient tool of production. Third, as sign and signified became distinct, reformers ignored traditional understandings of the poor that forged an identity between them and Christ. This cultural amnesia permitted reformers to disparage beggars and create new charitable institutions such as the Hospicio de Pobres and the Cuna de Huérfanos to contain them and inculcate a work ethic and respect for authority and order within them. In this way religious reformers participated directly (not just opened a space for) the disciplining of bodies. This aspect of religious reform coincided with secular projects to order and police the streets and plazas of Mexico City in an attempt to foster self-discipline among its citizens, rendering them pliant to authority and efficient in production.

Although reformed Catholicism promoted aspects of modernity, we must remember that intentions do not always produce desired results. As we have seen, the laity of Mexico City often deflected or creatively reworked the reformers' objectives. It is clear, however, that changes within Catholic practice in eighteenth-century Mexico promoted one aspect of modernity, the rise of the bounded individual. Pamela Voekel has cogently analyzed this process in her study of changing funeral and burial practices in New Spain. She argues that the movement toward simple funerals and cemetery burials in the last decades of the eighteenth century helped shatter the society of estates. Elaborate baroque funerals and burial in places of honor within church buildings had encoded social distinctions that sacralized the hierarchical nature of colonial Mexican society. The call for a simple funeral and for burial in a suburban cemetery undermined display of status in these religious rites and hence the church's sanctification of hierarchy. In this way reformed Catholicism promoted the rise of the modern autonomous individual unfettered by the weight of social rank and set the stage for the emergence of the modern republic composed of equal, autonomous, male individuals.[3]

Although the broad outlines of Voekel's argument are well founded, data from the wills show that the birth of the modern, bounded individual was a longer term process. Although the popularity of requests for simple funerals serves as a valid marker for the decline of the society of estates, an equally important indicator for Catholicism's impact on the rise of the bounded sense of self is confraternal participation. Traditionally, the confraternity had united believers in the mystical body of Christ, allowing suffrages performed by some confreres to benefit others both living and dead. The confraternity thus ameliorated the individual's responsibility for his or her own salvation. The confrere was a porous individual, one whose identity was in part subsumed under the larger identity of the confraternity and whose eternal fate could be significantly influenced by the good works of others. Therefore the decline in confraternity membership and the changing understandings of confraternal participation that began in Mexico City by the mid-eighteenth century, even before the advent of religious reform and the rise in popularity of simple funerals, demonstrates that the religious conditioning of the modern individual was a long-term process already in motion before reformers began to assiduously critique baroque Catholicism. The reformers' attempt to upend hierarchy through changes in funeral and burial practices thus responded to and furthered earlier transformations taking place within the realm of subjectivity rather than initiated them.

Furthermore, the political implications of the rise of the modern individual first occurred before the close of the colonial period, although they would come to fruition only with the establishment of the first Mexican republic. The individuals of Mexico City began to refashion the hierarchical relationship between crown and subject in the early years of the war for independence. Although the inhabitants of the capital remained largely quiescent during the insurrection, it is clear that members of the propertied class began to question the legitimacy of monarchical rule at that time. They voiced their political opinions in 1812 and 1813, when elections were held for the city council of Mexico City and for a new constitutional legislature, or *cortes*, in Spain. Napoleon's invasion of Spain and the consequent abdication of Ferdinand VII in 1808 set the stage for the Mexico City elections. In response to the French presence and the capture of their king, cities in Spain founded regional juntas to rule in the name of Ferdinand and resist the French armies. By 1810, the various juntas had united into the Regency, which set about the task of drafting a constitution. The document called for a constitutional monarchy that deprived the king of legislative and judicial authority and limited his court to a fixed budget. It also mandated the establishment of elective town councils in Spain and its dominions and gave seats in the new legislature to representatives from the Americas. The constitution was instituted in Mexico City in September 1812. Elections for the town council of Mexico City were held in November of the same year and those for representatives in the cortes in July 1813. Autonomists swept both elections. The propertied class of Mexico City, apparently disenchanted with direct monarchical rule, desired to distance the government of New Spain from imperial oversight. Although voters did not seek to sever ties with their king completely, they wanted to curtail his authority over the colony. Furthermore, their mere participation in the elections, the first popular elections ever held in Mexico, suggests that they approved of the constitution and the limitation of the monarch's power. In a sense, the simple act of casting a vote indicates that many denizens of Mexico City now considered themselves autonomous citizens of a sovereign political community rather than subjects of a king. In the end, however, these elections accomplished few practical results. The Regency refused to grant the colonies autonomy and any movement toward that goal was nipped in the bud when Ferdinand VII returned from captivity in 1814, resumed the throne, and abrogated the constitution.[4] Only with full independence in 1821 was Mexico able to distance itself formally from Spain and its king.

Although it is clear that transformations in religious culture participated in the emergence of the bounded individual in eighteenth-century Mexico City, Catholicism's role in fostering economic rationality and disciplined bodies is less evident. Although the modern epistemology underlying re-formed Catholicism opened greater space for the nonreligious use of eco-nomic resources and the forging of pliant, productive bodies, the testators of Mexico City, even many who accepted the desocialization of religious practice and the simultaneous rise of the bounded individual, rejected these aspects of the reformers' program. Many believers continued to perform devotions predicated upon the notions of sacred immanence and the salvific efficacy of performative and liturgical piety. They continued to grant precious gifts to saintly images and the eucharist, to request burial before them, to bequeath ornaments and funds to churches for their decoration, and to orchestrate liturgical gestures to gain merit for their souls. In short, they rejected the opportunity to economize on religious practice and redirect bodily energies away from pious ends. Of course, it is possible that the faithful of Mexico City practiced greater economic rationality in other spheres of their lives outside the religious realm or that they efficiently used their bodies for economic pro-duction even as they continued to seek the sacred corporeally in ornate church interiors and through liturgical gesture. But it seems unlikely that the Catholic who lavished funds on images and churchly ornaments and who punctuated the workday with symbolic devotions and weakened the flesh through self-mortification served as a paragon of thrift and productive gesture.

Although sometimes conflated, the three aspects of modernity analyzed here represent distinct processes. The rise of the modern sense of self as an autonomous individual relatively free from external influences does not neces-sarily entail the development of personal economy and bodily restraint. Many testators in Bourbon Mexico City, like María Guadalupe Antonia Sandoval García Bravo whose will began this conclusion, demonstrated an individu-alistic piety but nonetheless supported baroque exuberance in worship or designed liturgical gestures to connect with the sacred.[5] Personal economy and stilled bodies depend less on individual subjectivity than on conceptions of divinity. Because the sacred retained the ability to manifest itself physically within the world, sites of immanence continued to demand attention from believers in the form of gifts and pilgrimages. And because the body retained the ability to experience the sacred through the senses and invoke it through symbolic gestures, the faithful continued to devote corporeal energies to the search for union with divinity. In other words, the very nature of God funda-mentally shaped religious practice and thus in large measure conditioned the only partial realization of modernity in nineteenth-century Mexico.

APPENDIX

Note on Sources

The Rites of Dying and the Desacralization
of the Will in Bourbon Mexico

The last will and testament is a rich historical source, but requires much care
in its use. It was created in a relational process by testators and notaries (and
others present at its drafting).[1] Just as important, it was intimately related to
rites of dying. But its relationship with the rites of dying changed over the
Bourbon era, and this shift subtly influenced will writing and the will's content. The will, then, is not a stable serial source, and historians must understand the will's changing relational context to utilize it appropriately.

The will reveals much about piety and religious sensibilities because during the medieval and early modern eras it was as much a religious as a secular
document. In the last days and weeks before death, in the midst of numerous
other rites of dying, those who had property to distribute called a notary to
their bedsides to redact their final wishes. They included pious directives in
their wills to gain grace for their souls and improve their standing before
God. Testators also addressed their debts, credits, and financial concerns,
listed their children, bequeathed gifts to family, friends, and associates, and
named their heirs. The relationship between religious and mundane concerns
in wills was not stable. Over the eighteenth century the will began to lose its
sacral character. At one time a sacred document in itself inserted into the

broader rites of death, it began to be removed from the ceremonies of dying, and will writing began to lose its sacred aura. The will still served as a means to perform good works and to request suffrages for the soul, but the document itself and the act of will writing became desacralized. Furthermore, the notaries and testators of Mexico City began to shift the will's emphasis subtly from religious to mundane concerns by the end of the eighteenth century. The faithful of Mexico City still used the will to commission pious acts and gave no sign of abandoning a Christian understanding of life and death. But by the end of the eighteenth century, they lived in a more profane world and began subtly to privilege mundane over religious concerns. Religious practice and salvation were still of paramount importance, but mundane matters began to take precedence over religious ones in the last will and testament.

Death and the Will

The will was reintroduced in Europe during the eleventh and twelfth centuries. In antiquity, the testament had served a secular purpose—to distribute property among kith and kin. When it was resurrected after a hiatus of half a millennium in medieval Europe, its character had changed. The church revived it as a primarily religious document. Testators used it to bequeath alms to the church and poor, to commission masses for their souls, and to fund pious works. The reappearance of the will was closely associated with the rise of the doctrine of purgatory, that intermediate space between heaven and hell where those who died in Christ but who still had to make restitution for their sins were purified. The pious acts commissioned in the will sped one's passage through purgatory, for the merit earned from them accrued to the testator's soul.[2]

More than a means to issue pious directives, the act of writing a will was considered a sacred practice that, itself, conferred grace upon the testator much like any other sacramental. In fact, the will was closely linked to the testator's final confession, and the church mandated that all Christians redact wills as a necessary step toward salvation. In Spain, the Synod of Zaragosa in 1357 and the Council of Madrid in 1473 denied burial in hallowed ground to those who died intestate.[3] A treatise on will writing widely circulated in eighteenth-century Mexico reveals the sacred and obligatory nature of testamentary practice. The tract recommended that before dictating a will, the testator

commending yourself to God . . . resign your will to the divine
[will], ask for its aid, and with a firm desire to do what is of your
obligation and discharge of your conscience, with brave Christian
resolution, in order to perform (without attending to human concerns) what is of service to God and the good of your soul, proceed
to order your testament.[4]

Writing a will was a religious act of tremendous import that required the
testator to invoke God's aid. In essence, it was a form of prayer. Testators
removed themselves from worldly matters, meditated on death, and sought
to serve God.

Precisely for these reasons ecclesiastical courts rather than secular
ones exercised authority over the execution of testaments. The Council of
Trent (1545–63) reaffirmed the church's jurisdiction over testamentary cases
by ruling that bishops act as the ultimate executors of pious bequests.[5] In
Mexico the church stipulated that executors show a copy of the testament to
the deceased's parish priest before interment, so that he could take note of
the pious directives the testator had commissioned. It also required executors to complete the testament faithfully within one year of the testator's
death, though it strongly encouraged a speedier completion.[6] To ensure
that executors properly and quickly fulfilled their obligations, the Mexican
church instituted the Tribunal of Testaments, Chantries, and Pious Works.
Executors were required to submit a copy of the will and all relevant documentation concerning the completion of bequests to the Tribunal for review.
The Tribunal then determined the status of the will and, if complete, issued
a writ clearing the executors of further obligation.

The will, however, was not a strictly religious document. By at least the
beginning of the early modern period, it began to reflect testators' secular
interests. It enumerated debts and credits, listed property and bequests to
family and friends, and on occasion recorded the details of family life and
business contracts and conflicts. But the will did not become exclusively secular until the twentieth century—at least in Spain and Mexico. During the
eighteenth century, it retained much of its religious content. But mundane
concerns began to take precedence of place in the will. Furthermore, the will
began to lose its sacramental status as it was removed from long-standing
rites of dying.

Dying in eighteenth-century Mexico, as in Europe at that time, was a

social process. Friends, family, strangers, and priests performed public rituals around the deathbed that reminded the dying that salvation was not a
completely individual process and that the community also prayed for their
blissful repose. They encouraged the dying to repent for past sins, conclude
worldly affairs, and remain confident in God's mercy without arrogant
expectation of it.[7] In other words, they helped foster a "good death." A good
death was essential because, according to late medieval and early modern
clerical discourse, the disposition of the dying at the moment of death was
decisive in determining their eternal fate. The faithful who died repentant
and confident in God's mercy, even those who had lived wicked lives, passed
away in grace. Those who succumbed to temptation and despair at the cru-
cial moment, even if they had lived exemplary lives, deserved damnation.[8]
By the eighteenth century in Mexico, clerical discourse still upheld the decisive nature of the moment of death, but emphasized that the character of
one's entire life heavily influenced one's final disposition. The archbishop of
Mexico, Alonso Núñez de Haro y Peralta (1772–1800), commented in a sermon on the assumption of the Virgin that "the grace of a good death is a sole
effect of mercy [from God], though the merit of a good life contributes greatly
to obtain it."[9] In another sermon he rebuked those who delayed repentance
until the last, arguing that, though not impossible, it was "very difficult"
to make a true conversion at the moment of death.[10] In the eighteenth century, as the bounded continuous self emerged, the decisiveness of the final
moments before death was spread over a lifetime.[11]

Ideally, death rituals began when illness or infirmity became life threatening but before death was imminent. At this point, friends or relatives of the
dying informed the parish priest, who came to the moribund to hear the last
confession. Confession opened the gates of paradise, for the sacrament of penance possessed the power to absolve the faithful of the guilt of their sins (but
not the restitution required for them) and, thus, could reestablish a severed
relationship with God. With a thorough and contrite confession on the deathbed, the dying entered a state of grace that at least granted them a place in purgatory. The church considered confession *in extremis* of such great importance
that it repeatedly demanded that physicians urge their patients who suffered
grave illness to confess and that doctors refuse their services to any person
who did not confess within three days.[12] Furthermore, the church granted
permission to any priest to perform the sacrament at the deathbed even if he
did not possess an episcopal license to hear confession. It also required priests

to attend to the dying immediately, regardless of the time of day or distance to the home of the moribund. Priests found remiss in their duties faced a stiff fine.[13]

According to ecclesiastical prescriptions, the dying were to receive the viaticum, or the eucharist given at the deathbed, to prepare them for their journey to eternal life. A priest was to deliver the viaticum either at the same time as the moribund's final confession or some time after it. The consumption of Christ's body as death neared fortified the soul and created a special association between the agonies of the dying person and Christ's passion as commemorated and made present in the eucharist. The reception of the viaticum was also the most public of death rites. Community members could join the procession from the parish church to the home of the ill, witness the last communion, pray for the benefit of the dying, and in return for this good work receive 100–200 days of indulgence.[14]

According to ecclesiastical literature, during the period when the ill received confession and the viaticum, the parish priest or one of his assistants was to begin to visit the sick person regularly and with more frequency as the illness worsened. Most likely, however, this benefit was reserved for the wealthy or socially prominent. A widely used manual for pastors recommended that the priest place images of the crucifix, the Virgin, or other saints to whom the dying person had special devotion in view of the ill person and place a receptacle of holy water close by so those present could often asperse him or her. The presence of the images and the grace conferred by contact with blessed water aided the dying to dispel despair, ward off temptation, and remain faithful to God. The attending cleric was to aid the dying achieve a good death by reminding them of the examples of the saints, by exhorting them to bear illness with patience and resignation to God's will, and by instructing them about acts that gained grace, like contritely invoking Jesus's name for past sins and pardoning one's enemies.[15]

Once death was near, but ideally before the ill person lost consciousness, a priest again was to visit, this time to administer the sacrament of extreme unction. The anointing of the five sense organs lent strength to the dying to resist temptation and despair at the moment of greatest weakness, to diminish the fear of death, and encourage faith in God's mercy. It could even, if God chose, cure the ill.[16] This rite, unlike the reception of the viaticum, was private. A lone priest, without the accompaniment of the general faithful, anointed the eyes, ears, nose, mouth, hands, feet, and loins of the ill person with blessed oil by tracing a cross with his thumb over each area. After the anointing of the senses, the priest left holy water and a crucifix at the home so that the ill person could be aspersed frequently and could gaze upon the image of Christ's death as he or she died.[17] Confession, viaticum, and extreme unction were the official rites of dying that the vast majority of the urban population received.[18] For most of the populace, though, the parish clergy probably combined all three rites in one visit to save time and expense.

In addition to the sacraments of the church, other less formal practices to ensure a good death abounded. Customarily, the dying summoned household members to their deathbeds, decried their own futile attachment to worldly goods and causes, and exhorted those gathered to shun the vanities of this life and dedicate themselves to God.[19] The dying also commonly held a lighted "candle of good dying," a specially blessed candle that conferred a plenary indulgence on them when they held it and commended themselves to the Virgin during the last minutes of life.[20] If the moribund could not hold a candle, those attending the deathbed kept one burning close by. They repeatedly sprinkled the dying with holy water, gave them images of saints and the crucifix to kiss, and reminded them of God's mercy.

These standard rites and the parish priest's ideally frequent visits did not satisfy the desire or anxiety of some that they die a good death. A few people specifically requested that priests or friars attend them at the deathbed without pause. Juan Ángel de Urra, a well-off merchant, asked that when death approached a priest be called to "assist me . . . until I die." He earmarked fifty pesos to remunerate the cleric for his services.[21] Francisco Gregorio Cano specifically requested that two friars (but he did not indicate from which order) "help me die well" and "and assist me at the head of my bed [*cabecera*]" in return for twenty-five pesos each.[22] In contrast, Francisco Ruíz de Castañeda, a hacendado, asked that his attendants not watch over him until he died. Rather, he ordered them to distribute alms among Mexico City's Franciscan monasteries, a select group of hospitals, and many nunneries so that the friars and nuns would commend his soul to God as he died.[23] It is unclear how common the practice of requesting priests and friars to attend the deathbed was in eighteenth-century Mexico City. It was relatively expensive, and so was probably restricted to the wealthy.

Exactly when will writing fit into the rites of dying is uncertain. In most cases it probably came soon after the combined last rites, for it was the priest's duty at confession to exhort the dying to settle their worldly affairs by redacting a will.[24] Wherever it fell, it was associated with dying. With the exception of 1758, a majority of testators in the seven sample years wrote their wills when ill(see Table 9).[25] In fact, many were seriously ill, and a few perished before they could complete the instrument. Father Juan de Olivares Toralvo, an unbeneficed priest, died at nine o'clock at night while in the middle of redacting his will in the presence of the notary, his scribe, an attending physician, and another priest.[26] Miguel Ballesteros died after he finished dictating his will, but before all the witnesses necessary to certify the document arrived.[27] Juan Sánchez Pujarte did not die, but fell into a demented state before he could finish his will.[28] The vast majority of testators, though ill, did not wait until death was imminent before they called the notary and completed their wills without mishap. Some even recuperated afterwards.[29]

The church attempted to shift the practice of will writing away from the deathbed and convince the faithful to write their wills while healthy so they would have ample time to ponder the final disposition of their goods. One treatise on testaments published multiple times in Mexico City during the eighteenth century encouraged readers to imagine the conflicts among friends and family that could occur if they waited until the last moment and then wrote a hasty will with little forethought. Rivalries might emerge among the interested parties and lead to "formal hatreds" that consumed the testator's wealth before its distribution among heirs and pious works. It depicted the torment of those left without time to call the notary before death and unable to fulfill their Christian obligation to leave a will. On the other hand, it portrayed the moribund who had redacted a testament while in health as calm in the knowledge that they had already arranged their affairs.[30]

The dissemination of such arguments must in part account for the rise that began in 1717 in the percentage of testators who wrote their wills while healthy (see Table 9). The percentage climbed from 16.0 percent of all testators in 1696

TABLE 9 Percentage of Ill and Healthy Testators

	1696	1717	1737	1758	1779	1796	1813
Ill testators	70.1%	55.6%	57.4%	41.3%	51.8%	56.4%	65.2%
Testators with achaques (chronic illness)	6.7%	8.8%	6.8%	8.5%	5.4%	5.9%	4.4%
Healthy testators	16.0%	28.7%	25.3%	31.7%	32.9%	29.7%	24.1%

to 28.7 percent in 1717 and remained relatively high for the rest of the Bourbon period. This increase reflects a greater discipline on the part of testators in adhering to the church's recommendation to redact wills before illness or infirmity struck. At the same time, this trend also indicates an incipient removal of will writing from the rites of dying and the sundering of sacred associations it had with them. Even the arguments ecclesiastics used to encourage early will writing focused on mundane concerns, disputes over property and family enmity, rather than on religious issues.

The removal of will writing from the rites of dying and its loss of sacramental status, or the capacity of the act of will writing itself to confer grace on the testator, also helps account for the trend toward the declining resort to formal instruments to dispose of property at death. During the eighteenth century, the faithful had two options for arranging their affairs before death. One was the will; the other was the *poder para testar*, a legal document that gave an executor power of attorney to redact a will once the maker of the poder died. This document was usually shorter than a will, though it possessed an almost identical preamble and contained clauses concerning the maker's burial and his or her election of executors and heirs much like the will. People probably chose to redact a poder because it required less preparation than a will and placed the burden of dividing property on the executors. The church frowned on poderes and approved them only in cases of imminent death so the mortally ill could avoid dying intestate.[31] In practice, however, the poder was used in the same manner as the will, and occasionally people in good health wrote them. As shown in Table 10, the total number of people who redacted wills and poderes declined over the century, with the number of those writing poderes dropping precipitously. Given the differential frequency of will writing in plague and non-plague years, we must view the total number of wills and poderes according to whether an epidemic afflicted Mexico City in that year. For plague years, the total number of instruments written declined from a high of 606 in 1696 to a low of 292 in 1779, though the total written in 1813 was not significantly higher than in 1779. The decline in the total number of wills and poderes written in non-plague years is not as dramatic, but nonetheless significant, from a high of 299 in 1758 to 233 in 1796. Both data sets show a noticeable drop in the number of people who left a legal document to dispose of their estates by the end of the eighteenth century.

What caused this decline in the number of wills and poderes? The drop stemmed from and shaped the desacralization of will (and poder) writing.

TABLE 10 Number of Wills and Poderes Para Testar

	1696*	1717	1737*	1758	1779*	1796	1813*
Wills	360	177	331	198	230	203	281
Poderes para testar	246	73	208	101	62	30	17
Total number of wills and poderes	606	250	539	299	292	233	298

* Indicates Plague Year

In other words, the act of will writing lost its status as a sacramental act that conferred grace on testators. Will writing, once a ritual act considered necessary for salvation, became a more mundane activity intended for the mere disposal of property. The will still contained religious directives, but the act of will writing was no longer itself considered necessary for salvation. As the act of will writing lost its sacramental status, the faithful wrote wills and poderes less frequently.

Socioeconomic factors had little impact on this process. Mexico City's population grew during the eighteenth century. If the rate of will and poder writing had remained constant, the number of legal instruments written should have increased, not decreased. Mortality rates cannot account for this decline, either. The epidemic that ravaged Mexico City in 1779 was more virulent than the ones that struck in 1696 and 1813.[32] Assuming a constant rate of will writing, the number of wills redacted in 1779 should have been higher than in 1696 and 1813. Another possible cause of the decline in will and poder writing is the economic conditions prevailing in the capital in the latter part of the eighteenth century. If the city endured a recession and a consequent drain of wealth, fewer people would have possessed enough property to make the expense and inconvenience of writing a will worthwhile. But Mexico City experienced economic expansion, at least for the merchant, miner, and estate-owning elite, during most of the eighteenth century. True, the introduction of free trade in 1778 destabilized the profits of the capital's great wholesale merchants and certainly made the accumulation and retention of wealth more difficult. The reduction in will writing in 1779 from the previous plague year of 1737 may in part reflect this changing economic situation. But the more destabilizing effects of free trade were not felt until the 1780s. Hence, the decline in will and poder writing

TABLE 11 Will Characteristics

	1696	1717	1737
Wills with no pious or non-standard secular clauses (empty wills)	8.4% (n = 29)	2.9% (n = 5)	4.9% (n = 16)
Testators who issued a pious directive	59.0% (n = 203)	64.9% (n = 111)	59.9% (n = 194)
Average number of pious directives issued	2.3	2.7	2.2
Average value of pious bequests in pesos (does not include value of mass requests)	751	1264	1134
Median value of pious bequests in pesos (does not include value of mass requests)	100	500	275
Average number of secular bequests included	6.3	6.7	6.0
Wills in which the body opened with a pious bequest (among those wills that contained a pious bequest)	68.0% (n = 138)	56.8% (n = 63)	46.4% (n = 90)
Wills for which a cleric served as witness	19.5% (n = 67)	28.1% (n = 48)	22.8% (n = 74)

in 1796 from the previous non-plague year of 1758 may have been in part shaped by the advent of free trade. But declining economic fortunes cannot explain the stability in will and poder writing in 1779 and 1813, both of which were plague years. Heavy taxation and years of insurgency battered the Mexican economy in 1813. If relative prosperity influenced the incidence of will and poder writing, then the total number of final legal documents in 1813 should have been significantly lower than in 1779. In summary, the inability of socioeconomic factors to explain the decline in will and poder writing supports the argument that this drop stemmed from a changing perception of the will's purpose.

The decline in the number of testators who included no religious or secular clauses in their wills further indicates that the will was losing its sacramental aura over the Bourbon period. These empty wills consisted simply of the preamble, the election of executors and heirs, and the signature of the

1758	1779	1796	1813	Total
6.9% (n = 13)	5.0% (n = 11)	4.5% (n = 9)	1.1% (n = 3)	4.9% (n = 86)
69.8% (n = 132)	67.1% (n = 149)	57.9% (n = 117)	64.4% (n = 174)	62.7% (n = 1080)
2.4	2.2	1.8	2.0	2.2
968	971	2075	2175	1249
300	500	1000	1000	400
4.9	5.9	4.9	5.8	5.8
39.4% (n = 52)	49.0% (n = 73)	34.2% (n = 40)	31.6% (n = 55)	47.3% (n = 511)
28.6% (n = 54)	10.8% (n = 24)	7.4% (n = 15)	7.4% (n = 20)	17.5% (n = 302)

testator. They contain no special requests that truly necessitated the redaction of a will. Standard testamentary law provided guidelines for the distribution of property for those who died intestate, and empty wills did not contravene this law. Why then did some testators feel compelled to write a will when no legal reason existed to do so? They did so for religious reasons: to fulfill the church's precept that all good Christians compose a testament. For these testators, the simple act of writing a will was a pious practice. But the percentage of testators who wrote empty wills declined during the eighteenth century from a high of 8.4 percent of all testators in 1696 to a low of 1.1 percent in 1813 (see Table 11). By the early nineteenth century, the act of will writing had lost much of its religious nature. Although people continued to write wills that contained pious bequests, it was no longer religiously incumbent upon the faithful to draft a will if they had no property of which to dispose.

The Structure of the Will

The structure of the will in eighteenth-century Mexico was almost invariable. It began with a preamble, preceded to the commendation of the soul and disposition of the funeral and burial, moved on to the pious and secular bequests, then ended with the election of executors, heirs, and the signature of the testator and notary.

Preambles were formulaic. Each notary had his own formula, and the preambles he wrote hardly differed from one another. Despite the fact that preambles were always written in the first person as if the testator supplied the phrases used, notaries probably did not write them in the testator's presence. Three wills from three notaries in 1813 indicate that, when first called to record a will, the notary took notes concerning the testator's final wishes. He then left the home, wrote the will based on the notes, and later returned to read the will before the testator and witnesses and obtain the testator's signature. The will of José María Ruíz most clearly demonstrates this procedure. After drafting this will, the notary Manuel Ymaz y Cabanillas returned to the home of the testator to find that he had already died. At the end of the will, he wrote:

> I, the above signed notary, certify and verify that *having taken the notes* [emphasis mine] of the testament a little before twelve [o'clock] on this day and withdrawing to write up [*extender*] this instrument, when I returned to take the signature now at three close to four in the afternoon, I have found that the testator died around one. For this reason, only the witnesses who were present when the testator gave his will [*su otorgamiento*] and before whom I have read it, signed [it].[33]

Another notary, José María Moya, recorded a similar incident. He had come to the home of Francisco Guerra Manzanares to record his will on September 28. The next morning he returned "to read it in his presence and that of the witnesses who were present," but found that Francisco had died during the night.[34] Or consider the case of Nicolás de Vega who reported at the end of the will written for Barbara Castrejón that he and his scribe had recorded the testator's final requests during the afternoon and evening of August 2. When they returned at eleven in the morning on the next day with "the testament already written up [*extendido*]," they found Barbara unconscious and close to death. The will was never formally completed.[35] It is impossible to determine whether or not notaries wrote up wills in the absence of testators before 1813.

Regardless of where or when they drafted wills, notaries left their stamp upon them, most notably in the formulae of the preamble.

The preamble always began by calling on God to sanctify the will that followed. All notaries used the phrase "In the name of God Almighty amen" or a slight variant. This opening statement marked the will as a religious document and its creation a pious act. Ideally, testators had prepared before calling the notary by commending themselves to God and requesting his aid for the pending task. Writing a will with levity or without serious thought given to the final disposition of one's property would offend God, who was called upon to witness the act.

After the invocation, the notary recorded the testator's personal information. This usually included an honorific title,[36] the testator's full name, place of birth and residence, the names of his or her parents, whether or not he or she was a legitimate child, and, about a third of the time, his or her profession. Next came a statement on the testator's health or reason for writing a will. As seen above, most people wrote wills while ill. Most of the ill were so sick that they dictated their wills while confined to bed. Some of the sick, especially those who suffered from chronic illness (*achaques*), just over 6 percent of the testator population, were declared "up and about" (*en pie*). Other reasons for writing a will besides illness included pregnancy, profession in a religious order, and an upcoming journey that posed a risk of death. Few people wrote wills for these reasons: just over 6 percent of all testators gave wills on account of monastic profession, 2 percent for pending travels, and less than 1 percent because of pregnancy. A highly formulaic statement about the testator's mental competence immediately followed the health clause. It usually declared testators to be in possession of their "entire judgment, natural understanding, and complete memory," though the exact formula differed among notaries.

After the health clause came the statement of faith. Most notaries made this relatively simple. Ramón de Espinosa who practiced in 1696 employed a statement that differed little from that used by most notaries:

> believing as I firmly and truly believe the ineffable mystery of the most holy trinity, God the father, God the son, God the holy spirit, three distinct persons and only one divine essence and all the rest that our holy mother catholic roman church holds, believes, and confesses.[37]

A few notaries beginning in 1737 utilized more complex formulae. For instance, in 1779 José Bernardo de Navia wrote the following:

> believing as I really and truly believe and confess the most high mystery of the most holy, most amiable, and most merciful trinity, God the father, God the son, and God the holy spirit, three persons really distinct and only one divine consubstantial essence, in the most loving mystery of the incarnation of the divine word in the most pure and virginal womb [*entrañas*] of Our Lady, the Virgin Mary conceived without any stain of original sin, and likewise believing in all the other mysteries, arcane articles, and sacraments that our holy mother catholic apostolic church of Rome holds, believes, confesses and teaches.[38]

These longer and more complex statements became more common as the century progressed, but never served as the norm.

The next section of the preamble was the election of saints to intercede on behalf of the testator's soul before God. The invocation structure that Andrés Delgado Camargo used in 1779 was typical:

> electing as I elect for my intercessors, patrons, helpers, and advocates the most serene empress of heaven and earth Mary, the most holy mother of God and Our Lady conceived in grace from the first instant of her most pure being, the patriarch señor St. Joseph her most chaste and faithful husband, my holy guardian angel, and the other saints [*santos y santas*] of the celestial court so that they intercede before the divine presence of Our Lord Jesus Christ that he pardon my trespasses [*culpas*] and sins and place my soul on the path to salvation.[39]

This passage reveals typical conceptions of heaven and the afterlife in the eighteenth century. Heaven was a divine court that resembled royal courts in the mundane world. Christ, as part of the trinity, ruled heaven, and, as the second person of God, judged the souls of the deceased. The Virgin was empress and held special influence over her son. The total assembly of saints and angels acted as intercessors to obtain a favorable sentence from Christ the judge for their devotees. A favorable ruling from Christ, though, did not entitle the soul to immediate admission to glory. Rather, it only "placed the soul on the path to salvation." Purgatory stood between judgment and eternal bliss.

The next section of the preamble was a meditation on death. Its basic structure remained unchanged over the entire sample period. Antonio Alejo de Mendoza, a notary who practiced in 1737, used an almost universal formula: "and fearing death which is a natural thing for all living creatures and its hour uncertain."[40] Death is a "natural" occurrence that also naturally causes trepidation among the living. Because death is inevitable, the proper attitude toward it is Christian resignation to God's will. Resignation did not mean unpreparedness. Because the hour was uncertain, the good Christian was to ponder death frequently and continually prepare for judgment.

The last part of the preamble briefly stated why the testator had decided to write a will. This statement varied widely among notaries, and no pattern emerged. It usually included the ideas that the will served as a vehicle for the unburdening of the conscience and the good of the soul. But some notaries simply said that the will was a preventative measure against unspecified future contingencies.

After the preamble, came the commendation of the soul to God. The formulae of the commendation differed little among notaries. In 1696, José Anaya y Bonillo used the following: "I commend my soul to God Our Lord who created and redeemed it with the infinite price of his passion and death."[41] Other notaries used slightly different wording, for instance using the verb "to offer" instead of "to commend" or placed Christ's death in a more positive light by referring to its "infinite merits" rather than Christ's "infinite price." But the main ideas were constant. The commendation always acknowledged God as the creator of the soul and as its redeemer. Most notaries did not distinguish between the persons of the trinity in the commendation, preferring to present God in his unity. A few notaries, however, did make the distinction. José Bernardo de Navia, who practiced in 1779, was one of the most theologically precise. He wrote:

> I commend my soul to God Our Lord who created and redeemed it with the infinite treasure of the most precious blood, passion, and death of his only begotten son, Our Lord, Jesus Christ.[42]

Navia's orthodoxy is evident. He correctly attributed the creation and redemption of souls to God, the father, and the act that redeemed humankind to God, the son. Whatever its level of theological sophistication, the commendation almost always referred to the passion and death as the acts that established the possibility of salvation.

The commendation was the last formulaic section of the will that concerns us. After it came the disposition of the funeral and burial, and the pious and secular clauses. According to Spanish law, testators could freely bequeath up to one-fifth of their total property if they had obligatory heirs: the testator's children, the testator's grandchildren in representation of their deceased parents, or in the absence of both of these, the testator's parents. Those who had no obligatory heirs could dispose of their property without restriction.[43] Testators could distribute the unencumbered portion of their goods among pious causes, siblings, relatives, and friends, or they could add it to the inheritance of their obligatory heirs.

The most common pious causes were requests for masses and gifts to churches, religious orders, saints, the poor, and hospitals. As Table 11 shows, the percentage of testators who commissioned pious directives varied somewhat from year to year, but remained relatively stable over the Bourbon period, with a total of 62.7 percent of all testators issuing at least one. Among these testators, the average number of directives varied from a high of 2.7 in 1717 to a low of 1.8 in 1796. The general trend was downward. The average number of pious bequests hit its two lowest totals in 1796 and 1813. Does this mean that the population of Mexico City began to shun religious activities in their wills by the end of the eighteenth century? This conclusion seems untenable because 64.4 percent of testators issued pious directives in 1813 and because both the average and median values of pious bequests surged beginning in 1796, well outpacing inflation. Testators in the very late eighteenth and early nineteenth centuries issued fewer pious bequests, but they granted much larger gifts than their predecessors.

The subject of secular clauses in the will varied greatly. Testators commonly stated their marital status and named their living (and on occasion deceased) children in one clause. They usually made a perfunctory statement about their financial affairs, indicating that they had enumerated their debts, credits, and the extent of their goods in a separate document or had already informed their executors about these matters. But a large minority used the will itself to detail their financial situation. Testators also left gifts to family and friends, recorded details of legal and family disputes, and made arrangements for the care of children once they died. Table 11 shows that, like pious directives, the average number of secular bequests declined over the Bourbon period.

One reason for the shortening of the will by the late eighteenth century involves the emergence of a new type of clause. At that time testators often asked the notary to notarize blanks sheets of paper attached to the copy left in the testators' possession. They requested these pages so that they could amend their wills in the future without having to call the notary back to their homes. Testators could now enumerate their wishes without having to record them in the original copies kept by the notary. This new practice certainly led some testators to shorten the official copy of their wills to pay smaller notarial fees, which were based in part on the number of written pages contained in the notarized document.

Further indicating the desacralization of the will, the arrangement of pious and secular clauses within the testament changed over the eighteenth century (see Table 11). As mentioned above, the will was reintroduced into the death rites of medieval Europe as a religious document, but by at least the beginning of the early modern period it also contained secular clauses. Even with the inclusion of secular concerns, primacy of place was given to pious clauses. Only after the testator had completed his or her pious dispositions did he or she move on to secular issues.[44] This was still largely the case in Mexico City in 1696. Of those testators who included pious directives, 68 percent began the body of their wills with a religious clause. This percentage decreased over the period under study and, by 1813, a majority of testators who issued pious directives opened the body of the will with a secular clause. Although the faithful still used the will to issue pious directives, secular concerns began to take prominence of place as the will lost its sacramental status.

The closing, or the last section of the will in which the testator named his or her executors and heirs and in which the notary listed the witnesses (but never described their relationship with the testator), also reveals that will writing was losing its sacramental character over the eighteenth century. The election of witnesses to attend the signing of the testament shows a declining concern with sacralizing the event. Spanish law stipulated that five witnesses should attend the notarization of the will, but that if five could not be found, three would suffice. It was the testator's duty to call the necessary witnesses, but the repeated use of a small number of witnesses by each notary indicates that the notary often assumed this responsibility. Only men over the age of fourteen could act as witnesses, and heirs and the recipients of bequests were barred from doing so.[45] Not uncommonly, priests served as witnesses. But over the eighteenth century they did so with less frequency (see Table 11). This trend reflected and shaped the process of the desacralization of testamentary practice. The presence of a priest at the act of notarization marked the event as sacred and reflected the close connection between will writing and other sacred rites of dying that required ecclesiastical intervention. The decline in clerical attendance at the act of will writing demonstrates a growing separation of the will from these other rites and its consequent desacralization.

Conclusion

The practice of writing a will had been a sacred act until the eighteenth century in Mexico City. It formed an integral part of the sacred rites of dying, probably occurring soon after the reception of the combined last rites. During the eighteenth century the practice of will writing began to lose its sacramental character. This does not mean that the will became a completely secular instrument. The will still served as a vehicle for the faithful to commission pious acts. Rather, the very act of writing a will was losing its religious aura, its sacramental nature that conferred divine grace upon the testator. The rise in the number of testators who redacted their wills while healthy and, therefore, outside the sequence of death rites; the overall decline in the frequency of will and poder-para-testar writing; the drop in the number of testators who wrote empty wills with neither pious nor secular clauses; and the fall in the number of wills witnessed by priests all attest to the desacralization of the will. Salvation still required pious acts, but will writing was no longer one of them.

The changing structure of the will itself also suggests that mundane concerns began to challenge the primacy of religious ones in the will. Testators and notaries by the early nineteenth century began to open the body of the will with secular rather than religious clauses. Testators still commissioned pious acts in their wills, and good works and suffrages were still necessary for salvation. But this new arrangement of clauses within the testament indicates that mundane issues, though they certainly had not become the exclusive concern of the will, had gained at least an equal footing with pious ones.

These changes, however, do not indicate that the population of Mexico City had forsaken a fundamentally Christian understanding of life and death. The percentage of testators who made at least one pious bequest in their will remained high and even increased over the century, the average cash value of pious bequests more than doubled from 1696 to 1813, just outpacing the rate of inflation, and the average number of pious bequests per testator hardly changed over the century. Religious gestures were just as important in 1813 as in 1696. In the early nineteenth century, the faithful still knew salvation was the ultimate goal of life and they were willing to spend much of their wealth to achieve it. But they lived in a less sacred world and, even as they pondered their own deaths, they thought more about secular matters than their late seventeenth-century counterparts.

NOTES

INTRODUCTION

1. AN Notary # 637, vol. 4407, n.f., Mexico City, 11 Oct. 1696, will of Joseph Andres Linan notarized by Miguel Leonardo de Sevilla.

2. AN Notary # 210, vol. 1403, fols. 167–70, Mexico City, 5 July 1813, will of Andres Acosta notarized by Juan Mariano Diaz.

3. The bishop of Puebla, Francisco Fabián y Fuero, when speaking of the reasons why Catholics fast during Lent, stated that fasting creates a "consortium, union, and companionship with the mortification and cross of Christ" (consorcio, union y compañia de la mortificacion y Cruz de Christo). Francisco Fabián y Fuero, *Colección de providencias diocesanas del obispado de la Puebla de los Ángeles, hechas y ordenadas por su señoria ilustrísima el señor doctor don Francisco Fabián y Fuero* (Puebla: Real Seminario Palafoxiano, 1770), 216–18.

4. However, when necessary to distinguish between the two, I label gestures performed outside the mass and other sacraments as paraliturgy and those performed within the sacraments as liturgy.

5. The archbishop, a reformer, actually chided Catholics for their affection for splendor. Nonetheless, his explanation of the desired effect of splendor in baroque Catholicism is accurate. Alfonso Núñez de Haro y Peralta, *Sermones escogidos, pláticas epirituales privadas, y dos pastorales anteriormente impresas en México* (Madrid: Hija de Ibarra, 1806), vol. 1, 106–7.

6. John Bossy, *Christianity in the West, 1400–1700* (New York: Oxford University Press, 1985). Of course, this does not mean that ritual events could not express or foment division. Many times they did. But their intended purpose was community formation.

7. Clifford Geertz, "Religion as a Cultural System," in *The Interpretation of Cultures: Selected Essays by Clifford Geertz* (New York: Basic Books, 1973), 87–125.

245

8. Geertz, "Religion as a Cultural System."

9. See for instance, Catherine Bell, *Ritual Theory, Ritual Practice* (New York: Oxford University Press, 1992).

10. Pierre Bourdieu, *Outline of a Theory of Practice*, trans. Richard Nice (New York: Cambridge University Press, 1972).

11. William B. Taylor, *Magistrates of the Sacred: Priests and Parishioners in Eighteenth-Century Mexico* (Stanford: Stanford University Press, 1996), 60.

12. This literature has traced the development of the Mexican church from a largely ad hoc missionary organization staffed by the mendicant orders in the sixteenth century to an established set of institutions by the seventeenth century composed of episcopal and parish structures on the one hand and mendicant provinces on the other. John Frederick Schwaller, *Church and Clergy in Sixteenth-Century Mexico* (Albuquerque: University of New Mexico Press, 1987); Stafford Poole, C.M., *Pedro Moya de Contreras: Catholic Reform and Royal Power in New Spain, 1571–1591* (Berkeley: University of California Press, 1987); Solange Alberro, *Inquisición y sociedad en México, 1571–1700* (México: Fondo de Cultura Económica, 1988); and C. Bayle, S. J., "El concilio de trento en las indias españoles," *Razón y Fe: Revista Mensual Hispanoamericana* 131 (1945): 257–84. The literature has revealed the church's early accumulation of wealth due to pious bequests from the faithful and the economic might many ecclesiastical institutions wielded through the ownership of rural and urban estates and through the extension of loans to landowners and merchants. John Frederick Schwaller, *Origins of Church Wealth in Mexico: Ecclesiastical Revenues and Church Finances, 1523–1600* (Albuquerque: University of New Mexico Press, 1985); Michael P. Costeloe, *Church Wealth in Mexico: A Study of the "Juzgado de Capellanías" in the Archbishopric of Mexico, 1800–1856* (Cambridge: Cambridge University Press, 1967); Gisela von Wobeser, *El crédito eclesiástico en la Nueva España, siglo XVIII* (México: Universidad Nacional Autónoma de México, 1994); Arnold J. Bauer, "The Church in the Economy: Censos and Depósitos in the Eighteenth and Nineteenth Centuries," *Hispanic American Historical Review* 63 (1983): 707–33; Asunción Lavrin, "The Execution of the Law of Consolidación: Spain: Economic Aims and Results;" *Hispanic American Historical Review* 53 (1973): 27–49; Asunción Lavrin, "The Role of Nunneries in the Economy of New Spain in the Eighteenth Century," *Hispanic American Historical Review* 46 (1966): 371–93; Asunción Lavrin, "La riqueza de los conventos de monjas en Nueva España: estructura y evolución durante el siglo XVIII," *Cahiers des Amerique Latines* 8 (1973): 91–122; and Asunción Lavrin, "Problems and Policies in the Administration of Nunneries in Mexico, 1800–1835," *Americas* 28 (1971): 55–77. Last, it has demonstrated the diminishing power of the church vis-à-vis the state during the eighteenth century when the crown undermined ecclesiastical status and privilege in an attempt to centralize authority in an absolutist state bureaucracy. Nancy M. Farriss, *Crown and Clergy in Colonial Mexico, 1759–1821: The Crisis in Ecclesiastical Privilege* (London: University of London, Athlone Press, 1968); David A. Brading, *Church and State in Bourbon Mexico: The Diocese of Michoacán, 1749–1810* (New York: Cambridge University Press, 1994); Taylor, *Magistrates of the Sacred*.

13. This historiography is rich and continues to grow. The following are just a few examples. Robert Ricard, *The Spiritual Conquest of Mexico: An Essay on the Apostolate and the Evangelizing Methods of the Mendicant Orders in New Spain, 1523–1572*, trans. Lesly Byrd Simpson (Berkeley: University of California Press, 1966); Louise M. Burkhart, *The Slippery Earth: Nahua-Christian Moral Dialogue in Sixteenth-Century Mexico* (Tucson: University of Arizona Press, 1989); James Lockhart, *The Nahuas After the Conquest: A Social and Cultural History of the Indians of Central Mexico* (Stanford: Stanford University Press, 1992); Nancy M. Farriss, *Maya Society Under Colonial Rule: The Collective Enterprise of Survival* (Princeton: Princeton University Press, 1984); Inga Clendinnen, *Ambivalent Conquests: Maya and the Spaniards in Yucatan, 1517–1570* (New York: Cambridge University Press, 1987); and Taylor, *Magistrates of the Sacred*. For the Peruvian case, see Sabine MacCormack, *Religion in the Andes: Vision and Imagination in Early Colonial Peru* (Princeton: Princeton University Press, 1991); Kenneth Mills, *Idolatry and Its Enemies: Colonial Andean Religion and Extirpation, 1640–1750* (Princeton: Princeton University Press, 1997).

14. Nora E. Jaffary, *False Mystics: Deviant Orthodoxy in Colonial Mexico* (Lincoln: University of Nebraska Press, 2004); Ellen Gunnarsdóttir, *Mexican Karismata: The Baroque Vocation of Francisca de los Ángeles, 1674–1744* (Lincoln: University of Nebraska Press, 2004).

15. See, for instance, Linda A. Curcio-Nagy, "Giants and Gypsies: Corpus Christi in Colonial Mexico City," in *Rituals of Rule, Rituals of Resistance: Public Celebrations and Popular Culture in Mexico*, ed. William H. Beezley, Cheryl English Martin, and William French (Wilmington: Scholarly Resources, 1994); Linda A. Curcio-Nagy, "Native Icon to City Protectress to Royal Patroness: Ritual, Political Symbolism, and the Virgin of Remedies," *Americas* 52, no. 3 (1996): 367–91; Clara García Ayluardo, "A World of Images: Cult, Ritual, and Society in Colonial Mexico City," in *Rituals of Rule, Rituals of Resistance*. Of course, the Virgin of Guadalupe has received much scholarly attention. Among the best works on Guadalupe during the colonial period are Stafford Poole, *Our Lady of Guadalupe: The Origins and Sources of a Mexican National Symbol, 1531–1797* (Tucson: University of Arizona Press, 1995); David A. Brading, *Mexican Phoenix: Our Lady of Guadalupe: Image and Tradition Across Five Centuries* (New York: Cambridge University Press, 2001); and Taylor, *Magistrates of the Sacred*, especially chap. 11.

16. For a notable exception, see Osvaldo F. Pardo, *The Origins of Mexican Catholicism: Nahua Rituals and Christian Sacraments in Sixteenth-Century Mexico* (Ann Arbor: University of Michigan Press, 2004). Pardo examines the changes within Catholic ritual itself in early postconquest Mexico.

17. David Brading was the first historian to examine religious reform. As part of a larger study of church-state relations in Bourbon Mexico, he investigated the program advocated by what he terms "Jansenist" bishops and lay thinkers. He argues that these elites criticized the "excesses" of baroque Catholicism, which, in their minds, opened religion to ridicule. In place of dramatic and lavish baroque practices, Brading states that reformers promoted a subdued, interior religious life based on individual contemplation of God and charitable works. Given Brading's larger concerns, his treatment of religious reform is necessarily brief and he does

not examine how the ideas of a handful of elite thinkers played out in the lives of Catholics at large. Brading, *Church and State.*

18. Pamela Voekel, *Alone Before God: The Religious Origins of Modernity in Mexico* (Durham: Duke University Press, 2002).

19. Bureaucratization and racial categorization are also hallmarks of modernity. For intriguing studies of these aspects of modernity in the Latin American context, see Irene Silverblatt, *Modern Inquisitions: Peru and the Colonial Origins of the Civilized World* (Durham: Duke University Press, 2004); and Jorge Cañizares-Esguerra, *Nature, Empire, and Nation: Explorations of the History of Science in the Iberian World* (Stanford: Stanford University Press, 2006), especially chap. 4.

20. Movements to curtail the power of the church and the influence of religion by nineteenth-century liberals and twentieth-century revolutionaries in Mexico stemmed from this belief. See, for instance, Marjorie Becker, *Setting the Virgin on Fire: Lázaro Cárdenas, Michoacán Peasants, and the Redemption of the Mexican Revolution* (Berkeley: University of California Press, 1995); and Adrian A. Bantjes, "Burning Saints, Molding Minds: Iconoclasm, Civic Ritual, and the Failed Cultural Revolution," in *Rituals of Rule.*

21. Dale K.Van Kley, *The Religious Origins of the French Revolution: From Calvin to the Civil Constitution, 1560–1791* (New Haven: Yale University Press, 1996).

22. Max Weber, *The Protestant Ethic and the Spirit of Capitalism*, trans. Talcott Parsons (New York: Routledge, 1930).

23. Rodney Stark, *The Victory of Reason: How Christianity Led to Freedom, Capitalism, and Western Success* (New York: Random House, 2005). Stark argues that other conditions, such as freedom from tyrannical states, were necessary for the rise of capitalism. Nonetheless, the centrality of reason to Christianity remains Stark's essential condition for economic rationality.

24. The connection between religion and embodiment has been treated. See Philip A. Mellor and Chris Schilling, *Re-forming the Body: Religion, Community and Modernity* (London: Sage Publications, 1997). But this work does not discuss religion's role in disciplining the body.

25. Michel Foucault, *Discipline & Punish: The Birth of the Prison*, trans. Alan Sheridan (New York: Vintage Books, 1979).

26. See the appendix "Note on Sources" for a fuller discussion of the shifting balance between secular and sacred in the will in Bourbon Mexico City.

27. Studies that rely on wills are numerous. Michel Vovelle pioneered the use of wills for the study of piety. He examined the process of secularization in Provence largely by counting the incidence of mass requests and the average number of masses requested in southern France in the eighteenth century. Michel Vovelle, *Piété baroque et déchristianisation en Provence au XVIIIe siecle: Les attitudes devant la mort d'apres les clauses des testatments* (Paris: Plon, 1973). Many historians have employed Vovelle's methodology to examine secularization in other areas of Europe. They, along with Vovelle, also quantify aspects of funerary rites that appear in wills, but the heart of their analyses centers on mass requests. For the use of this methodology in Spain, see María José de la Pascua, *Vivir la muerte en el Cádiz del setecientos, 1675–1801* (Cádiz: Fundación Municipal de Cultura del

Ayuntamiento de Cádiz, 1990); Julio Antonio Vaquero Iglesias, *Muerte e ideología en las Asturias del siglo XIX* (Madrid: Siglo Veintiuno de España Editores, S.A., 1991); Pere Saborit Badenes, *Morir en el Alto Palencia: la religiosidad popular a través de los testamentos, siglos XVI–XVIII* (Segorbe: Ayuntamiento de Segorbe, 1991); Roberto J. López, *Oviedo: muerte y religiosidad en el siglo XVIII: un estudio de mentalidades colectivas* (Oviedo: Consejería de Educación, Cultura y Deportes, 1985); Roberto J. López, *Comportamientos religiosos en Asturias durante el antiguo régimen* (Gijón: Silverio Cañada, 1989); and Antonio Peñafiel Ramón, *Testamento y buena muerte: un estudio de mentalidades en la Murcia del siglo XVIII* (Murcia: Academia Alfonso X el Sabio, 1987). Susan Nicasio also analyzed the average number of masses requested per testator in her study of secularization in eighteenth-century Italy. Unlike Vovelle, De la Pascua, and Vaquero Iglesias, she found no diminution in masses. Susan Nicasio, " . . . For the Benefit of My Soul: A Preliminary Study of the Persistence of Tradition in Eighteenth-Century Mass Obligations," *Catholic Historical Review* 78 (1992): 175–96. Other historians have quantified other types of pious bequests. Philip Hoffman, the first historian to use the will to study the local processes of the Catholic Reformation, employed a count of the percentage of testators who commissioned at least one pious directive in their wills and the average value of pious bequests to gauge enthusiasm for reform in seventeenth- and eighteenth-century Lyon (France). Philip Hoffman, *Church and Community in the Diocese of Lyon, 1500–1789* (New Haven: Yale University Press, 1984). Sara Nalle, studying the religious culture in Cuenca (Spain) during the era of the Catholic Reformation, analyzed petitions for masses in much the same fashion as Vovelle and his followers. Sara Nalle, *God in la Mancha: Religious Reform and the People of Cuenca, 1500–1650* (Baltimore: Johns Hopkins University Press, 1992). Kathryn Norberg, in a study of the changing nature of charity in Grenoble (France) during the Catholic Reformation, counted the percentage of testators who bequeathed charitable gifts to examine the impact Catholic Reformation discourse had on almsgiving. Kathryn Norberg, *Rich and Poor in Grenoble, 1600–1814* (Berkeley: University of California Press, 1985). In her study of cemetery reform and piety in Mexico, Pamela Voekel quantified a limited number of pious indicators as well. Voekel, *Alone Before God*. Not all historians, however, have counted pious directives. Some have examined changes in the formulae of will preambles. The most well-known example is Pierre Chaunu, *La mort a Paris XVIe, XVIIe et XVIIIe siecles* (Paris: Fayard, 1978); for an English summary and critique of his work, see Ann W. Ramsey, "Piety in Paris during the League, 1585–1590: An Urban Community in Transition" (Ph.D. diss., Columbia University, 1991), 66–94. For another example of discourse-based will analysis, see Lorraine C. Attreed, "Preparation for Death in Sixteenth-Century Northern England," *Sixteenth Century Journal* 13 (1982): 37–66. These scholars have come under attack for not taking into account the formulaic nature of will preambles. For examples of this criticism, see Eamon Duffy, *The Stripping of the Altars: Traditional Religion in England, 1400–1580* (New Haven: Yale University Press, 1992), 504–23; and J. D. Alsop, "Religious Preambles in Early Modern English Wills as Formulae," *Journal of Ecclesiastical History* 40 (1989): 19–27. Although much testamentary discourse, including the vast majority of the preamble, is formulaic, this criticism misses the mark. The stock language notaries used in will preambles reflects religious concerns and understandings at a particular time. Tracing shifts in the use of these linguistic structures sheds light upon broad-based changes in beliefs and conceptions of the divine over time. Despite the utility of studying formulaic discourse in the will, I have chosen to examine pious directives issued by testators in the body of the document. I have done so for two reasons. First, I wanted to examine the religious habits of individual testators, not simply changes in general patterns of belief. Second, pious directives afford a greater breadth of data than the language of preambles.

28. Carlos Eire is one of the few historians who have discussed number symbolism in mass requests. Carolos Eire, *From Madrid to Purgatory: The Art and Craft of Dying in Sixteenth-Century Spain* (New York: Cambridge University Press, 1995). Another historian who has employed a subtle methodology in the study of wills is Ann W. Ramsey, *Liturgy, Politics, and Salvation: The Catholic League in Paris and the Nature of Catholic Reform, 1540–1630* (Rochester, NY: University of Rochester Press, 1999).

29. I, however, did not read illegible wills or those written far outside Mexico City. Furthermore, I include only one will in the sample from the small number of testators who redacted multiple wills. In most cases, testators who wrote multiple wills did not change pious bequests from one version to the next. Rather, secular concerns like the naming of different executors usually necessitated the writing of a new will.

30. For information on the virulence of these epidemics, see Juan Javier Pescador, *De bautizados a fieles difuntos: familia y mentalidad en una parroquia urbana: Santa Catarina de México, 1568–1820* (México: El Colegio de México, 1992), 94–106.

31. AN Notary # 13, vol. 55, fols. 434–38, Mexico City, 10 Aug. 1696, will of Cristobal Leonel Urtado de Mendoza y Castilla notarized by Jose Anaya y Bonillo; AN Notary # 13, vol. 55, fols. 494–98, Mexico City, 12 Sept. 1696, joint will of Cristobal Leonel Hurtado de Mendoza y Castilla and Maria de Moya y Contreras notarized by Jose Anaya y Bonillo.

32. AN Notary # 122, vol. 793, fols. 485–88, Mexico City, 1 Dec. 1696, will of Antonio Marcos de Mendieta notarized by Juan de Condarco y Caceres; AN Notary # 122, vol. 793, fols. 494–98, Mexico City, 5 Dec. 1696, will of Antonia de Mendieta notarized by Juan de Condarco y Caceres; and AN Notary # 122, vol. 793, fols. 498–502, Mexico City, 6 Dec. 1696, will of Phelipe de Rivas Angulo notarized by Juan de Condarco y Caceres.

33. AN Notary # 73, vol. 512, fols. 210–11, Mexico City, 3 Aug. 1737, will of Juan Moredo notarized by Juan Francisco Benitez Trigueros; AN Notary # 73, vol. 512, fols. 211–12, Mexico City, 3 Aug. 1737, will of Joseph Comelles notarized by Francisco Benitez Trigueros.

34. AN Notary # 206, vol. 1373, fols. 733–37, Mexico City, 10 Dec. 1779, will of Francisco Palacio Castillo notarized by Andres Delgado Camargo; AN Notary # 206, vol. 1373, fols. 776–78, Mexico City, 31 Dec. 1779, will of Manuel de Bolea notarized by Andres Delgado Camargo.

35. There is one study of notaries in Mexico City, but it is at best perfunctory. Bernardo Pérez Fernández del Castillo, *Historia de la escribanía en la Nueva España y del notariado en México* (México: Editorial Porrúa, 1988).

36. Priests were 10 percent of all testators; artisans, 6 percent; bureaucrats, 5 percent; soldiers, 2 percent; professionals, 7 percent; and rural landowners, 5 percent.

CHAPTER 1

1. These figures come from Enrique Florescano, *Precios del maíz y crisis agrícolas en México, 1708–1810*, rev. ed. (México: Colegio de México, 1986), 95; and John E. Kicza, *Colonial Entrepreneurs: Families and Business in Bourbon Mexico City* (Albuquerque: University of New Mexico Press, 1983), 2–3. These figures are debated however. Herbert S. Klein estimates the population of Mexico City in 1790 at 105,000 and in 1811 at 113,000. Herbert S. Klein, "The Demographic Structure of Mexico City in 1811," *Journal of Urban History* 23 (1996): 67. For the impact of disease, see Donald B. Cooper, *Epidemic Disease in Mexico City, 1761–1813: An Administrative, Social, and Medical Study* (Austin: University of Texas Press, 1965), 67–68, 180–81. According to Juan Javier Pescador, who has studied the epidemics that afflicted Mexico City during the seventeenth and eighteenth centuries, the frequency and intensity of epidemic disease increased during the second half of the eighteenth century. He states that the nine plagues that struck Mexico City from 1670 to 1770 were relatively mild with the exception of the measles epidemic of 1692–93 and the typhus epidemics of 1696–97, 1737, and 1761–62. In contrast, the five epidemics that ravaged Mexico City from 1770 to 1820 were more severe in terms of proportional mortality rates, the smallpox outbreak of 1779 ranking as the most devastating. Juan Javier Pescador, *De bautizados a fieles difuntos: Familia y mentalidad en una parroquia urbana: Santa Catarina de México, 1568–1820* (México: Colegio de México, 1992), 90–106.

2. Klein, "Demographic Structure," 68.

3. For merchants in Mexico City, see Kicza, *Colonial Entrepreneurs*, especially 13–31, 45–55, 77–81, 101–33; for miners and agriculturists in Mexico City, see David A. Brading, *Miners and Merchants in Bourbon Mexico, 1763–1810* (New York: Cambridge University Press, 1971), 215. Many of the financial elite often participated in trade and owned mines and/or haciendas at the same time or belonged to families that engaged in diverse economic activities. Therefore, sharply delineating miners, merchants, and hacienda owners is often times inaccurate.

4. John Kicza estimates that in the late eighteenth century four hundred families that each managed assets over 100,000 pesos resided in Mexico City. Kicza, *Colonial Entrepreneurs*, 17.

5. In contrast to these 517 secular priests resident in Mexico City who did *not* hold parish positions, only fifty-nine priests held a parish office, either as a pastor or assistant. Alexander von Humboldt, *Ensayo político sobre el reino de la Nueva España* (México: Porrua, S.A., 1966), 129. William Taylor states that few parish priests held *capellanías*, or endowed foundations for the celebration of masses for the dead. Most of these were held by secular priests who did not hold a parish

benefice. William Taylor, *Magistrates of the Sacred: Priests and Parishioners in Eighteenth-Century Mexico* (Stanford: Stanford University Press, 1996), 78, 126–27, 146–48.

6. In a report to Rome written in 1767, Archbishop Manuel Rubio y Salinas reported that Mexico City possessed twenty-three male and fifteen female religious houses. These numbers would change by the end of the eighteenth century because of the expulsion of the Jesuits. Mariano Cuevas, *Historia de la iglesia en México* (México: Ediciones Cervantes, 1942), vol. 4, 96.

7. Humboldt, *Ensayo político*, 129.

8. Archbishop Manual Rubio y Salinas included this figure in his report to the papacy in 1767. It is not clear how he counted churches. This number must include the churches of parishes, monastic houses, hospitals, and colegios. It does not include collateral chapels of church buildings. Cuevas, *Historia de la iglesia*, vol. 4, 96.

9. Michael Scardaville estimates that one-third of the population of Mexico City in 1790 was unemployed and forced to beg. Michael Scardaville, "Crime and the Urban Poor: Mexico City in the Late Colonial Period" (Ph.D. diss., University of Florida, 1977), 48. For a vivid description of the hardships faced by the poor of eighteenth-century Mexico City, see Gabriel Haslip-Viera, *Crime and Punishment in Late Colonial Mexico City, 1692–1810* (Albuquerque: University of New Mexico Press, 1999), 25–35.

10. The population of the entire colony of New Spain doubled during the last half of the eighteenth century and increased demand on the maize and wheat supply. Prices for these basic commodities almost doubled, but the nominal wages of laborers remained virtually unchanged during this same period. Michael Scardaville, "(Hapsburg) Law and (Bourbon) Order: State Authority, Popular Unrest, and the Criminal Justice System in Bourbon Mexico City," *Americas* 50 (1994), 508; Timothy E. Anna, *The Fall of the Royal Government in Mexico City* (Lincoln: University of Nebraska Press, 1978), 141–48; Susan Deans-Smith, *Bureaucrats, Planters, and Workers: The Making of the Tobacco Monopoly in Bourbon Mexico* (Austin: University of Texas Press, 1992), 191–96.

CHAPTER 2

1. AN Notary # 707, vol. 4765, n.f., Mexico City, 9 Oct. 1779, will of María Manuela de Jesus Cadena Galindo notarized by Francisco Juan de Velasco.

2. In his study of saints in late antiquity Peter Brown argues that Christians reworked Roman cosmology, which had posited a sharp, unbridgeable distinction between the earthly, mundane world and the realm of divine order located beyond the moon. Upon death, the spirit entered the divine realm, whereas the corpse decayed on earth. The Christian martyrs—martyrdom being the only path to sainthood at the time—breached this chasm. Though their souls resided with God in heaven, they maintained links to their physical remains on earth. The corpses of saints became conduits for the manifestation of divine power within the world. Peter Brown, *The Cult of Saints: Its Rise and Function in Latin Christianity* (Chicago: University of Chicago Press, 1981).

3. On the early history of images, see Hans Belting, *Likeness and Presence: A History of the Image before the Era of Art*, trans. Edmund Jephcott (Chicago: University of Chicago Press, 1994); D. A. Brading, *Mexican Phoenix: Our Lady of Guadalupe: Image and Tradition across Five Centuries* (Cambridge: Cambridge University Press, 2001), 14–17.

4. Brading, *Mexican Phoenix*, 18–20.

5. For a description of devotions to relics and images, see Benedicta Ward, *Miracles and the Medieval Mind: Theory, Record and Event, 1000–1215* (Philadelphia: University of Pennsylvania Press, 1982); William Christian, *Local Religion in Sixteenth-Century Spain* (Princeton: Princeton University Press, 1981); and Donald Weinstein and Rudolph Bell, *Saints & Society: The Two Worlds of Western Christendom, 1000–1700* (Chicago: University of Chicago Press, 1982).

6. Lee Palmer Wandel, *The Eucharist in the Reformation: Incarnation and Liturgy* (New York: Cambridge University Press, 2006), 20–21.

7. Miri Rubin, *Corpus Christi: The Eucharist in Late Medieval Culture* (Cambridge: Cambridge University Press, 1991); and Charles Zika, "Hosts, Processions and Pilgrimages: Controlling the Sacred in Fifteenth-Century Germany," *Past & Present* 118 (1988): 25–64.

8. Ward, *Miracles*; and Bob Scribner, "Cosmic Order and Daily Life: Sacred and Secular in Pre-Industrial German Society," in *Religion and Society in Early Modern Europe, 1500–1800*, ed. Kaspar von Greyerz (Boston: George Allen & Unwin, 1984).

9. Early reformers, such as John Hus and John Wyclif, questioned the use of images and relics and the doctrine of the eucharist. But their critiques were not systematic. Erasmus of Rotterdam ridiculed Christians who relied on relics and images for protection rather than placing their faith in Christ. But he never publicly questioned the corporeal presence of Christ in the eucharist and, in the end when the Church censored his work, he equivocated. He denied that he condemned the cult of saints and declared that he had simply criticized excesses and abuses surrounding it. Martin Luther's stance on these matters was inconsistent. He delegitimized the religious value of images and relics, but refused to have them removed from churches. He was indecisive concerning the eucharist. He never unequivocally repudiated the doctrine of transubstantiation—the idea that the substance of Christ's body and blood replaced those of the bread and wine at consecration. He preferred the notion of consubstantiation—that the essence of Christ's body and blood commingles with those of the bread and wine after consecration—because it required fewer miracles. But he refused to make a final decision on the matter, stating that it was a mystery beyond human comprehension.

10. For the history of early modern critiques of God's bodily presence in the world, see Carlos M. N. Eire, *War Against the Idols: The Reformation of Worship from Erasmus to Calvin* (New York: Cambridge University Press, 1986). For images during the Reformation, see Belting, *Likeness and Presence*, 458–70. For a discussion of the eucharist during the Reformation, see Bernard M. G. Reardon, *Religious Thought in the Reformation*, 2nd ed. (New York: Longman, 1995), 32, 72–73, 189–90.

11. Ann Woodson Ramsey, *Liturgy, Politics, and Salvation: The Catholic League in Paris and the Nature of Catholic Reform, 1540–1630* (Rochester: University of Rochester Press, 1999).

12. H. J. Schroeder, O. P., *Canons and Decrees of the Council of Trent* (Rockford, IL: Tan Books and Publishers, Inc., 1978), 73.

13. Schroeder, *Canons*, 151.

14. Ibid., 214–17.

15. Ann W. Ramsey, "Piety in Paris during the League, 1585–1590: An Urban Community in Transition" (Ph.D. diss., Columbia University, 1991), 224–25; and Owen Chadwick, *The Popes and the European Revolution* (Oxford: Clarendon Press, 1981), 59–60.

16. Philip M. Soergel, *Wondrous in His Saints: Counter-Reformation Propaganda in Bavaria* (Berkeley: University of California Press, 1993), 230–32.

17. Christian, *Local Religion*, 181–83.

18. For a history of the Third Mexican Provincial Council, see Stafford Poole, C.M., *Pedro Moya de Contreras: Catholic Reform and Royal Power in New Spain, 1571–1591* (Berkeley: University of California Press, 1987). Poole does not address the history of devotions. He is more concerned with the institutional aspects of Catholic reform and the expansion of royal authority over the church.

19. *Concilio III Provincial Mexicano, celebrado en México el año 1585* . . . (Barcelona: Manuel Miró y D. Marsa, 1870), 327.

20. Ibid., 185, 327–32.

21. Ibid., 332.

22. This hypothesis is corroborated by a statement concerning the dressing of images made in the decrees of the Fourth Mexican Provincial Council. This later council mandated that all items "once placed on the holy images could not be applied to profane uses." *Concilio IV provincial mexicano celebrado año de 1771* (Querétaro: Escuela de Artes, 1898), 167.

23. *Concilio III*, 331.

24. For a brief introduction to devotions to miraculous relics and images in Mexico, see Antonio Rubial García, "Tierra de prodigios: lo maravilloso cristiano en la Nueva España de los siglos XVI y XVII," in *La iglesia católica en México,* ed. Nelly Sigaut (Zamora: El Colegio de Michoacán, 1997); Antonio Rubial García, "Icons of Devotion: The Appropriation and Use of Saints in New Spain," in *Local Religion in Colonial Mexico,* ed. Martin Austin Nesvig (Albuquerque: University of New Mexico Press, 2006).

25. For a history of Corpus in Mexico City, see Linda A. Curcio-Nagy, "Giants and Gypsies: Corpus Christi in Colonial Mexico City," in *Rituals of Rule, Rituals of Resistance: Public Celebrations and Popular Culture in Mexico,* ed. William H. Beezley, Cheryl English Martin, and William French (Wilmington, DE: Scholarly Resources, 1994), especially pages 4–14 for a description of the celebrations in the sixteenth and seventeenth centuries; for Corpus in the northern provincial city of San Luis Potosí, see Alfonso Martínez Rosales, "Los gigantes de San Luis Potosí," *Historia Mexicana* 37, no. 4 (1988): 585–612; for Corpus in the Andes and it meanings for the indigenous population, see Carolyn Dean, *Inka Bodies and the*

Body of Christ: Corpus Christi in Colonia Cuzco, Peru (Durham: Duke University Press, 1999).

26. Clara García Ayluardo, "A World of Images: Cult, Ritual, and Society in Colonial Mexico City," in *Rituals of Rule, Rituals of Resistance*; Rosalva Loreto López, "La fiesta de la Concepción y las identidades colectivas, Puebla (1619–1636)," in *Manifestaciones religiosas en el mundo colonial Americano*, vol. 2, *Mujeres, instituciones y culto de María*, ed. Clara García Ayluardo and Manuel Ramos Medina (México: INAH, Condumex, UIA, 1993); Linda A. Curcio-Nagy, "Native Icon to City Protectress to Royal patrones: Ritual, Political Symbolism, and the Virgin of Remedies," *Americas* 52 (1996): 367–91.

27. Fracisco de Florencia and Juan Antonio Oviedo, *Zodiaco mariano en que el sol de justicia Christo con la salud en las alas visita como Signos, y Casas proprias para beneficio de los hombres los templos y lugares dedicados a los cultos de su SS. Madre . . .* (México: Antiguo Colegio de San Ildefonso, 1755). For an analysis of the *Zodiaco Mariano*, see Thomas Calvo, "El zodiaco de la nueva Eva: el culto mariano en la América Septentrional hacia 1700," in *Manifestaciones religiosas*, vol. 2.

28. Juan de Abreu, *Desagravios dolorosos de Maria por los agravios ignominiosos de Christo . . .* (México: Los Herederos de Miguel de Rivera, 1726), 25.

29. Manuel Eduardo Perez Bonilla, *Practicas devotas en honor del sacratisimo corazon de nuestro señor Jesucristo . . .* (México: Mariano Joseph de Zúñiga y Ontiveros, 1805), 44–45.

30. Perez Bonilla, *Practicas devotas en honor del sacratisimo corazon*, 151.

31. Wax, candles, candle holders, lamps, and oil—or monetary donations to purchase them—accounted for sixty-five of the 213 gifts given to the host and images.

32. The other eight were either liturgical items used in the mass or monetary gifts for the adornment of the host. The wording of these clauses indicated that the gift was made to the eucharist and not the church or chapel where the mass was performed.

33. AN Notary # 218, vol. 1419, fols. 34–36, Mexico City, 5 Feb. 1696, will of Maria de Cobarrubias notarized by Ramon Espinosa. Santa María la Redonda became the seat of a parish in the parish reform of 1772.

34. AN Notary # 563, vol. 3893, n.f., Mexico City, 6 Dec. 1696, will of Juan Mudarra notarized by Martin del Rio.

35. AN Notary # 588, vol. 4013, fols. 4–19, Mexico City, 19 Jan. 1737, will of Catarina Paez de la Cadena notarized by Francisco de Rivera Butron.

36. Herbert Thurston, "Candles," in *Catholic Encyclopedia* (New York: Encyclopedia Press, 1913). Of course, the Paschal candle, the large beeswax candle lighted at the Easter Vigil in representation of Christ's resurrection, most clearly demonstrates this function. It burned during liturgical services from Easter Sunday to the feast of the Ascension, recalling the presence of the glorified Christ in the world.

37. Theodor Klauser, *A Short History of the Western Liturgy: An Account and Some Reflections*, 2nd ed., trans. by John Halliburton (New York: Oxford University Press, 1979), 100–101.

38. For regulations on lights before the tabernacle, see Miguel Venegas, S. J., *Manual de párrocos para administrar los santos sacramentos* . . . (México: Joseph Bernardo de Hogal, 1731), 53.

39. John Harper, *The Forms and Orders of the Western Liturgy: From the Tenth to the Eighteenth Century: A Historical Introduction and Guide for Students and Musicians* (Oxford: Clarendon Press, 1991), 146–52. In processions of the viaticum that returned to the church after visiting the home of the dying, all lights were extinguished if the priest had distributed all the consecrated hosts he had brought with him. Venegas, *Manual de párrocos*, 65.

40. Note the numeric symbolism of seven masses to the Virgin of (seven) Sorrows. See Chapter 3 of this book on the importance of numeric symbolism in pious directives. AN Notary # 210, vol. 1403, fols. 18–22, Mexico City, 12 Jan. 1813, will of Mariana Josefa Salazar notarized by Juan Mariano Diaz.

41. For other contemporary religious uses of the term holocaust, see Stephanie L. Kirk, *Convent Life in Colonial Mexico: A Tale of Two Communities* (Gainesville: University Press of Florida, 2007), 23–24, 41.

42. AN Notary # 645, vol. 4440, fols. 1–5, Mexico City, 8 April 1758, will of Juan Angel de Puras notarized by Juan Antonio de la Serna.

43. AN Notary # 391, vol. 2593, fols. 115–18, Mexico City, 4 March 1737, will of Nicolas Cayetano Abrego notarized by Felipe Muñoz de Castro.

44. AN Notary # 408, vol. 2684, n.f., Mexico City, 20 Nov. 1779, will of Maria Manuela Villavicencio notarized by Nicolas de Meraz y Velasco.

45. AN Notary # 680, vol. 4571, fols. 112–17, Mexico City, 1 Oct. 1717, will of Antonio de Ruilova y Villegas notarized by Juan Bautista de Ulibarri.

46. Ward, *Miracles*, 35, 73, 80, 85, 116.

47. Testators sampled for this study gave fourteen gifts of clothing to images.

48. AN Notary # 356, vol. 2319, n.f., Mexico City, 17 July 1779, will of Rosalia de Aguirre notarized by Pedro Jose Lopez de Rivera.

49. AN Notary # 383, vol. 2546, fols. 222–25, Mexico City, 10 Dec. 1696, will of Xpttoval Martines de Sepeda notarized by Diego de Marchena.

50. Marina Warner, *Alone of All Her Sex: The Myth and Cult of the Virgin Mary* (New York: Alfred A. Knopf, 1976), 326–29.

51. AN Notary # 270, vol. 1729, fols. 1–3, Mexico City, 6 Jan. 1758, will of Manuel Paulin notarized by Jose Gomez.

52. Testators sampled for this study gave twenty-four gifts of jewelry.

53. AN Notary # 122, vol. 793, fols. 280–84, Mexico City, 2 Sept. 1696, will of Maria Mariana de la Encarnacion y Lorenzana notarized by Juan de Condarco y Caceres.

54. AN Notary # 155, vol. 924, fols. 301–304, Mexico City, 2 July 1813, will of Juana Maria de Quintanar notarized by Francisco Calapiz y Aguilar.

55. See appendix "Note on Sources."

56. Testators sampled for this study gave forty-six cash gifts to adorn the host and images.

57. AN Notary # 383, vol. 2546, fols. 213–16, Mexico City, 26 Nov. 1696, will of Juan Augustin de Esquibel y Maldonado notarized by Diego de Marchena.

58. AN Notary # 574, vol. 3945, n.f., Mexico City, 23 Dec. 1758, will of Pedro Rodriguez notarized by Manuel Antonio Rodriguez.

59. Testators sampled for this study gave twenty-eight monetary gifts with no stipulation about their use.

60. AN Notary # 395, vol. 2628, fols. 226–33, Mexico City, 26 Nov. 1717, will of Francisco de Algarra y Sanchez notarized by Jose Valerio de Morales.

61. Fifty-three percent of testators sampled for this study, or 942 of them, left the choice of burial site to their executors. The remainder chose from a wide variety of churches. The most popular choices were the monastery of San Francisco with 138 testators, the monastery of Nuestra Señora de la Merced with fifty-five, the Cathedral of Mexico City with forty-four, and the monastery of Santo Domingo with forty-two. Other churches drew far fewer testators.

62. Seventy-nine testators, or 4.5 percent of all testators, requested such a burial.

63. AN Notary # 453, vol. 3109, fols. 44–46, Mexico City, 22 Oct. 1696, will of Mariana Nuñez de Rojas notarized by Juan Francisco Neri.

64. AN Notary # 665, vol. 4506, fols. 41–42, Mexico City, 6 Nov. 1717, will of Antonia de Sosa Altamirano notarized by Jose de Trujillo; and AN Notary # 80, vol. 524, n.f., Mexico City, 8 April 1758, will of Francisco Martinez notarized by Jose Antonio Bravo.

65. AN Notary # 252, vol. 1648, fols. 137–39, Mexico City, 19 June 1696, will of Diego de Arellano notarized by Francisco Gonzalez de Peñafiel.

66. AN Notary # 321, vol. 2166, fols. 23–25, Mexico City, 20 Feb. 1796, will of Maria Catarina Celis notarized by Tomas Hidalgo.

67. AN Notary # 669, vol. 4518, fols. 131–35, Mexico City, 16 June 1758, will of Joseph de Zeballos Quebedo notarized by Antonio de la Torre.

CHAPTER 3

1. AN Notary # 122, vol. 793, fols. 49–59, Mexico City, 16 February 1696, will of Ines Velarde notarized by Juan de Condarco y Caceres.

2. In speaking of the rationale for fasting, the Bishop of Puebla, Francisco Fabián y Fuero, remarked that through abstinence Christians formed a "union and company with the mortification and cross of Christ." Francisco Fabián y Fuero, *Colección de providencias diocesanas del obispado de la Puebla de Los Ángeles, hecas y ordenadas* (Puebla: Real Seminario Palafoxiano, 1770), 216–18. Devotional treatises also spoke of unions. One devoted to the Virgin included a prayer to Mary in which the reader was to petition: "present to your divine son my pain, uniting it with yours, to achieve pardon and grace for me." Fernando Martagon, *Exercisios espirituales para desagraviar a Maria Santísima nuestra Señora de los Dolores* (México: Marian Joseph de Zúñiga y Ontiveros, 1807), 93. This type of union forged through symbolic performances should not be confused with the unions experienced by mystics, who through rigorous regimes of withdrawal from the world, self-mortification, and meditation, dissolved their egos, perceived visions, and intensely felt God's presence. For a history of mysticism in the Americas see, Nora E. Jaffary, *False Mystics: Deviant Orthodoxy in Colonial Mexico*

(Lincoln: University of Nebraska Press, 2004); and Nancy E. Van Deusen, *Between the Sacred and the Worldly: The Institutional and Cultural Practice of Recogimiento in Colonial Lima* (Stanford: Stanford University Press, 2001), 17–20, 24–26, 115–19, 127–30.

3. The Catholic church endorsed seven sacraments, the formal ecclesiastical rites that confer sacred grace on recipients. They are baptism, the eucharist, confession, confirmation, marriage, holy orders, and extreme unction.

4. Michael Brescia argues in an insightful article that historians of Mexico, focusing more on infrequent but spectacular religious events like Corpus Christi processions, have largely ignored the faithful's most basic and common religious activity, the mass. Michael Brescia, "Liturgical Expressions of Episcopal Power: Juan de Palafox y Mendoza and the Tridentine Reform in Colonial Mexico," *Catholic Historical Review* 90 (2004): 497–501.

5. Catholics were required to attend mass on all fifty-two Sundays of the year and at least on forty-four feast days, though some of these feast days must have fallen on Sundays. *Concilio III Provincial Mexicano, celebrado en México el año 1585 . . .* (Barcelona: Manuel Miró y D. Marsa, 1870), 147–53. Of course, not everyone fulfilled their obligation. Nonetheless, many certainly did. Moreover, most people probably attended other masses on additional days.

6. Lee Palmer Wandel, *The Eucharist in the Reformation: Incarnation and Liturgy* (New York: Cambridge University Press, 2006), 20–29; Ann W. Ramsey, *Liturgy, Politics, and Salvation: The Catholic League in Paris and the Nature of Catholic Reform, 1540–1630* (Rochester: University of Rochester Press, 1999), 48–54.

7. For a liturgists' argument in favor of expanding the definition of liturgy to include lay organized and led ritual actions outside the bounds of the sacraments, see C. Clifford Flanigan, Kathleen Ashley, and Pamela Sheingorn, "Liturgy as Social Performance: Expanding the Definitions" in *The Liturgy of the Medieval Church*, ed. Thomas J. Heffernan and E. Ann Matter (Kalamazoo: Western Michigan University, 2001).

8. On the question of images and the eucharist as loci of the real presence of divinity, see William A. Christian, *Local Religion in Sixteenth-Century Spain* (Princeton: Princeton University Press, 1981), 23–69; and Miri Rubin, *Corpus Christi: The Eucharist in Late Medieval Culture* (New York: Cambridge University Press, 1991), 12–77.

9. Other concerns, such as a desire for sociability and/or the wish to display social status, as well as the need to attain grace, certainly influenced Catholics to perform religious activities.

10. Wandel, *The Eucharist in the Reformation*, 20–22.

11. H. J. Schroeder, O. P., *Canons and Decrees of the Council of Trent* (Rockford, IL: Tan Books and Publishers, Inc., 1978), 145–46.

12. Wandel, *The Eucharist in the Reformation*, 231–41.

13. As Osvaldo Pardo shows, local variation within the practice of the sacraments was common. For instance, friars in sixteenth-century Mexico truncated baptismal rites for indigenous converts and were reluctant to grant them access to the eucharist. Osvaldo F. Pardo, *The Origins of Mexican Catholicism: Nahua Rituals*

and Christian Sacraments in Sixteenth-Century Mexico (Ann Arbor: University of Michigan Press, 2004). The process of standardizing the liturgy began only in earnest at the end of the century. It is likely that standardization took much time to complete. It is unclear how far this process had progressed by the eighteenth century in Mexico.

14. On Trent's identification of the priest with Christ, see Wandel, *The Eucharist in the Reformation*, 224–27.

15. Caroline Walker Bynum, *Holy Feast and Holy Fast: The Religious Significance of Food to Medieval Women* (Berkeley: University of California Press, 1987).

16. Miri Rubin argues that women and men practiced eucharistic devotions during the late medieval period and critiques Bynum for essentializing female piety. Rubin, *Corpus Christi*, 9.

17. Susan Verdi Webster, *Art and Ritual in Golden-Age Spain: Sevillian Confraternities and the Processional Sculpture of Holy Week* (Princeton: Princeton University Press, 1998), 25–29; Christopher F. Black, *Italian Confraternities in the Sixteenth Century* (New York: Cambridge University Press 1989), 26–30.

18. Maureen Flynn, *Sacred Charity: Confraternities and Social Welfare in Spain, 1400–1700* (Ithaca: Cornell University Press, 1989), 126–34; Christian, *Local Religion*, 185–86; Alicia Bazarte Martínez, *Las cofradías de españoles en la ciudad de México, 1526–1860* (México: Universidad Autónoma Metropolitana, 1989).

19. *Concilio III*, 195.

20. David A. Brading, *The First America: The Spanish Monarchy, Creole Patriots, and the Liberal State, 1492–1867* (New York: Cambridge University Press, 1991), 236–37; Brescia, "Liturgical Expressions of Episcopal Power," 507.

21. José Boneta y Liplana, *Gritos del purgatorio y medios para callarlos: libro primero y segundo* (Puebla: Diego Fernandez de Leon, 1708), 234–35, unpaginated novena.

22. Cayetan de Cabrera y Quintero, *Hebdomadario trino, ejercicios devotos, y obsequiosos desagravios a la santísima, amablilissima, y missericordiosissima TRINIDAD . . .* (México, Viudad de Don Joseph Bernardo de Hogal, 1745), 14, 29, 35–36, 48, 51, 63, 69, 72.

23. Joseph Vicente de Ochoa Villaseñor, *Escala del cielo que con piadoso afecto ofrece a los fieles de Jesucristo . . .* (México: Felipe de Zúñiga y Ontiveros, 1793), 47–48, 55.

24. Not all colonial Mexicans practiced self-flagellation and other intense forms of mortification, or they certainly did not relish them. In her biography of Francisca de los Ángeles, a beata and mystic from Querétaro, Ellen Gunnarsdóttir points out that, although her spiritual advisor, Fray Antonio Margil de Jesús practiced intense mortifications and recommended these pious practices to her, Francisca found them spiritually unfulfilling and tended to avoid them. Ellen Gunnarsdóttir, *Mexican Karismata: The Baroque Vocation of Francisca de los Ángeles, 1674–1744* (Lincoln: University of Nebraska Press, 2004), 124–25.

25. For the history of this catechism, see Ernest J. Burrus, S. J., "The Author of the Mexican Council Catechisms," *Americas* 15 (1958): 171–81.

26. Every faithful Christian is strongly obliged to have wholehearted devotion to the holy cross of Jesus Christ, our light; because on it he sought to die to redeem us of our sins and the evil enemy. And therefore you are to be become accustomed

to sign and cross yourself, making three crosses. The first on the forehead, so that God may free us from evil thoughts. The second on the mouth, so that God may free us from evil words. The third on the chest, so that God may free us from evil deeds. Saying the following: by the sign of the holy cross, free us Lord, Our God, from our enemies. In the name of the father, and of the son, and of the holy spirit. Amen Jesus. Gerónimo Ripalda, *Catecismo y exposicion breve de la doctrina christiana* . . . (Puebla: Pedro de la Rosa, 1784), 1–3. The earliest complete Spanish version of this work I encountered in the National Library in Mexico is the 1784 edition.

27. Ripalda, *Catecismo*, 38–39.

28. Juan de Abreu, *Desagravios dolorosos de Maria por los agravios ignominiosos de Christo* . . . (México: Herederos de Miguel de Rivera, 1726), 5, 8, 9, 11, 17, 21, 23.

29. Abreu, *Desagravios dolorosos de Maria*, unpaginated introduction.

30. *Ejercicios espirituales de el divino infante Jesús, disposición, que una alma devota de este misterio, ha observado en el santo adviento* . . . (México: Felipe de Zúñiga y Ontiveros, 1774), 12, 21, 30–33, 37–38, 46, 52–53, 60.

31. For the Saturday office of the Virgin, see John Harper, *The Forms and Orders of Western Liturgy: From the Tenth to the Eighteenth Century: A Historical Introduction and Guide for Students and Musicians* (Oxford: Clarendon Press, 1991), 134–35.

32. The Third Mexican Provincial Council recommended this practice. *Concilio III*, 334. The Fourth Mexican Provincial Council stated that churches should retain the custom, indicating that it was actually practiced. *Concilio IV provincial mexicano celebrado año de 1771* (Querétaro: Escuela de Artes, 1898), 168.

33. Abreu, *Desagravios dolorosos de Maria*, 4.

34. Manuel Eduardo Perez Bonilla, *Practicas devotas en honor del sacratisimo corazon de nuestro señor Jesucristo* . . . (México: Mariano Joseph de Zúñiga y Ontiveros, 1805), 53.

35. Abreu, *Desagravios dolorosos de Maria*, 16.

36. *Ejercicios espirituales de el divino infante Jesús*, 14–15.

37. AN Notary # 122, vol. 793, fols. 485–88, Mexico City, 1 Dec. 1696, will of Antonio Marcos de Mendieta notarized by Juan de Condarco y Caceres.

38. AN Notary # 129, vol. 827, fols. 38–42, Mexico City, 7 June 1717, will of Francisco del Castillo notarized by Juan de la Colina.

39. AN Notary # 669, vol. 4530, fols. 698–701, Mexico City, 15 Oct. 1779, will of Josepha Rodriguez de Pinillos notarized by Antonio de la Torre.

40. The seven pains, or sorrows, of Mary are the prophecy of Simeon, the flight into Egypt, the loss of Jesus in the temple, the meeting with Jesus on the road to Calvary, the Crucifixion, the Deposition, and the Entombment. Marina Warner, *Alone of All Her Sex: The Myth and Cult of the Virgin Mary* (New York: Alfred A. Knopf, 1976), 218. For a description of the corona, see *Formula, y modo de rezar con utilidad, y provecho la Corona de las cinco llagas, meditando juntamente, los dolorores agudissimos que traspasseron el corazon de la santissima Virgen* . . . (México: Francisco de Rivera Calderón, 1718), unpaginated.

41. Flynn, *Sacred Charity*, 44–72.

42. AN Notary # 29, vol. 216, fols. 118–28, Mexico City, 27 July 1758, will of Diego Joseph Ramirez del Corral notarized by Mariano Arroyo.

43. AN Notary # 254, vol. 1664, n.f., Mexico City, 18 June 1717, will of Joseph Francisco de Urbina notarized by Juan Clemente Guerrero.

44. There were a total of three such gifts in 1696, five in 1717, and eight in 1737.

45. D. M. Hope, "The Medieval Western Rites," in *The Study of Liturgy*, ed. Cheslyn Jones, Geoffrey Wainwright, and Edward Yarnold, S.J. (New York: Oxford University Press, 1978), 238.

46. See, for example, the rite of burial and the rite of giving communion after the mass proper, Miguel Venegas, *Manual de párrocos para administrar los santos sacramentos y exercer otras funciones ecclesiasticas conforme al ritual romano* (México: Joseph Bernardo de Hogal, 1731), 54, 92–98.

47. AN Notary # 158, vol. 960, fols. 50–51, Mexico City, 4 Sept. 1813, will of Jacinto del Conal y Rozo notarized by Jose Cano y Moctezuma.

48. AN Notary # 23, vol. 186, fols. 313–17, Mexico City, 23 Dec. 1737, will of Francisco Jose Ponce de Leon Enrriquez Ladron de Guevara notarized by Jose Antonio de Anaya.

49. AN Notary # 235, vol. 1466, fols. 333–34, Mexico City, 5 Nov. 1737, will of Jose Domingo de la Peña notarized by Toribio Fernandez de Cosgaya.

50. AN Notary # 666, vol. 4510, fols. 1–3, Mexico City, 2 Feb. 1717, will of Maria Antonia Lujan y Quiroz notarized by Manuel de la Torre.

51. AN Notary # 589, vol. 4024, fols. 42–46, Mexico City, 5 April 1758, will of Marselo Ygnacio Flores notarized by Jose de Rivera Butron.

52. AN Notary # 670, vol. 4534, vol. 48–50, Mexico City, 5 June 1779, will of Juan de Mata Barbosa notarized by Jose Antonio Troncoso.

53. AN Notary # 30, vol. 260, n.f., Mexico City, 15 June 1779, will of Domingo Antonio Gil y Fernandez notarized by Jose Joaquin Arroyo Bernardo de Quiros.

54. AN Notary # 218, vol. 1419, fols. 2–8, Mexico City, 13 Jan. 1696, will of Jose Nuñez de Azebado notarized by Ramon de Espinosa.

55. AN Notary # 738, vol. 5229, fols. 26–27, Mexico City, 6 April 1813, will of Jose Antonio Rodriguez notarized by Manuel Ymaz y Cabanillas.

56. Fabián y Fuero, *Colección de providencias*, 462–64.

57. AN Notary # 709, vol. 4768, fols. 14–17, Mexico City, 19 Aug. 1779, will of Francisco Galindo y Quiñones notarized by Francisco Jose de Villaseca.

58. See for example, AN Notary # 589, vol. 4024, fols. 30–37, Mexico City, 18 Feb. 1758, will of Francisco Picaro notarized by Jose de Rivera Butron. In addition to five masses in honor of the "most holy wounds" of Christ and five masses in honor of the "most holy cross," Francisco requested three masses in honor of the trinity, nine masses in honor of the nine choirs of angels, twelve masses in honor of the twelve apostles, four masses in honor of the four evangelists, and seven masses in honor of the holy spirit, probably in reference to its seven gifts. Other examples include, but are not limited to, AN Notary # 350, vol. 2289, fols. 250–53, Mexico City, 19 Aug. 1758, will of Joseph Xiptoval Zeron notarized by Diego Jacinto Leon; AN Notary # 19, vol. 134, fols. 178–87, Mexico City, 5 Dec. 1737, will of Francisco Martínez Chavarelo notarized by Juan Antonio Arroyo; and AN Notary # 459,

vol. 3132, n.f., Mexico City, 27 Oct. 1779, will of Lorenzo Francisco Timoteo Benavides notarized by Jose Bernardo de Navia.

59. In their joint will, a husband and wife requested five masses to the "five lords and ladies of the holy family [*los cinco señores*]" and five to the "most painful wounds of our Lord Jesus Christ and to his most holy sacramentalized body," and five "to the five great sorrows of his most holy mother the Virgin Mary." AN Notary # 590, vol. 4027, fols. 3–5, Mexico City, 9 Feb. 1758, joint will of Manuel Gernando de Pinzon y Liñan and Francisca de Galdiano y Lopez notarized by Jose Leonardo Rodriguez.

60. In fact, more than one testator made this explicit in their wills. Nine also refers to the number of months Christ spent in the Virgin's womb and the nine choirs of angels.

61. AN Notary # 312, vol. 2130, n.f., Mexico City, 21 Oct. 1737, will of Maria Theresa de Montemaior notarized by Juan del Horno.

62. AN Notary # 29, vol. 236, fols. 196–99, Mexico City, 14 Sept. 1779, will of Sor Maria Josefa del Niño Jesus (Maria Josefa Fernandez Pinta) notarized by Mariano Buenaventura Arroyo.

63. AN Notary # 425, vol. 2820, fols. 115–18, Mexico City, 31 July 1813, will of Maria Dolores de la Cruz Saravia notarized by Jose Maria Moya.

64. AN Notary # 480, vol. 3264, fols. 41–43, Mexico City, 2 June 1779, joint will of Francisca Garcia del Valle y Araujo and Baltazar de Vidaurre notarized by Jose Manuel Ochoa.

65. AN Notary # 350, vol. 2307, fols. 161–64, Mexico City, 11 May 1779, will of Josefa Joaquina Ramirez notarized by Diego Jacinto Leon.

CHAPTER 4

1. AN Notary # 254, vol. 1664, n.f., Mexico City, 18 Sept. 1717, will of Maria Josepha de Abendaño y Orduña notarized by Juan Clemente Guerrero.

2. It is difficult to estimate the number of masses celebrated in Bourbon Mexico City. Karen Melvin records that the Carmelite monastery in Toluca, a provincial city northwest of Mexico City, performed about ten thousand masses a year from 1761–80. It did so with a population of about only twenty friars. Karen Melvin, "Urban Religions: Mendicant Orders in New Spain's Cities, 1570–1800 (Ph.D. diss., University of California, Berkeley, 2005). Given Mexico City's greater size, wealth, and number of monasteries and priests, it is likely that many times that number of masses were celebrated each year in New Spain's capital. The number of masses, however, probably fell short of that recited in the great cities of Europe at the same time. In Barcelona, over three thousand masses for the dead were celebrated each day in 1700. R. Po-Chia Hsia, *The World of Catholic Renewal, 1540–1770*, 2nd ed. (New York: Cambridge University Press, 2005), 54.

3. William B. Taylor, *Magistrates of the Sacred: Priests and Parishioners in Eighteenth-Century Mexico* (Stanford: Stanford University Press, 1996), 266.

4. Of course, Protestantism was not monolithic, and each Protestant church followed different principles in the decoration of sacred space. Nonetheless, they generally

utilized more sedate ornamentation in their churches. Carlos M. N. Eire, *War Against the Idols: The Reformation of Worship from Erasmus to Calvin* (New York: Cambridge University Press, 1986); Hans Belting, *Likeness and Presence: A History of the Image before the Era of Art*, trans. Edmund Jephcott (Chicago: University of Chicago Press, 1994), 458–70.

5. H. J. Schroeder, *Canons and Decrees of the Council of Trent* (Rockford: Tan Books and Publishers, Inc., 1978), 147.

6. Donna Pierce, "At the Crossroads: Cultural Confluence and Daily Life in Mexico, 1521–1821" in *Painting a New World: Mexican Art and Life, 1521–1821*, ed. Donna Pierce, Rogelio Ruiz Gomar, and Clara Bargellini (Denver: Denver Museum of Art, 2004), 34. On the advance of naturalism, see Rogelio Ruiz Gomar, "Unique Expressions: Painting in New Spain," in *Painting a New World*, 47–77.

7. Clifford Howell, S. J., "From Trent to Vatican II" in *The Study of Liturgy*, ed. Cheslyn Jones, Geoffrey Wainwright, and Edward Yarnold, S. J. (New York: Oxford University Press, 1978), 244–45; George Grayson Wagstaff, "Music for the Dead: Polyphonic Settings of the Officium and Missa pro Defunctis by Spanish and Latin American Composers before 1630" (Ph.D. diss., University of Texas at Austin, 1995), 9–10, 492. For a history of Mexico City's professional cathedral choir, see Jesús Alejandro Ramos Kittrell, "Dynamics of Ritual and Ceremony at the Metropolitan Cathedral of Mexico, 1700–1750" (Ph.D. diss., University of Texas at Austin, 2006). Ramos Kittrell argues that the performance of the divine office in the cathedral of Mexico City may not have been as splendorous as one imagines. Tithe revenue supported the choir, but this income proved insufficient to fund the professional musicians and signers adequately in the first half of the eighteenth century. It should be noted, however, that the choir continued to perform its duties. Furthermore, music was only one aspect of the splendorous nature of baroque religiosity. As we will see, the faithful of Mexico City spent lavishly to promote other aspects of the liturgy and adorn church interiors.

8. Hsia, *The World of Catholic Renewal*, 159–71.

9. For an overview of baroque architecture and art in New Spain, see George Kubler and Martin Soria, eds., *Art and Architecture in Spain and Portugal and Their American Dominions, 1500 to 1800* (Baltimore: Penguin Books, 1959), 69–82, 165–69; Guillermo Tovar de Teresa, *México barroco* (Mexico: SAHOP, 1981); and Robert J. Mullen, *Architecture and Its Sculpture in Viceregal Mexico* (Austin: University of Texas Press, 1997), 114–205.

10. Kubler and Soria, *Art and Architecture*, 168–69; Mullen, *Architecture and Its Sculpture*, 90–93, 118, 168–72.

11. There are some stylistically "pure" churches. For example, the convent of La Enseñanza is fully churrigueresque.

12. *Concilios Provinciales Primero y Segundo, Celebrados en la muy noble y muy leal ciudad de México . . .* (México: Imprenta de el Superior Gobierno, de el Br. D. Joseph Antonio de Hogal, 1769), 93.

13. *Concilio III Provincial Mexicano, celebrado en México el año 1585 . . .* (Barcelona: Manuel Miró y D. Marsa, 1870), 208.

14. Juan Joseph de Escalona y Calatayud, *Instrucción a la perfecta vida: máximas para su logro a personas de todos estados. Mandadas escribir a un clerigo sacerdote, domiciliario del Obispado de Michaocàn, y sacadas a luz para el aprovechamiento de sus ovejas* (México: Joseph Bernando de Hogal, 1737), 34–35.

15. Testators often gave gifts to support the construction of churches or monastic houses and to provide sustenance for friars and nuns. They also gave gifts to churches, orders, and confraternities without specifying the donation's purpose. I have not included these types of gift in this discussion of the baroque.

16. See Chapter 3 for a discussion of numeric and temporal symbolism in chantries and chaplaincies.

17. In my sample, gifts of money or fungible parts of estates accounted for 138 of the 271 gifts donated to religious institutions to increase the splendor of worship.

18. AN Notary # 563, vol. 3893, n.f., Mexico City, 6 Dec. 1696, will of Juan Mudarra notarized by Martin del Rio.

19. AN Notary # 563, vol. 3893, n.f., Mexico City, 12 Aug. 1696, will of Francisco Martinez de Lerarsar y Saracho notarized by Martin del Rio.

20. AN Notary # 19, vol. 134, fols. 5–10, Mexico City, 3 Jan. 1737, will of Juan de Iraizos notarized by Juan Antonio Arroyo.

21. "Culto" is a difficult word to translate into English. In one sense, it means honor and reverence the faithful pay to God and the saints. The translation in English depends on the recipient of the honor. If God, the translation is "worship"; if a saint, then "veneration"; technically worship is only due to God. Culto can be internal, mental, and spiritual on the one hand or external and physical on the other, or both simultaneously. It then can be an internal psychological state or the accumulation of material objects given to a church, image, or the eucharist to honor God and the saints. No easy English translation captures these subtleties. The English phrases internal piety/devotion and external piety/devotion come closest to the Spanish meaning. Culto can also refer broadly to devotions directed toward one particular advocation. In this sense, the English term "cult" is most appropriate, for example the cult of the Virgin or the cult of the saints.

22. AN Notary # 669, vol. 4530, fols. 570–76, Mexico City, 15 June 1779, will of Thomas Dias de Vargas notarized by Antonio de la Torre.

23. A corporal is a linen cloth upon which the eucharist is placed; purifiers are slotted spoons used to strain the wine before consecration. AN Notary # 32, vol. 275, n.f., Mexico City, 13 May 1796, will of Mª Josefa del Niño Jesus notarized by Ignacio de Arteaga.

24. AN Notary # 563, vol. 3893, n.f., Mexico City, 25 Oct. 1696, will of Gonzalo de Cervantes Casaus notarized by Martin del Rio.

25. AN Notary # 133, vol. 838, fols. 75–77, Mexico City, 1 July 1737, will of Miguel Ramon de Cruz notarized by Juan Jose de la Cruz y Aguilar.

26. AN Notary # 350, vol. 2307, fols. 364–66, Mexico City, 18 Oct. 1779, will of Manuel Ordoñez y Aguilar notarized by Diego Jacinto de Leon.

27. AN Notary # 311, vol. 2126, fols. 113–16, Mexico City, 1 July 1737, will of Marcos Reinel Hernandez notarized by Juan Hurtado de Castillo.

28. In my sample, testators gave seventy-seven gifts of images to religious institutions.

29. For a sophisticated discussion of contemporary home use of images by Protestants in the United States, see David Morgan, *Visual Piety: A History and Theory of Popular Religious Images* (Berkeley: University of California Press, 1998). Morgan argues that religious images compel emotional responses in viewers. They either serve to elicit empathy or function as a call to compassion. Empathy consists of the faithful's identification with the toils and suffering of the religious figure represented. Compassion consists of the faithful's request for aid from the holy figure. Colonial Mexican Catholics clearly engaged images in both ways.

30. The best study of early modern communal devotion to images and relics is William A. Christian's *Local Religion in Sixteenth-Century Spain* (Princeton: Princeton University Press, 1981).

31. AN Notary # 417, vol. 2729, fols. 14–16, Mexico City, 30 Jan. 1779, will of Maria Fran^{ca} Saens de Rosas notarized by Jose Ignacio Montes de Oca.

32. AN Notary # 637, vol. 4407, n.f., Mexico City, 5 Oct. 1696, will of Melchora Montejo notarized by Miguel Leonardo de Sevilla.

33. AN Notary # 480, vol. 3264, fols. 41–43, Mexico City, 2 June 1779, joint will of Fran^{ca} Garcia del Valle y Araujo and Balthazar de Vidaurre notarized by Jose Manuel Ochoa.

34. AN Notary # 350, vol. 2307, fols. 340–41, Mexico City, 6 Oct. 1779, will of Christoval Mariano de Leon notarized by Diego Jacinto de Leon.

35. AN Notary # 707, vol. 4765, n.f., Mexico City, 30 May 1779, will of Theresa de Rivero y Zuñiga notarized by Francisco Juan de Velasco.

36. AN Notary # 480, vol. 3264, fols. 35–38, Mexico City, 8 May 1779, Josefa de Salcedo notarized by Jose Manuel Ochoa.

37. AN Notary # 567, vol. 3910, fols. 312–16, Mexico City, 19 Oct. 1737, will of Maria Ana Gonzales de Valdeosera notarized by Francisco Romero Zapata.

38. AN Notary # 329, vol. 2205, n.f., Mexico City, 16 April 1779, will of Cayetano Elias de Araballo notarized by Pablo Jimenez Ribadeneyra.

39. AN Notary # 710, vol. 4781, fols. 108–11, Mexico City, 24 Sept. 1813, will of Felipe Bentacur notarized by Ignacio Valle.

40. In my sample, six testators financed chapels and altars. I have excluded testators who merely gave a small sum of money to help finance the construction of a church. Many testators did so, but this type of pious bequest does not unequivocally represent the baroque proclivity to adorn sacred space.

41. AN Notary # 21, vol. 175, fols. 5–7, Mexico City, 23 Jan. 1737, will of Joseph Miguel de Reyna notarized by Francisco Javier de Ariza y Valdes.

42. AN Notary # 19, vol. 134, fols. 801–21, Mexico City, 14 Dec. 1737, will of Juana de Arriaga Mendizabal Mexia de Vera notarized by Juan Antonio Arroyo.

43. AN Notary # 13, vol. 76, fols. 210–12, Mexico City, 21 March 1717, will of Beatriz de Figueroa notarized by Jose de Anaya y Bonillo.

44. AN Notary # 29, vol. 253, fols. 28–35, Mexico City, 16 July 1796, will of Mª de Jesus (Paulin y Solis) notarized by Mariano Buenaventura de Arroyo.

45. The three ministers María speaks of are the priest, deacon, and subdeacon. Both the deacon and subdeacon had to take solemn vows, so were no longer in minor orders. But they had not yet been ordained priests. The subdeacon sang the

epistle, the deacon sang the gospel, and the priest intoned the canon of the mass. AN Notary # 425, vol. 2820, fols. 13–17, Mexico City, 9 Feb. 1813, will of Maria Guadalupe Marin del Castillo notarized by Jose Maria Moya.

46. AN Notary # 504, vol. 3394, fols. 133–47, Mexico City, 27 Dec. 1737, will of Fernando Garcia de Rojas notarized by Jose Manuel de Paz.

47. AN Notary # 66, vol. 476, fols. 34–37, Mexico City, 8 July 1737, will of Margarita Josepha de la Consepsion notarized by Luis de Benavides.

48. AN Notary # 350, vol. 2289, fols. 405–7, Mexico City, 4 Dec. 1758, will of Francisco Ygnacio de Gojendola notarized by Diego Jacinto de Leon.

49. AN Notary # 155, vol. 924, fols. 283–86, Mexico City, 26 June 1813, will of Francisco Reyes notarized by Francisco Calapiz y Aguilar.

50. Schroeder, *Canons and Decrees*, 150.

CHAPTER 5

1. AN Notary # 70, vol. 491, fols. 429–33, Mexico City, 23 Nov. 1737, will of Joseph de Arze y Carriedo notarized by Manuel de Benjumea Jimenez.

2. William A. Christian, *Local Religion in Sixteenth-Century Spain* (Princeton: Princeton University Press, 1981).

3. Linda Curcio-Nagy, "Giants and Gypsies: Corpus Christi in Colonial Mexico City," in *Rituals of Rule, Rituals of Resistance: Public Celebrations and Popular Culture in Mexico*, ed. William H. Beezley, Cheryl English Martin, and William E. French (Wilmington: Scholarly Resources, 1994), 2–4; Linda Curcio-Nagy, *The Great Festivals of Colonial Mexico City: Performing Power and Identity* (Albuquerque: University of New Mexico Press, 2004), 28–30. At times disputes over precedence shattered the ideal of social harmony processions were designed to create and reinforce. See, for instance, Clara García Ayluardo, "A World of Images: Cult, Ritual, and Society in Colonial Mexico City," in *Rituals of Rule*, 84–85.

4. For a description of processions to end plague, see David A. Brading, *Mexican Phoenix: Our Lady of Guadalupe: Image and Tradition across Five Centuries* (New York: Cambridge University Press, 2001), 120–27.

5. See for instance, *Catecismo para uso de los párrocos hecho por el IV concilio provincial mexicano celebrado año de 1771* (México: Joseph de Jauregui, 1772), 21–23, 86–87, 301–2.

6. See for example, Colin Morris, *The Discovery of the Individual, 1050–1200* (New York: Harper & Row, Publishers, 1972); Philippe Aries, *The Hour of Our Death*, trans. Helen Weaver (New York: Alfred A. Knopf, 1981); David Warren Sabean, *Power in the Blood: Popular Culture and Village Discourse in Early Modern Germany* (New York: Cambridge University Press, 1984); John Bossy, *Christianity in the West, 1400–1700* (New York: Oxford University Press, 1985); Georges Duby, ed., *A History of Private Life*, vol. 2, *Revelations of the Medieval World* (Cambridge: Harvard University Press, 1988), especially 511–14; Aaron Guervich, *The Origins of European Individualism*, trans. Katharine Judelson (Cambridge, MA: Blackwell Publishers, 1995); Lynn Hunt, "Psychoanalysis, The Self, and Historical Interpretation," *Common Knowledge* 6, no. 2 (1997): 10–19; and for a controversial account of selfhood and

embodiment, see Morris Berman, *Coming to Our Senses: Body and Spirit in the Hidden History of the West* (New York: Simon and Schuster, 1989).

7. Natalie Zemon Davis argues that, although individualism was emerging in early modern Europe, individual subjects still defined themselves in reference to familial and other group identities. Natalie Zemon Davis, "Boundaries and the Sense of Self in Sixteenth-Century France," in *Reconstructing Individualism: Autonomy, Individuality, and the Self in Western Thought*, ed. Thomas C. Heller et al. (Stanford: Stanford University Press, 1986).

8. *Catecismo para uso de los párrocos*, 319–20.

9. The seven corporeal acts of mercy are to visit the ill, feed the hungry, give drink to the thirsty, cloth the naked, lodge the pilgrim, redeem captives, and bury the dead. The seven spiritual acts of mercy are to teach the ignorant, give good advice to those in need, correct those who err, pardon offenses, console the grieving, suffer patiently the weakness of one's neighbors, and pray for the living and the dead. Taken from Gerónimo Ripalda, *Catecismo y exposición breve de la doctrina christiana por el P. Mro. Gerónimo de Ripalda con un tratado muy útil del órden con que el christiano debe ocupar el tiempo y emplear el día* (Puebla: Pedro de la Rosa, 1784), 19–21.

10. Luther held that faith in Christ, alone, sufficed to gain salvation. Calvin, on the other hand, dismissed any human endeavor to win admission into glory as futile. Salvation in his mind was a gift from God that humans could do nothing on their own to merit. Bernard M. G. Reardon, *Religious Thought in the Reformation*, 2nd ed. (New York: Longman, 1995), 52–57, 175–80.

11. Joseph Boneta y Liplana, *Gritos del purgatorio y medios para callarlos. Libro primero y sugundo dedicados a la Virgen Santíssima del Carmen* (Puebla de los Angeles: Diego Fernandez de Leon, 1708), 156–57.

12. *New American Bible* 25:35–40.

13. Bossy, *Christianity in the West*, especially 57–60, 144–49. Of course, ideal and real practice did not always conform and, although the sacraments and other religious activities may have produced a change of heart among participants, such a state was probably fleeting.

14. For a discussion of changing meanings of charity in the early modern era, see Linda Martz, *Poverty and Welfare in Habsburg Spain: The Example of Toledo* (New York: Cambridge University Press, 1983); Kathryn Norberg, *Rich and Poor in Grenoble, 1600–1814* (Berkeley: University of California Press, 1985); and Maureen Flynn, *Sacred Charity: Confraternities and Social Welfare in Spain, 1400–1700* (Ithaca: Cornell University Press, 1989).

15. It probably persisted in early modern Europe as well.

16. Juan Joseph de Escalona y Calatayud, *Instrucción a la perfecta vida: maximas para su logro a personas de todos estados* (México: Joseph Bernardo de Hogal, 1737), 6–7.

17. *Exercicios espirituales de el divino infante Jesús, disposición, que una alma devota de este misterio, ha observado en el santo adviento, comenzando desde el dia veinte y dos de noviembre, hasta cumplir treinta y tres dias, que son los previos a la pascua* (México: Felipe de Zúñiga y Ontiveros, 1774), 43–44, 70–71, 109–10.

18. AC Edictos, Caja 2, 26 March 1584.

19. *Concilio III provincial mexicano celebrado en México el año 1585* . . . (Barcelona: Manuel Miró y D. Marsa, 1870), 223, 303, 310–11.

20. In my sample, testators gave a total of 284 gifts to orphans: 177 to women, 103 to men, and four to orphans without specifically naming them.

21. The average monetary gift to female orphans was 1,130 pesos, with a median gift of four hundred pesos. The average for male orphans was 610 pesos, with a median of three hundred pesos.

22. AN Notary # 692, vol. 4690, fols. 516–17, Mexico City, 2 Sept. 1696, will of Antonio de Nebro notarized by Francisco de Valdes.

23. AN Notary # 83, vol. 528, fols. 45–48, Mexico City, 4 Sept. 1813, will of Francisco Antonio Narbaez y Sanchez notarized by Francisco Javier Benitez.

24. AN Notary # 340, vol. 2247, fols. 182–86, Xochimilco, 1 April 1696, joint will of Antonio Ruiz Morandiel and Maria Gonzales de Selisco notarized by Jose de Ledesma.

25. In my sample, testators gave 183 gifts to the poor.

26. A total of twenty-three gifts required the recipient to commend the benefactor's soul to God, and two asked recipients to pray for the testator.

27. Any time a testator bequeathed something to a specific person, whether the recipient was a relative, friend, servant, or associate, I coded the gift as a secular bequest, even if the testator described the person as poor.

28. Sixty-nine out of 183 gifts to the poor, or 37.7 percent, carried restrictions on recipients.

29. AN Notary # 509, vol. 3416, n.f., Mexico City, 2 Nov. 1758, will of Fernando Zorrila notarized by Felipe Antonio de la Peña.

30. He described his gift as one-third of 13,000 pesos. AN Notary # 73, vol. 512, fols. 168–70, Mexico City, 17 June 1737, will of Juan Angel de Urra notarized by Juan Francisco Benitez Trigueros.

31. AN Notary # 23, vol. 186, fols. 313–17, Mexico City, 23 Dec. 1737, will of Francisco Joseph Ponce de Leon Enrriquez Ladron de Guebara notarized by Jose Antonio de Anaya.

32. AN Notary # 206, vol. 1358, fols. 129–34, Mexico City, 25 Aug. 1758, will of Pedro Gordillo notarized by Andres Delgado Camargo. The term "solemn poor" refers to a legal status granted to petitioners who demonstrated their poverty to the crown or other royal officials. The solemn poor could pursue cases in royal courts free of charge or at a reduced cost. For a detailed discussion of the solemn poor in Quito, see Cynthia E. Milton, *The Many Meanings of Poverty: Colonialism, Social Compacts, and Assistance in Eighteenth-Century Ecuador* (Stanford: Stanford University Press, 2007), 65–97, 215–44.

33. A total of thirty-six gifts to the poor in my sample were made through religious institutions.

34. In a decree criticizing mendicancy, archbishop of Mexico Francisco Lorenzana revealed the vital importance of the city's religious orders in the distribution of food to the poor. He stated that the "lazy" poor "only know monasteries and convents [*conventos*] for soup." Francisco Antonio Lorenzana, *Cartas Pastorales y edictos del Illmo Señor D. Francisco Antonio Lorenzana y Buitron, Arzobispo de*

Mexico (México: Imprenta del Superior Gobierno, del Br. D. Joseph Antonio de Hogal, 1770), 168.

35. Testators in my sample bequeathed seventy-eight gifts to the poor to be distributed by their executors. Testators did not mention a form of distribution for sixty-five gifts.

36. AN Notary # 413, vol. 2706, fols. 8–11, Mexico City, 31 Jan. 1758, joint will of Juan de la Vega y Bela and Francisca de Puga y Villanueba notarized by Jose de Morales Mariano.

37. AN Notary # 129, vol. 827, fols. 38–42, Mexico City, 7 June 1717, will of Francisco del Castillo notarized by Juan de la Colina.

38. In my sample, testators gave 179 gifts to hospitals.

39. Josefina Muriel de la Torre, *Hospitales de la Nueva España*, 2 vols. (México: Instituto de Historia, 1956).

40. AN Notary # 745, vol. 5281, n.f., Mexico City, 22 March 1758, will of Joseph Freyre notarized by Ambrosio Zevallos.

41. One peso of interest from the capital fund established for the hospital of San Pedro was to be used to purchase two private masses each year on the feast of St. Augustine. Pedro wrote two wills before different notaries in 1737. Both wills contain these two pious clauses. AN Notary # 70, vol. 491, fols. 59–62, Mexico City, 15 Feb. 1737, will of Pedro de Borja Altamirano y Reinoso notarized by Manuel de Benjumea Jimenez; and AN Notary # 19, vol. 134, fols. 776–81, Mexico City, 2 Dec. 1737, will of Pedro de Borja Altamirano y Reynoso notarized by Juan Antonio Arroyo. The second will includes one fewer pious directive and names only two executors rather than three as the earlier will had done.

42. Not all confraternities were open to everyone. Some only admitted people who came or were descended from people who had come from particular regions of Spain. Others were only open to specific racial groups. For a study of Afro-Mexican confraternities, see Nicole von Germeten, *Black Blood Brothers: Confraternities and Social Mobility for Afro-Mexicans* (Gainesville: University Press of Florida, 2006).

43. William Monter, *Ritual, Myth and Magic in Early Modern Europe* (Athens: Ohio University Press, 1984), 15.

44. Christopher F. Black, *Italian Confraternities in the Sixteenth Century* (New York: Cambridge University Press, 1989), 7.

45. *Concilios provinciales primero y segundo celebrados en la muy noble y muy leal ciudad de México . . . en los años de 1555 y 1565. . . .* (México: Joseph Antonio de Hogal, 1769), 150–51.

46. In its twenty-second session (1562), the Council of Trent granted bishops the authority to regulate confraternal activities and finances. H. J. Schroeder, *Canons and Decrees of the Council of Trent* (Rockford, IL: Tan Books and Publishers, Inc., 1978), 156–57. For the relationship between bishops and confraternities in Mexico, see Alicia Bazarte Martínez, *Las cofradías de españoles en la ciudad de México* (México: Universidad Autónoma Metropolitana, 1989), 31–32.

47. AGN Bienes Nacionales, vol. 1028, exp. 40, n.f., Mexico City, 11 May 1694, "Autos fhos sobre que se aprueben las constituciones de la Cofradía que nuevamente se a ynstituido y fundado en la Parrochia de Sta. Catharina Virgen y Martir . . ."

48. AGN Templos y Conventos, vol. 160, exp. 35, fols. 731–35, Mexico City, 1672, "Constituciones de la cofradia de Sn Benito sita en la Yglecia de Sn Francisco, Mexico."

49. Asunción Lavrin, "Cofradías novohispanas: economías material y espiritual," in *Cofradías, capellanías y obras pías en la América colonial*, ed. Pilar Martínez López-Cano, Gisela von Wobeser, and Juan Guillermo Muñoz (México: Universidad Nacional Autónoma de México, 1998), 57.

50. AGN Bienes Nacionales, vol. 1028, exp. 1, n.f., Mexico City, 1683, "Autos fechos sobre la Aprovacion de las nuevas constituciones reformadas de la cofradia de La presiosa Sangre de Xpto Señor Nuestro fundada en la Parrochia de Sta Catarina Martir de esta ciudad."

51. For a discussion of the diverse activities of confraternities, see James R. Banker, *Death in the Community: Memorialization and Confraternities in an Italian Commune in the Late Middle Ages* (Athens: University of Georgia Press, 1988); Black, *Italian Confraternities;* Maureen Flynn, *Sacred Charity;* Susan Verdi Webster, *Art and Ritual in Golden-Age Spain: Sevillian Confraternities and the Processional Sculpture of Holy Week* (Princeton: Princeton University Press, 1998); and for the case of Mexico, Bazarte Martínez, *Las cofradías de españoles.* For the role confraternities performed in the creation of sacred communities, see Flynn, *Sacred Charity*, 13; and Bossy, *Christianity in the West*, 58–60. For ritual feasting, Sara Nalle, *God in la Mancha: Religious Reform and the People of Cuenca, 1550–1650* (Baltimore: Johns Hopkins University Press, 1992), 158. For the agape, Theodor Klauser, *A Short History of the Western Liturgy: An Account and Some Reflections*, trans. John Halliburton (New York: Oxford University Press, 1979), 7–8.

52. AN Notary # 637, vol. 4407, n.f., Mexico City, 22 Dec. 1696, will of Felix Vela del Castillo notarized by Miguel Leonardo de Sevilla.

53. Ibid.

54. Asunción Lavrin, "La congregación de San Pedro: una cofradía urbana del México colonial, 1604–1730," *Historia Mexicana* 29 (1980): 570–76.

55. Miguel Venegas, *Manual de párrocos para administrar los santos sacramentos y exercer otras funciones eclesiasticas conforme al ritual romano* (México: Joseph Bernardo de Hogal, 1731), 92–98.

56. AN Notary # 9, vol. 30, fols. 196–202, Mexico City, 16 Sept. 1696, will of Antonio de Aguilar notarized by Antonio de Anaya.

57. AN Notary # 563, vol. 3893, n.f., Mexico City, 7 Dec. 1696, will of Felipa Juarez de Salazar notarized by Martin del Rio.

CHAPTER 6

1. For an overview of the Bourbon reforms in Spain, see John Lynch, *Bourbon Spain, 1700–1801* (Cambridge: Basil Blackwell Inc., 1989).

2. David A. Brading, *Miners and Merchants in Bourbon Mexico, 1763–1810* (New York: Cambridge University Press, 1971), 129–68; production figures are listed in a table on page 131. Production increased from about three million pesos per year in 1700 to twenty-seven million in 1800. These two years, however, marked

particularly low and high points in output. Nonetheless, growth in production was exponential.

3. In the twelve-year period from 1728 to 1739, a total of sixty-nine ships legally docked in Veracruz. From 1784 to 1795, 521 ships did so. John E. Kicza, *Colonial Entrepreneurs: Families and Business in Bourbon Mexico City* (Albuquerque: University of New Mexico Press, 1983), 49.

4. Brading, *Miners and Merchants*, 114–18, 152.

5. Richard L. Garner, *Economic Growth and Change in Bourbon Mexico* (Gainesville: University of Florida Press, 1993).

6. The average price for a fanega of wheat in 1797 was thirteen pesos. Due to drought, the price rose to twenty-six pesos in 1803 and thirty-six pesos in 1811. Timothy E. Anna, *The Fall of the Royal Government in Mexico City* (Lincoln: University of Nebraska Press, 1978), 141–42; Enrique Florescano, *Precios del maíz y crisis agrícolas en México, 1708–1810*, rev. ed. (México: Colegio de México, 1986), 193–213; Garner, *Economic Growth and Change*, 27–33. Richard Garner's data indicate that wages kept pace with inflation over the eighteenth century. But his data are admittedly thin and are taken from both rural and urban areas. Garner, *Economic Growth and Change*, 33–36. Wage data for workers in the Mexico City Tobacco Manufactory, which employed around 9,000 workers, show a decline in nominal wages and therefore an even larger decline in real wages. On the other hand, salaries for bureaucrats of the tobacco monopoly increased or remained even. But even those salaries that rose did not increase enough to keep pace with inflation. Of course, well-paid bureaucrats spent a much smaller portion of their personal income on foodstuffs than wage workers. Susan Deans-Smith, *Bureaucrats, Planters, and Workers: The Making of the Tobacco Monopoly in Bourbon Mexico* (Austin: University of Texas Press, 1992), 191–96.

7. Garner, *Economic Growth and Change*, 215–45; Brading, *Miners and Merchants*, 29.

8. Pamela Voekel, "Peeing on the Palace: Bodily Resistance to Bourbon Reforms in Mexico City," *Journal of Historical Sociology* 5 (1992): 185–86. See also Silvia Marina Arrom, *Containing the Poor: The Mexico City Poor House, 1774–1871* (Durham: Duke University Press, 2000), 14–26, 43–75; Gabriel Haslip-Viera, "The Underclass," in *Cities & Society in Colonial Latin America*, ed. Louisa Schell Hoberman and Susan Migden Socolow (Albuquerque: University of New Mexico Press, 1986), 305–6; Michael Scardaville, "(Hapsburg) Law and (Bourbon) Order: State Authority, Popular Unrest, and the Criminal Justice System in Bourbon Mexico City," *Americas* 50 (1994): 509–10.

9. For Bourbon reforms of other religious festivals, including carnival, in Mexico, see Juan Pedro Viqueira Albán, *Propriety and Permissiveness in Bourbon Mexico*, trans. Sonya Lipsett Rivera and Sergio Rivera Ayala (Wilmington: Scholarly Resources, 1999), 97–129.

10. For a description of Corpus Christi festivities in Mexico City, see Linda A. Curcio-Nagy, "Giants and Gypsies: Corpus Christi in Colonial Mexico City," in *Rituals of Rule, Rituals of Resistance: Public Celebrations and Popular Culture in Mexico*, ed. William H. Beezley, Cheryl English Martin, and William French (Wilmington: Scholarly Resources, 1994), especially 8–14; for Corpus Christi celebrations in

San Luís Potosí, see Alfonso Martínez Rosales, "Los gigantes de San Luis Potosí," *Historia Mexicana* 37 (1988): 585–612.

11. Curcio-Nagy, "Giants and Gypsies," 20; Martínez Rosales, "Los gigantes," 594; Voekel, "Peeing on the Palace," 198–99. Royal officials issued similar decrees regarding holy week processions and other public religious celebrations. See Clara García Ayluardo, "A World of Images: Cult, Ritual, and Society in Colonial Mexico City," in *Rituals of Rule, Rituals of Resistance*, 90.

12. Because of the *Patronato Real*, the privilege granted to the Spanish monarchy by Pope Julius II in 1508 that gave the sovereign the right to appoint bishops and assign benefices in the Americas, the crown wielded considerable influence over the secular clergy in New Spain. The monarch could install pliant clerics in high ecclesiastical offices and remove unruly priests from their posts. The papal grant, however, did not extend to the regular clergy. Because the orders, particularly the mendicants, operated numerous parishes in rural Mexico and many schools and monasteries in urban areas, much of the local Mexican church lay outside direct crown supervision.

13. David A. Brading, "Tridentine Catholicism and Enlightened Despotism in Bourbon Mexico," *Journal of Latin American Studies* 15 (1983): 6–10; David A. Brading, *The First America: The Spanish Monarchy, Creole Patriots, and the Liberal State, 1492–1867* (New York: Cambridge University Press, 1991), 492.

14. Brading, "Tridentine Catholicism," 10–11; Brading, *First America*, 497–98; Arnold J. Bauer, "Church in the Economy of Spanish America: Censos and Depósitos in the Eighteenth and Nineteenth Centuries," *Hispanic American Historical Review* 63 (1983): 727; Karen Melvin, "Urban Religions: Mendicant Orders in New Spain's Cities, 1570–1800" (Ph.D. diss., University of California, Berkeley, 2005), 165–95.

15. He had already done the same in Spain in 1798.

16. The faithful could create chantries and chaplaincies in one of two ways. They could place a lien valued at a certain amount on their real estate, thus obliging themselves and all future owners to pay five percent of the established lien each year to a priest or ecclesiastical corporation to recite the specified masses. Or they could donate a cash sum to an ecclesiastical corporation that would then loan the principal to a respectable landowner, merchant, or miner. The recipient was thus obligated to pay interest on the loan that supported the celebration of masses.

17. The elite who held these loans and liens vociferously protested to the crown, but to little avail. By the time the law was abrogated in 1809, the elite of New Spain had already remitted twelve million pesos to the royal treasury. Asunción Lavrin, "The Execution of the Law of Consolidación in New Spain: Economic Aims and Results," *Hispanic American Historical Review* 53 (1973): 27–49; Brian R. Hamnett, "The Appropriation of Mexican Church Wealth by the Spanish Bourbon Government: The Consolidación de Vales Reales, 1805–1809," *Journal of Latin American Studies* 1 (1972): 85–113; Margaret Chowning, "The Consolidación de Vales Reales in the Bishopric of Michoacán," *Hispanic American Historical Review* 69 (1989): 451–78.

18. Bauer, "The Church in the Economy," 729; Hamnett, "Appropriation of Mexican Church Wealth," 91–93; Lavrin, "Execution of the Law of Consolidación," 38.

19. Other Bourbon reforms included establishing the Intendant System and re-placing creole functionaries with peninsular ones to more tightly tie the colonial bureaucracy with crown rather than local interests. Brading, *Miners and Merchants*, 33–92. The causes of the insurgencies were many and differed according to the different populations who participated in them. Demographic growth and consequent land pressures, shifting patterns of land tenure that heightened economic instability, resentment engendered by the Bourbon reforms, the spread of Enlightenment political thought that challenged the justification for monarchical rule, and the desacralization of kingship all played a part. John Tutino, *From Insurrection to Revolution in Mexico: Social Bases of Agrarian Violence, 1750–1940* (Princeton: Princeton University Press, 1986), 41–212; Brian Hamnett, *Roots of Insurgency: Mexican Regions, 1750–1824* (New York: Cambridge University Press, 1986); Hugh M. Hammil, *The Hidalgo Revolt: Prelude to Mexican Independence* (Gainesville: University of Florida Press, 1966); Pamela Voekel, *Alone Before God: The Religious Origins of Modernity in Mexico* (Durham: Duke University Press, 2002); Eric Van Young, *The Other Rebellion: Popular Violence, Ideology, and the Mexican Struggle for Independence, 1810–1821* (Stanford: Stanford University Press, 2001).

20. Anna, *Fall of Royal Government*, 71–73, 84–86, 94, 98–100.

CHAPTER 7

1. On the rise of reformed piety in Spain, see William J. Calahan, *Church, Politics, and Society in Spain, 1750–1874* (Cambridge: Harvard University Press, 1984); and Richard Herr, *The Eighteenth-Century Revolution in Spain* (Princeton: Princeton University Press, 1958), 11–34, 400–432.

2. Alonso Núñez de Haro y Peralta, *Sermones escogidos, pláticas espirituales privadas, y dos pastorales, anteriormente impresas en México . . .* (Madrid: Imprenta de la hija de Ibarra, 1806), vol. 2, 260.

3. Ibid., 256–57.

4. Núñez de Haro y Peralta, *Sermones*, vol. 1, 211.

5. Núñez de Haro y Peralta, *Sermones*, vol. 3, 261–63.

6. Paul Saenger, "Books of Hours and the Reading Habits of the Later Middle Ages," in *The Culture of Print: Power and the Uses of Print in Early Modern Europe*, ed. Roger Chartier, trans. Lydia G. Cochrane (Princeton: Princeton University Press, 1989), 145–46.

7. Patricia Seed, *To Love, Honor and Obey in Colonial Mexico: Conflicts over Marriage Choice, 1574–1821* (Stanford: Stanford University Press, 1988), 47–55.

8. On the use of catechisms and the role of understanding in Christianity in the late medieval and early modern periods, see Jean Delumeau, *Catholicism between Luther and Voltaire: A New View of the Counter-Reformation*, trans. Jeremy Moiser (Philadelphia: Westminster Press, 1977). Delumeau argues that the early modern period was the time of the "Christianization" of Europe; the emphasis on teaching doctrine finally dispelled the paganism of the medieval period. This view of medieval Christianity is now held in disrepute. For a more nuanced treatment of

late medieval Christianity, see Eamon Duffy, *The Stripping of the Altars: Traditional Religion in England, 1400–1580* (New Haven: Yale University Press, 1992). Duffy argues that the medieval Church employed a number of means, particularly participation in the liturgy, to teach the tenets of Christianity. Nonetheless, there is no doubt that the second half of the sixteenth century saw a marked increase in formal catechism training. For a study of the catechistical endeavor in Spain, see Sara T. Nalle, *God in La Mancha: Religious Reform and the People of Cuenca, 1500–1650* (Baltimore: Johns Hopkins University Press, 1992).

9. H. J. Schroeder, *Canons and Decrees of the Council of Trent* (Rockford, IL: Tan Books and Publishers, Inc., 1978), 196.

10. *Concilio III Provincial Mexicano, celebrado en México el año 1585 . . .* (Barcelona: Manuel Miró y D. Marsa, 1870), 32–33, 38.

11. For the history of these two catechisms, see Ernest J. Burrus, S. J., "The Author of the Mexican Council Catechisms," *Americas* 15 (1958): 171–81.

12. *Catecismo para uso de los párrocos, hecho por el IV Concilio Provincial Mexicano . . .* (México: Josef de Jaúregui, 1772). The Ripalda catechism does contain prayers and doctrines that Catholics should know. In fact, right after the instructions for the sign of the cross, Ripalda lists the Our Father, Hail Mary, Creed, and Salve Regina. But he simply includes these prayers. He does not explain them. Gerónimo Ripalda, *Catecismo y exposicion breve de la doctrina christiana . . .* (Puebla: Pedro de la Rosa, 1784), 4–38.

13. Richard Boyer, in his study of plebeian culture in colonial Mexico, has argued that the catechizing endeavor of the colonial church was at best a partial success. Many plebeians prosecuted by the Inquisition could not recite their prayers with complete accuracy. Richard Boyer, *Lives of the Bigamists: Marriage, Family, and Community in Colonial Mexico* (Albuquerque: University of New Mexico Press, 1995), 220–29.

14. William B. Taylor, *Magistrates of the Sacred: Priests and Parishioners in Eighteenth-Century Mexico* (Stanford: Stanford University Press, 1996), 158–62.

15. *Concilio provincial mexicano IV, celebrado en la ciudad de México el año 1771* (Querétaro: Escuela de Artes, 1898), 3–4.

16. Schroeder, *Canons*, 195; and *Concilio III*, 25–26.

17. *Concilio IV*, 2–3. Sermons delivered by priests on Sundays and feast days must have constituted the primary method of dissemination of the episcopate's discourse on piety. But as we will see in Chapter 8, many priests continued to participate in the practices of baroque Catholicism. This suggests that the lower clergy was an imperfect medium for the advocacy of religious reform. For a brief introduction to preaching in eighteenth-century Mexico, see Carlos Herrejón Peredo, "El sermón en Nueva España durante la segunda mitad del siglo XVIII," in *La iglesia católica en México*, ed. Nelly Sigaut (Zamora: El Colegio de Michoacán, 1997). Herrejón Peredo argues that sermons in the second half of the eighteenth century emphasized the interiority of religious engagement.

18. Núñez de Haro y Peralta, *Sermones*, vol. 1, 284.

19. In fact, the Tridentine church encouraged devotions like reading prayer books, lighting candles, signing hymns, and praying the rosary during mass. Clifford

Howell, S. J., "From Trent to Vatican II," in *The Study of Liturgy*, ed. Cheslyn Jones, Geoffrey Wainwright, and Edward Yarnold (New York: Oxford University Press, 1978), 244–45; Theoder Klauser, *A Short History of the Western Liturgy: An Account and Some Reflections*, 2nd ed., trans. John Halliburton (New York: Oxford University Press, 1979), 120; and Owen Chadwick, *The Popes and the European Revolution* (Oxford: Clarendon Press, 1981), 72.

20. Núñez de Haro y Peralta, *Sermones*, vol. 1, 220.

21. Saenger, "Books of Hours," 149; Joseph Boneta y Laplana, *Gritos del purgatorio y medios para callarlos. Libro primero y sugundo* (Puebla de los Angeles: Diego Fernandez de Leon, 1708), 178–79.

22. *Catecismo para uso*, 292–94.

23. AC Edictos, caja 5, 1756, Sede Vacante.

24. Francisco Antonio Lorenzana, *Cartas pastorales y edictos del Illmo Señor D. Francisco Antonio Lorenzana y Buitrón, Arzobispo de México* (México: Joseph Antonio de Hogal, 1770), 50.

25. *Concilio IV*, 111–12.

26. The elevation of priests above parishioners began at least by the Fourth Lateran Council in 1215, when the church officially restricted the celebration of the mass to the ordained clergy. The Council of Trent and the Tridentine church continued this trend toward exalted priestly status. Nonetheless, during the late medieval and baroque periods, the laity retained easy access to the sacred in its many manifestations. Reformed Catholicism sought to limit these opportunities for the laity.

27. Núñez de Haro y Peralta, *Sermones*, vol. 2, 167.

28. AC Actas, vol. 49, 8 April 1768.

29. Ibid., 26 April 1768.

30. Núñez de Haro y Peralta, *Sermones*, vol. 2, 155–57.

31. Francisco Fabián y Fuero, *Colección de providencias diocesanas del obispado de la Puebla de los Ángeles . . .* (Puebla: Real Seminario Palafoxiano, 1770), 308–10.

32. Lorenzana, *Cartas*, 68.

33. Ibid., 188–90.

34. Ibid., 49–50.

35. Fabián y Fuero, *Colección de providencias*, 474–82. Apparently, priests in his see had been refusing to administer the viaticum because they could not arrange processions to travel to distant areas.

36. Núñez de Haro y Peralta, *Sermones*, vol. 1, 209–10.

37. Ibid., 218.

38. Ibid., 106–7.

39. Ibid., 77–79.

40. Fabián y Fuero, *Colección de providencias*, 477–78.

41. Núñez de Haro y Peralta, *Sermones*, vol. 2, 142.

42. Núñez de Haro y Peralta, *Sermones*, vol. 1, 104; Ibid., vol. 2, 96–97.

43. Fabián y Fuero, *Colección de providencias*, 477–78.

44. *Concilio IV*, 164–65.

45. Núñez de Haro y Peralta, *Sermones*, vol. 1, 290.

46. The campaign to devalue public acts of penitential piety was universal in Catholic countries in the eighteenth century. See Chadwick, *Popes*, 33–36.

47. *Concilio IV*, 161.

48. It is clear, however, that Afro-Mexican confraternities often practiced self-flagellation. Nicole von Germeten, *Black Blood Brothers: Confraternities and Social Mobility for Afro-Mexicans* (Gainesville: University Press of Florida, 2006), 23–40. Von Germeten argues that this fact may have created the perception that linked penitentes with socially marginalized populations. But it is clear that members of the elite participated in public self-flagellation as well. In fact, in seventeenth-century Spain, socially prominent groups monopolized public self-flagellation. Maureen Flynn, *Sacred Charity: Confraternities and Social Welfare in Spain, 1400–1700* (Ithaca: Cornell University Press, 1989), 127–33.

49. *Concilio IV*, 161.

50. Caroline Walker Bynum, *Holy Feast and Holy Fast: The Religious Significance of Food to Medieval Women* (Berkeley: University of California Press, 1987).

51. See Schroeder, *Canons*, 254; *Concilio III*, 341–46. Catholics over the age of twenty-one were required to take only one meal at midday on indicated days throughout the liturgical year. Furthermore, they were to refrain from consuming eggs, cheese, milk, and lard during the forty days of Lent and to abstain from meat every Friday and Saturday during the year.

52. *Concilio III*, 341–43.

53. *Concilio IV*, 172.

54. Fabián y Fuero, *Colección de providencias*, 216–18.

55. Ibid., 514.

56. Lorenzana, *Cartas*, 19.

57. AC Edictos, caja 6, 13 Feb. 1787.

58. See *Concilio III*, 422. Some printed documents on the church in the nineteenth century are included in the edition of the proceedings of the Third Mexican Provincial Council I consulted. The cathedral chapter of Mexico allowed all to partake of any food (from meat and dairy products) on days of partial abstinence, but did not dispense the faithful to eat freely on fast days.

59. Fabián y Fuero, *Colección de providencias*, 37–39.

60. Lorenzana, *Cartas*, 16–17.

61. *Concilio IV*, 157.

62. Núñez de Haro y Peralta, *Sermones*, vol. 1, 269.

63. Lorenzana, *Cartas*, 172.

64. Ibid., 168.

65. Ibid., 167.

66. Ibid., 166–67.

67. Núñez de Haro y Peralta, *Sermones*, vol. 1, 257–58.

68. In the same sermon Archbishop Núñez de Haro spoke of the early Christians' practice of charity: "They did not distribute their alms to lazy and non-humble persons, who, because they did not subject themselves to service or work, found

themselves in a voluntary and criminal misery. [It is] these . . . that so abound in this populous city." Núñez de Haro y Peralta, *Sermones*, vol. 1, 255.

69. Lorenzana, *Cartas*, 172–73, 186; BN Colección de Libros Raros y Curiosos, Francisco Antonio Lorenzana y Buitron, "Sermon derigido a sus feligreses al despedirse como arzobispo de México para hacerse cargo del arzobispado de Toledo," 7 March 1772, xiv.

70. Lorenzana, *Cartas*, 188. Executors were required to submit proof of completion of wills to an ecclesiastical tribunal. Lorenzana ordered the judge of this court to accept only receipts from the Hospicio de Pobres as valid evidence for the completion of bequests to the unspecified poor. Whether this edict was observed in practice is unclear.

71. Lorenzana, *Cartas*, 172–73.

72. Using his own funds, Lorenzana founded the Cuna in January 1766. The original house proved too small, so Lorenzana moved the Cuna to more ample quarters in 1772. For brief histories of the Cuna, see Pilar Gonzalbo Aizpuru, "La casa de niños expósitos de la Ciudad de México: una fundación del siglo XVIII." *Historia Mexicana* 31 (1982): 409–30; and Felipe Arturo Avila Espinosa, "Los niños abandonados de la casa de niños expósitos de la Ciudad de México: 1767–1821," in *La familia en el mundo iberoamericano*, ed. Pilar Gonzalbo Aizpuru and Cecilia Rabell (México: Instituto de Investigaciones Sociales, Universidad Nacional Autónoma de México, 1994).

73. Lorenzana, *Cartas*, 123–27.

74. Lorenzana, *Cartas*, 135.

75. Michel Foucault, *Discipline & Punish: The Birth of the Prison*, trans. Alan Sheridan (New York: Vintage Books, 1979).

76. See Chapter 6.

77. Archbishop Núñez de Haro, however, recommended the dissolution of hundreds of rural, indigenous confraternities in the archdiocese of Mexico. His reasoning seems to have been motivated by economic rather than religious concerns. For two accounts of confraternal reform in Bourbon New Spain see Clara García Ayluardo, "Confraternity, Cult and Crown in Colonial Mexico City, 1700–1810" (Ph.D. diss., Cambridge University, 1989), 268–78; and Francis Joseph Brooks, "Parish and Cofradía in Eighteenth-Century Mexico" (Ph.D. diss., Princeton University, 1976).

78. García Ayluardo, "Confraternity, Cult and Crown," 248–68.

79. Ibid., 258.

80. Lorenzana, *Cartas*, 75.

81. Ibid., 76.

82. García Ayluardo, "Confraternity, Cult and Crown," 37, 181–82. Promoting the blessed sacrament confraternities, the Fourth Mexican Provincial Council mandated that they be given precedence of place in processions, regardless of the date of their foundation, the criterion most often used to determine placement of confraternities in processions. *Concilio IV*, 67. Matthew D. O'Hara, however, has found that blessed sacrament confraternities did not always bow to the will of their parish priests. Spanish confraternities in the Mexico City parish of Santa

Cruz y Soledad, including the parish's blessed sacrament confraternity, refused to supply funds to their pastor, Gregorio Pérez Cancio, for the building of a new church. Disputes between confreres and pastor eventually led to Pérez Cancio's arrest. Matthew D. O'Hara, "Stone, Mortar, and Memory: Church Construction and Communities in Late Colonial Mexico City," *Hispanic American Historical Review* 86 (2006): 673–77. Similarly, the blessed sacrament confraternity of the parish of Santiago in the provincial city of Querétaro defied its pastor over questions of autonomy from parish oversight. Brian C. Belanger, "Secularization and the Laity of Colonial Mexico: Querétaro, 1598–1821" (Ph.D. diss., Tulane University, 1990), 112–20.

83. García Ayluardo, "Confraternity, Cult, and Crown," 276–78. I calculated the minimum number of confraternities suppressed in Mexico City from the table of all confraternities extant in the capital contained in Alicia Bazarte Martínez, *Las cofradías de españoles en la ciudad de México* (México: Universidad Autónoma Metropolitana, 1989), 64–67. I speak of a minimum number because this table significantly undercounts the number of confraternities in Mexico City in 1794. William Taylor has argued that the archbishop did not suppress rural confraternities, but merely degraded their status to informal organizations. Taylor, *Magistrates of the Sacred*, 307–11. Perhaps the same occurred in Mexico City. Archbishop Núñez de Haro y Peralta suppressed eight confraternities in Querétaro during two episcopal visitations. He amalgamated all of these suppressed confraternities into the blessed sacrament confraternity of the city's main parish of Santiago. Belanger, "Secularization and the Laity," 106–13.

CHAPTER 8

1. AN Notary # 522, vol. 3511, fols. 170–77, Mexico City, 11 Dec. 1813, will of Jose Buenaventura Santa Maria y Liparza notarized by Juan Manuel Pozo.

2. Ibid.

3. David A. Brading, "Tridentine Catholicism and Enlightened Despotism in Bourbon Mexico," *Journal of Latin American Studies* 15 (1983): 1–22; David A. Brading, *The First America: The Spanish Monarchy, Creole Patriots, and the Liberal State, 1492–1867* (New York: Cambridge University Press, 1991), 492–513; David A. Brading, *Church and State in Bourbon Mexico: The Diocese of Michoacán, 1749–1810* (New York: Cambridge University Press, 1994); William B. Taylor, *Magistrates of the Sacred: Priests and Parishioners in Eighteenth-Century Mexico* (Stanford: Stanford University Press, 1996); Pamela Voekel, *Alone Before God: The Religious Origins of Modernity in Mexico* (Durham: Duke University Press, 2002); Ellen Gunnarsdóttir, *Mexican Karismata: The Baroque Vocation of Francisca de los Ángeles, 1674–1744* (Lincoln: University of Nebraska Press, 2004), especially pages 219–25; and Juan Pedro Viqueira Albán, *Propriety and Permissiveness in Bourbon Mexico*, trans. Sonya Lipsett-Rivera and Sergio Rivera Ayala (Wilmington: Scholarly Resources, 1999), 103–28.

4. Voekel, *Alone Before God*, 66–71.

5. See Chapter 6 of this volume.

6. Juan Javier Pescador, *De bautizados a fieles difuntos: Familia y mentalidad en una parroquia urbana: Santa Catarina de México, 1568–1820* (México: El Colegio de México, 1992), 98–106.

7. Antonio Rubial García, *La santidad controvertida: hagiografía y conciencia criolla alrededor de los venerables no canonizados de Nueva España* (México: Fondo de Cultura Económica, 1999), 84–85.

8. I consulted the reprinted edition published in 1807. Fernando Martagon, *Exercicios espirituales para desagraviar á Maria Santisima, Nuestra Señora de los Dolores* (México: Mariano Joseph de Zúñiga y Ontiveros, 1807), 33–34.

9. Ibid., 55–56, 64–65.

10. Ibid., 178–79.

11. Martagon instructed his readers to fast and practice self-mortification if they could do so conveniently and if their health permitted. He required that they receive approval from their "spiritual father" to practice these penitences. He also asked readers to recite seven Hail Marys each morning "in memory and reverence of the seven principle sorrows that Our Lady suffered." Martagon, *Exercicios espirituales*, 3, 6.

12. *Devocionario para honrar al glorioso San Antonio de Padua y solicitar su poderosa protección, tanto en los dias de su novena como en el dia trece de cada mes* (México: Mariano Ontiveros, 1821).

13. José Vicente de Ochoa Villaseñor, *Escala del cielo que con piadoso afecto ofrece a los fieles de Jesucristo* (México: Felipe de Zúñiga y Ontiveros, 1793), 50–54, 60.

14. First published in 1726, it was reprinted in 1728, 1732, 1736, 1745, 1751, 1756, 1769, and 1784.

15. Karen Melvin, "Urban Religions: Mendicant Orders in New Spain's Cities, 1570–1800" (Ph.D. diss., University of California, Berkeley, 2005), 203–43.

16. Taylor, *Magistrates of the Sacred*, on priestly education, 88–92; on preaching and teaching, 160–62; on the qualifications of the urban clergy, 88.

17. Voekel, *Alone Before God*, 124–25.

18. BN LaFragua 1276, "Sermon que en la solemne funcion con que se dio principio a real congregacion del alumbrado y vela continua del Santisimo Sacramento del altar, celebrado en la Yglesia parroquial de San Sebastian de la ciudad de Mexico, en donde se ha establecido, el dia de 11 de Marzo de 1793, predicó el Sr. Dr. D. Joseph Ruiz de conejares, Canónigo de la Santa Yglesia Metropolitana de la misma ciudad."

19. William B. Taylor, "Between Nativitas and Mexico City: An Eighteenth-Century Pastor's Local Religion," in *Local Religion in Colonial Mexico*, ed. Martin Austin Nesvig (Albuquerque: University of New Mexico Press, 2006). Quotation taken from page 92.

20. For a brief history of San Felipe de Jesús, see Rubial García, *Santidad controvertida*, 133–35.

21. AGN Reales Cedulas Originales, vol. 195, exp. 109, fols. 223–33.

22. David Brading argues that in the end the processions were allowed to continue. Brading, *Church and State*, 169–70.

23. In 1779 priests accounted for 10.4 percent of all testators and 13.2 percent of those who issued at least one baroque pious directive; in 1796 9.4 percent of testators and 6.3 percent of those who commissioned a baroque directive; and in 1813 10 percent of testators and 11.9 percent of those who included a baroque pious directive.

24. Michel Vovelle, *Piété baroque et déchristianisation en Provence au XVIIIᵉ siecle: Les attitudes devant la mort d'apres les clauses des testaments* (Paris: Plon, 1973), 94–100; John McManners, *Death and the Enlightenment: Changing Attitudes to Death among Christians and Unbelievers in Eighteenth-Century France* (New York: Clarendon Press, 1981), 299–302; María José de la Pascua, *Vivir la muerte en el Cádiz del setecientos, 1675–1801* (Cádiz: Fundación Municipal de Cultura del Ayuntamiento de Cádiz, 1990), 153–64; Voekel, *Alone Before God,* 62–71.

25. AN Notary # 85, vol. 561, n.f., Mexico City, 12 June 1813, will of Barbara Rodriguez de Velasco Ximenes notarized by Joaquin Barrientos.

26. AN Notary # 81, vol. 525, fols. 22–26, Mexico City, 28 Nov. 1779, will of Yldephonzo Antonio de Yniesta Vejarano notarized by Antonio Barrantes.

27. AN Notary # 417, vol. 2746, fols. 258–63, Mexico City, 9 June 1796, will of Antonia Tenorio de la Vanda y Victoria notarized by Jose Ignacio Montes de Oca.

28. AN Notary # 19, vol. 134, fols. 499–503, Mexico City, 5 Aug. 1737, will of Francisco Manuel Chirlin notarized by Juan Antonio Arroyo.

29. AN Notary # 519, vol. 3465, fols. 53–56, Mexico City, 11 Feb. 1796, will of Jose de Noriega notarized by Felipe Francisco Oton Pasalle.

30. AN Notary # 519, vol. 3349, fols. 62–65, Mexico City, 23 Feb. 1779, will of Juan Francisco de Segura notarized by Felipe Francisco Oton Passalle.

31. AN Notary # 235, vol. 1466, fols. 16–18, Mexico City, 17 Jan. 1737, will of Joseph Estensoro de la Peña y Cortasar notarized by Toribio Fernandez de Cosgaya.

32. AN Notary # 479, vol. 3258, fols. 17–20, Mexico City, 2 Aug. 1758, will of Fernando Rodriguez de Araujo notarized by Manuel Jose de Ochoa.

33. AN Notary # 417, vol. 2763, fols. 284–86, Mexico City, 23 Oct. 1813, will of Pedro Guerrero notarized by Jose Ignacio Montes de Oca.

34. AN Notary # 84, vol. 542, fols. 294–312, Mexico City, 19 Dec. 1796, will of Antonia Gomez Rodriguez de Pedrozo notarized by Antonio Burillo.

35. AN Notary # 602, vol. 4068, fols. 58–59, Mexico City, 13 Aug. 1813, will of Bernardo Palacio notarized by Antonio Ramirez Arellano.

36. AN Notary # 359, vol. 2325, fols. 187–97, Mexico City, 11 Oct. 1796, will of Pedro Andrade Moctezuma Mellado y San José notarized by Jose Lopez Valdes.

37. AN Notary # 569, vol. 3931, fols. 68–72, Mexico City, 2 May 1737, will of Pedro de la Canadilla notarized by Juan Romo de Vera.

38. AN Notary # 460, vol. 3137, fols. 14–18, Mexico City, 15 Sept. 1796, will of Maria Barbara Jimenez notarized by Manuel Jose Nuñez Morillon.

39. The vast majority of the population of Mexico City in the late eighteenth century earned less than three hundred pesos per year. For instance, a cigarette roller in the royal tobacco manufactory could earn from seventy to 140 pesos a year, a cigar roller from 140 to 280 pesos a year. Administrators, clerks, and bureaucrats usually made more. The administrator of the tobacco manufactory earned a salary of two thousand pesos per year in 1801, whereas the accountant of the manufactory, the

second highest paid official, earned 1,500 pesos per year. Of course, the majority of the population did not hold such "white-collar" positions. Susan Deans-Smith, *Bureaucrats, Planters, and Workers: The Making of the Tobacco Monopoly in Bourbon Mexico* (Austin: University of Texas Press, 1992), 191–97.

40. AN Notary # 519, vol. 3465, fols. 209–14, Mexico City, 22 June 1796, will of Antonio de Vivanco Gutierrez notarized by Felipe Francisco Oton Pasalle.

41. AN Notary # 199, vol. 1316, fols. 38–43, Mexico City, 28 Jan. 1696, will of Juana Mexia Altamirano notarized by Juan Diaz de Rivera.

42. AN Notary # 417, vol. 2746, fols. 356–62, Mexico City, 26 Aug. 1796, will of Francisco Mejia notarized by Jose Ignacio Montes de Oca.

43. AN Notary # 210, vol. 1403, fols. 144–49, Mexico City, 19 June 1813, will of Jacinto Francisco Tesorel y Paredes notarized by Juan Mariano Diaz.

44. AN Notary # 588, vol. 4013, fols. 4–19, Mexico City, 19 Jan. 1737, will of Catarina Paez de la Cadena notarized by Francisco de Rivera Butron.

45. AN Notary # 410, vol. 2701, fols. 30–35, Mexico City, 4 Dec. 1779, will of Maria Anna Josefa de Palacio notarized by Jose Antonio Martinez del Campo.

46. AN Notary # 741, vol. 5246, fols. 81–89, Mexico City, 8 Jan. 1696, Mexico City, will of Juan de Dios de Medina y Picaso notarized by Juan de Zearreta.

47. AN Notary # 31, vol. 264, fols. 36–38, Mexico City, 3 Aug. 1779, will of Bernardo Juan Arias notarized by Ignacio Javier de Alba.

48. AN Notary # 143, vol. 867, fols. 48–58, Mexico City, 13 June 1779, will of Domingo Antonio Lopez notarized by Jose Carbello.

49. AN Notary # 483, vol. 3283, fols. 38–40, Mexico City, 2 May 1813, will of Ignacio Herrera y Estrada notarized by Jose Basilio Ortiz.

50. AN Notary # 155, vol. 924, fols. 511–20, Mexico City, 8 Oct. 1813, will of Esteban Diaz Gonzalez notarized by Francisco Calapiz y Aguilar.

51. He died in 1800.

52. See Chapter 7.

53. In 1696 only ten testators requested an anti-baroque simple funeral, in 1717 five, in 1737 sixteen, in 1758 ten, in 1779 fifteen, in 1796 eighteen, and in 1813 fifty-five.

54. Voekel, *Alone Before God*, 84–105.

55. In 1796 76.2 percent of baroque testators signed their wills and 88.9 percent of reformed testators did so.

56. Jean Franco, *Plotting Women: Gender and Representation in Mexico* (New York: Columbia University Press, 1989), xv.

57. Voekel, *Alone Before God*, 144–45.

58. Charles C. Noel, "Missionary Preachers in Spain: Teaching Social Virtue in the Eighteenth Century," *American Historical Review* 90 (1985): 869.

59. In 1696, eight notaries (out of a total of thirty who notarized baroque wills) notarized 60.2 percent of baroque wills, but only 50.4 percent of all wills. They are José Anaya y Bonillo, Juan de Condarco y Cáceres, Juan Díaz de Rivera, Ramón de Espinosa, Martín del Río, Francisco de Solís y Alcázar, Miguel Leonardo de Sevilla, and Isidro Javier de Velasco. In 1717, five notaries (out of a total of twenty-one who notarized baroque wills) notarized 45.5 percent of baroque wills, but only 35.2 percent of all wills. They are José Anaya y Bonillo, Pedro Gil Guerrero, Felipe

Muñoz de Castro, José Manuel de Paz, and José de Trujillo. In 1737, nine notaries (out of a total of thirty-six who notarized baroque wills) notarized 57.3 percent of baroque wills, but only 39.3 percent of all wills. They are Juan Antonio Arroyo, José Antonio de Anaya, Luis de Benavides, Manuel de Bensumea Jiménez, José Victoriano Delgado, Felipe Muñoz de Castro, Francisco Romero Zapata, Juan Romo de Vera, and Francisco Rivera Butrón. In 1813, five notaries (out of a total of twenty-two who notarized baroque wills) notarized 59.3 percent of baroque wills, but only 41.4 percent of all wills. They are Francisco Calapiz y Aguilar, José Ignacio Montes de Oca, Joé María Moya, Ignacio Valle, and Manuel Ymaz y Cabanilas.

60. In 1758, two notaries (out of twenty-nine who notarized baroque wills) notarized 21.4 percent of baroque wills and 16.4 percent of all wills. They are Mariano Buenaventura de Arroyo and Diego Jacinto de Leon. The seven notaries who notarized 48.7 percent of baroque wills in 1779 are Iganacio Javier de Alba, Diego Jacinto de Leon, José Bernardo de Navia, José Manuel Ochoa, Felipe Francisco Otón Pasalle, Antonio de la Torre, and José Antonio Troncoso. In 1796, five notaries (out of twenty-eight who notarized baroque wills) notarized 41.1 percent of baroque wills and 36.7 percent of all wills. They are Francisco Calapiz y Águilar, José López Váldes, José Ignacio Montes de Oca, Felipe Francisco Otón Pasalle, and Juan José Ramírez de Arellano.

61. In 1758, Mariano Buenaventura de Arroyo notarized eight wills, of which five contained baroque directives. In that year, he accounted for 8.9 percent of baroque wills, but only 4.2 percent of all wills. In 1779 José Antonio Troncosco notarized six wills, of which four contained baroque directives. He accounted for 5.9 percent of baroque wills, but only 2.7 percent of all wills. And in 1796, José López Váldes notarized seven wills, of which four contained baroque directives. He accounted for 6.3 percent of baroque wills, but only 3.5 percent of all wills.

62. In addition to Juan Romo de Vera, nine notaries showed strong tendencies toward reformed wills. In 1779, José Bernardo de Navia notarized four reformed wills, or 26.7 percent of reformed wills, but only 5.9 percent of all wills. In 1796, Antonio de Casas y Orellana notarized three reformed wills, or 16.7 percent of reformed wills, but only 1.5 percent of all wills. In the same year, José Basilio Ortiz notarized three reformed wills, or 16.7 percent of reformed wills, but only 4 percent of all wills. In 1813, six notaries exhibited an inclination to notarize wills for reformed testators. They are Joaquin Barrientos, Francisco Calapiz y Aguilar, Juan Mariano Díaz, Juan Manuel Pozo, Antonio Ramírez Arellano, and Ignacio Valle. In all they notarized thirty-two reformed wills, or 58.2 percent of reformed wills, but only 36.2 percent of all wills.

CHAPTER 9

1. AN Notary # 350, vol. 2307, fols. 466–78, Mexico City, 22 Dec. 1779, will of Juan de Sierra Uruñuela notarized by Diego Jacinto de Leon.

2. A few testators bequeathed money to fund dowries for orphaned girls. Because these gifts were given to anonymous recipients (those who did not live in the household of the testator), I have not included them here.

3. Although occurring centuries later, this pattern of decline in personalized care for orphans after the foundation of the orphanage in Mexico City follows a trend established in Europe during the fourteenth century when foundling homes were widely established. John Boswell, *The Kindness of Strangers: The Abandonment of Children in Western Europe from Late Antiquity to the Renaissance* (New York: Vintage Books, 1988), especially pages 414–27.

4. Josefina Muriel de la Torre, *Hospitales de la Nueva España* (México: Universidad Nacional, Instituto de Historia, 1956), vol. 1, 37–46.

5. Ibid., vol. 2, 31.

6. Of the three orders, the Brothers of Charity experienced the greatest difficulties. The order of San Hipólito, the only religious order native to Mexico, had begun in the sixteenth century as an association of charitable lay people dedicated to the care of any and all in the capital who needed aid, but in time came to specialize in care for the mentally ill. Its founder, Bernardino Álvarez, wrote a simple rule for the devout laity who assisted in the hospital and petitioned the papacy to recognize the group as a religious order. Papal recognition did not come until 1700, when Innocent XII placed the order of San Hipólito under the rule of St. Augustine. Strangely, the Brothers of Charity abandoned monastic discipline shortly after papal recognition. During the first half of the eighteenth century, the conduct of the order scandalized the public. The order could not attract novices, its membership aged, and its hospitals deteriorated. The order underwent a period of reform in the 1770s, but relapsed into chaos by the turn of the century. Luisa Zahino Peñafort, *Iglesia y sociedad en México, 1765–1800: Tradición, reforma, y reacciones* (México: Universidad Nacional Autónoma de México, 1996), 133–38; Muriel, *Hospitales de la Nueva España*, vol. 1, 227.

7. AN Notary # 519, vol. 3449, fols. 454–67, Mexico City, 24 Nov. 1779, will of Jose Augustin de Lecumberry notarized by Felipe Francisco Oton Passalle.

8. AN Notary # 519, vol. 3449, fols. 348–51, Mexico City, 2 Sept. 1779, will of Andres Martinez Campillo notarized by Felipe Francisco Oton Passalle.

9. AN Notary # 350, vol. 2307, fols. 198–99, Mexico City, 15 June 1779, will of Andres Ambrosio de Llanos y Valdes notarized by Diego Jacinto de Leon.

10. AN Notary # 522, vol. 3511, fols. 86–89, Mexico City, 3 July 1813, will of Policarpo Cristomo Davila notarized by Juan Manuel Pozo.

11. Michael Scardaville, "Crime and the Urban Poor: Mexico City in the Late Colonial Period" (Ph.D. diss., University of Florida, 1977), 70.

12. Silvia Marina Arrom, *Containing the Poor: The Mexico City Poor House, 1774–1871* (Durham: Duke University Press, 2000). The rejection of the Hospicio's aims in Mexico City coincides with the condition of poor relief in Spain during the late eighteenth century. William Callahan has argued that the crown, after a popular uprising that forced Charles III to flee Madrid in 1766, began to establish workhouses for the confinement of the poor throughout the peninsula because it suddenly viewed beggars as a major threat to the established order. Despite the royal initiative to establish workhouses, the crown left the financial support of these institutions to the general populace. According to Callahan, the Spanish population withheld its support and continued to distribute alms to the poor on a face-to-face basis. William Callahan, "The Problem of Confinement: An Aspect of

Poor Relief in Eighteenth-Century Spain," *Hispanic American Historical Review* 51 (1971): 1–24.

13. Scardaville, "Crime and the Urban Poor," 48.

14. Alexander von Humboldt, *Ensayo político sobre el reino de la Nueva España* (México: Editorial Porrúa, 1966), 577.

15. Arrom, *Containing the Poor*, 81; and Scardaville, "Crime and the Urban Poor," 70.

16. Scardaville, "Crime and the Urban Poor," 69.

17. Arrom, *Containing the Poor*, 57.

18. Although Patricia Seed does not address the question of the relative openness of colonial Mexican families, she does argue that parental authority over children's marital decisions increased in the late eighteenth century. This may represent a hardening of the family unit and an unwillingness to accept undesirable elements into the family. Patricia Seed, *To Love, Honor, and Obey in Colonial Mexico: Conflicts over Marriage Choice, 1574–1821* (Stanford: Stanford University Press, 1988).

19. Dorothy Tanck de Estrada, "The 'Escuelas Pías' of Mexico City, 1768–1820," *Americas* 31 (1974): 51–71.

20. Quoted from Tanck de Estrada, "The 'Escuelas Pías' of Mexico City," 53.

21. AN Notary # 143, vol. 867, fols. 48–58, Mexico City, 13 June 1779, will of Domingo Antonio Lopez notarized by Jose Carbello.

22. AN Notary # 155, vol. 924, fols. 520–33, Mexico City, 9 Oct. 1813, will of Maria Rita Yañes notarized by Francisco Calapiz y Aguilar.

23. Arrom, *Containing the Poor*, 11–22.

24. Like the presence of planets in distant solar systems, the rise of the modern sense of the bounded individual is difficult to observe directly. But just as a planet's presence can be deduced by variations it causes in a star's movement, the bounded individual can be inferred by changes in more observable cultural practices—practices like participation in confraternities.

25. The steady decline in claims to confraternal membership by testators continues a pattern begun in the seventeenth century. Nicole von Germeten demonstrates that participation rates in confraternities in Mexico City declined somewhat even over the seventeenth century. In fact the decades of 1680s and 1690s marked the low point for confraternal participation. Nicole von Germeten, "Death in Black and White: Testaments and Confraternal Devotion in Seventeenth-Century Mexico City," *Colonial Latin American Historical Review* 12 (2003): 283–89.

26. AN Notary # 93, vol. 587, fols. 27–28, Mexico City, 9 Aug. 1813, will of Maria Luisa de la Puente y Becerra notarized by Manuel Bravo Torija; AN Notary # 155, vol. 924, fols. 255–57, Mexico City, 12 June 1813, will of Luis Martinez notarized by Francisco Calapiz y Aguilar; AN Notary # 155, vol. 924, fols. 373–76, Mexico City, 12 Aug. 1813, will of Maria Barbara Fernandez notarized by Francisco Calapiz y Aguilar; AN Notary # 158, vol. 950, n.f., Mexico City, 26 Feb. 1813, will of Francisco Xavier Paez notarized by José Cano y Moctezuma; AN Notary # 610, vol. 4088, n.f., Mexico City, 1 Sept. 1813, will of Ana Maria Andrade notarized by Mariano Gonzalez de la Rosa.

27. AN Notary # 600, vol. 4055, fols. 143–48, Mexico City, 16 Jan. 1779, will of Marcos Francisco Maldonado notarized by Bernardo de Rivera Buitron.

28. John McManners, *Death and the Enlightenment: Changing Attitudes to Death among Christians and Unbelievers in Eighteenth-Century France* (New York: Clarendon Press, 1981), 233; William J. Callahan, "Las cofradías y hermandades de España y su papel social y religioso dentro de una sociedad de estamentos," in *Cofradías, capellanías y obras pías en la América colonial,* ed. Pilar Martínez López-Cano, Gisela von Wobeser, and Juan Guillermo Muñoz (México: Universidad Nacional Autónoma de México, 1998), 36.

29. AGN Reales Cédulas Originales, vol. 146, exp. 194, fols. 374–79, Madrid, 20 July 1790. The original petition to found the order was dated 1786.

30. Three testators, or 8.6 percent of all testators who claimed membership in a confraternity in 1717, employed this hybrid discourse.

31. AN Notary # 65, vol. 471, fols. 11–16, Mexico City, 19 June 1717, will of Bartholome de Arellano notarized by Juan de Balbuena.

32. AN Notary # 475, vol. 3249, fols. 104–8, Mexico City, 25 April 1717, will of Maria de Vargas notarized by Diego de Olaiz.

33. AN Notary # 669, vol. 4530, fols. 698–701, Mexico City, 15 Oct. 1779, will of Josefa Rodriguez de Pinillos notarized by Antonio de la Torre.

34. AN Notary # 480, vol. 3264, fols. 35–38, Mexico City, 8 May 1779, will of Josefa de Salcedo notarized by Jose Manuel Ochoa.

35. AN Notary # 745, vol. 5281, n.f., Mexico City, 10 April 1758, will of Raphael de Zeballos notarized by Ambrosio Zevallos.

36. AN Notary # 132, vol. 832, fols. 23–25, Mexico City, ? Nov. 1737, will of Marcos de Mendoza notarized by Jose Caballero.

37. AN Notary # 425, vol. 2820, fols. 98–101, Mexico City, 9 July 1813, will of Maria Manuela Jimenez de Velasco notarized by Jose Maria Moya.

38. Pamela Voekel, *Alone Before God: The Religious Origins of Modernity in Mexico* (Durham: Duke University Press, 2002), 162–66.

CONCLUSION

1. AN Notary # 738, vol. 5229, fols. 89–91, Mexico City, 24 Dec. 1813, will of Maria Guadalupe Antonia Sandoval Garcia Bravo notarized by Manuel Ymaz y Cabanillas.

2. María included two other liturgical gestures in her will. She established two chantries, each worth five thousand pesos. She stipulated that the priest responsible for the first chantry celebrate a mass dedicated to Our Lady of Sorrows every Friday of the year. The priest charged with the second chantry was to say mass every Saturday in honor of Our Lady of Solitude.

3. Pamela Voekel, *Alone Before God: The Religious Origins of Modernity in Mexico* (Durham: Duke University Press, 2002).

4. Virginia Guedea, "Las primeras elecciones populares en la ciudad de México, 1812–1813," *Mexican Studies* 7 (1991): 1–28; Virginia Guedea, "El pueblo de México y la

política capitalina, 1808 y 1812," *Mexican Studies* 10 (1994): 27–61. Guedea offers a detailed narrative of both elections and states that creoles won all seats available. Her analysis is flawed by an equation of creoles with autonomists and separatists. Nonetheless, she does demonstrate that many of the elected favored autonomy.

5. María Guadalupe Antonia Sandoval García Bravo's liturgical gesture directly involved her body—the burial of her corpse. Most testators who included liturgical gestures in their wills, however, did so in requests for masses at which their bodies were not present. Nonetheless, as I argue in Chapter 3, liturgical gestures in mass requests are ontologically identical to those performed by or on bodies. Hence the presence of liturgical elements in mass requests strongly suggests that those testators performed bodily liturgical gestures in life.

NOTES ON SOURCES

1. See the introduction for a discussion of this process.
2. Ann W. Ramsey, "Piety in Paris during the League, 1585–1590: An Urban Community in Transition" (Ph.D. diss., Columbia Unversity, 1991), 307–8, 313–19, 328; Julio Antonio Vaquero Iglesias, *Muerte e ideología en las Austurias del siglo XIX* (Madrid: Siglo Veintiuno de España Editores, S.A., 1991), 109.
3. Philippe Aries, *The Hour of Our Death*, trans. Helen Weaver (New York: Alfred A. Knopf, 1981), 198; Carlos M. N. Eire, *From Madrid to Purgatory: The Art and Craft of Dying in Sixteenth-Century Spain* (New York: Cambridge University Press, 1995), 20–23. The requirement that a Christian must redact a will in order to receive burial in consecrated ground seems never to have been promulgated in Mexico. None of the four provincial councils held in New Spain during the colonial period mentions this stipulation.
4. *Dificultad imaginada, facilidad verdadera en la práctica de testamentos reducida a ocho documentos en que se manifiesta la facilidad conque se pueden tener en sana salud ortorgados los testamentos....* (México: Viuda de Miguel de Ribera Calderón, 1714), 4–5.
5. H. J. Schroeder, *Canons and Decrees of the Council of Trent* (Rockford: Tan Books and Publishers, Inc., 1978), 156–57.
6. *Concilio III provincial mexicano celebrado en México en año 1585....* (Barcelona: Manuel Miró y D. Marsa, 1870), 272–75; *Concilio IV provincial mexicano celebrado año de 1771* (Querétaro: Escuela de Artes, 1898), 142.
7. For more on the social nature of death, see John Bossy, *Christianity in the West, 1400–1700* (New York: Oxford University Press, 1985), 26–27; John McManners, *Death and the Enlightenment: Changing Attitudes to Death among Christians and Unbelievers in Eighteenth-Century France* (New York: Clarendon Press, 1981), 231.
8. Aries, *Hour of Our Death*, 99–110, 300–310; Eire, *From Madrid*, 32–33.
9. Alonso Núñez de Haro y Peralta, *Sermones escogidos, pláticas espirituales privadas, y dos pastorales anteriormente impresas en México del Excelentísimo Señor D. Alonso Núñez de Haro y Peralta....* (Madrid: Hija de Ibarra, 1806), vol. 2, 170.
10. Núñez de Haro, *Sermones*, vol. 1, 169–73.

11. For more on this shift in notions surrounding death, see Aries, *Hour of Our Death*, 300–310; Vaquero, *Muerte*, 15–19. For more on the rise of the bounded individual in Bourbon Mexico, see Chapter 9.

12. *Concilios provinciales primer y segundo celebrados en la muy noble y muy leal ciudad de México, presidiendo el Illmo y Rmo Señor S. F. Alonso de Montúfar en los años 1555 y 1565. . . .* (México: Joseph Antonio de Hogal, 1769), 55–56; *Concilio III*, 401–2; *Concilio IV*, 195.

13. *Catecismo para uso de los párrocos hecho por el IV concilio provincial mexicano, celebrado año de 1771* (México: Joseph de Jauregui 1772), 121; *Concilios*, 191; *Concilio IV*, 297. The Third Mexican Provincial Council set the fine at fifty pesos.

14. For detailed prescriptions on the arrangement of the procession, the preparation of the moribund's residence for reception of the eucharist, and the procedure for the rite itself see, Agustín Vetancurt, *Manual de administrar lòs santos sacramentos conforme a la reforma de Paulo V y Urbano VIII. . . .* (México: Francisco Rodríguez Lupercio, 1674), 31–36; Miguel Venegas, *Manual de párrocos para administrar los santos sacramentos y exercer otras funciones ecclesiasticas conforme al ritual romano* (México: Joseph Bernardo de Hogal, 1731), 60–68.

15. Venegas, *Manual de párrocos*, 78–83.

16. *Concilio IV*, 27–28.

17. Vetancurt, *Manual de administrar*, 36–40; Venegas, *Manual de párrocos*, 71–77.

18. While conducting research, I briefly examined death records from three parishes in Mexico City: the Sagrario, Santa Catarina Mártir, and Santa Veracruz. This cursory examination revealed that when a parish actually recorded who received the last rites almost all those listed had in fact received them. Of course, the more time-consuming rites that required a priest's presence were probably confined to the few who could pay for them.

19. Archbishop Núñez de Haro fulminated against those who gave such instructions on the deathbed, but who failed to convert their hearts to God. Núñez de Haro, *Sermones*, vol. 1, 183.

20. Vetancurt, *Manual de administrar*, 103–4.

21. AN Notary # 73, vol. 512, fols. 168–70, Mexico City, 17 June 1737, will of Juan Angel de Urra notarized by Juan Francisco Benitez Trigueros.

22. AN Notary # 235, vol. 1466, fols. 207–10, Mexico City, 3 Aug. 1737, will of Francisco Gregorio Cano notarized by Toribio Fernandez de Cosgaya.

23. AN Notary # 391, vol. 2593, fols. 344–50, Mexico City, 18 Sept. 1737, will of Francisco Ruiz de Castañeda notarized by Felipe Muñoz de Castro.

24. Venegas, *Manual de párrocos*, 80. Priests were under the same obligation in eighteenth-century France. McManners, *Death*, 239.

25. Surprisingly, epidemic disease played little role in the percentage of testators who wrote their wills while ill from 1717 to 1796. The incidence of will writing while ill in the plague years of 1737 and 1779 is consistent with that of 1717 and 1796, two non-plague years. Fear of contracting disease must have inspired healthy people to write wills in these plague years.

26. AN Notary # 9, vol. 30, fols. 264–66, Mexico City, 9 Dec. 1696, will of Juan de Olivares Toralbo notarized by Antonio de Anaya.

27. AN Notary # 73, vol. 512, fols. 38–40, Mexico City, 15 Feb. 1737, will of Miguel Ballesteros notarized by Juan Francisco Benitez Trigueros.

28. AN Notary # 13, vol. 55, fols. 427–28, Mexico City, 3 Aug. 1696, will of Juan Sanchez Pujarte notarized by Jose Anaya y Bonillo.

29. For instance, Antonio Cabello, a merchant, first redacted his will when ill. A year later he informed the notary who had proved his testament that he wished to write another. Because, now healthy and with time to ponder the disposition of his goods at length, he considered his first will inadequate. AN Notary # 459, vol. 3132, n.f., Mexico City, 9 Sept. 1779, will of Antonio Cabello notarized by Jose Bernardo Navia.

30. *Dificultad imaginada*, 1–17.

31. Ibid., 53–54.

32. Juan Javier Pescador, *De bautizados a fieles difuntos: familia y mentalidad en una parroquia urbana: Santa Catarina de Mexico, 1568–1820* (México: El Colegio de México, 1992), 94–106.

33. AN Notary # 738, vol. 5229, fols. 57–59, Mexico City, 22 Aug. 1813, will of Jose Maria Ruiz notarized by Manuel Ymaz y Cabanillas.

34. AN Notary # 425, vol. 2820, fols. 138–40, Mexico City, 28 Sept. 1813, will of Francisco Guerra Mansanares notarized by Jose Maria Moya. This was dated according to the day the testator gave his final disposition, not on the day he was to sign the completed will.

35. AN Notary # 711, vol. 4790, fols. 66–69, Mexico City, 3 Aug. 1813, will of Barvara Castrejon notarized by Nicolas de Vega.

36. The honorific titles "don" and "doña" were ubiquitous by the eighteenth century and reveal little about a testator's social status.

37. For example, see AN Notary # 218, vol. 1419, fols. 77–79, Mexico City, 27 April 1696, will of Luisa de Torres y Castro notarized by Ramon de Espinosa.

38. For example, see AN Notary# 459, vol. 3132, n.f., Mexico City, 17 Feb. 1779, will of Jose Antonio Abiles notarized by Jose Bernardo de Navia.

39. For example, see AN Notary # 206, vol. 373, fols. 255–62, Mexico City, 23 April 1779, will of Manuel de Coellar y Ocon notarized by Andres Delgado Camargo.

40. For example, see AN Notary # 392, vol. 2608, fols. 88–92, Mexico City, 13 May 1737, will of Joseph de Lopeola notarized by Antonio Alejo de Mendoza.

41. For example, see AN Notary # 13, vol. 55, fols. 528–30, Mexico City, 29 Oct. 1696, will of Angela de Contheras Matiengo notarized by Jose Anaya y Bonillo.

42. For example, see AN Notary # 459, vol. 3132. n.f., Mexico City, 29 Aug. 1779, will of Josef Fernando Bustamante notarized by Jose Bernardo de Navia.

43. Pedro Murillo Velarde, *Práctica de testamentos en que se resuelven los casos mas frequentes que se ofrecen en la disposición de las últimas voluntades* (México: Joseph de Jauregui, 1790), 26; *Dificultad imaginada*, 27. Testators whose obligatory heirs were their parents could freely bequeath one-third of their property.

44. Eire, *From Madrid*, 19–20.

45. *Dificultad imaginada*, 33–36; *Práctica de testamentos*, 3.

BIBLIOGRAPHY

ARCHIVES AND ABBREVIATIONS

Archivo de la Catedral Metropolitana (Mexico City)   AC

Archivo General de la Nación (Mexico City)   AGN

Archivo General de Notarías (Mexico City)   AN

Biblioteca Nacional (Mexico City)   BN

PRINTED PRIMARY SOURCES

Abreu, Juan de. *Desagravios dolorosos de Maria, por los agravios ignominiosos de Christo.* México: Herederos de Miguel de Rivera, 1726.

Bolaños, Joaquin. *La portentosa vida de la Muerte: emperatriz de los sepulcros, vengadora de los agravios del Altísimo, y muy señora de la humana naturaleza.* México: Herederos de Joseph de Jauregui, 1792.

Boneta y Liplana, Joseph. *Gritos del purgatorio y medios para callarlos: Libro primero y segundo.* Puebla: Diego Fernández de Leon, 1708.

Cabrera y Quintero, Cayetano de. *Hebdomadario trino, exercicios devotos, y obsequiosos desagravios a la Santissima, Amabilissima, y Misericordiosissima Trinidad: por la execrable ingratitud y grossero olvido de los mortales en el mas pronto obsequio, devocion, y agradecimiento debido à tan soberano mysterio.* México: Viuda de don Joseph Bernardo de Hogal, 1745.

Calderon de la Barca, Frances. *Life in Mexico.* Berkeley: University of California Press, 1982.

Catecismo para uso de los párrocos hecho por el IV concilio provincial mexicanao, celebrado año de 1771. México: Joseph de Jauregui, 1772.

Concilio III provincial mexicano celebrado en México el año 1585, confirmado en Roma por el Papa Sixto V, y mandado observar por el gobierno español en diversa reales órdenes. Barcelona: Manuel Miró y D. Marsa, 1870.

Concilio IV provincial mexicano celebrado año de 1771. Querétaro: Escuela de Artes, 1898.

Concilios provinciales primero y segundo, celebrados en la muy noble y muy leal ciudad de México, presidiendo el Illmo y Rmo Señor D. F. Alonso de Montúfar en los años de 1555 y 1565 . . . México: Joseph Antonio de Hogal, 1769.

Devocionario para honrar al glorioso San Antonio de Padua y solicitar su poderosa protección, tanto en los dias de su novena como en el dia trece de cada mes. México: Mariano Ontiveros, 1821.

Dia ocho del mes, en que haciendo dulce recuerdo de la Purissima Concepcion de Maria Santissima Señora Nuestra, implora su poderoso patrocinio para alcanzar la divina gracia. México: Joseph Jauregui, 1775.

Dificultad imaginada, faciliada verdadera en la prática de testamentos reducida a ocho documentos en que se manifiesta la facilidad conque se pueden tener en sana salud otorgados los testamentos . . . México: Viuda de Miguel de Ribera Calderón, 1714.

Escalona y Calatayud, Juan Joseph de. *Instrucción à la perfecta vida; máximas para su logro à personas de todos estados. Mandadas escribir à un clerigo sacerdote, domiciliario del Obispado de Michaocàn, y sacadas a luz para el aprovechamiento de sus ovejas.* México: Joseph Bernardo de Hogal, 1737.

Exercicios espirituales de el Divino Infante Jesus: disposicion, de una alma devota de este mysterio, ha observado en el Santo Adviento, comenzando desde el dia veinte y dos de noviembre, hasta cumplir treinta y tres dias, que son los previos à la Pasqua. A devocion de un zeloso del aprovechamiento de las almas. México: Felipe de Zúñiga y Ontiveros, 1774.

Fabián y Fuero, Francisco. *Colección de providencias diocesanas del obispado de la Puebla de los Angeles hechas y ordenadas por su señoria ilustrisima el señor doctor don Francisco Fabian y Fuero, obispo de dicha ciudad y obispado del consejo de su mag. &c.* Puebla: Real Seminario Palafoxiano, 1770.

Florencia, Francisco de, and Juan Antonio Oviedo. *Zodiaco mariano: en que el sol de justicia Christo con la salud en las alas vista como signos, y casas propias para beneficio de los hombres los templos, y lugares dedicados à los cultos de su SS. Madre por medio de las mas celebres, y milagrosas imagenes de la misma Señora, que se veneran en esta America Septentrional, y reynos de la Nueva España.* México: Nueva Imprenta del Real y mas antinguo Colegio de San Ildefonso, 1755.

Formula, y modo de rezar con utilidad, y provecho la Corona de las cinco Llagas, meditando, juntamente, los Dolores agudissimos que traspassaron el Coraçon de la SS. Virgen al abrir estas llagas preciosas de su hijo. México: Francisco Rivera Calderon, 1718.

Humbolt, Alexander von. *Ensayo político sobre el reino de la Nueva España.* México: Editorial Porrua, S.A., 1966.

Lorenzana, Francisco Antonio. *Cartas pastorales y edictos del Illmo Señor D. Francisco Antonio Lorenzana y Buitron, Arzobispo de México.* México: Joseph Antonio de Hogal, 1770.

Martagon, Fernando. *Exercicios espirituales para desagraviar á María Santísima Nuestra Señora de los Dolores*. México: Mariano de Zúñiga y Ontiveros, 1807.

Murillo Velarde, Pedro. *Prática de testamentos en que se resuelven los casos mas frequentes que se ofrecen en la disposición de la últimas voluntades*. México: Joseph de Jauregui, 1790.

Núñez de Haro y Peralta, Alfonso. *Sermones escogidos, pláticas espirituales privadas, y dos pastorales anteriorment impresas en México del Excelentísimo Señor D. Alfonso Núñez de Haro y Peralta, virrey interino, gobernador y capitan general que fue de Nueva España* . . . Madrid: Hija de Ibarra, 1806.

Ochoa Villaseñor, Joseph Vicente de. *Escala del cielo que con piadoso afecto ofrece a los fieles de Jesu Christo*. México: Felipe de Zúñiga y Ontiveros, 1793.

Perez Bonilla, Manuel Eduardo. *Practicas devotas en honor del sacratisimo corazon de nuestro señor Jesu Christo*. México: Mariano Joseph de Zúñinga y Ontiveros, 1805.

Ripalda, Gerónimo de. *Catecismo y exposición breve de la doctrina christiana por el P. Mro. Gerónimo de Ripalda con un tratado my útil del órden con que el christiano debe ocupar el tiempo y emplear el día*. Puebla: Pedro de la Rosa, 1784.

Schroeder, H. J. *Canons and Decrees of the Council of Trent*. Rockford: Tan Books and Publishers, Inc., 1978.

Valdéz, Francisco. *Novena devota consagrada al culto del santo arcangel, uno de los siete principes que asisten ante el trono del Altísimo Omnipotente Dios, el señor san Rafael*. México: María Fernández de Jauregui, 1810.

Venegas, Miguel. *Manual de párrocos para administrar los santos sacramentos y exercer otras funciones ecclesiasiticas conforme al ritual romano*. México: Joseph Bernardo de Hogal, 1731.

Vetancurt, Agustín. *Manual de administrar los santos sacramentos conforme a la reforma de Paulo V y Urbano VIII sacado de los manuales de los padres Fr. Miguel de Zarate y Fr. Pedro de Contreras, hijos de la provincia del Santo Evangelio de México*. México: Francisco Rodríguez Lupercio, 1674.

SECONDARY SOURCES

Alberro, Solange. *Inquisición y sociedad en México, 1571–1700*. México: Fondo de Cultura Económica, 1988.

Alsop, J. D. "Religious Preambles in Early Modern English Wills as Formulae." *Journal of Ecclesiastical History* 40 (1989): 19–27.

Anna, Timothy E. *The Fall of Royal Government in Mexico City*. Lincoln: University of Nebraska Press, 1978.

Aries, Philippe. *The Hour of Our Death*. Translated by Helen Weaver. New York: Alfred A. Knopf, 1981.

Arnold, Linda. *Bureaucracy and Bureaucrats in Mexico City, 1742–1835*. Tucson: University of Arizona Press, 1988.

Arrom, Silvia Marina. *Containing the Poor: The Mexico City Poor House, 1774–1871*. Durham: Duke University Press, 2000.

Attreed, Lorraine C. "Preparation for Death in Sixteenth-Century Northern England." *Sixteenth Century Journal* 13 (1982): 37–66.

Avila Espinosa, Felipe Arturo. "Los niños abandonados de la casa de niños expósitos de la Ciudad de México: 1767–1821." In *La familia en el mundo iberoamericano.* Edited by Pilar Gonzalbo Aizpuru and Cecilia Rabell. México: Instituto de Investigaciones Sociales, Universidad Nacional Autónoma de México, 1994.

Baez Macias, Eduardo. "Planos y censos de la ciudad de México, 1753." *Boletín del Archivo General de la Nación.* 2nd series. 7 (1966): 407–84.

———. "Planos y censos de la ciudad de México, 1753." *Boletín del Archivo General de la Nación.* 2nd series. 8 (1967): 485–1150.

Banker, James R. *Death in the Community: Memorialization and Confraternities in an Italian Commune in the Late Middle Ages.* Athens: University of Georgia Press, 1988.

Bantjes, Adrian A. "Burning Saints, Molding Minds: Iconoclasm, Civic Ritual, and the Failed Cultural Revolution." In *Rituals of Rule, Rituals of Resistance: Public Celebrations and Popular Culture in Mexico.* Edited by William H. Beezley, Cheryl English Martin, and William E. French. Wilmington: Scholarly Resources, 1994.

Bauer, Arnold J. "The Church in the Economy of Spanish America: Censos and Depósitos in the Eighteenth and Nineteenth Centuries." *Hispanic American Historical Review* 63 (1983): 707–33.

Bayle, C. "El concilio de trento en las indias españoles." *Razón y Fe: Revista Mensual Hispanoamericana* 131 (1945): 257–84.

Bazarte Martínez, Alicia. *Las cofradías de españoles en la ciudad de México.* México: Universidad Autónoma Metropolitana, 1989.

Becker, Marjorie. *Setting the Virgin on Fire: Lázaro Cárdenas, Michoacán Peasants, and the Redemption of the Mexican Revolution.* Berkeley: University of California Press, 1995.

Belanger, Brian Conal. "Secularization and the Laity in Colonial Mexico: Querétaro, 1598–1821." Ph.D. diss., Tulane University, 1990.

Bell, Catherine. *Ritual Theory, Ritual Practice.* New York: Oxford University Press, 1992.

Belting, Hans. *Likeness and Presence: A History of the Image before the Era of Art.* Translated by Edmund Jephcott. Chicago: University of Chicago Press, 1994.

Berman, Morris. *Coming to Our Senses: Body and Spirit in the Hidden History of the West.* New York: Simon and Schuster, 1989.

Black, Christopher F. *Italian Confraternities in the Sixteenth Century.* New York: Cambridge University Press, 1989.

Bobb, Bernard E. *The Viceregency of Antonio María Bucareli in New Spain, 1771–1779.* Austin: University of Texas Press, 1962.

Bossy, John. *Christianity in the West, 1400–1700.* New York: Oxford University Press, 1985.

Boswell, John. *The Kindness of Strangers: The Abandonment of Children in Western Europe from Late Antiquity to the Renaissance.* New York: Vintage Books, 1988.

Bourdieu, Pierre. *Outline of a Theory of Practice.* Translated by Richard Nice. New York: Cambridge University Press, 1972.

Boyer, Richard. *Lives of the Bigamists: Marriage, Family, and Community in Colonial Mexico.* Albuquerque: University of New Mexico Press, 1995.

Brading, David A. *Church and State in Bourbon Mexico: The Diocese of Michoacán, 1749–1810*. New York: Cambridge University Press, 1994.

———. *The First America: The Spanish Monarchy, Creole Patriots, and the Liberal State, 1492–1867*. New York: Cambridge University Press, 1991.

———. *Mexican Phoenix: Our Lady of Guadalupe: Image and Tradition Across Five Centuries*. New York: Cambridge University Press, 2001.

———. *Miners and Merchants in Bourbon Mexico, 1763–1810*. New York: Cambridge University Press, 1971.

———. "Tridentine Catholicism and Enlightened Despotism in Bourbon Mexico." *Journal of Latin American Studies* 15 (1983): 1–22.

Brescia, Michael M. "Liturgical Expressions of Episcopal Power: Juan de Palafox y Mendoza and Tridentine Reform in Colonial Mexico." *The Catholic Historical Review* 90 (2004): 497–518.

———. "Material and Cultural Dimensions of Episcopal Authority: Tridentine Donation and the Biblioteca Palafoxiana in Seventeenth-Century Puebla de los Ángeles, Mexico." *Colonial Latin American Historical Review* 8 (1999): 207–27.

Brooks, Francis Joseph. "Parish and Cofradía in Eighteenth-Century Mexico." Ph.D. diss., Princeton University, 1976.

Brown, Peter. *The Cult of Saints: Its Rise and Function in Latin Christianity*. Chicago: University of Chicago Press, 1981.

Burkhart, Louise M. *The Slippery Earth: Nahua-Christian Moral Dialogue in Sixteenth-Century Mexico*. Tucson: University of Arizona Press, 1989.

Burrus, Ernest J. "The Author of the Mexican Council Catechisms." *Americas* 15 (1958): 171–81.

Bynum, Caroline Walker. *Holy Feast and Holy Fast: The Religious Significance of Food to Medieval Women*. Berkeley: University of California Press, 1987.

Callahan, William J. *Church, Politics, and Society in Spain, 1750–1874*. Cambridge: Harvard University Press, 1984.

———. "Las cofradías y hermandades de España y su papel social y religioso dentro de una sociedad de estamentos." In *Cofradías, capellanías y obras pías en la América colonial*. Edited by Pilar Martínez López-Cano, Gisela von Wobeser, and Juan Guillermo Muñoz. México: Universidad Nacional Autónoma de México, 1998.

———. "The Problem of Confinement: An Aspect of Poor Relief in Eighteenth Century Spain." *Hispanic American Historical Review* 51 (1971): 1–24.

Calvo, Thomas. "Santuarios y devociones: entre dos mundos, siglos XVI-XVIII." In *La iglesia Católica en México*. Edited by Nelly Sigaut. Zamora: El Colegio de Michoacán, 1997.

———. "El zodiaco de la nueva Eva: el culto mariano en la América septentrional hacia 1700." In *Manifestaciones religiosas en el mundo colonial americano*. Vol. 2, *Mujeres, instituciones y culto a María*. Edited by Clara García Ayluardo and Manuel Ramos Medina. México: UIA, INAH, Condumex, 1994.

Cañizares-Esguerra, Jorge. *Nature, Empire, and Nation: Explorations of the History of Science in the Iberian World*. Stanford: Stanford University Press, 2006.

Chadwick, Owen. *The Popes and the European Revolution*. Oxford: Clarendon Press, 1981.

Chartier, Roger. *The Cultural Origins of the French Revolution*. Translated by Lydia G. Cochrane. Durham: Duke University Press, 1991.

Chaunu, Pierre. *La mort a Paris XVIe, XVIIe et XVIIIe siecles*. Paris: Fayard, 1978.

Chowning, Margaret. "The Consolidación de Vales Reales in the Bishopric of Michoacán." *Hispanic American Historical Review* 69 (1989): 451–78.

———. *Rebellious Nuns: The Troubled History of a Mexican Convent, 1752–1863*. New York: Oxford University Press, 2006.

Christian, William A. *Apparitions in Late Medieval and Renaissance Spain*. Princeton: Princeton University Press, 1981.

———. *Local Religion in Sixteenth-Century Spain*. Princeton: Princeton University Press, 1981.

Clendinnen, Inga. *Ambivalent Conquests: Maya and the Spaniards in Yucatan, 1517–1570*. New York: Cambridge University Press, 1987.

Cohn, Samuel K., Jr. *Death and Property in Sienna, 1205–1800: Strategies for the Afterlife*. Baltimore: Johns Hopkins University Press, 1988.

Cooper, Donald B. *Epidemic Disease in Mexico City, 1761–1813: An Administrative, Social, and Medical Study*. Austin: University of Texas Press, 1965.

Cope, R. Douglas. *The Limits of Racial Domination: Plebeian Society in Colonial Mexico City, 1660–1720*. Madison: University of Wisconsin Press, 1994.

Costeloe, Michael P. *Church Wealth in Mexico: A Study of the "Juzgado de Capellanías" in the Archbishopric of Mexico, 1800–1865*. New York: Cambridge University Press, 1967.

Cuevas, Mariano. *Historia de la iglesia mexicana*. Vol. 4. México: Ediciones Cervantes, 1942.

Curcio-Nagy, Linda A. "Giants and Gypsies: Corpus Christi in Colonial Mexico City." In *Rituals of Rule, Rituals of Resistance: Public Celebrations and Popular Culture in Mexico*. Edited by William H. Beezley, Cheryl English Martin, and William French. Wilmington: Scholarly Resources Inc., 1994.

———. *The Great Festivals of Colonial Mexico City: Performing Power and Identity*. Albuquerque: University of New Mexico Press, 2004.

———. "Native Icon to City Protectress to Royal Patroness: Ritual, Political Symbolism, and the Virgin of Remedies." *Americas* 52, no. 3 (1996): 367–91.

Dean, Carolyn. *Inka Bodies and the Body of Christ: Corpus Christi in Colonia Cuzco, Peru*. Durham: Duke University Press, 1999.

Deans-Smith, Susan. *Bureaucrats, Planters, and Workers: The Making of the Tobacco Monopoly in Bourbon Mexico*. Austin: University of Texas Press, 1992.

Delumeau, Jean. *Catholicism Between Luther and Voltaire: A New View of the Counter-Reformation*. Translated by Jeremy Moiser. Philadelphia: Westminster Press, 1977.

Desan, Suzanne. *Reclaiming the Sacred: Lay Religion and Popular Politics in Revolutionary France*. Ithaca: Cornell University Press, 1990.

Duby, Georges, ed. *A History of Private Life*. Vol. 2: *Revelations of the Medieval World*. Cambridge: Harvard University Press, 1988.

Duffy, Eamon. *The Stripping of the Altars: Traditional Religion in England, 1400–1580*. New Haven: Yale University Press, 1992.

Eire, Carlos M. N. *From Madrid to Purgatory: The Art and Craft of Dying in Sixteenth-Century Spain*. New York: Cambridge University Press, 1995.

———. *War Against the Idols: The Reformation of Worship from Erasmus to Calvin*. New York: Cambridge University Press, 1986.

Farr, James R. *Authority and Sexuality in Early Modern Burgundy, 1550–1730*. New York: Oxford University Press, 1995.

Farriss, Nancy M. *Crown and Clergy in Colonial Mexico, 1759–1821: The Crisis of Ecclesiastical Privilege*. London: University of London, Athlone Press, 1968.

———. *Maya Society Under Colonial Rule: The Collective Enterprise of Survival*. Princeton: Princeton University Press, 1984.

Flanigan, C. Clifford, Kathleen Ashley, and Pamela Sheingorn, "Liturgy as Social Performance: Expanding the Definitions." In *The Liturgy of the Medieval Church*. Edited by Thomas J. Heffernan and E. Ann Matter. Kalamazoo: Western Michigan University, 2001.

Florescano, Enrique. *Precios del maíz y crisis agrícolas en México, 1708–1810*. México: Ediciones Era, S. A., 1986.

Flynn, Maureen. *Sacred Charity: Confraternities and Social Welfare in Spain, 1400–1700*. Ithaca: Cornell University Press, 1989.

Foucault, Michel. *Discipline & Punish: The Birth of the Prison*. Translated by Alan Sheridan. New York: Vintage Books, 1979.

———. *The Order of Things: An Archaeology of the Human Sciences*. New York: Vintage Books, 1994.

Franco, Jean. *Plotting Women: Gender and Representation in Mexico*. New York: Columbia University Press, 1989.

Frijhoff, W. "Official and Popular Religion in Christianity: The Late Middle-Ages and Early Modern Times, 13th–18th Centuries." In *Official and Popular Religion: Analysis of a Theme for Religious Studies*. Edited by Pieter Hendrik Vrijhof and Jacques Waardenburg. New York: Mouton Publishers, 1979.

García Ayluardo, Clara. "Confraternity, Cult and Crown in Colonial Mexico City: 1700–1810." Ph.D. diss., University of Cambridge, 1989.

———. "A World of Images: Cult, Ritual, and Society in Colonial Mexico City." In *Rituals of Rule, Rituals of Resistance: Public Celebrations and Popular Culture in Mexico*. Edited by William H. Beezley, Cheryl English Martin, and William French. Wilmington: Scholarly Resources Inc., 1994.

Garner, Richard L., with Spiro E. Stefanou. *Economic Growth and Change in Bourbon Mexico*. Gainesville: University of Florida Press, 1993.

Geertz, Clifford. "Religion as a Cultural System." In *The Interpretation of Cultures: Selected Essays by Clifford Geertz*. New York: Basic Books, 1973.

Gilley, Sheridan. "Catholic Revival in the Eighteenth Century." *Studies in Church History* 7 (1990): 99–108.

Gonzalbo Aizpuru, Pilar. "La casa de niños expósitos de la Ciudad de México: una fundación del siglo XVIII." *Historia Mexicana* 31 (1982): 409–30.

———. *Historia de la educación en la época colonial: la educación de los criollos y la vida urbana*. México: Colegio de México, 1995.

Guedea, Virginia. "Las primeras elecciones populares en la ciudad de México, 1812–1813." *Mexican Studies/Estudios Mexicanos* 7 (1991): 1–28.

———. "El pueblo de México y la política capitalina, 1808 y 1812." *Mexican Studies/Estudios Mexicanos* 10 (1994): 27–61.

Gunnarsdóttir, Ellen. *Mexican Karismata: The Baroque Vocation of Francisca de los Ángeles, 1674–1744.* Lincoln: University of Nebraska Press, 2004.

Gurevich, Aaron. *The Origins of European Individualism.* Translated by Katharine Judelson. Cambridge, MA: Blackwell Publishers, 1995.

Hamill, Hugh M., Jr. *The Hidalgo Revolt: Prelude to Mexican Independence.* Gainesville: University of Florida Press, 1966.

Hamnett, Brian R. "The Appropriation of Mexican Church Wealth by the Spanish Bourbon Government: The Consolidacion de Vales Reales, 1805–1809." *Journal of Latin American Studies* 1 (1972): 85–113.

———. *Roots of Insurgency: Mexican Regions, 1750–1824.* New York: Cambridge University Press, 1986.

Harper, John. *The Forms and Orders of the Western Liturgy: From the Tenth to the Eighteenth Century: A Historical Introduction and Guide for Students and Musicians.* Oxford: Clarendon Press, 1991.

Haslip-Viera, Gabriel. *Crime and Punishment in Late Colonial Mexico City, 1692–1810.* Albuquerque: University of New Mexico Press, 1999.

———. "The Underclass." In *Cities & Society in Colonial Latin America.* Edited by Louisa Schell Hoberman and Susan Migden Socolow. Albuquerque: University of New Mexico Press, 1986.

Heller, Thomas C. et al. *Reconstructing Individualism: Autonomy, Individuality, and the Self in Western Thought.* Stanford: Stanford University Press, 1986.

Herr, Richard. *The Eighteenth-Century Revolution in Spain.* Princeton: Princeton University Press, 1958.

Herrejón Peredo, Carlos. "El sermon en Nueva España durante la segunda mitad del siglo XVIII." In *La iglesia Católica en México.* Edited by Nelly Sigaut. Zamora: El Colegio de Michoacán, 1997.

Hoffman, Philip T. *Church and Community in the Diocese of Lyon, 1500–1789.* Yale Historical Publications, Miscellany, 132. New Haven: Yale University Press, 1984.

Hope, D. M. "The Medieval Western Rites." In *The Study of Liturgy.* Edited by Cheslyn Jones, Geoffrey Wainwright, and Edward Yarnold. New York: Oxford University Press, 1978.

Howell, Clifford. "From Trent to Vatican II." In *The Study of Liturgy.* Edited by Cheslyn Jones, Geoffrey Wainwright, and Edward Yarnold. New York: Oxford University Press, 1978.

Hunt, Lynn. "Psychoanalysis, the Self, and Historical Interpretation." *Common Knowledge* 6, no. 2 (1997): 10–19.

Jaffary, Nora E. *False Mystics: Deviant Orthodoxy in Colonial Mexico.* Lincoln: University of Nebraska, 2004.

Kicza, John E. *Colonial Entrepreneurs: Families and Business in Bourbon Mexico City.* Albuquerque: University of New Mexico Press, 1983.

Kirk, Stephanie L. *Convent Life in Colonial Mexico: A Tale of Two Communities.* Gainesville: University Press of Florida, 2007.

Klauser, Theodor. *A Short History of the Western Liturgy: An Account and Some Reflections.* Translated by John Halliburton. 2nd ed. New York: Oxford University Press, 1979.

Klein, Herbert S. "The Demographic Structure of Mexico City in 1811." *Journal of Urban History* 23 (1996): 55–93.

Kubler, George and Martin Soria. *Art and Architecture in Spain and Portugal and Their American Dominions, 1500 to 1800.* Baltimore: Penguin Books, 1959.

Lavrin, Asunción. "El capital eclesiástico y las élites sociales en Nueva España a finales del siglo XVIII." In *Orígenes y desarrollo de la burguesía en América Latina, 1700–1955.* Edited by Enrique Florescano. México: Editorial Nueva Imagen, 1985.

———. "Cofradías novohispanas: economías material y espiritual." In *Cofradías, capellanías y obras pías en la América colonial.* Edited by Pilar Martínez López-Cano, Gisela von Wobeser, and Juan Guillermo Muñoz. México: Universidad Nacional Autónoma de México, 1998.

———. "La congregación de San Pedro: Una cofradía urbana del México colonial, 1604–1730." *Historia Mexicana* 29 (1980): 562–601.

———. "Ecclesiastical Reform of Nunneries in New Spain in the Eighteenth Century." *Americas* 22 (1965): 182–203.

———. "The Execution of the Law of Consolidación in New Spain: Economic Aims and Results." *Hispanic American Historical Review* 53 (1973): 27–49.

———. "Problems and Policies in the Administration of Nunneries in Mexico, 1800–1835." *Americas* 28 (1971): 55–77.

———. "La riqueza de los conventos de monjas en Nueva España: Estructura y evolución durante el siglo XVIII." *Cahiers des Ameriques Latines* 8 (1973): 91–122.

———. "The Role of the Nunneries in the Economy of New Spain in the Eighteenth Century." *Hispanic American Historical Review* 46 (1966): 371–93.

Le Goff, Jacques. *The Birth of Purgatory.* Translated by Arthur Goldhammer. Chicago: University of Chicago Press, 1984.

Lehmann, Hartmut. "The Cultural Importance of the Pious Middle Classes in Seventeenth-Century Protestant Society." In *Religion and Society in Early Modern Europe, 1500–1800.* Edited by Kaspar von Greyerz. Boston: George Allen & Unwin, 1984.

Leonard, Irving A. *Baroque Times in Old Mexico: Seventeenth-Century Persons, Places, and Practices.* Ann Arbor: University of Michigan Press, 1959.

Lockhart, James. *The Nahuas After the Conquest: A Social and Cultural History of the Indians of Central Mexico.* Stanford: Stanford University Press, 1992.

López, Roberto J. *Comportamientos religiosos en Asturias durante el antiguo régimen.* Gijón: Silverio Cañada, 1989.

———. *Oviedo: muerte y religiosidad en el siglo XVIII: un studio de mentalidades colectivas.* Oviedo: Consejería de Educación, Cultura y Deportes del Principado de Asturias, 1985.

Loreto López, Rosalva. "La fiesta de la Concepción y las identidades colectivas, Puebla (1619–1636)." In *Manifestaciones religiosas en el mundo colonial Americano.*

Vol. 2, *Mujeres, instituciones y culto a María*. Edited by Clara García Ayluardo and Manuel Ramos Medina. México: INAH, Condumex, UIA, 1993.

Luria, Keith P. *Territories of Grace: Cultural Change in the Seventeenth-Century Diocese of Grenoble*. Berkeley: University of California Press, 1991.

Lynch, John. *Bourbon Spain, 1700–1808*. Cambridge: Basil Blackwell Inc., 1989.

MacCormack, Sabine. *Religion in the Andes: Vision and Imagination in Early Colonial Peru*. Princeton: Princeton University Press, 1991.

Malvido, Elsa. "Los novicios de san francisco en la ciudad de México: la edad de hierro, 1649–1749." *Historia Mexicana* 36 (1987): 699–738.

Martínez, Elías. "Los franciscanos y la independencia de Méjico." *Abside* 24 (1960): 129–62.

Martínez Gil, Fernando. *Muerte y sociedad en la España de los Austrias*. Madrid: Silgo Veintiuno Editores, 1993.

Martínez Rosales, Alfonso. "Los gigantes de San Luis Potosí." *Historia Mexicana* 37 (1988): 585–612.

Martz, Linda. *Poverty and Welfare in Habsburg Spain: The Example of Toledo*. New York: Cambridge University Press, 1983.

Maza, Francisco de la. *La ciudad de México en el siglo XVII*. 3rd ed. México: Fondo de Cultura Económica, 1995.

Mantecón Movellán, Tomás Antonio. "Reformismo borbónico, iglesia y vida religiosa durante el siglo XVIII: el control de las cofradías religiosas, una aproximación a su estudio." *Hispania* 50 (1990): 1191–1206.

McManners, John. *Death and the Enlightenment: Changing Attitudes to Death among Christians and Unbelievers in Eighteenth-Century France*. New York: Clarendon Press, 1981.

Mellor, Philip A. and Chris Shilling. *Re-forming the Body: Religion, Community and Modernity*. Thousand Oaks: Sage Publications, 1997.

Melvin, Karen. "Urban Religions: Mendicant Orders in New Spain's Cities, 1570–1800." Ph.D. diss., University of California, Berkeley, 2005.

Mills, Kenneth. *Idolatry and Its Enemies: Colonial Andean Religion and Extirpation, 1640–1750*. Princeton: Princeton University Press, 1997.

Milton, Cynthia E. *The Many Meanings of Poverty: Colonialism, Social Compacts, and Assistance in Eighteenth-Century Ecuador*. Stanford: Stanford University Press, 2007.

Monter, William. *Ritual, Myth and Magic in Early Modern Europe*. Athens: Ohio University Press, 1984.

Morgan, David. *Visual Piety: A History and Theory of Popular Religious Images*. Berkeley: University of California Press, 1998.

Moreno de los Arcos, Roberto. "Los territorios parroquiales de la ciudad arzobispal, 1325–1981." *Gaceta oficial del Arzobispado de México* 22 (1982): 152–73.

Morris, Colin. *The Discovery of the Individual, 1050–1200*. New York: Harper & Row, Publishers, 1972.

Mullin, Robert J. *Architecture and Its Sculpture in Viceregal Mexico*. Austin: University of Texas Press, 1997.

Muriel de la Torre, Josefina. *Hospitales de la Nueva España.* 2 vols. México: Universidad Nacional, Instituto de Historia, 1956.

Nalle, Sara T. *God in La Mancha: Religious Reform and the People of Cuenca, 1500–1650.* Baltimore: Johns Hopkins University Press, 1992.

Nesvig, Martin Austin, ed. *Local Religion in Colonial Mexico.* Albuquerque: University of New Mexico Press, 2006.

Nicasio, Susan V. " . . . For the Benefit of My Soul: A Preliminary Study of the Persistence of Tradition in Eighteenth-Century Mass Obligations." *Catholic Historical Review* 78 (1992): 175–96.

Noel, Charles C. "Missionary Preachers in Spain: Teaching Social Virtue in the Eighteenth-Century." *American Historical Review* 90 (1985): 866–92.

Norberg, Kathryn. *Rich and Poor in Grenoble, 1600–1814.* Berkeley: University of California Press, 1985.

O'Hara, Matthew D. "A Flock Divided: Religion and Community in Mexico City, 1749–1800." Ph.D. diss., University of California, San Diego, 2003.

———. "Stone, Mortar, and Memory: Church Construction and Communities in Late Colonial Mexico City." *Hispanic American Historical Review* 86 (2006): 647–80.

Pardo, Osvaldo F. *The Origins of Mexican Catholicism: Nahua Rituals and Christian Sacraments in Sixteenth-Century Mexico.* Ann Arbor: University of Michigan Press, 2004.

Pascua, María José de la. *Vivir la muerte en el Cádiz del setecientos, 1675–1801.* Cádiz: Fundación Municipal de Cultura del Ayuntamiento de Cádiz, 1990.

Peñafiel Ramón, Antonio. *Testamento y buena muerte: un estudio de mentalidades en Murcia del siglo XVIII.* Murcia: Academia Alfonso X El Sabio, 1987.

Pérez Fernández del Castillo, Bernardo. *Historia de la escribanía en la Nueva España y del notariado en México.* 2nd ed. México: Editorial Porrúa, S.A., 1988.

Pescador, Juan Javier. *De bautizados a fieles difuntos: familia y mentalidad en una parroquia urbana: Santa Catarina de México, 1568–1820.* México: El Colegio de México, 1992.

———. "Vanishing Woman: Female Migration and Ethnic Identity in Late-Colonial Mexico City." *Ethnohistory* 42 (1995): 617–26.

Pierce, Donna. "At the Crossroads: Cultural Confluence and Daily Life in Mexico, 1521–1821." In *Painting a New World: Mexican Art and Life, 1521–1821.* Edited by Donna Pierce, Rogelio Ruiz Gomar, and Clara Bargellini. Denver: Frederick and Jan Mayer Center for Pre-Columbian and Spanish Colonial Art, Denver Art Museum, 2004.

Pierce, Donna, Rogelio Ruiz Gomar, and Clara Bargellini. *Painting a New World: Mexican Art and Life, 1521–1821.* Denver: Frederick and Jan Mayer Center for Pre-Columbian and Spanish Colonial Art, Denver Art Museum, 2004.

Po-Chia Hsia, R. *The World of Catholic Renewal, 1540–1770.* 2nd ed. New York: Cambridge University Press, 2005.

Poole, Stafford. *Our Lady of Guadalupe: The Origins and Sources of a Mexican National Symbol, 1531–1797.* Tucson: University of Arizona Press, 1995.

———. *Pedro Moya de Contreras: Catholic Reform and Royal Power in New Spain, 1571–1591.* Berkeley: University of California Press, 1987.

————. "The Third Mexican Provincial Council of 1585 and the Reform of the Diocesan Clergy." In *The Church and Society in Latin America: Selected Papers from the Conference at Tulane University, New Orleans, Louisiana, April 29–30, 1982.* Edited by Jeffrey A. Cole. New Orleans: Center for Latin America Studies, Tulane University, 1984.

Ramos Kittrell, Jesús Alejandro. "Dynamics of Ritual and Ceremony at the Metropolitan Cathedral of Mexico, 1700–1750." Ph.D., diss., University of Texas at Austin, 2006.

Ramsey, Ann W. *Liturgy, Politics, and Salvation: The Catholic League in Paris and the Nature of Catholic Reform, 1540–1630.* Rochester, NY: University of Rochester Press, 1999.

————. "Piety in Paris during the League, 1585–1590: An Urban Community in Transition." Ph.D. diss., Columbia University, 1991.

Reardon, Bernard M. G. *Religious Thought in the Reformation.* 2nd ed. New York: Longman, 1995.

Ricard, Robert. *The Spiritual Conquest of Mexico: An Essay on the Apostolate and the Evangelizing Methods of the Mendicant Orders in New Spain, 1523–1572.* Translated by Lesley Byrd Simpson. Berkeley: University of California Press, 1966.

Rodríguez G. de Ceballos, Alfonso. "Usos y funciones de la imagen religiosa en los virreinatos americanos." In *Los siglos de Oro en los virreinatos de América, 1550–1700.* Madrid: Sociedad Estatal para la Conmemoración de los Centenarios de Felipe II y Carlos V, 1999.

Rosell, Lauro E. *Iglesias y conventos coloniales de México: Historia de cada uno de los que existen en la ciudad de México.* 2nd ed. México: Editorial Patria, 1961.

Rubial García, Antonio. "Icons of Devotion: The Appropriation and Use of Saints in New Spain." In *Local Religion in Colonial Mexico.* Edited by Martin Austin Nesvig. Albuquerque: University of New Mexico Press, 2006.

————. *Una monarquía criolla: La provincia agustina en el siglo XVII.* México: Consejo Nacional para la Cultura y las Artes, 1990.

————. *La santidad controvertida: Hagiografía y conciencia criolla alrededor de los venerables no canonizados de Nueva España.* México: Fondo de Cultura Económica, 1999.

————. "Los santos milagreros y malogrados de la Nueva España." In *Manifestaciones religiosas en el mundo colonial americano.* Vol. 1, *Espiritualidad barroca colonial: santos y demonios en América.* Edited by Clara García Ayluardo and Manuel Ramos Medina. México: UIA, INAH, Condumex, 1993.

————. "Tierra de prodigios: lo maravilloso cristiano en la Nueva España de los siglos XVI y XVII." In *La iglesia Católica en México.* Edited by Nelly Sigaut. Zamora: El Colegio de Michoacán, 1997.

Rubin, Miri. *Corpus Christi: The Eucharist in Late Medieval Culture.* New York: Cambridge University Press, 1991.

Ruiz Gomar, Rogelio. "Unique Expressions: Painting in New Spain." In *Painting a New World: Mexican Art and Life, 1521–1821.* Edited by Donna Pierce, Rogelio Ruiz Gomar, and Clara Bargellini. Denver: Frederick and Jan Mayer Center for Pre-Columbian and Spanish Colonial Art, Denver Art Museum, 2004.

Sabean, David Warren. *Power in the Blood: Popular Culture & Village Discourse in Early Modern Germany*. New York: Cambridge University Press, 1984.

Saborit Badenes, Pere. *Morir en el alto Palancia: la religiosidad popular a través de los testamentos, siglos XVI-XVIII*. Segorbe: Ayuntamiento de Segorbe, 1991.

Saenger, Paul. "Books of Hours and the Reading Habits of the Later Middle Ages." In *The Culture of Print: Power and the Uses of Print in Early Modern Europe*. Edited by Roger Chartier. Translated by Lydia G. Cochrane. Princeton: Princeton University Press, 1989.

Saucedo, Zarco María del Carmen. "Triunfo parténico de la religiosidad criolla." *Revista Complutense de Historia de América* 19 (1993): 93–107.

Scardaville, Micheal C. "Crime and the Urban Poor: Mexico City in the Late Colonial Period." Ph.D. diss., University of Florida, 1977.

———. "(Hapsburg) Law and (Bourbon) Order: State Authority, Popular Unrest, and the Criminal Justice System in Bourbon Mexico City." *Americas* 50 (1994): 510–25.

Schwaller, John Frederick. *Church and Clergy in Sixteenth-Century Mexico*. Albuquerque: University of New Mexico Press, 1987.

———. "The Implementation of the Ordenanza del Patronasgo in New Spain." In *The Church and Society in Latin America: Selected Papers from the Conference at Tulane University, New Orleans, Louisiana, April 29–30, 1982*. Edited by Jeffrey A. Cole. New Orleans: Center for Latin America Studies, Tulane University, 1984.

———. *Origins of Church Wealth in Mexico: Ecclesiastical Revenues and Church Finances, 1523–1600*. Albuquerque: University of New Mexico Press, 1985.

Scribner, Bob. "Cosmic Order and Daily Life: Sacred and Secular in Pre-Industrial German Society." In *Religion and Society in Early Modern Europe, 1500–1800*. Edited by Kaspar von Greyerz. Boston: George Allen & Unwin, 1984.

———. "Popular Piety and Modes of Visual Perception in Late-Medieval and Reformation Germany." *Journal of Religious History* 15 (1989): 448–69.

Sedgwick, Alexander. *Jansenism in Seventeenth-Century France: Voices from the Wilderness*. Charlottesville: University Press of Virginia, 1977.

Seed, Patricia. *To Love, Honor, and Obey in Colonial Mexico: Conflicts over Marriage Choice, 1574–1821*. Stanford: Stanford University Press, 1988.

Los siglos de Oro en los virreinatos de América, 1550–1700. Madrid: Sociedad Estatal para la Conmemoración de los Centenarios de Felipe II y Carlos V, 1999.

Silverblatt, Irene. *Modern Inquisitions: Peru and the Colonial Origins of the Civilized World*. Durham: Duke University Press, 2004.

Soergel, Philip M. *Wondrous in His Saints: Counter-Reformation Propaganda in Bavaria*. Berkeley: University of California Press, 1993.

Stark, Rodney. *The Victory of Reason: How Christianity Led to Freedom, Capitalism, and Western Success*. New York: Random House, 2005.

Steele, Thomas J. *Santos and Saints: The Religious Folk Art of Hispanic New Mexico*. Santa Fe: Ancient City Press, 1994.

Strauss, Gerald. "Lutheranism and Literacy: A Reassessment." In *Religion and Society in Early Modern Europe, 1500–1800*. Edited by Kaspar von Greyerz. Boston: George Allen & Unwin, 1984.

Tanck de Estrada, Dorothy. "The 'Escuelas Pías' of Mexico City, 1768–1820." *Americas* 31 (1974): 51–71.

Taylor, William B. "Between Nativitas and Mexico City: An Eighteenth-Century Pastor's Local Religion." In *Local Religion in Colonial Mexico*. Edited by Martin Austin Nesvig. Albuquerque: University of New Mexico Press, 2006.

———. *Magistrates of the Sacred: Priests and Parishioners in Eighteenth-Century Mexico*. Stanford: Stanford University Press, 1996.

Tovar de Teresa, Guillermo. *México barroco*. México: SAHOP, 1981.

Thurston, Herbert. "Candles." *Catholic Encyclopedia*. New York: Encyclopedia Press, 1913.

Trexler, Richard C. "Reverence and Profanity in the Study of Early Modern Religion." In *Religion and Society in Early Modern Europe, 1500–1800*. Edited by Kaspar von Greyerz. Boston: George Allen & Unwin, 1984.

Tutino, John. *From Insurrection to Revolution in Mexico: Social Bases of Agrarian Violence, 1750–1940*. Princeton: Princeton University Press, 1986.

Van Duesen, Nancy E. *Between the Sacred and the Worldly: The Institutional and Cultural Practice of Recogimiento in Colonial Lima*. Stanford: Stanford University Press, 2001.

Van Kley, Dale K. *The Religious Origins of the French Revolution: From Calvin to the Civil Constitution, 1560–1791*. New Haven: Yale University Press, 1996.

Van Young, Eric. *The Other Rebellion: Popular Violence, Ideology, and the Mexican Struggle for Independence, 1810–1821*. Stanford: Stanford University Press, 2001.

Vaquero Iglesias, Julio Antonio. *Muerte e ideología en las Austurias del siglo XIX*. Madrid: Siglo Veintiuno de España Editores, S.A., 1991.

Venard, Marc. "Popular Religion in the Eighteenth Century." In *Church and Society in Catholic Europe of the Eighteenth Century*. Edited by William J. Callahan and David Higgs. New York: Cambridge University Press, 1979.

Viqueira Albán, Juan Pedro. *Propriety and Permissiveness in Bourbon Mexico*. Translated by Sonya Lipsett-Rivera and Sergio Rivera Ayala. Wilmington, DE: Scholarly Resources Inc., 1999 [1987].

Voekel, Pamela. *Alone Before God: The Religious Origins of Modernity in Mexico*. Durham: Duke University Press, 2002.

———. "Peeing on the Palace: Bodily Resistance to Bourbon Reforms in Mexico City." *Journal of Historical Sociology* 5 (1992): 183–208.

Von Germeten, Nicole. *Black Blood Brothers: Confraternities and Social Mobility for Afro-Mexicans*. Gainesville: University Press of Florida, 2006.

———. "Death in Black and White: Testaments and Confraternal Devotion in Seventeenth-Century Mexico City." *Colonial Latin American Historical Review* 12 (2003): 275–301.

Vovelle, Michel. *Piété baroque et déchristianisation en Provence au XVIIIe siecle: Les attitudes devant la mort d'apres les clauses des testaments*. Paris: Plon, 1973.

Wagstaff, George Grayson. "Music for the Dead: Polyphonic Settings of the Officium and Missa pro defunctis by Spanish and Latin American Composers before 1630." Ph.D. diss., University of Texas at Austin, 1995.

Wandel, Lee Palmer. *The Eucharist in the Reformation: Incarnation and Liturgy*. New York: Cambridge University Press, 2006.

Ward, Benedicta. *Miracles and the Medieval Mind: Theory, Record and Event, 1000–1215*. Philadelphia: University of Pennsylvania Press, 1987.

Warner, Marina. *Alone of All Her Sex: The Myth and Cult of the Virgin Mary*. New York: Alfred A. Knopf, 1976.

Warren, Richard A. *Vagrants and Citizens: Politics and the Masses in Mexico City from Colony to Republic*. Wilmington, DE: Scholarly Resources Inc., 2001.

Weber, Max. *The Protestant Ethic and the Spirit of Capitalism*. Translated by Talcott Parsons. New York: Routledge, 1930.

Webster, Susan Verdi. *Art and Ritual in Golden-Age Spain: Sevillian Confraternities and the Processional Sculpture of Holy Week*. Princeton: Princeton University Press, 1998.

Weinstein, Donald, and Rudolph M. Bell. *Saints & Society: The Two Worlds of Western Christendom, 1000–1700*. Chicago: University of Chicago Press, 1982.

White, James F. *Roman Catholic Worship: Trent to Today*. New York: Paulist Press, 1995.

Wirth, Jean. "Against the Acculturation Thesis." In *Religion and Society in Early Modern Europe, 1500–1800*. Edited by Kaspar von Greyerz. Boston: George Allen & Unwin, 1984.

Wobeser, Gisela von. *El crédito eclesiástico en la Nueva España, siglo XVIII*. México: Universidad Nacional Autónoma de México, 1994.

Wright, L. P. "The Military Orders in Sixteenth and Seventeenth Century Spanish Society: The Institutional Embodiment of a Historical Tradition." *Past & Present* 43 (1969): 34–70.

Wybrew, Hugh. "Ceremonial." In *The Study of Liturgy*. Edited by Cheslyn Jones, Geoffrey Wainwright, and Edward Yarnold. New York: Oxford University Press, 1978.

Zahino Peñafort, Luisa. *Iglesia y sociedad en México, 1765–1800: tradición, reforma y reacciones*. México: Universidad Nacional Autónoma de México, 1996.

Zárate Toscano, Verónica. *Los nobles ante la muerte en México: actitudes, ceremonias y memoria (1750–1850)*. México: El Colegio de México, Centro de Estudios Históricos, Instituto Mora, 2000.

Zemon Davis, Natalie. "Boundaries and Sense of the Self in Sixteenth-Century France." In *Reconstructing Individualism: Autonomy, Individuality, and the Self in Western Thought*. Edited by Thomas C. Heller, et al. Stanford: Stanford University Press, 1986.

Zika, Charles. "Hosts, Processions and Pilgrimages: Controlling the Sacred in Fifteenth-Century Germany." *Past & Present* 118 (1988): 25–64.

INDEX